THE HiGH NORTH

THE HIGH NORTH

CANNABIS IN CANADA

EDITED BY
Andrew D. Hathaway AND
Clayton James Smith McCann

© UBC Press 2022

All rights reserved. No part of this publication may be reproduced, stored in a retrieval system, or transmitted, in any form or by any means, without prior written permission of the publisher, or, in Canada, in the case of photocopying or other reprographic copying, a licence from Access Copyright, www.accesscopyright.ca.

31 30 29 28 27 26 25 24 23 22   5 4 3 2 1

Printed in Canada on FSC-certified ancient-forest-free paper (100% post-consumer recycled) that is processed chlorine- and acid-free.

Library and Archives Canada Cataloguing in Publication

Title: The high North / edited by Andrew D. Hathaway and Clayton James Smith McCann.

Other titles: High north (2022)

Names: Hathaway, Andrew D., editor. | McCann, Clayton James Smith, editor.

Identifiers: Canadiana (print) 20220167400 | Canadiana (ebook) 20220167478 | ISBN 9780774866705 (hardcover) | ISBN 9780774866729 (PDF) | ISBN 9780774866736 (EPUB)

Subjects: LCSH: Drug legalization – Canada. | LCSH: Cannabis – Law and legislation – Canada. | LCSH: Cannabis – Canada – History. | LCSH: Marijuana – Law and legislation – Canada. | LCSH: Marijuana – Canada – History.

Classification: LCC HV5822.M3 .H54 2022 | DDC 362.29/50971 – dc23

Canadä

UBC Press gratefully acknowledges the financial support for our publishing program of the Government of Canada (through the Canada Book Fund), the Canada Council for the Arts, and the British Columbia Arts Council.

This book has been published with the help of a grant from the Canadian Federation for the Humanities and Social Sciences, through the Awards to Scholarly Publications Program, using funds provided by the Social Sciences and Humanities Research Council of Canada.

Printed and bound in Canada by Friesens
Set in Segoe and Warnock by Artegraphica Design Co.
Copy editor: Lesley Erickson
Proofreader: Judith Earnshaw
Indexer: Margaret de Boer
Cover designer: Alexa Love

UBC Press
The University of British Columbia
2029 West Mall
Vancouver, BC V6T 1Z2
www.ubcpress.ca

*For those we've met along the way
who share our love of cannabis and contributed
their voices to the struggle to be heard.*

Contents

Foreword / ix
RYAN STOA

Introduction: Can Someone Tell Me What Just Happened? / 3
ANDREW D. HATHAWAY and CLAYTON JAMES SMITH McCANN

PART 1 Cannabis in Context: Historical, Political, and Economic Factors

1 From Prohibition to Legalization: Cannabis Use and the Law / 29
CATHERINE CARSTAIRS

2 Cannabis-Policy Integration and Alignment: Missed Opportunities and Obstacles to Collaborative Governance / 52
JARED J. WESLEY

3 Displacing the Illicit Cannabis Market: Challenges and Trade-Offs / 73
JASON CHILDS and GEORGE HARTNER

4 Medical Cannabis Dispensaries: A Conduit for Change? / 97
JENNA VALLERIANI

PART 2 Cannabis and Public Health: A Multidisciplinary View

5 Cannabis Legalization: Déjà Vu All over Again? / 113
MICHAEL DEVILLAER

6 Cannabis Substitution: The Canadian Experience / 146
MICHELLE ST. PIERRE, SARAH DANIELS, and ZACH WALSH

7   Cannabis and Mental Health: A Sociological Perspective / 164
    ANDREW D. HATHAWAY

8   Help Wanted: The Plight of Workers and Consumers under Canada's Legal Cannabis Production Regime / 188
    CLAYTON JAMES SMITH McCANN

PART 3   Cannabis Subjectivities: An Array of Voices

9   Women in Corporate Cannabis Work / 213

    From a Good:House to Good:Farm / 213
    An interview with JEANNETTE VANDERMAREL

    Building Consumer Trust in a Nascent Industry / 219
    KARINA LAHNAKOSKI

    Cannabis Jobs in Canada / 223
    ALISON McMAHON

10 Last Stop before Hopeless / 231
    KELLY INSLEY

11 Dusting Off the Path – Tsi Nionkwarihotens / 242
    KANENHARIYO SETH LEFORT with CLAYTON JAMES SMITH McCANN

12 Slow Cannabis / 266
    KELLY COULTER

13 Illicit Cannabis Market Folklore / 272

    Guilty Republic / 274
    CLAYTON JAMES SMITH McCANN

    For the Discriminating Traveller / 280
    "SAL"

14 Cannabis Activism in Canada: Reflections on a Movement in Transition / 286
    JODIE EMERY

Postscript: "Craft" Cannabis and a New Kind of Canadian Farm / 312
ANDREW D. HATHAWAY and CLAYTON JAMES SMITH McCANN

List of Contributors / 326

Index / 329

Foreword

RYAN STOA

More than three years have passed since the Cannabis Act legalized the recreational use of cannabis in Canada. Nonetheless, the Canadian cannabis landscape remains disorienting and frustrating to navigate. The legal cannabis industry suffers under the weight of regulations that are out of touch with the industry's complicated history, present realities, and future potential. Large, well-capitalized companies draw attention from investors but struggle to establish that scaling up is possible, much less desirable. Those who suffered the most in the prohibition era are poorly represented in the new cannabis industry. In the face of these challenges, the illicit market thrives, an implicit acknowledgment that the legal market is not meeting the needs of potential consumers.

No one said this would be easy. Decades of prohibition and heavy-handed prosecutions gave rise to an underground cannabis trade characterized by indoor cultivation sites or remote farms, and an illicit but resilient distribution network that delivered product to all corners of the country. The transition to a system in which production and distribution are both more centralized and more scrutinized was never going to be met with a universal endorsement. One wonders if the legal cannabis industry even draws from the ranks of the veterans of the war on drugs, or if it represents a mostly new, competing vision of Canadian cannabis.

There are many forces at play, of course, pulling the Canadian cannabis industry in a dazzling array of directions. The venture capitalists and corporate investors predict a green rush – a billion-dollar industry held back by prohibition but primed for growth and disruption. Social-equity activists see the cannabis industry's potential for restorative justice, channelling the benefits and opportunities of legalization into rebuilding communities hit the hardest by the war on drugs. Cultivators and environmentalists envision an agrarian renaissance, with the legal cannabis industry paving the way for the rejuvenation of the local, sustainable family farm. Regulators and political officials grapple with a monumental task – to regulate a disorganized and rapidly evolving industry in a very short time. Health advocates imagine an industry capable of delivering compassion and relief to struggling patients. Scientists marvel at the power and potential of the cannabis plant, eager for more breakthroughs and innovations that might come with further research. Consumers, finally, enjoy the proliferation of new products and contribute to the sophistication of cannabis consumption.

It is a credit to cannabis itself that such a diverse group of stakeholders has so much at stake. By bringing so many disparate voices under its canopy, the cannabis sector has established itself as a social and economic force to be reckoned with. It has also created tension, however, and many questions about the Canadian cannabis landscape remain unanswered or mired in misunderstanding. Fundamentally: What happened? Where are we? Where should we be going?

In *The High North: Cannabis in Canada,* Andrew D. Hathaway and Clayton James Smith McCann bring us together to explore these questions, among many others. The chapter authors in this book identify critical challenges facing the cannabis industry and ask us to consider how Canada might overcome them. As one of the first industrialized countries to legalize cannabis, Canada is tasked with forging a way forward and overcoming these challenges in order to illuminate a similar path for many other countries around the world. Much is at stake.

THE HiGH NORTH

Introduction

Can Someone Tell Me What Just Happened?

ANDREW D. HATHAWAY and CLAYTON JAMES SMITH McCANN

There is a scene in the anarchic masterpiece *Mad Max* in which a police chase culminates in a multi-vehicle crash. The motorcycle cop goes into a skid, lays down his bike, and slides to avoid hitting a car. Ashen-faced at the chaotic scene of mayhem, the driver gasps: "Oh my God! What's happened?"

The earnest cop, "Jim Goose," removes the face shield of his helmet. Tanned and youthful, he smiles and replies: "I don't know, man. I just got here myself." And then he laughs.

Well, here we are, indeed! But what to make of the historic changes ushered in when legal cannabis became a reality in Canada on October 17, 2018? What happened and what will happen are controversial and contentious. Reactions ranged from overjoyed to cynical to cautious to alarmed to outraged to indifferent, to name just a few.

Does the legalization of cannabis signify the culmination of a victorious agrarian or cultural revolution? Or does it represent an all-too-rare capitulation by the criminal justice system, a recognition that prohibition does not work? Is it an admission that the war on drugs has done more harm than good? Does legalization demonstrate the supremacy of science and reason over ignorance and fear? Or is it just a ploy to woo young voters? To be more cynical, is it a shameless cash grab by ex-cops and politicians who profited by waging war on (some) drugs and who now profit as prominent shareholders and investors in legal cannabis production? Is legal cannabis just another sign of social Armageddon, marked by licentiousness, mass immigration, and the rest? Does it mark the dawning of a new Age of Aquarius? Or is it the inevitable result of the corrupting influence of modern neoliberal market forces?

Whatever cannabis has been and is becoming, its social meaning is something firmly rooted in "the social lives of things" (Appadurai 1996). To understand the social lives of things, anthropologists examine their relationships with people and other objects in the different times and places that have influenced their meaning. The social history of cannabis in Canada, of course, is distinctively Canadian but inseparable from its larger cultural significance in North America and elsewhere.

A Green So Delicious It Hurts[1]

Despite the "startling lack of toxicity" known to distinguish cannabis from other psychoactive substances, its more common name is believed to be derived from the Portuguese word *maraguango,* for "intoxicant" (Lee 2012). The term *cola,* used by growers to describe the long bud cluster at the top of the plant, is Spanish for "tail." Terms used elsewhere, and in the ancient world, are less mundane, reflecting a sense of reverence and gratitude for the powers bestowed on users. *Dawamesc* is Arabic for "medicine of immortality." And the terms used by Indian *sadhus* (holy men) for cannabis once described it as the "joy giver" and the "leaf of heroes."

When migrant Indian labourers were indentured to the "Spice Island" of Jamaica in the 1800s, they called it *ganja* – the same term later made famous by reggae legend Bob Marley. Early jazz musicians in the United States called it *tea* and *gage, muggles* and *Mary Warner* to hoodwink the authorities and claim it as a symbol of subcultural belonging to a world outside the law.

Hippies called it *weed* and *pot* and even more overtly politicized its meaning as a symbol of defiance and countercultural allegiance. The growing prevalence of the use of a banned substance over decades ushered in the advent and diffusion of drug culture, including intimate shared knowledge of the historically transgressive act and the meaning of getting high and being high.

Sociologist Howard Becker (1963) long ago described the social process of learning to become a "marihuana user" in a deviant subculture devoted to the drug.[2] In participation with more experienced users, one learns how to produce its mind-altering effects and recognize them and enjoy them as connected to its use. To become a regular user, one must have access to a steady source of supply and learn how to control one's behaviour after using the drug in encounters with authorities and respected others liable to disapprove.

Becker (1963) argued that the user also learns to understand drug-use behaviour as nondeviant, or normal, in terms that depart from the norms and values of a society that views marijuana use as harmful and immoral. Understanding drug use, from the point of view of users, thus requires an understanding of (sub)cultural forms of knowledge that partially determine use behaviour and experience in its situated context as an inherently social act.[3] But what are we to make of the societal reaction that signifies transgression in the meaning of drug use?

By the late 1970s, marijuana use had become the most widely committed crime in North America – a crime that disproportionately made criminals of youth and those already marginalized by race and class distinctions. Critics have contended that the prohibition served to justify the targeting of *others* seen as a threat to law and order and as a scapegoat to protect the vested interests of elites. Thus, winning the war on drugs was less important than the ends served by its function to maintain the status quo. "The drug war is a holy war," quipped Joseph McNamara, "and in a holy war you don't have to win" (Lee 2012, 160).[4]

Born of temperance-era virtues, marijuana prohibition in Canada and the United States employed themes of social chaos, degradation, and disorder to trigger the anxieties of the property-holding classes. Fears evoking class and racial conflict were augmented in the Reefer Madness era by a moral panic over marijuana's designation as the *assassin of youth*. "Officer Warns Insidious Weed Is Even Supplied to School Children," exclaimed a 1938 headline in the *Toronto Star* (Boyd and Carter 2014).

Today, the war on marijuana – as we once knew it – may be over, the insidious weed having transformed into a respectable commodity called *cannabis* that can be legally bought and sold. And yet eight decades after the height of Reefer Madness, there has been a resurgence of concerns about psychosis, the effects of use on adolescent brain development, and rising diagnoses of cannabis use disorder (CUD).[5] Moreover, the related health care burden is reportedly costing the economy billions of dollars every year.

In Canada, the architects of legalization, eight decades after Reefer Madness, have made claims of a not too different sort. The former deputy prime minister Anne McLellan led the task force informing the creation of the regulatory system allowing legal access to cannabis for recreational use.

She is also of the view that only "stupid people" use the drug (e.g., see CBC 2003; Emery 2016).

Official statements by Bill Blair,[6] the former minister for border services and organized crime, suggested the illicit cannabis market finances organized crime in the "billions of dollars." In his former role as police chief of the City of Toronto, Blair observed that he had seen marijuana ruin lives. His more recent statements are consistent with past claims of the RCMP, which has referred to marijuana as "the most dangerous narcotic in Canada today" (Poole 1998, 68), and those of Public Health and Safety Minister Ralph Goodale,[7] who warned Canadians of the dangers of buying cannabis from dealers selling "poison product that could kill them."

The emerging stance of government – that legalizing cannabis serves public health objectives while advancing social justice – has thus been somewhat undermined by claims not far removed from the blatant propaganda of the Reefer Madness era. To be clear, it is our position that legalization is a pyrrhic victory, a win that inflicts a devastating toll on the victor, one tantamount to a defeat. The outcome for Canadians is thereby one that negates a true sense of achievement, which damages more long-term progress.

Okay! Time to Move along Folks. There Is Nothing to See Here.
The war on drugs has long been substantiated by hyperbole, othering, and outright lies that serve to reinforce distinctions between "good drugs" and "bad drugs." The good-drugs-versus-bad-drugs theme is being transformed now that cannabis is becoming a respectable commodity – while still being sold by bad guys "on the streets." Participants in the illicit market, who continue to profit from the sale of an unregulated drug, are characterized as *really* bad guys of a different character than those who are abiding by the rules.

Has the government's objective of diverting cannabis profits into the deep pockets of new corporate profiteers spurred a reinvestment in myth making? How do these claims stand up to evaluation based on evidence that provides a more informed and nuanced point of view? The illicit cannabis market – quite unlike the one emerging in which the profiteers are good people who pay taxes and wear suits – is commonly portrayed in a distorted way, suggesting that it is run by violent criminals selling dangerous drugs to kids.

A 2011 report by the Canadian Justice Department provides a more informed view. The data on arrests for cultivation show that only a small fraction of the cannabis market was connected to organized crime. In five hundred investigations (1997–2005), just 5 percent of grow-ops were linked to organized crime or street gangs. Firearms were located at 6 percent of busted sites, a rate approximately consistent with the national proportion of licensed gun owners in Canada. While only 3 percent of the investigated grow-ops were found to be growing more than one thousand plants, over half had five or less. Forty percent were issued fines (Boyd and Carter 2014).

The connection between cannabis and organized crime is thereby not substantiated by the facts. Historically, however, exaggerating the connection has reliably resulted in larger law-enforcement budgets supporting more surveillance of illicit substance users. Our bloated criminal justice system requires more lawyers, judges, bailiffs, and corrections officers, among other opportunists, to protect the turf of a new brand of profiteers. The scapegoats of the past are issued pardons, if deserving, rather than expungement of their sins.[8]

The new class of criminal created – that is, those guilty of diverting profits properly intended for the regulated market – is strikingly familiar, populated disproportionately by youth, racialized minorities, and the lower classes. Their social characteristics further justify the surveillance and policing of groups excluded from the legal market.

Successfully displacing illegal vendors also requires the legitimation of claims that target uninformed consumers. Unregulated cannabis is depicted as more dangerous and inferior to products being sold by corporations. To justify the higher cost, for those who can afford it, buying legal cannabis is represented as putatively safer because of child-proof packaging and point-of-sale restrictions. The public must be malleable enough to be receptive to the notion that these safeguards will reduce use by youth – and unsuspecting pets and children – and prevent the sale of cannabis laced with fentanyl and other so-called street drugs.

Suggesting that "street dealers" subscribe to business models in which it is advisable to sell adulterated cannabis requires a violent transformation of reality implying that the drug is sold by dangerous criminals and street thugs. The term *folk market,* though more accurate, does not have the same ring to it as connecting organized crime and violence to the sale of drugs on the unregulated market.[9]

Critical reflection on claims making by the powerful (claims that serve the economic interests of elites) elicits themes familiar to sociologists and anthropologists. As we shall see, however, the legal cannabis phenomenon is fertile ground for insights from across the social sciences. All social scientists, to some degree, concern themselves with the social construction of reality and its relationship to power (Berger and Luckmann 1991; Goode and Ben-Yehuda 1994). As something firmly rooted in the social lives of things, cannabis is rife with cultural significance, symbols, rituals, and meanings that are in the process of being rapidly transformed.

From a constructionist perspective, science itself is understood as just another perspective, or way of looking at the world, in which objectivity or fact cannot be separated from our cultural understandings.[10] Conducted from its standpoint as a perspective of perspectives, a constructionist inquiry's primary objective is to render strange and problematic ways of looking at phenomena that are ordinarily taken for granted. To imagine different ways of looking at the world is to imagine that things can be otherwise. Inquiry of this nature is political in that it serves to diminish the power of authority and legitimacy, which are produced and reinforced by unquestioning belief.

When political realities are taken for granted, or understood as matters of technical necessity, the language of scientific experts is commonly co-opted to serve the interests of the powerful by concealing from the public that moral and political decisions are being made. To foster the development of many perspectives, the best defence is to be skeptical of every perspective. Constructionists must situate claims making within its social context of culture and structure. We must acknowledge that all claims – and, indeed, all research products – cannot be separated from the cultural and social realities in which they are produced. Because the meanings of all things are situational and relative, we need to understand what claims mean within their larger social context.

Social problems are the products of collective definition. Social scientists possess the kind of knowledge needed to serve as a corrective for ignorance and misinformation and to further understanding of the makeup of the problem. This position is in no way inconsistent with the idea that all sources of knowledge are social constructions that ought to be treated as claims in their own right. Recognizing the sociocultural context of claims making helps situate it structurally, and politically, in a world where there is an increasing obligation of social scientists to challenge ideas and ideologies that many people take for granted. Rather than obsessing about theory, our objective is to facilitate informed investigation and critique.

Ethnographic Inquiry and Representation

The High North: Cannabis in Canada is a curated collection that seeks, in its interdisciplinarity, to create something novel. We favour Roland Barthes's

(1972, cited in Clifford 1986, 1) interpretation: "To do something interdisciplinary it's not enough to choose 'a subject' (a theme) and gather around it two or three sciences. Interdisciplinarity consists in creating a new object that belongs to no one." Our approach is broadly ethnographic in that we as editors invited an array of contributions and set out to discover emergent themes and patterns (Altheide 1987). As Eric Weissman (2017) notes, such work inevitably crosses academic boundaries in seeking to derive information from people and their experiences. The central task of the ethnographer is to make sense of how people become engaged in thinking critically about their world. But how can social research be effective, Weissman (2017, 57) asks: "In a world where truth is unstable and objective reality constantly socially constructed?"

This definition of the situation opens the door to innovative forms of inquiry and methodologies that bridge the social sciences and literary work done in the humanities and outside academia to inform, augment, and challenge scientific ways of knowing. Much of this volume is accordingly devoted to discovering insights through a myriad of methods, some of which have been described elsewhere using such terms as *autoethnography, ethnographic autobiography, reflexive ethnography,* and *public ethnography* and in research that employs ethnographic observation and sees the inherent value in producing "messy texts" (Denzin 1997).

Autoethnography is an approach to research and writing that seeks to describe and analyze personal experience to understand cultural experience (Ellis, Adams, and Bochner 2011). This approach challenges objective research standards for representing others and treats research as a political, socially just, and socially conscious act. Recognizing research as both a process and a product, the autoethnographer uses tenets of autobiography and ethnography to do and write autoethnography.

When the intent and purposes of relating a life story are anthropological, other authors suggest that the work be labelled ethnographic autobiography (Wolcott 2004). More specifically, an ethnographic autobiography is a life story told to an anthropologist or used in ways that implicate a sociocultural rather than a psychological interpretation.

Reflexive ethnography is an approach to research guided by a critical understanding of the philosophical basis of ethnographic authority (Davies 2012). It attempts to strike a balance between postmodernist relativism, which overemphasizes reflexivity in ways that hinder research, and a realist perspective that values the scientific method. This is an ethnographic standpoint that reflects postmodern insights by incorporating different standpoints to expose the tyranny of hegemonic metanarratives.

The areas of overlap between academic subjects and those of most appeal to the general public are described elsewhere as public ethnography (Gans 2010). This approach differs from academic ethnography when its sites and subjects are relevant to what the public wants and needs to know and when it is written in nontechnical language.

More generally, along with Norman Denzin (1997), we acknowledge the importance of reflexive, messy texts that break with representations that are typical for traditional, realist writing forms. Such authorship is sensitive to how reality is socially constructed and understands that writing is a form of narrative or a way of framing reality. Messy texts are unapologetically political and tell stories that are multivoiced and many sited, with a tendency to be open-ended and resistant to theoretical holism. They tend to make the reader work and refuse to impose meaning. These are more than subjective accounts of experiences.

Like James Clifford (1986), we contend that ethnographic writing is something that itself is situated and determined contextually, rhetorically, institutionally, generically, politically, and historically. So, yes, indeed, the task is daunting. In addition to conventional academic sources that shed light on these phenomena, we sought to achieve fuller polyvocality by curating a living, breathing collection of accounts by nonacademic authors too. By seeking voices typically ignored, or rendered marginal, in the lead up to and aftermath of legalization in October 2018, we wanted to tell stories that may never have been told. Clifford (1986, 13) asks: "Who speaks? Who writes? When and where? With or to whom? Under what institutional and historical constraints?" Put in another way, we ought to be attentive to the struggle reflected and produced by age-old questions surrounding the proper role of the researcher or philosopher or author.

To quote Mikhail Bakhtin (1981, 33): "After all, the boundaries between fiction and nonfiction, between literature and non-literature and so forth are not laid up in heaven." Clifford (1986) speaks of the crisis in representation as a postcolonial awakening in anthropology among those tasked with representing others in their cultural descriptions by crafting the "expected texts." Instead, researchers are encouraged to "seek out and establish new modes of contact across cultures" by breaking the conventions of the academy that serve to reinforce hegemony, such as the socially advantaged speaking for disadvantaged others. The challenge posed by Dan Rose (1993, 216), and we agree, is for ethnographers to strive to develop "new relations within other cultures, such that we begin to draft new forms of texts, and explore new modes of experience."

Rose (1993, 217) writes: "The future of ethnography lies in a more sophisticated and self-conscious relationship" in which ethnographic texts, "whether in sociology, anthropology, psychology, critical legal studies, planning, or folklore, will be a polyphonic, heteroglossic, multigenre construction." Thus, we endeavoured, as Rose (1993, 218) urges, to assemble a selection of "critical, theoretical, humanist mini-essays that advance ... particular disciplines" and tried to capture "the conversations, voices, attitudes, visual genres, gestures, reactions, and concerns of the daily life of the people with whom the author participates." Accordingly, this volume, if successful in the eyes of readers and contributors, convincingly achieves the cohabitation of "analytic, fictive, poetic, narrative, and critical genres."

Before proceeding, it is fitting to acknowledge the incisive words of Australian Indigenous rights activist Lilla Watson, who is often quoted for reminding would-be allies: "If you have come here to help me, you are wasting your time. But if you have come because your liberation is bound up with mine, then let us work together."[11]

Our approach to this endeavour is to situate our efforts within social scientific discussions and recurring debates in academia about the role of the researcher in producing public scholarship. Whatever our commitment to "truth telling" and our apparent obligation to contribute to resolving social problems, presuming to perform such a role is ultimately fraught with contradictions, challenges, and criticisms. There was a time not all that long ago when Canadian poets were feted in public occasions that attracted widespread media attention: "The assumption was that poets could speak articulately to the nation at large about matters that affect our collective life" (Wayman 2014, 79).

But how might a collective life be spoken to when there are so many issues that divide us? And, moreover, how could one ever hope to speak for and do justice to oppressed groups such as the Indigenous people living in third world conditions within our own borders, or the one in four Canadians who face housing insecurity and go hungry every day? How might we tackle and atone for Canada's contribution to global carbon emissions or our ignoble distinction of being, on a per-capita basis, among the worst polluters on the planet – despoiling fisheries, forests, pristine shorelines, lakes, and streams?

At minimum, the invocation to engage in public sociology, anthropology, and ethnography (or any of the other disciplines) requires that social scientists must seek to "break down the public appearance of a united and consensual society" (Hathaway 2015b). This, in turn, requires maintaining academic freedom to be critical and at liberty to refuse to take the world for granted. In a moving tribute to his colleague Kerry Preibisch, Gerardo Otero honours her commitment to advancing "organic public sociology" with a clear value standpoint to "bridge the tension ... between science and politics ... value neutrality and value relevance" (Otero 2017, 355).

With a nod to Gramsci's notion of the organic intellectual, the primary role of researchers must be to challenge or question "conventional wisdoms" that underpin assumptions about policy formation that put people at risk of structural violence. This role includes debunking myths and scare tactics to reframe hegemonic, prejudicial cultural images and calls on us to problematize the complicity of academia in serving the technocratic aims of the neoliberal state (Hathaway 2015b).

Ethnographic institutional critique, contends Eric Weissman, is a means to further social justice aims that contradict and conflict with dominant neoliberal values. His research on homelessness speaks truth to power by demonstrating that access to power is enhanced by shelter, safe community, and having a say in one's affairs and a chance to "get back in the game of being a citizen." Citizenship is predicated on participation by self-transformative political subjects and through constructive criticism of material conditions (Weismann 2017, 61). We are similarly committed to advancing ethnographic practice through immersion in often overlooked communities to enhance understanding of their versions of reality by ensuring that their story has been told – and told by them.

Subjective lived experience is a person's history (Scott 1991, 1992). That is to say, as Clifford (1983, 129) does, it is the culmination of "clues, traces, gestures, and scraps of sense" that inform the construction of "stable interpretations." Experience is best described as knowing. Joan Scott (1992, 27) observes that until the eighteenth century, "experience and experiment were closely connected terms, designating how knowledge was arrived at through testing and observation."

Knowledge gained by experience is the most authentic truth on which to anchor subsequent reasoning and analysis (Williams 2013). There is immediacy to personal experience as something ordinarily accepted as irrefutably real. One's lived experience is reality. It is a form of truth. And we should care very much about seeking out the truth or, more accurately perhaps, the truths of lived experience that often go untold.

As a wise man once said, "I'm not sure I can tell the truth ... I can only tell what I know."[12] Experience is the ring of truth listeners seek from a storyteller. It is what researchers are pursuing when they ask someone to tell what they know about a given way of life. Indeed looking for the truth in accounts of reality is the very essence of the work of social scientists. It is the kind of interaction that has enabled humans to flourish for millennia through the exchange of lived experience from one person to another. And it is experience adorning the cave walls of Chauvet and Altamira in southern France and northern Spain.

Experience provides a way of knowing that includes potential revelation of unspoken truths that challenge "hegemonic constructions of social worlds" (Scott 1992, 24). Speaking truth to power requires seeking out these truths with regard for relational, historical processes that shape understandings we "know" to be true. Ethnographers, notes Clifford (1983, 140), must also learn to "share our texts," and the writing credit, with our collaborators, "for whom the term 'informants' is no longer accurate, if [indeed] it ever was."

Claims about the truth reflect both power and resistance (Burawoy et al. 1991); and it is usually the loudest, the richest, or strongest in any social interaction who assume the "right" to speak. Countering this tendency asserts the need to hear all voices in what Rose (1993, 219) calls "multiple, heterophonic sites of a struggle." Far from being the exclusive domain of academics, understanding of the history and cultural experience of cannabis in Canada requires attention be paid to the experience of otherwise neglected voices bearing witness to the "green rush."

The present volume is an extension of our research on the subject of cannabis in Canada, especially Clayton McCann's long-term research program of creating linked humanizing projects that tell the stories of coworkers who have laboured in precarity, not *as if* but *because* they are tales of his own. These are themes explored in well-known works of sociology and anthropology such as Alice Goffman's *On the Run* (2015) and, less recently, Philippe Bourgois's *In Search of Respect* (2003). More generally, and to the point, the goal of thick description can also be a conduit to advocate for change. In this vein, Michael Burawoy entreated the ethnographer to represent culture as not merely "arenas where laws are played out but a constellation of institutions located in time and space that shape domination and resistance" (Burawoy 1991, 281).

It's a Pleasure! Introducing Cannabis the Commodity

The use of cannabis is pleasurable, and pleasure is subversive. Pleasure is freedom. And freedom is pleasure. When pleasure is commodified, however, that same pleasure binds consumers to their duty to consume (Jameson 1983). Is altered consciousness false consciousness? More to the point, several hundred years of "grow or die" indoctrination under capitalism were not about promoting freedom. As the apparent love child of the Reformation and colonial expansion, capitalism was not the first established system of exploitation and oppression to valorize expansionist imperatives, of course.

The birth of capitalism was predicated on establishing a global slave trade, itself preceded by trade routes that predated the Roman Empire. Trade had to be protected from the pirates, and the locals had to consent or be coerced, through force if necessary, to desire and supplicate themselves to the new gods. The dismantling of peasant communes, often violent, took place in the colonies supplying the slave labour, colonies fuelling capitalism's early growth. Capitalism – and hence freedom, as the world has come to know it – feeds on the flesh of slaves, devoured through brutality, genocide, and ecological destruction.

Travelling pathways carved by torchlight from the jungles of antiquity to today's glass-and-steel corridors of power, cannabis (the new commodity) has been domesticated and reinvented in another form. The cannabis consumer has been seduced into believing that capitalism is the provider of a pleasure made permissible for those who pay and play by the new rules. As Herbert Marcuse (1969) sagely noted fifty years ago: "The so-called consumer economy and the politics of corporate capitalism have created a second nature of man which ties him libidinally and aggressively to the commodity form."

Consumption is constructed as the necessary interval between periods of production; the social practice of consumers is the just reward for production time well used (Appadurai 1996). The collective consciousness is, accordingly, conditioned to demand what we desire and desire what we demand. Consumption is a necessary part of the performance that shows we are deserving of the pleasure – at least for those who organize their lives in such a way as to afford to pay the bills, with some left over to participate in capitalism's rituals of conspicuous consumption.

Consumption rituals express ideas of order and disorder (see, e.g., Geertz 1966; Blackman 2011) that protect the interests of the owners of production. The place of cannabis in modern history, in this light, treads a path well-travelled by commodities such as sugar and other intoxicants such as alcohol and tobacco. In the case of sugar, Sidney Mintz (1986, 44) observes that "more elaborate and heterogeneous consumer demand" came with increasing product differentiation. New consumption habits served to demonstrate "a critical connection between the will to work and the will to consume" (Mintz 1986, 64).

William Marling (1998) notes a seismic shift in consumer culture in the 1920s, on the heels of Prohibition, a shift that ushered in new meanings tied to alcohol consumption and cigarette smoking, especially by women. Within a few years, social relations based on gender changed dramatically: "In 1920 only the bravest women claimed a right to smoke, but by 1927 women smoked in restaurants, theater lobbies, and at parties" (Marling 1998, 4). New consumption habits in that era and thereafter were greatly influenced by the consumer's never-ending fascination with technological innovation. New spending "began to chase 'qualities' of color, lightness, and newness. Momentum shifted from mass production to mass marketing and then to consumers" (Marling 1998, xi).

Commodities are said to "have momentum if their durability, economy, and familiarity make them a part of people's habits" (Marling 1998, 40). And, investment has momentum. Once investors have a stake, they will continue to invest more to protect their investment and to overcome competitors. Thus what constitutes "good food" (or a good intoxicant) is, ultimately, "a social, not a biological matter" (Mintz 1986, 8). Or, to put it differently, it has been pointed out that "one did not succeed entrepreneurially by making *better* crack" (Grief 2017, 154).

Organization and Objectives

To better understand cannabis's shift from a banned drug to a commodity from a multifaceted and critical perspective, *The High North: Cannabis in Canada* brings together illuminating insights from across the social sciences. The move to legalize and regulate in October 2018 provided new opportunities and a sense of urgency to document this dramatic transformation from a multitude of standpoints. Contributors from outside academia bring perspectives and voices seldom heard to the discussion as we enter a new era of cannabis-policy reform.

This collection came together after much deliberation to determine the volume's intended scope and content. Its multidisciplinary focus and inclusion of perspectives from outside academia are designed for a wide readership. The editors invited original chapter contributions from cannabis researchers at Canadian universities with academic training in history, psychology, sociology, economics, political science, and anthropology. We requested interviews or written contributions from nonacademic activists and industry insiders, including legal and illegal cannabis production workers. In collaboration, our collective aim has been to make a timely, novel contribution to the literature, written for an audience of scholars and laypersons, to stimulate more nuanced discussion and debate.

The collection is organized into three parts. The first part helps contextualize recent policy developments by examining the history of cannabis in Canada and some of the many challenges presented by the move to legalize and regulate its use. These readings offer insight into the social, historical, political, and economic factors underlying Canada's distinctive experience with cannabis through a multifaceted, multidisciplinary lens.

Part 1, "Cannabis in Context" opens with Catherine Carstairs's examination of the social history of cannabis throughout the twentieth century – from the ban in 1923 to the emergence of a counterculture that celebrated marijuana, to early efforts at marijuana law reform, and to more recent policy developments. Chapter 1 helps situate the contemporary context of cannabis legalization by providing a deep history of the emergence of prohibition laws in Canada, a process that ran parallel and was connected to claims-making activities in the United States. Themes of race and social order in law-making trickled up to become nationalized, later sparking the emergence of countercultural social movements. Historians, notes Carstairs, are like magpies with an affinity for collecting bits and pieces and odd scraps of information. Her work in Chapter 1 sets the stage for what comes after, revisiting key sources and gathering fresh insights that illuminate the history of cannabis in Canada. Ninety-five years of prohibition left a legacy of drug-war bureaucracy on an unprecedented scale.

De-escalating and dismantling the ban against cannabis has been a governmental exercise fraught with extraordinary challenges. In Chapter 2, Jared Wesley explains the unique political context in which cannabis was legalized in Canada, wherein provincial jurisdiction and local policy control are shown to take priority over harmonizing measures that might be fruitfully adopted under federal regulations. The analysis provides a striking contrast and some parallels to American policy developments. The states have largely developed their own measures, wherever cannabis is legal for consumption by adults, within a context of ongoing federal prohibition. The political realities of legalizing cannabis in Canada called for the integration and alignment of a multitude of levels of government and law enforcement agencies, resulting in a bureaucratic landscape that is daunting. Wesley examines the extent of (mis)alignment and collaboration between federal and provincial/territorial governments in cannabis policy development. His training as a political scientist and practical experience working outside academia in intergovernmental relations provide a unique perspective on the alignment of theory and practice as applied to complex, nationwide policy-making challenges like cannabis legalization. He overviews a number of the factors that contributed to the federal government's decision to develop its own policy framework, leaving the provinces and territories to devise a patchwork of new policies that replicate existing alcohol and tobacco regulations.

The challenge of repealing and replacing prohibition with a regulated market is further amplified by the economic imperative of competing with existing, and definitively displacing, illicit sources of supply. Chapter 3 critiques the faulty economic reasoning behind policy decisions that establish legal markets for cannabis as though consumers have no other choice. Jason Childs and George Hartner analyze the market structures adopted by Canadian provinces for legal distribution to cannabis consumers. The academic training of the authors as economists informs their research focus on assessment of the relative effectiveness of each model for displacing the illicit cannabis market. In addition to the need for more effective integration pointed to by Wesley, they contend that policy development suffered from a lack of time. Using national-level data to evaluate the rollout of a regulated system of cannabis supply, they examine marketplace behaviour of consumers as determined by competing vectors such as price, variety, and quality of product. Their analyses of data from the National Cannabis Survey shed new light on factors that determine choices made by cannabis consumers with new options to consider in a market where illegal and legal sources coexist.

The insights gained in Chapters 2 and 3 contribute to a better understanding of political and economic factors to facilitate more critical inquiry of public policy and governance in neoliberal societies. Shifting the focus of inquiry to use of cannabis as medicine, and sources of supply beyond the regulated market, Chapter 4 examines the essential and yet largely overlooked role of medical cannabis dispensaries in providing a model for safe and reliable access. Jenna Valleriani traces the emergence and growth of North America's "medical marijuana movement," with particular attention to Canada's evolving medical access programs in the twenty-first century. Her chapter documents the history of medical dispensaries with reference to how local governments have responded to use of cannabis as medicine and service providers still considered at the fringes of public health and law. She concludes that legalization has not provided necessary support for sick Canadians seeking safe, affordable access to cannabis in an era dominated by new political and financial vested interests. In addition to improved integration across governments and government departments, Valleriani calls for less restrictive, more inclusive regulations for the licensing of medical cannabis dispensaries.

In sum, Part 1 contributes to a better understanding of the bigger picture from a vantage point informing the critical perspective that resonates throughout the book. Part 2, "Cannabis and Public Health" provides a closer look at new public health priorities, challenges and opportunities as cannabis undergoes transition to a regulated market. These chapters – by researchers from across the social sciences with background training in psychology, sociology, and anthropology – cover topics ranging from health and safety regulations to the use of cannabis for treating opiate addiction. Part 2 concludes with research by the editors. The last two chapters, respectively, examine cannabis use and mental health and the heretofore neglected conditions facing workers in legal cannabis production.

Chapter 5 by Michael DeVillaer inspects the bureaucratic process that (mis)guided the development of federal legislation and regulations governing the legal cannabis industry. DeVillear situates legalization within a political economy in which psychiatric drug treatment and pharmaceutical companies are the major players in a profit-driven industry. He observes that government, in practice, has tended to prioritize protecting corporate interests, and paid lip service to its mandate of protecting health and safety. The resulting business-friendly model, being legitimized by public health authorities and related institutions, effectively facilitates co-option of state policy by profiteers whose practices are harming public health.

Chapter 6 provides another window to critique how public health has been co-opted by claims makers who focus on the harms of using cannabis while largely disregarding benefits of use. Zach Walsh and his students, Michelle St. Pierre and Sarah Daniels, conducted in-depth interviews with Canadian researchers about the use of cannabis as a substitute for opioids. The authors note that legalization has provided opportunities to conduct more rigorous and systematic research into the conditions under which the use of cannabis has measurable benefits to public health. The use of cannabis as a substitute for more addictive drugs has long been controversial, yet it has evident potential as an adjunct to more conventional addiction treatment options. The authors argue for expanding harm reduction interventions, and point out that focusing on harms of substance use overlooks the benefits described by many users. This tendency is evident in policy discussions evoking a distorted view of cannabis dependence and biased assumptions about mental health effects.

To provide a less distorted view of mental health effects, Chapter 7 reviews the research literature observing a tendency to treat the use of cannabis itself as a comorbidity or substance use disorder, or in other equally pathologizing terms. The author, Andrew Hathaway, contends there is a need for more sociologically informed research on cannabis use patterns, experiences, and outcomes, as the user understands them. Studies using interviews and surveys show that users commonly interpret its mental health benefits as primary reasons for cannabis use. The interpretation of such research that takes seriously the perspectives and experiences of people who use drugs significantly differs between scientific disciplines. Within the social sciences interpretations vary depending on one's training as a humanist or positivist and related disciplinary canons or commitments about what counts as scientific evidence or "proof." Overcoming stigma and discrimination that equates the use of cannabis to a form of mental illness is as much contingent on supplanting ideology as the resolution of empirical disputes.

Chapter 8 by Clayton McCann adjusts our focus from cannabis and mental wellness to environmental health. Despite the evident potential of regulating the supply source to optimize health benefits while reducing harm, McCann contends and documents the myriad concerns raised by large-scale cannabis production for the legal market that present significant new challenges and risks. Drawing on experience and ethnographic research over several years before and after legalization, he traces the dramatic transformation of the plant from an illegal crop into a corporate commodity. Echoing concerns raised in Chapter 5, the author critiques the use of harmful products, neglect of regulations, and lack of government protections in this burgeoning new industry. In closing, he proposes a *clean cannabis manifesto* that calls for the enforcement of much stricter regulations, and regulatory oversights prioritizing safeguards that ensure the health and safety of both workers and consumers.

In sum, the contributions in Part 2, through a variety of disciplinary lenses and methodological approaches, argue for a rethink of assumptions guiding cannabis policy development. The authors call on policy makers to pay more than mere *lip service* to the goal of harm reduction when it comes to regulating legal cannabis production and consumption of these products. Collectively, the chapters in Part 2 call for adopting a more critical and nuanced understanding of the evidence informing Canada's new "public health approach."

Part 3 extends the ethnographic orientation of Chapter 8 so as to give the last word to nonacademic voices that tell the social history of cannabis in Canada. Inspired by feminist and postcolonial methodologies, each of the six chapters underscores the need for more engagement with messy texts and narratives reflecting lived experience. Part 3 is bookended (in Chapters 9 and 14) by the contributions of female industry insiders Jeannette VanderMarel, Karina Lahnakoski, and Alison McMahon and well-known social activist Jodie Emery, each of whom have very different and important tales to tell. The wide array of narratives presented in between include voices seldom heard in drug-policy discussions, such as those of socially excluded, dislocated, and alienated persons seen as disposable by society.

A core constituency of this group, as described in Chapter 10 by Kelly Insley, consists of literally and figuratively institutionalized persons, including the chronically ill and addicted and the neurodivergent "medical cannabis patient." In their refusal to be categorized and easily disposed of by social institutions, there is a sense of subjectivity, a human thread they share that is repressed by institutionally acceptable personas and subject positions. A different kind of subjectivity is shown in Chapter 11 by Kanenhariyo Seth LeFort, who offers unique insight into an Indigenous worldview. This serves as a gateway to broader understanding by helping us to situate cannabis law reform within a larger framework of anticolonial legal struggle. In so doing, it provides a counternarrative that highlights the complex relationship between Indigenous sovereignty and the conflicting principles of (neo)liberal democracy.

Chapters 12 by Kelly Coulter and Chapter 13 by Clayton McCann present cannabis cultural folklore as a form of narrative that tells of lived experience as a tool to deconstruct the myths of the black market. Bearing the marks of authenticity of a cultural achievement that contradicts official claims and policy pronouncements, these selections do not merely debunk the claims and language of bureaucrats and technocrats – they are also products of a world with different meanings. The people of the plant are far from normal in a world that appears to be seeking to normalize cannabis. It remains to be seen if and how public policy demands to standardize and regulate consumers of these products will manage to effectively accommodate their differences.

Envisaging the Future: Some Preliminary Remarks
With an eye to protecting the legacy of Canada's cannabis folk market, we envisage a sustainable future for craft cannabis prioritizing the protection of the environment, fair trade, and labour standards. With legalization came the corporatization of cannabis and, with it, the compulsion to accumulate the large sums of finance capital required to make money from money (Røyvrik 2013). The corporation is the principal sociolegal arrangement under late capitalism in Western society. Thus, in many ways, it is the "scaffolding – or form – of life," comprising legal-rational and cultural formations (Rose 1993, 198).

When the Government of Canada began investing in corporate cannabis production, there could be no other outcome. And now the record shows that legalization has been sold to Canadians and investors based on claims that new producers would be willing and able to actually produce cannabis. Not so, as we shall show. The documented "pump and dump" schemes are a byproduct of intensified demand for capital accumulation that obscures the aggregate of skills, history, and knowledge that created the demand and supply to begin with.

Karl Marx used the term *commodity fetishism* to describe neglect of the labour that produced the product because of an obsession with the commodity itself. Workers' labour is exploited when they are rendered into interchangeable parts of the production process through deskilling and industrialization. It has been observed, however, that exploitation and corruption are not inevitable conditions of legal cannabis production.

With Ryan Stoa (2018; see also Schaneman 2020), we envisage a way forward that is organized, protected, and sustainable. Cannabis cultivation has important implications for natural resources and ecosystems because of pollutants, irrigation, energy consumption, and soil integrity, all of which are variables that affect human health (Seddon and Floodgate 2020). The adoption of the appellation model practised in French wine-growing regions is a solution that will create "a legally protected geographical indication of origin" for local cannabis production.

In addition to ensuring quality and regulations protecting the environment, workers, and consumers, Stoa notes a number of advantages for communities, not the least of which are job creation and tourism with profits that benefit local rural economies. Cultivation standards within appellations better encourage compliance to conserve and protect water, soil integrity, and use of renewable energy sources. Regulations can include incentives to transition to cleaner production techniques and technologies and to prevent the use of toxic pesticides and fertilizers.

There is no good reason, observes Stoa, that craft cannabis can't be just as popular and profitable as craft breweries in the beer industry. The creation of a localized identity around regional cannabis production would provide legal protection of the intellectual property of growers and a guarantee of authenticity for buyers. Creating access to markets for small, family-owned farms would create ancillary trade organizations and co-ops and supports a lengthy chain of connected local insurance, commercial, retail, and financial services.

Channelling billions of dollars of cannabis revenue into small-scale farming ventures would spur rural renewal. In Canada, much like the United States, there is little standing in the way of a concerted "public effort to create an agricultural model for the cannabis industry that serves the public interest" (Stoa 2018, 190). Bill C-45, the legislation governing legalization, permits Health Canada to regulate this sector. No laws need to be changed to reduce the well-documented social harm attributable to low-cost, low-quality cannabis flooding the market.[13]

Another social cost of legalization in its present manifestation is the considerable loss of agricultural knowledge and heritage in Canada, as it has hastened to adopt the mobile corporate model:

> As has frequently been observed, financial markets move their investments around at a pace that is out of all proportion to the commodity exchanges that not so long ago underlay the basics of international financial fluctuations. Financial markets may be regarded as exploiting countries or firms ... They shift capital to a country (currency purchases, loans to the state, acquisition of an interest in local firms), but can withdraw it at any moment (this possibility being stipulated as a condition of investment). (Boltanski and Chiapello 2005, 365–66)

This devotion to private enterprise in business all but assures the eventual migration of resources and skills to the United States after federal legalization.

Perhaps the time is right to adopt a more responsible approach to legalization that is modelled on Stoa's vision of a cooperative community of family farms. These arguments are revisited at the end of this volume. But, to be clear, it is our position that the time is right. The time is now.

Notes

1. Charles Baudelaire, as quoted in Jameson (1983).
2. Use of terms like *user* – as opposed to *drug consumer* and other variations such as *people who use drugs* – are increasingly disputed for their stigmatizing attributes, as are dated terms such as *marihuana* or *marijuana*, which are considered vestiges of an overtly racist past. These objections notwithstanding, we have opted to preserve the terms used in historical sources (and by the contributors) rather than replacing them with recent terminology that might be deemed more scientific or politically correct.
3. Likewise, terms such as *drug addiction, dependence, abuse, substance use disorder,* and *misuse* are socially constructed designations that are widely disputed in the literature and subject to change in science, as they are in daily common use. Their use throughout this book is at the discretion of the authors, and of we the editors, to suit our present purpose. We make no claim suggesting that these are the right terms, most appropriate or best terms, scientifically or otherwise. They are just the terms that we have used, and we accept that others may object to them and favour other terms.
4. Joseph McNamara was a well-known US police chief and a vocal critic of the war on drugs.
5. The discovery of CUD has significantly contributed to a "net widening" effect through the use of screening tools that adopt a lower threshold for delineating problematic use (Hathaway 2015a).
6. Statement in the House by Bill Blair, Liberal MP for Scarborough Southwest (Ontario), September 22nd, 2017, Canadian Parliament, https://openparliament.ca/politicians/bill-blair/?page=47.
7. Kathleen Harris, "Pot Consumers Paying Less Than $7 a Gram, Statistics Canada Survey Finds," *CBC News,* February 8, 2018. https://www.cbc.ca/news/politics/statistics-canada-cannabis-pot-price-1.4524891.
8. According to the Government of Canada (2020), "The purpose of a record suspension/pardon is to remove barriers to reintegration that can be associated with a criminal record. If an application for a record suspension/pardon is approved, the entire criminal record is to be kept separate and apart. The criminal record can only be disclosed, ceased or revoked in certain circumstances ... For expungement, the Government recognizes that those whose record of conviction constitutes a historical injustice should not be viewed as 'former offenders.' Their conviction was for an act that should never have been a crime and had the conviction occurred today, it would likely be inconsistent with the Canadian Charter of Rights and Freedoms."
9. The terms *folk market* and *folk knowledge,* as we use them in this book, refer to the informal supply and distribution networks and cultural understandings shared by those with life experience in interaction with other users and suppliers. These shared skills and knowledge have been informally passed on from one generation to the next for many decades in Canada and many Western countries; in other cultures, they extend back for hundreds, even thousands, of years.
10. For a more detailed discussion of constructionist inquiry with particular attention to drug policy and science, see Hathaway (2015a).

11 Of further note, Watson has also stated that she is "not comfortable being credited for something that had been born of a collective process." Her preference instead is that the quotation be credited to "Aboriginal activists group, Queensland, 1970s."
12 Quote attributed to Richard Price, a Cree Hunter in the province of Quebec, c. 1930s.
13 In their global review, Seddon and Floodgate (2020) observe that high-THC products (shatter, resin, rosin, hashish, and nano-emulsification) can inadvertently deliver a highly toxic load of pollutants from pesticides and fertilizers in higher concentration because of the process of extraction. Potential outcomes of exposure to these toxins are rising mortality, morbidity, and ER visits. They also note that the high concentration of consumption in a small portion of the consuming population can be problematic, from a public health perspective. In Canada and globally, it is well established that Pareto's Law applies; the bulk of cannabis consumption (80 percent) is concentrated in a small proportion (20 percent) of users.

Works Cited

Altheide, David L. 1987. "Ethnographic Content Analysis." *Qualitative Sociology* 10 (1): 65–77.

Appadurai, Arjun. 1996. *Modernity at Large: Cultural Dimensions of Globalization*. Minneapolis: University of Minnesota Press.

Bakhtin, Mikhail M. 1981. *The Dialogic Imagination: Four Essays*, edited by Michael Holquist, translated by Caryl Emerson and Holquist, 33. Austin: University of Texas Press.

Barthes, Roland. 1972. "Jeunes chercheurs" (Research: The young). *Communications* 19: 1–5.

Becker, Howard S. 1963. *Outsiders: Studies in the Sociology of Deviance*. New York: Free Press.

Berger, Peter L., and Thomas Luckmann. 1991. *The Social Construction of Reality: A Treatise in the Sociology of Knowledge*. London: Penguin.

Blackman, Shane. 2011. "Rituals of Intoxication: Young People, Drugs, Risk and Leisure." In *The New Politics of Leisure and Pleasure*, edited by Peter Bramham and Stephen Wagg, 97–118. New York: Palgrave Macmillan.

Boltanski, Luc, and Eve Chiapello. 2005. *The New Spirit of Capitalism*. London: Verso.

Bourgois, Philippe. 2003. *In Search of Respect: Selling Crack in El Barrio*. Cambridge: Cambridge University Press.

Boyd, Susan C., and Connie Carter. 2014. *Killer Weed: Marijuana Grow Ops, Media, and Justice*. Toronto: University of Toronto Press.

Burawoy, Michael. 1991. "The Extended Case Method." In *Ethnography Unbound: Power and Resistance in the Modern Metropolis*, edited by Michael Burawoy, Alice Burton, Ann Arnett Ferguson, and Kathryn J. Fox, 271–90. Berkeley: University of California Press.

Burawoy, Michael, Alice Burton, Ann Arnett Ferguson, and Kathryn J. Fox. 1991. *Ethnography Unbound: Power and Resistance in the Modern Metropolis*. Berkeley: University of California Press.

CBC. 2003. "More Teens Smoke Pot Than Cigarettes: Survey." *CBC.ca*, October 29. https://www.cbc.ca/news/canada/ottawa/more-teens-smoke-pot-than-cigarettes-survey-1.378918.
Clifford, James. 1983. "On Ethnographic Authority." *Representations* 2: 118–46.
–. 1986. *Writing Culture: The Poetics and Politics of Ethnography*. Berkeley: University of California Press.
Davies, Charlotte Aull. 2012. *Reflexive Ethnography: A Guide to Researching Selves and Others*. London: Routledge.
Denzin, Norman K. 1997. *Interpretative Ethnography: Ethnographic Practices for the 21st Century*. Thousand Oaks, CA: Sage.
Ellis, Carolyn, Tony E. Adams, and Arthur P. Bochner. 2011. "Autoethnography: An Overview." *Historical Social Research* 36 (4): 273–90.
Emery, Marc. 2016. "Naming Anne McLellan as Chair of Marijuana Legalization Task Force Is Breathtakingly Offensive." *Georgia Straight*, July 24. https://www.straight.com/news/742231/marc-emery-naming-anne-mclellan-chair-marijuana-legalization-task-force-breathtakingly.
Gans, Herbert J. 2010. "Public Ethnography, Ethnography as Public Sociology." *Qualitative Sociology* 33 (1): 97–104.
Geertz, Clifford. 1966. "Religion as a Cultural System." In *Anthropological Approaches to the Study of Religion*, edited by Michael Banton, 1–46. London: Tavistock.
Goffman, Alice. 2015. *On the Run: Fugitive Life in an American City*. New York: Picador.
Goode, Erich, and Nachman Ben-Yehuda. 1994. *Moral-Panics: The Social Construction of Deviance*. Oxford: Blackwell.
Government of Canada. 2020. "Frequently Asked Questions about Expungement." https://www.canada.ca/en/parole-board/services/expungements/commonly-asked-questions.html.
Greif, Mark. 2017. "Learning to Rap." In *Against Everything: Essays*, 133–66. New York: Vintage.
Hathaway, Andrew D. 2015a. *Drugs and Society*. Don Mills, ON: Oxford University Press.
–. 2015b. "Public Criminology in an Age of Austerity: Reflections from the Margins of Drug Policy Research." *Radical Criminology* 5, On Public Criminology, II: 169–91.
Jameson, Frederic. 1983. "Pleasure: A Political Issue." In *Formations of Pleasure*, edited by the Editorial Collective, 1–14. London: Routledge/Kegan Paul.
Lee, Martin A. 2012. *Smoke Signals: A Social History of Marijuana – Medical, Recreational and Scientific*. New York: Simon and Schuster.
Marcuse, Herbert. 1969. *An Essay on Liberation*. Vol. 319. Boston: Beacon Press.
Marling, William. 1998. *The American Roman Noir: Hammett, Cain, and Chandler*. Athens: University of Georgia Press.
Mintz, Sidney Wilfred. 1986. *Sweetness and Power: The Place of Sugar in Modern History*. New York: Penguin.
Otero, Gerardo. 2017. "In Pursuit of Real Utopias: Kerry Preibisch as an Organic Public Sociologist." *Canadian Review of Sociology* 54 (3): 353–59.

Poole, Michael. 1998. *Romancing Mary Jane: A Year in the Life of a Failed Marijuana Farmer.* Vancouver: Douglas and McIntyre.

Rose, Dan. 1993. "Ethnography as a Form of Life: The Written Word and the Work of the World." In *Anthropology and Literature,* edited by P.J. Benson, 192–224. Urbana: University of Illinois Press.

Røyvrik, Emil A. 2013. *The Allure of Capitalism: An Ethnography of Management and the Global Economy in Crisis.* New York: Berghahn Books.

Schaneman, Bart. 2020. "California Outdoor Marijuana Cultivators to Designate Products by Growing Region." *MJBizDaily,* October 17. https://mjbizdaily.com/california-outdoor-marijuana-cultivators-to-designate-products-by-growing-region/.

Scott, Joan W. 1991. "The Evidence of Experience." *Critical Inquiry* 17 (4): 773–97.

—. 1992. "Experience." In *Feminists Theorize the Political,* edited by Judith Butler and Joan Scott, 22–40. New York and London: Routledge.

Seddon, Toby, and William Floodgate. 2020. *Regulating Cannabis: A Global Review and Future Directions.* London: Palgrave Macmillan.

Stoa, Ryan. 2018. *Craft Weed: Family Farming and the Future of the Marijuana Industry.* Cambridge, MA: MIT Press.

Wayman, Tom. 2014. *The Order in Which We Do Things: The Poetry of Tom Wayman,* selected and with an introduction by Owen Percy. Waterloo, ON: Wilfrid Laurier Press.

Weissman, Eric. 2017. *Tranquility on the Razor's Edge.* Oakville, ON: Rock Mills Press.

Williams, Raymond. 2013. *Keywords (Routledge Revivals): A Vocabulary of Culture and Society.* London: Routledge.

Williams, Eric. E. 1944. *Capitalism and Slavery.* Chapel Hill, NC: The University of North Carolina Press.

Wolcott, Harry F. 2004. "The Ethnographic Autobiography." *Auto/biography* 12 (2): 93.

PART 1

CANNABIS IN CONTEXT

HISTORICAL, POLITICAL, AND ECONOMIC FACTORS

1

From Prohibition to Legalization

Cannabis Use and the Law

CATHERINE CARSTAIRS

In 2018, Canada became the second country in the world, after Uruguay, to legalize the use of marijuana. Ironically, Canada was also a global leader in criminalizing cannabis back in 1923, part of an effort to position itself as an international leader in the fight against drugs. When possession of the drug became illegal, most Canadians had never even heard of marijuana, much less tried it. Today, cannabis use is widespread: grandmothers take it for their sore knees, hipsters pride themselves on their knowledge of strains, and teenagers smoke it surreptitiously at school. In the interim, Canadians have vigorously debated what the best approach might be to this complex drug, which can be used as a medicine, a tool for spiritual enlightenment, and a fun recreational high.

As use increased from the late 1960s to the present, some Canadians were outraged that young people were receiving criminal convictions that would affect their futures for smoking a drug that many regarded as harmless (Erickson 1980; Giffen, Endicott, and Lambert 1991), while others feared that smoking marijuana would lead students to lose interest in their studies and damage their lungs. Many recognized that penalties were unevenly applied, and in the past few decades there has been growing recognition that Black and Indigenous people in Canada were much more likely to be convicted of marijuana possession despite having similar rates of use. There has also been concern about the extent to which criminalization contributes to organized crime. This chapter explores the history of marijuana use in

Canada as well as the debates that have taken place over the meanings of this use and the appropriate legal and policy response.

Historians often think of themselves as magpies – inquisitive birds that like to gather and sort through all kinds of material. Above all, historians adore the archives – we love to get our hands on original correspondence and unpublished reports that allow us to get as close to the origins of an event as possible. In addition to archival documentation of the criminalization of cannabis in 1923, my research draws on the legal and sociological literature on marijuana use in Canada, newspapers and magazines and published reports, and records of debates in the House of Commons.

Since one goal of this research is to explore not just how the law changed but how Canadians responded to marijuana use over the years, research included gathering reports by governments and nongovernmental organizations, surveys, polls, anecdotal reports, and first-person accounts. And since historians are trained to treat all information sources with some skepticism, the analysis is prefaced by observing that surveys may be biased, polling data is frequently unreliable, authors are often blinded by their point of view, and first-person accounts are just that – only one person's account. The account presented here was devised by carefully weighing and qualifying the evidence. I hope it will encourage further research, recognizing that much remains to be done to fully flesh out the fascinating history of marijuana use in Canada.

The Origins of Prohibition

Why cannabis was added to the Schedule of Restricted Drugs remains somewhat of a mystery. Many scholars have suggested that it was the publication of Emily Murphy's antiopium screed, *The Black Candle*, in 1922 that persuaded the government to add marijuana to Canada's schedule of restricted drugs (Green and Miller 1975; Giffen, Endicott, and Lambert 1991; Booth 2003). Certainly, Murphy made some outrageous claims. She asserted that marijuana users "become raving maniacs" and "are liable to kill or indulge in any sort of violence" (Murphy 1922, 333). This ludicrous statement has been comic fodder for marijuana activists ever since, but it seems unlikely that it had much influence at the time. Canada was in the midst of an antidrug panic in the early 1920s, closely tied with the drive to ban Chinese immigrants from entering Canada. It was also positioning itself as a leader in the international movement against opium. In the early 1920s, Canada significantly strengthened its drug laws: in 1921, maximum sentences for trafficking and possession increased from one year to seven; in

1922, legislation allowed judges to order the deportation of any aliens convicted of possession or trafficking and introduced minimum penalties; and, in 1923, the right to an appeal was restricted, and codeine and marijuana were added to the Schedule of Restricted Drugs (Giffen, Endicott, and Lambert 1991).

There was no debate in the House of Commons about the addition of cannabis. There are few records pertaining to this issue in Library and Archives Canada and no mention of the decision in the press. But controlling cannabis had been under international discussion for more than a decade, although it did not become part of an international convention until 1925, when the Geneva Convention limited Indian hemp to "medical and scientific" consumption (Bewley-Taylor 2001; McAllister 2000). Egypt was the first country in the world to ban the sale and production of cannabis in the late nineteenth century, and in the 1910s, a number of US states passed laws against cannabis, although the federal Marijuana Tax Act would not be passed until 1937 (Kozma 2011; Johnson 2017). In 1929, the assistant chief of Canada's Narcotic Division, K.C. Hossick, wrote that Canada had to include cannabis on the schedule of restricted drugs because Canada had ratified the 1912 Hague Convention (Carstairs 2006). This was not true. It was not until 1925 that cannabis came under international control, and Canada had banned cannabis two years earlier. Even so, Hossick's reference to the international treaties is a sign that the idea for adding the drug came from international discussions.

Alexander B. Morrison, the assistant deputy minister of the Health Protection Branch, Health and Welfare Canada, later wrote that "it appears that Col. Sharman (Chief of the Narcotic Division) returned from meetings of the League of Nations convinced that cannabis would soon fall under international control. In anticipation ... he moved to have it added to the list of drugs controlled under Canadian law" (Morrison 1974, 10). This explanation seems far more likely than Murphy's book chapter. While Murphy's earlier articles in *Maclean's* had helped to incite Canada's drug panic, the book itself attracted little attention. By this point, officials in the Division of Narcotic Control had little respect for Murphy's ravings about cannabis and were unlikely to take her views on the matter seriously. Finally, the marijuana chapter was a minor inclusion in a long book devoted to the problems of opium and cocaine.

The inclusion of marijuana on the schedule meant that people found in possession of cannabis would be sentenced to a minimum of six months in prison. But this had little initial impact, as there were no convictions for the possession of marijuana in Canada for over a decade, and even then, they were unusual. From 1930 to 1946, only twenty-five people were convicted of marijuana offences in Canada (Green and Miller 1975). The drug was rarely mentioned in the press until the mid-1930s, when the antimarijuana campaign in the United States exploded, associating marijuana use with criminality, murder, and insanity. Even then, the drug attracted little attention in Canada, although the cultivation of cannabis was prohibited in 1938. That decade, the RCMP requested landowners who were growing hemp as a windbreaker to destroy the plant. Almost none of them were aware of the potentially psychoactive properties of the weed. In his autobiography, Clifford Harvison, a former commissioner of the RCMP, reported that one of the few protests came from an older woman who grew the plant to feed her canaries, believing that it improved their singing. When the RCMP tried to destroy the plants, she threatened them with a broom (Harvison 1967). As late as the mid-1950s, a study of convicted drug criminals in British Columbia found that few had ever tried the drug (Stevenson 1956). The RCMP reported that most of the cannabis arrests prior to 1962 were of musicians and other visitors from the United States (Green and Miller 1975).

The Marijuana Renaissance
Marijuana use began to grow in the United States in the 1950s through beatnik communities. Small numbers of Canadians also started to experiment with the drug. In 1966, a small study of marijuana users in Vancouver found that they were young adults and well educated. Many identified as artists. They had little in common with and little interaction with the heroin users in Vancouver (Paulus and Williams 1966). By the mid-1960s, there was a growing number of musicians, beatniks, and bohemians using the drug in southern Ontario (Coleclough and Hanley 1968). A drug seller interviewed by *Maclean's* reported that he first started using cannabis as a university student when he got a job as a waiter at an after-hours jazz club in Toronto. Eventually, he paid his way through school by selling pot to other middle-class users, including doctors, lawyers, and people working in radio and television. He reported that he liked the feeling of being high – the distortions in perception, the loss of sense of time, the intensification of emotion. By contrast, he didn't like alcohol, which made him feel like he was losing control (Stein 1964).

When the baby boomers came of age in the late 1960s, cannabis became a drug of choice. Marijuana became part of the countercultural experience:

a way to open one's mind to new ways of being and understanding. Part of marijuana's appeal was its illicit status. It allowed baby boomers to reject the "establishment" and the habits of their parents. Marijuana advocates touted that their drug would make the user more open to new experiences while alcohol diminished one's understanding of the world around them. As the LSD guru Timothy Leary put it in his *Politics of Ecstasy*, alcohol consumption brought about the "State of Emotional Stupor" while marijuana would lead to "The State of Sensory Awareness" (Leary 1968, 45). The Beatles, Janis Joplin, Bob Dylan, and The Doors, among others, sang anthems to marijuana's positive effects. Movies such as *Easy Rider* glorified travel and adventure, including smoking marijuana. Alternative newspapers praised the drug, and new stores in the Yorkville district of Toronto served as destinations for "heads" seeking roach clips, hookahs, and a range of flavoured rolling papers. Customers were welcome to use the "Trippers' Room" in the basement, where coloured lights danced (Delaplante 1967). At music festivals and be-ins, the smell of marijuana wafted through the air. Across the country, communities such as Kitsilano (Vancouver), Yorkville (Toronto), and Carré St. Louis (Montreal) became centres of hippie life, places where marijuana smoking was common (Loo 1998; Henderson 2011; Bourdieu 2012; Marquis 2014).

Young people interviewed by the Le Dain Commission of Inquiry into the Non-Medical Use of Drugs, which was created in 1969 to investigate the new drug culture, claimed that marijuana revealed "a greater sense of the universe" and enthused that "things you never noticed ... now jump out ... and every event becomes suddenly deep" (Canada 1969a, 110). Another suggested that drug use created "new insights" and "social relationships" that threatened the status quo (Canada 1969b, 168). Another member of the public waxed about the "joy," "ecstasy," and "grace" that came from smoking pot and declared that "one sees reality in a new way ... that is sometimes very scary and sometimes very beautiful, but in a way that is extremely meaningful to the individual" (Canada 1969c, 32).

Marijuana convictions skyrocketed from the mid-1960s through the mid-1970s. This partially reflected increased use of the drug, but it was also the result of increased enforcement capacity. From 1969 to 1971, the RCMP nearly doubled the size of its drug squad. It also provided training to municipal police forces on how to deal with drug offences and started turning simple possession over to better-staffed municipal police departments (Erickson 1980). Prior to this time, the vast majority of people convicted under Canada's drug laws were heroin users. Most were poor, many came from troubled homes, and they had usually been in trouble with the law before they were convicted of drug possession (Carstairs 2006).

The people arrested for marijuana offences beginning in the mid-1960s came from a different demographic. The overwhelming majority were twenty-five years of age or younger. Many were well educated and middle class. And yet, some were receiving long sentences, despite the fact that the mandatory minimums had been removed in 1961. In 1968, for example, a twenty-five-year-old graduate student was sentenced to six months for possession. A few months later, a twenty-year-old student from Manitoba was sentenced to a year for the same offence. The disparities in sentencing practices were alarming – many people were receiving suspended sentences or fines while others were going to jail, depending on which judge was hearing the case (Whitaker 1969).

Protesting the Crackdown
Middle-class youth were outraged by the long sentences given out for marijuana possession, as were some of their parents. In the House of Commons, several middle-aged legislators were highly critical of the impact marijuana convictions would have on youth. Arnold Peters, the New Democrat MP from Timiskaming, proclaimed that it would be a "travesty of justice" to put in jail all of the people who were experimenting with marijuana and pronounced that the "police have been awfully stupid ... in regard to this problem" (Canada 1968, 8098). The Conservative MP from Calgary North, Eldon Woolliams, also complained that young lives were being destroyed by severe penalties and compared the situation to prohibition (Canada 1969d, 516–17). Legislators expressed concern about the impact of a criminal record on a young person's life (Canada 1970). In 1967, a Gallup Poll reported that 59 percent of Canadians supported the decriminalization or legalization of marijuana (Giffen, Endicott, and Lambert 1991).

In 1969, amendments to the drug act made it possible for prosecutors to proceed by summary conviction. This made it far more likely that possession of marijuana would be punished by a fine rather than a jail term. Subsequent revisions to the Criminal Code in 1972 meant that many people convicted of cannabis offences could be given an "absolute" or "conditional" discharge, which meant that they paid no fines and served no time. An absolute discharge meant that the defendant would not have a criminal record, while a conditional discharge allowed the record to be expunged after a year. Most cannabis offenders after 1969 received fines, although over the course of the 1970s the number of people sentenced to serve time increased (Green and Miller 1975; Erickson 1980; Boyd 1982; Hathaway and Erickson 2003). Until 1985, when the government stopped recording sentencing outcomes for different drugs, approximately two-thirds of cannabis offences received a fine, rather than a jail term (Hathaway and Erickson 2003).

The interim report of the Le Dain Commission (1970) recommended that marijuana be transferred from the Narcotic Control Act to the Food and Drugs Act and that the penalty for a first-time marijuana possession offence be reduced to a fine of one hundred dollars. In their subsequent report on cannabis, the commissioners failed to agree. The majority thought that the charge of cannabis possession should be repealed and the penalties for trafficking, importing, and exporting reduced. Commissioner Marie-Claude Bertrand recommended legalization, while Commissioner Ian L. Campbell believed that possession of marijuana should remain a crime, with reduced penalties, to send the message that marijuana was a harmful substance (Martel 2006).

Similar debates were occurring in the United States and other countries around the world (Fischer et al. 2003). While President Nixon announced a war on drug abuse and put pressure on countries around the world to crack down on the cultivation and exportation of drugs, many other Americans were fighting to liberalize the law. In 1972, the Nixon-appointed Shafer Commission on Marijuana and Drug Abuse came out strongly in favour of decriminalization (Dufton 2017). From 1973 to 1978, twelve American states encompassing nearly one-third of the population embraced the decriminalization or legalization of marijuana. During the 1976 election, Jimmy Carter supported decriminalization while Gerald Ford held that possession should not be a crime (Dufton 2013).

Marcel Martel (2006) argues that the Liberal government did not seriously consider the idea of legalizing marijuana, partly because this would have violated the Single Convention on Narcotic Drugs, 1961, of which Canada was a signatory, and because of US opposition. Instead, politicians, including Allan MacEachen (minister of national health and welfare from 1965 to 1968) and John C. Munro (minister of health from 1968 to 1972), favoured moving marijuana from the Narcotic Control Act to the Food and Drugs Act. In 1972, after the release of the Le Dain Commission report on cannabis, Munro announced that cannabis would be transferred to the Food and Drugs Act, or another law would take it out of the Narcotic Control Act in fall 1972.

But that fall, another election took place, and the Liberals returned with a minority government. The new minister of national health and welfare,

Marc Lalonde, hesitated, preferring to wait for the final report of the Le Dain Commission. When the Liberals were elected with a majority government in 1974, a bill was introduced to the Senate which would have transferred marijuana to the Food and Drugs Act. But there was substantial opposition to changing the law. Law enforcement, including the RCMP, argued that marijuana was a gateway drug, suggesting that the young people now using marijuana would graduate to LSD or heroin use. They argued that even though marijuana was not physically addictive, it created a psychological dependence that could be even worse. They asserted that marijuana use led to memory loss, lethargy, loss of self-respect, and distortions in perception.

Even worse, the RCMP claimed that marijuana led to acts of violence and that people found in possession of marijuana, in contrast to people found in possession of heroin, were sometimes found to have firearms in their possession (Martel 2006). The fierce debate in the Senate intimidated the Liberals, as did a stream of angry letters from the public. The bill was killed by a government more concerned by inflation and unemployment (Martel 2006). The Liberals continued to express support for decriminalization. In 1977, Prime Minister Pierre Trudeau told a group of university students that "if you have a joint and you're smoking it for your own pleasure, the government's policy is that you shouldn't be hassled" (MacGregor 1979, 26). In the 1980 Speech from the Throne, the Liberals announced that they planned to reduce the penalties, but the legislation was never introduced (Gray 1982).

While little legislative change was enacted, the number of Canadians who reported having tried the drug mounted rapidly. In 1970, only 3.5 percent of Canadians reported that they had ever used marijuana, and only 1 percent said that they had used in the past year. By 1978, 17.2 percent reported lifetime use (Brochu et al. 2011). A *Globe and Mail* poll in 1979 reported that one in four Canadians had tried the drug, including nearly half of the population under thirty-five years of age (*Globe and Mail* 1979). Marijuana became an ever more common feature of daily life: newsstands now featured *High Times*, a magazine devoted to marijuana culture while movies like Cheech and Chong's *Up in Smoke* (1978) made marijuana even more mainstream. The National Organization for the Reform of Marijuana Laws (NORML), established in the United States in 1971, came to Canada in 1977 (*Globe and Mail* 1977a; Dufton 2017). Margaret Trudeau's tell-all memoir of her life with the prime minister described how she smoked pot at the PM's official residence, 24 Sussex Drive. And a *Globe and Mail* reporter revealed that he had shared a joint with a cabinet minister and an MP at the Speaker's Christmas Party (Trudeau 1979; *Globe and Mail* 1977b).

The Antipot Backlash
But despite the growing normalization of pot smoking, some parents, teachers, and doctors were growing alarmed. In 1980, the Ontario Medical Association rescinded its support for decriminalization in light of "recent medical evidence" that suggested that cannabis was not "an innocuous drug" (Korcock 1980). There was growing concern about the long-term effects on brain function and on the impact of marijuana on respiratory and reproductive health (Fehr et al. 1980). By the end of the 1970s, a parental movement had sprung up in the United States to mobilize against the growing drug culture. By the time Ronald Reagan was elected in 1980, these parental groups had succeeded in repealing decriminalization in many US states. They had also been successful at getting antiparaphernalia legislation passed across the country (Dufton 2013). In 1980, the Headmasters' Council of Ontario published a small booklet on marijuana warning that the age of first-time users was falling and that the marijuana being used was ten times stronger than the marijuana being used a decade ago. They were worried that marijuana use could create immediate danger in shop classes and science labs (Headmasters' Council 1980).

The headmasters warned that the grades of regular marijuana users fell and that they withdrew from academics and extracurriculars. They threatened that regular use could lead to brain damage, sexual dysfunction, chromosomal breakage, and lung disease. They concluded: "Use of (cannabis) products presents a very real threat to the health, welfare and safety of the young people of this country and that steps to discourage and prevent its use must be taken." They recommended that penalties for marijuana use increase and that the federal government take steps to better educate young people about marijuana (Headmasters' Council 1980). In 1980, the Addiction Research Foundation of Ontario published *Cannabis: Adverse Effects on Health*, claiming that marijuana use could lead to apathy and psychotic symptoms, that it was more carcinogenic than cigarettes, and that it could affect fertility (Fehr et al. 1980). Two years later, a group of Willowdale parents formed Parents Against Drugs, while the Parents Resource Institute for Drug Education (PRIDE) Canada was formed in Saskatchewan in 1983 (Kleinman 1985; RCMP and PRIDE 1990; *Vancouver Sun* 1988).

In the 1980s, a variety of programs were launched to prevent youthful marijuana use. The best known of these was Nancy Reagan's "Just Say No" campaign, which had her align with Proctor & Gamble to support the formation of "Just Say No" clubs in schools across the United States. The campaign had some impact in Canada. A "Just Say No" organization started in Quebec in 1986. With the support of provincial premiers, a parade float travelled across the country, and a 1–800 number was established, although the organizer subsequently got in trouble for bounced cheques and unpaid bills (Henderson 1986; Harris 1986). Antidrug campaigns received significant celebrity support. Nine-year-old television star Soleil Moon Frye (Punky Brewster) became the national chairperson of the "Just Say No" foundation, while in 1984 the entire cast of the award-winning television show *Fame* participated in an antimarijuana commercial (McCormack 1984). David Hasselhoff of the show *Knight Rider* filmed a public service announcement in which his talking car K.I.T.T. lectured young people on the cancer-causing properties of marijuana, while the television personality Mr. T threatened to "shake some sense" into children who took drugs (Alexandra 2017; Mettler 2018). The RCMP and PRIDE produced a leaflet instructing parents how to create a parent group to educate themselves about drugs, establish a speaker's bureau, and lobby against stores that sold drug paraphernalia and pro-drug T-shirts (RCMP and PRIDE 1990).

Influenced by Reagan's drug war in the United States, Mulroney's Conservative government launched its own antidrug crusade in 1987, although the Canadian Drug Strategy would put more emphasis on treatment and prevention than on enforcement (Erickson 1999). Antidrug education exploded. After the death of Benji Hayward in 1988, a fourteen-year-old who drowned in Toronto Harbour after smoking marijuana and taking LSD at a Pink Floyd concert, the government of Ontario redoubled its efforts at drug-based education, making drug education compulsory from Grade 4 through high school (Black 1989). Programs included DARE, which was developed by Los Angeles police and the Los Angeles unified school district in 1983. DARE had police officers go into schools on a weekly basis to teach students to say no to drugs (Ennett et al. 1994).

In Montreal, Capitaine Cosmos went to French-language schools along with police officers to deliver a DARE-like program (Curran 1988). The Canadian Association of Chiefs of Police developed a drug education program they called Canadian Offensive for Drug Education (CODE), which included three videos geared for different age groups, but this seems to have had little uptake (Panzeri 1990). Health and Welfare Canada developed a partnership with YTV to launch advertisements showing youth across Canada engaging in spectacular athletic feats. Called the "Really

Me" campaign, they made no mention of drugs; they were supposed to subtly encourage Canadian youth to avoid getting high (Kennedy 1989). The "Really Me" campaign also included posters, sweatshirts, and print advertisements (Kennedy 1991).

Marijuana use in Canada declined significantly; surveys from the Addiction Research Foundation of Ontario, which performed the only consistent survey of drug use in Canada, found that the number of students who reported using cannabis declined from 32 percent in 1979 to 16 percent in 1987 (Erickson 1999). Perhaps the antidrug publicity made a difference, although research on the new drug education programs suggests they had little impact (West and O'Neal 2004). It seems more likely that this generation, raised in an era when crack cocaine was taking over, was more cautious about drug use. Also, after fifteen years of widespread marijuana use, this generation was probably less likely to regard marijuana as a powerful symbol of youthful rebellion.

A Countercultural Resurgence

The reduction in marijuana use proved to be short-lived – pot culture began to flourish again in the 1990s. A new generation of musicians began to rap about their use of the drug, including Dr. Dre, Snoop Dogg, and Cypress Hill, while "stoner bands" like the Grateful Dead and Phish experienced renewed popularity (Heisler 2012; Waddell 2004). People were getting high at music festivals such as Lollapalooza, and marijuana (along with MDMA) was a favoured drug in the growing rave scene. Films such as Richard Linklater's *Dazed and Confused* glamourized the marijuana use of the 1970s, while by the end of the decade even mainstream television such as *That 70s Show* simulated marijuana use. Skateboarders and snowboarders toked regularly. Canadians seemed more amused than ashamed when the International Olympic Committee removed (and then returned) Canadian snowboarder Ross Rebagliati's gold medal in 1998 for marijuana use (Howard 1998). A new generation of legalization advocates emerged. Marc Emery, Canada's so-called Prince of Pot, began publishing *Cannabis Culture* magazine (initially titled *Cannabis Canada*) in 1995. Four years later, he started Pot TV, an internet television channel. In 2000, Emery founded the BC Marijuana Party. In the following election, the party fielded candidates in every single constituency (Mulgrew 2006).

In Quebec, Marc-Boris St. Maurice founded a provincial marijuana party, Bloc Pot, in 1998. Later, he founded the Marijuana Party of Canada that fielded seventy-one candidates in the 2000 election. He also opened compassion clubs in Montreal and Quebec City (Beausoleil 2017). David Malmo-Levine, a crimson- and sometimes green-haired activist, helped form the Harm Reduction Club in Vancouver in 1996 and fought a losing Supreme Court case in 2003, which he hoped would overturn Canada's marijuana laws (MacCharles 2003; CBC 1998). In the early 2000s, people gathered in parks, Highway 420, and other locations to smoke up on April 20 (4/20) in support of marijuana legalization (Laroque 2004; Galloway 2004).

Some Canadians were beginning to take pride in Canada's reputation for high-quality cannabis. In the late 1980s, thanks in part to increased international enforcement efforts, domestic marijuana began to displace marijuana imported from abroad (Lafrieniére and Spicer 2002; Johnson 2017). While marijuana had previously been grown outside, new hydroponic technology led to an explosion of grow-ops (Mulgrew 2006). These grow-ops increased in size, and by the 1990s Canada had become a cannabis exporter, with BC bud a luxury brand (Lafrieniére and Spicer 2002). Canadian flags with a marijuana leaf instead of a maple leaf became a common feature at demonstrations and in retail stores (*Victoria Colonist* 1996; *Calgary Herald* 1995). Canadians were also reporting much higher levels of use. In 2005, the Canadian Addiction Survey found that 44.5 percent of Canadians reported that they had used marijuana while 14.1 percent reported using it in the past year. Nearly 70 percent of people between the ages of eighteen and twenty-four reported that they had used cannabis over the course of their lifetime. People with higher incomes reported higher rates of lifetime use, as did people with higher levels of education – 44.2 percent of people with a university degree had used cannabis compared to only 34.9 percent of people who had not completed high school (Patton and Adlaf 2005).

Medical marijuana advocates began flexing their muscles. Marijuana had long been used as a medicine, although by the late nineteenth century other drugs had displaced marijuana in most products (Booth 2003). The argument that marijuana was a helpful medicine re-emerged in the 1970s when some doctors and marijuana advocates asserted that the drug could help with glaucoma and chemotherapy-induced nausea. In 1976, Robert Randall became the first American to get a legal exemption to use marijuana to control his glaucoma. In the 1980s, it became clear that marijuana could also combat the weight loss associated with AIDS (Dufton 2017; Hathaway and Rossiter 2007). In 1996, California became the first US state to allow patients' access to medical marijuana (Hannah and Mallison 2018; Ferraiolo 2007). Indeed, medical marijuana referendums were remarkably successful across the United States – as of July 2021, medical marijuana was legal in thirty-six states (National Conference of State Legislators 2021).

As the medical marijuana movement grew, Canadians learned about people like Lynn Harichy, a thirty-six-year-old with MS who was featured in *Chatelaine*. Hariachy had been diagnosed with MS at eighteen. By thirty-five, she suffered from periods of blindness and her limbs went numb. When a friend gave her a joint, she found that her pain disappeared. By smoking a joint a day, she was able to regain her concentration, and her physical symptoms lessened (Onstad 1997). In Vancouver, a young woman by the name of Hilary Black began working for Marc Emery. Many customers were looking for pain relief, and Black began to bring the herb to the ill and housebound. Eventually, she opened Canada's first "compassion club" in 1997, distributing cannabis for free or at reduced rates to people suffering from cancer, AIDS, and MS (*Canadian Press* 1997; Ore 2018). From the beginning, Canadians expressed strong support for medical marijuana – a 1997 poll showed that 83 percent of Canadians supported the legal use of marijuana for medical purposes (Erickson 1999).

In the late 1990s, a number of court cases forced the government's hand on medical marijuana. In 1998, James Wakeford, who was suffering from AIDS, sought an exemption from the laws prohibiting him from possessing marijuana. The court recommended that he be given an exemption under the Controlled Drugs and Substances Act (Grayson 2008). Terry Parker used marijuana to control his epileptic seizures. He was charged with possession but argued that the drug was medically necessary. The *R v Parker* decision insisted that Canadians be able to access medical marijuana without being subject to criminal penalties (Solomon and Clarizio 2015). The Canadian government subsequently established a medical marijuana program, although there were substantial complaints about a confusing application process and delays, as well as resistance from physicians (Jones and Hathaway 2008; Lucas 2009; Solomon and Clarizio 2015). As a result, few of the Canadians who defined their marijuana use as "medicinal" obtained legal supplies, preferring to access the drug through the illicit market (Fischer et al. 2016). In the 2000s, numerous court challenges forced changes to the medical cannabis program, which gradually improved access (Solomon and Clarizio 2015).

The Clamour for Reform in the Twenty-First Century
Beginning in the late 1990s, support for changing the law came from a wide range of organizations. In 1999, the Canadian Association of Chiefs of

Police recommended decriminalization. The following year, the Centre for Addiction and Mental Health, Canada's most prestigious research institute for drug and alcohol issues, recommended removing cannabis from the realm of criminal law. Two years later, the *Canadian Medical Association Journal* recommended decriminalization (Fischer et al. 2003). In 2000, the Senate established a special committee on illegal drugs, which recommended in 2002 that cannabis be legalized, along with amnesty for all people who had been convicted of possession. The Senate Committee on Illegal Drugs expressed significant concern about the uneven application of the law, including the possibility that "the law was applied discriminatorily" (Senate Special Committee on Illegal Drugs 2002).

The committee pointed to the fact that more than 2.5 million Canadians used marijuana in 1999 but that only 21,281 people were charged with possession, meaning that only a small percentage of Canadians were charged with a crime that many more committed. The Senate Committee concluded that "this certainly raises concerns regarding fairness" in addition to calling into question whether or not the law was functioning as a deterrent. They also pointed out cannabis was not harmful for the vast majority of users and that the laws prohibiting cannabis had not prevented Canada from having one of the highest rates of use in the world (Senate Special Committee on Illegal Drugs 2002). This was followed by a House of Commons committee that recommended the decriminalization of possession and cultivation of no more than thirty grams of cannabis for personal use (Hathaway and Erickson 2003).

In 2003, the Liberals introduced Bill-38, which would have decriminalized the possession of fifteen grams of cannabis. Possession of small amounts would no longer be a criminal offence and would be punished with a small fine of one hundred to four hundred dollars. The bill would have increased penalties for cultivation. The bill died when the government was prorogued. In 2004, the Martin government reintroduced the bill, now known as Bill C-17, but the bill was referred to committee, and the government fell before the bill returned to Parliament. There was strong pressure from the United States against decriminalization. The US drug czar John Walters pledged to "respond to the threat" that this posed to the United States (Hyshka 2009; Klein 2003, 12). With the election of Conservative Stephen Harper, the opportunity for reform passed. In 2010, Harper's National Drug Strategy announced that Canada was getting "tougher" on drug crimes. And in 2012, Bill C-10 increased the penalties for minor drug offences (Khenti 2015).

From Prohibition to Legalization

TABLE 1.1
Lifetime cannabis use, Canada, 1970–2017

Year	Report	(%)
1970	Le Dain Commission	3.4
1978	Unclear – Reported in Senate Committee on Illicit Drugs	17.0
1994	Alcohol and Other Drugs Survey	23.0
2004	Canadian Alcohol and Drug Use Monitoring Survey	44.5
2008	Canadian Alcohol and Drug Use Monitoring Survey	43.9
2012	Canadian Alcohol and Drug Use Monitoring Survey	41.5
2017	Canadian Tobacco, Alcohol and Drugs Survey	46.6

Sources: Canada 2002; Health Canada 2013, 2015, 2017.

TABLE 1.2
Cannabis consumption in the past twelve months, fifteen years of age and over, Canada, 1985–2017

Year	Report	(%)
1985	Health Promotion Survey	5.6
1989	National Alcohol and Other Drugs Survey	6.5
1990	Health Promotion Survey	5.0
1993	General Social Survey	4.2
1994	National Alcohol and Other Drugs Survey	7.4
2004	Canadian Alcohol and Drug Use Monitoring Survey	14.1
2008	Canadian Alcohol and Drug Use Monitoring Survey	11.4
2010	Canadian Alcohol and Drug Use Monitoring Survey	10.7
2012	Canadian Alcohol and Drug Use Monitoring Survey	10.2
2013	Canadian Tobacco, Alcohol and Drugs Survey	11.0
2015	Canadian Tobacco, Alcohol and Drugs Survey	12.0
2017	Canadian Tobacco, Alcohol and Drugs Survey	15.0

Sources: Canada 2002; Health Canada 2013, 2015, 2017.

Even so, marijuana use continued to rise, as suggested by both lifetime and past-year prevalence statistics reported over several decades (see Tables 1.1 and 1.2).

In 2017, Health Canada's Canadian Tobacco, Alcohol and Drugs Survey reported that 47 percent of Canadians over the age of fifteen reported that they had used cannabis at some point, while 15 percent of them had used in the past year. A 2013 UNICEF report found that Canadian teenagers used marijuana more frequently than teenagers in any other wealthy country

(UNICEF 2013). As the Liberal Party pointed out in its 2015 platform statement, young Canadians were using marijuana despite the law. Too many people were acquiring criminal records, and it was costly for the judicial system. At the same time, the marijuana trade was reported to be fuelling organized crime "and greater threats to public safety, like human trafficking and hard drugs" (Liberal Party 2015).

In the early decades of the twenty-first century, Canadians began to express alarm about the extent to which the marijuana trade was feeding organized crime (Stop the Violence 2013; Easton 2004). For very different reasons, both police and marijuana advocates drew attention to the possible links: the police wanted more money for enforcement, while marijuana advocates argued that a legal supply would undercut organized crime (Foot 2004). While the degree to which organized crime makes money off marijuana is debatable – journalist Jerry Langton, who has written extensively on organized crime in Canada, argues that marijuana is too bulky, too smelly, and too unprofitable for organized crime to bother with although they do make money threatening producers in their territories – the concern was real (Langton 2018; see also Boyd and Carter 2014).

In 2017, the Liberals introduced Bill C-45 into the House of Commons to legalize marijuana. While the legislation passed easily in the House, with the support of the NDP and the Bloc Québécois, there were some delays in the Senate, but the legislation was finally approved in June 2018. After some time to allow the provinces to develop systems of sale and control, cannabis became legal in Canada on October 17, 2018. But an important issue remained. As many as half a million Canadians have a criminal record for cannabis possession. A criminal record can prevent people from travelling outside of Canada, can prohibit someone from volunteering in schools, or prevent someone from being hired in certain jobs. Back in 2002, when the Senate Committee on Illicit Drugs reported, it recommended an amnesty for all people convicted of marijuana possession. As the group Cannabis Amnesty has argued, the lack of an amnesty has a particular impact on Black and Indigenous people in Canada (LeBlanc 2018; Harris 2019).

Drug laws have long been enforced in racially discriminatory ways (Carstairs 2006; Mosher 1988). Beginning in 1995 with the *Report of the Commission on Systemic Racism in the Ontario Criminal Justice System* (Cole, Gittens, and CSROCJS 1995), there was growing concern about the degree to which Black youth were disproportionately targeted by police for marijuana offences and were more likely to spend time in prison when sentenced (Roberts and Doob 1997; Ontario 1995). A 2002 study showed that while Black youth were less likely to use marijuana in Toronto than their white counterparts, they were far more likely to be arrested for drug offences: 65 percent of Black youth who dealt drugs had been arrested at some point, compared to only 35 percent of the white youth who dealt drugs (Wortley and Tanner 2005).

In 2002, the *Toronto Star* did a series on race and policing. It used data produced by the Toronto Police Service's Criminal Information Processing System and showed that Black Torontonians were much more likely to be arrested for drug possession than other city residents. When charged with possession, Blacks were much more likely to be taken to the police station (48.2 percent) than whites (23.5 percent) and were twice as likely to be held overnight (Rankin, Quinn, and Sheppard 2002; Wortley and Tanner 2005). In 2018, a study by *Vice* magazine, in cooperation with University of Toronto criminologists Akwasi Owusu-Bempah and Alex Luscombe, showed that from 2015 to 2017, Indigenous people in Regina were nine times more likely to be arrested for cannabis possession than white people, despite similar rates of use. Black people in Halifax were five times more likely to be arrested for possession than whites. In Ottawa, people identifying as Indigenous, Black, and "middle eastern" were overrepresented in cannabis arrests (Browne 2018). The Liberal government passed amnesty legislation in 2019, but critics complain that the legislation was too restrictive and did not go far enough to remedy the racial injustices (CBC, 2021).

Canadian attitudes toward marijuana use have significantly changed from 1923, when the decision was made to criminalize the drug, to 2018 when the decision was made to legalize marijuana use. The normalizing trend observed for decades is, in large part, attributed to its increasing familiarity and accommodation by nonusers of the drug (Hathaway 1997; Hathaway et al. 2016). Few Canadians had any experience with marijuana in 1923. By the early twenty-first century, the vast majority of Canadians either used themselves or had friends or family members who used it. Marijuana seemed to hold out new possibilities – not only can you use it to get high, it can be used to reduce the aches or pains of people suffering from chronic diseases.

The problems associated with criminalization, such as organized crime, seemed to be a greater risk than the illusory benefit of reducing use through legal penalties. For Canadians concerned about racial prejudice, it also seemed increasingly clear that the drug laws were being used against minority groups. While the 1923 criminalization took place in near silence, the

2018 legalization was met with celebration. Media interviewed people lined up for legal pot across the country, and there was a feeling of festivity in the air. And yet, concerns remain, especially about the long-term impact of marijuana use on teenagers. While legalization seems fairly secure, it will be interesting to see how the debate over the health benefits and risks of marijuana use evolves over the next decade.

Works Cited

Alexandra, Rae. 2017. "The Insane World of Vintage Anti-marijuana PSAs." *KQED Arts*, December 4. https://www.kqed.org/pop/97017/the-insane-world-of-vintage-anti-marijuana-psas.

Beausoleil, Jean-Marc. 2017. *Monsieur Boris et le cannabis*. Montreal: Québec Amérique.

Bewley-Taylor, David R. 2001. *The United States and International Drug Control, 1909–1997*. London: Continuum.

Black, Debra. 1989. "Drug Education Put to the Test." *Toronto Star*, October 11.

Booth, Martin. 2003. *Cannabis: A History*. London: Doubleday.

Boudrieu, Michael. 2012. "'The Struggle for a Different World': The 1971 Gastown Riot in Vancouver." In *Debating Dissent: Canada and the 1960s*, edited by Gregory Kealey, Lara Campbell, and Dominique Clément, 117–34. Toronto: University of Toronto Press.

Boyd, Neil. 1982. "Taking a Well-Earned Potshot." *Maclean's*, January 19, 10.

Boyd, Susan C., and Connie Carter. 2014. *Killer Weed: Marijuana Grow Ops, Media, and Justice*. Toronto: University of Toronto Press.

Brochu, Serge, Cameron Duff, Mark Asbridge, and Patricia Gail Erickson. 2011. "'There's What's on Paper and Then There's What Happens, Out on the Sidewalk': Cannabis Users Knowledge and Opinions of Canadian Drug Laws." *Journal of Drug* 41 (1), 1: 95–115.

Browne, Rachel. 2018. "Black and Indigenous People Are Overrepresented in Canada's Weed Arrests." *Vice News*, April 18. https://news.vice.com/en_ca/article/d35eyq/black-and-indigenous-people-are-overrepresented-in-canadas-weed-arrests.

Calgary Herald. 1995. "Displays Emphasis on Marijuana Worrisome." February 28.

Canada. 1968. *House of Commons Debates, Official Report*. March 26. Ottawa: Queen's Printer.

—. 1969a. *Transcripts of Hearings of the Canada Commission of Inquiry into the Non-Medical Use of Drugs*. October 18. Toronto: St Lawrence Hall.

—. 1969b. *Transcripts of Hearings of the Canada Commission of Inquiry into the Non-Medical Use of Drugs*. October 31. Toronto: Queen Elizabeth Theatre.

—. 1969c. *Transcripts of Hearings of the Canada Commission of Inquiry into the Non-Medical Use of Drugs*. October 17. Toronto: McLaughlin College.

—. 1969d. *House of Commons Debates, Official Report*. November 4. Ottawa: Queen's Printer.

—. 1970. *House of Commons Debates, Official Report.* April 7. Ottawa: Queen's Printer.
—. 2002. *Report of the Senate Committee on Illegal Drugs: Cannabis.* https://sencanada.ca/content/sen/committee/371/ille/rep/summary-e.htm.
—. 2004. *Canadian Alcohol and Drug Use Monitoring Survey Health Canada.* Ottawa: Office of Controlled Substances and Tobacco Directorate.
—. 2008. *Canadian Alcohol and Drug Use Monitoring Survey Health Canada.* Ottawa: Office of Controlled Substances and Tobacco Directorate.
—. 2010. *Canadian Alcohol and Drug Use Monitoring Survey Health Canada.* Ottawa: Office of Controlled Substances and Tobacco Directorate.
—. 2012. *Canadian Alcohol and Drug Use Monitoring Survey.* Ottawa: Office of Controlled Substances and Tobacco Directorate. https://www.canada.ca/en/health-canada/services/health-concerns/drug-prevention-treatment/drug-alcohol-use-statistics/canadian-alcohol-drug-use-monitoring-survey-summary-results-tables-2012.html.
—. 2013. *Canadian Tobacco, Alcohol and Drugs Survey.* Ottawa: Office of Controlled Substances and Tobacco Directorate. https://www.canada.ca/en/health-canada/services/canadian-tobacco-alcohol-drugs-survey/2013-summary.html.
—. 2015. *Canadian Tobacco, Alcohol and Drugs Survey.* Ottawa: Office of Controlled Substances and Tobacco Directorate. https://www.canada.ca/en/health-canada/services/canadian-tobacco-alcohol-drugs-survey/2015-summary.html.
—. 2017. *Canadian Tobacco, Alcohol and Drugs Survey.* Ottawa: Office of Controlled Substances and Tobacco Directorate. https://www.canada.ca/en/health-canada/services/canadian-tobacco-alcohol-drugs-survey/2017-summary.html.
Canadian Press. 1997. "Vancouver Club Supplies Medicinal Marijuana." July 19.
Carstairs, Catherine. *Jailed for Possession: Illegal Drug Use, Regulation and Power in Canada, 1920–61.* Vancouver: UBC Press, 2006.
CBC. 2021. "3 Years after Legalization, number of Cannabis Charges Pardoned is Low: Expert," October 24. https://www.cbc.ca/radio/checkup/after-3-years-was-legalizing-cannabis-a-good-idea-1.6220073/3-years-after-legalization-number-of-cannabis-charges-pardoned-is-low-expert-1.6222785.
—. 1998. "Canada's Most Flamboyant Pot Activist." *Big Life,* December 2. CBC Digital Archives. https://www.cbc.ca/archives/entry/canadas-most-flamboyant-pot-activist.
Cole, David P., Margaret Gittens, and CSROCJS Ontario. 1995. *Report of the Commission on Systemic Racism in the Ontario Criminal Justice System.* Toronto: The Commission.
Coleclough, A., and Lloyd G. Hanley. 1968. "Marijuana Users in Toronto." In *Deviant Behavior in Canada,* edited by W.E. Mann, 257–91. Toronto: Social Science.
Curran, Peggy. 1988. "Five-Year Education Program Seeks to Enlist Teens to Wage War on Drugs." *Montreal Gazette,* November 5.
Delaplante, Don. 1967. "Yorkville Story Pushes Petition: Claims Top People Use Pot." *Globe and Mail,* August 8.
Dufton, Emily. 2013. "Parents, Peers and Pot: The Rise of the Drug Culture and the Birth of the Parent Movement, 1976–1980." *Trans-Scripts* 3: 211–36.

—. 2017. *Grass Roots: The Rise and Fall and Rise of Marijuana in America.* New York: Basic Books.
Easton, Stephen T. 2004. "Marijuana Growth in British Columbia." Fraser Institute Occasional Paper 74.
Ennett, Susan T., Nancy S. Tobler, Christopher L. Ringwalt, and Robert L. Flewelling. 1994. "How Effective Is Drug Abuse Resistance Education? A Meta-analysis of Project DARE Outcome Evaluations." *American Journal of Public Health* 84 (9): 1394–1401.
Erickson, Patricia. 1980. *Cannabis Criminals.* Toronto: Addiction Research Foundation.
—. 1999. "A Persistent Paradox: Drug Law and Policy in Canada." *Canadian Journal of Criminology* 41: 275–76.
Fehr, Kevin O'Brien, Oriana Josseau Kalant, Harold Kalant, and Eric Single. 1980. *Cannabis: Adverse Effects on Health.* Toronto: Addiction Research Foundation.
Ferraiolo, Kathleen. 2007. "From Killer Weed to Popular Medicine: The Evolution of American Drug Control Policy, 1937–2000." *Journal of Policy History* 19 (2): 147–79.
Fischer, Benedikt, Kari Ala-Leppilampi, Eric Single, and Amanda Robins. 2003. "Cannabis Law Reform in Canada: Is the 'Saga of Promise Hesitation and Retreat' Coming to an End." *Canadian Journal of Criminology and Criminal Justice* 45 (3), 3: 265–98.
Fischer, Benedikt, Sharan Kuganesan, and Robin Room. 2015. "Medical Marijuana Programs: Implications for Cannabis Control Policy – Observations from Canada." *International Journal of Drug Policy* 26: 15–19.
Foot, Richard. 2004. "Pot." *Vancouver Sun,* March 4.
Galloway, Gloria. 2004. "Potheads Ready to Roll on Day They Call 4:20." *Globe and Mail,* April 20.
Giffen, P. James, Shirley Endicott, and Sylvia Lambert. 1991. *Panic and Indifference: The Politics of Canada's Drug Law.* Ottawa: Canadian Centre on Substance Abuse.
Globe and Mail. 1977a. "Four Lawyers Launch Campaign for Easing of Marijuana Penalties." March 3.
—. 1977b. "Hill Offers Sanctuary to Pot Smokers." January 24.
—. 1979. "Marijuana." June 21.
Gray, John. 1982. "The Marijuana Predicament." *Globe and Mail,* January 26.
Grayson, Kyla. *Chasing Dragons: Security, Identity and Illicit Drugs in Canada.* Toronto: University of Toronto Press, 2008.
Hannah, A. Lee, and Daniel J. Mallison. 2017. "Defiant Innovation: The Adoption of Medical Marijuana Laws in the American States." *Policy Studies Journal* 46 (2): 402–23.
Harris, Lewis. 1986. "High-Rolling Anti-drug Group in Shambles, Critics Say." *Montreal Gazette,* July 10.
Harvison, Clifford. 1967. *The Horsemen.* Toronto: McClelland and Stewart.
Hathaway, Andrew D. 1997. "Marijuana and Tolerance: Revisiting Becker's Sources of Control." *Deviant Behavior* 18 (2): 103–24.
Hathaway, Andrew D., and Patricia G. Erickson. 2003. "Drug Reform Principles and Policy Debates: Harm Reduction Prospects for Cannabis in Canada." *Journal of Drug Issues* 33 (3): 467–96.

Hathaway, Andrew, Amir Mostaghim, Kat Kolar, Patricia G. Erickson, and Geraint Osborne. 2016. "A Nuanced View of Normalisation: Attitudes of Cannabis Non-users in a Study of Undergraduate Students at Three Canadian Universities." *Drugs: Education, Prevention and Policy* 23 (3): 238–46.

Hathaway, Andrew D., and Kate Rossiter. 2007. "Medical Marijuana, Community Building, and Canada's Compassionate Societies." *Contemporary Justice Review* 10 (3): 283–96.

Health Canada. 2013. *Canadian Tobacco, Alcohol and Drugs Survey (CTADS): 2013 Summary.* https://www.canada.ca/en/health-canada/services/canadian-tobacco-alcohol-drugs-survey/2013-summary.html.

–. 2015. *Canadian Tobacco, Alcohol and Drugs Survey (CTADS): 2015 Summary.* https://www.canada.ca/en/health-canada/services/canadian-tobacco-alcohol-drugs-survey/2015-summary.html.

–. 2017. *Canadian Tobacco, Alcohol and Drugs Survey (CTADS): Summary of Results 2017.* https://www.canada.ca/en/health-canada/services/canadian-tobacco-alcohol-drugs-survey/2017-summary.html.

Heisler, Steve. 2012. "Phish Stoner Story." *Vice,* April 24. https://www.vice.com/en_ca/article/9bn37p/phish-stoner-story.

Henderson, Rachelle. 1986. "Anti-drug Campaign Teaches Children How to 'Just Say No.'" *Montreal Gazette,* May 21.

Henderson, Stuart. 2011. *Making the Scene: Yorkville and Hip Toronto in the 1960s.* Toronto: University of Toronto Press.

Howard, Ross. 1998. "Rebagliati Gets Hero's Welcome." *Globe and Mail,* February 18.

Hyshka, Elaine. 2009. "The Saga Continues: Canadian Legislative Attempts to Reform Cannabis Law in the Twenty-First Century." *Canadian Journal of Criminology and Criminal Justice* 51: 73–91.

Johnson, Nick. 2017. *Grass Roots: A History of Cannabis in the American West.* Corvallis: Oregon State University Press.

Jones, Craig, and Andrew D. Hathaway. 2008. "Marijuana Medicine and Canadian Physicians: Challenges to Meaningful Drug Policy Reform." *Contemporary Justice Review* 11 (2): 165–75.

Kennedy, Janice. 1989. "Really Me: Teens Beat Challenges for YTV Series of Anti-drug Vignettes." *Montreal Gazette,* December 30.

–. 1991. "Growing Up Hooked." *Ottawa Citizen,* March 26.

Khenti, Akwatu. 2014. "The Canadian War on Drugs: Structural Violence and Unequal Treatment of Black Canadians." *International Journal of Drug Policy* 25 (2): 190–95.

Klein, Naomi. 2003. "Canada: Hippie Nation?" *The Nation* 277 (3): 12.

Kleinman, Cindy. 1985. "Parents Against Drugs." *Toronto Star,* July 16.

Korcok, Milan. 1980. "Marijuana Warnings: New Evidence against the 'Soft' Drug." *Canadian Medical Association Journal* 123: 575–80.

Lafrieniére, Gérald, and Leah Spicer. 2002. "Illicit Drug Trends in Canada, 1980–2001: A Review and Analysis of the Enforcement Data." Prepared for the Special Senate Committee on Illegal Drugs, Library of Parliament, June 26. https://sencanada.ca/content/sen/committee/371/ille/library/drugtrends-e.htm.

Langton, Jerry. 2018. "Even with Legalized Marijuana, Organized Crime Isn't Going Away." *Globe and Mail,* May 26.

Laroque, Corey. 2004. "Pot Rally at 4:20, Near the 420, on 4/20." *Niagara Falls Review,* April 13.

Leary, Timothy. 1968. *The Politics of Ecstasy.* New York: Putnam.

LeBlanc, Daniel. 2018. "Canadians Convicted of Simple Cannabis Possession Will Soon Be Able to Apply for a Pardon." *Globe and Mail,* October 17. https://www.theglobeandmail.com/cannabis/article-amnesty-program-for-canadians-convicted-of-simple-cannabis-possession/.

Le Dain Commission of Inquiry into the Non-Medical Use of Drugs. 1970. *Interim Report of the Commission of Inquiry into the Non-Medical Use of Drugs.* Ottawa: Queen's Printer.

Liberal Party. "A New Plan for a Strong Middle Class." https://liberal.ca/wp-content/uploads/sites/292/2020/09/New-plan-for-a-strong-middle-class.pdf.

Loo, Tina. 1998. "Flower Children in Lotusland." *The Beaver* 78 (1): 36–41.

MacCharles, Tonda. 2003. "Highest Court Backs Pot Law." *Toronto Star,* December 24.

MacGregor, Roy. 1979. "Pot Legislation: Promises to Keep." *Maclean's,* April 2, 26.

Marquis, Greg. 2014. "Constructing an Urban Drug Ecology in 1970s Canada." *Urban History Review* 41 (1): 27–40.

Martel, Marcel. 2006. *Not This Time: Canadians, Public Policy and the Marijuana Question, 1961–1975.* Toronto: University of Toronto Press.

McAllister, William B. 2000. *Drug Diplomacy in the Twentieth Century.* London: Routledge.

McCormack, Pat. 1984. "Marijuana Is Good for ... Nothing." *Toronto Star,* May 25.

Mettler, Katie. 2018. "Mr. T Dressed as Santa; Nancy Reagan Sat on His Lap." *Washington Post,* 21 December.

Morrison, Alexander. 1974. "Regulatory Control of the Canadian Government over the Manufacturing, Distribution and Prescribing of Psychotropic Drugs." In *Social Aspects of the Medical Use of Psychotropic Drugs,* edited by Ruth Cooperstock, 9–20. Toronto: Alcoholism and Drug Addiction Research Foundation.

Mosher, Clayton. 1998. *Discrimination and Denial: Systemic Racism in Ontario's Legal and Criminal Justice Systems, 1892–1961.* Toronto: University of Toronto Press.

Mulgrew, Ian. 2006. *Bud Inc.: Inside Canada's Marijuana Industry.* Toronto: Vintage Canada.

Murphy, Emily. 1922. *The Black Candle.* Toronto: Thomas Allen.

National Conference of State Legislators. 2021. "State Marijuana Laws." http://www.ncsl.org/research/health/state-medical-marijuana-laws.aspx.

Onstad, Katrina. 1997. "Rx: Marijuana." *Chatelaine* 70 (11): 164–66.

Ontario. 1995. "Commission on Systemic Racism in the Ontario Criminal Justice System." Ontario: The Commision.

Ontario Secondary School Teachers' Federation. 1980. "The Marijuana Issue: A Headmaster's Perspective." Toronto: Micromedia. https://www.worldcat.org/title/marijuana-issue-a-headmasters-perspective/oclc/612808036&referer=brief_results.

Ore, Jonathan. 2018. "How Compassion Club Founder Hilary Black Changed the Course of Cannabis Law in Canada." CBC Radio, October 20.

Panzeri, Allen. 1990. "Alberta Schools Reject Police Anti-drug Videos." *Edmonton Journal*, February 21.

Patton, David, and Edward M. Adlaf. 2005. "Cannabis Use and Problems." *Canadian Addiction Survey*, 48–54. Ottawa: Canadian Centre on Substance Abuse.

Paulus, Ingeborg, and Hugh Williams. 1966. "Marijuana and Young Adults." *BC Medical Journal* 8 (6): 240–44.

Rankin, Jim, Jennifer Quinn, and Michelle Sheppard. 2002. "Singled Out." *Toronto Star*, October 19.

RCMP and PRIDE. 1990. *Youth and Drugs: What Parent Groups Can Do to Create Drug Resistant Communities.* Ottawa: RCMP.

Roberts, Julian V., and Antony N. Doob. 1997. "Race, Ethnicity and Criminal Justice in Canada." *Crime and Justice* 21: 469–522.

Senate Special Committee on Illegal Drugs. 2002. *Cannabis: Our Position for a Canadian Public Policy.* https://sencanada.ca/content/sen/committee/371/ille/rep/summary-e.htm.

Solomon, Robert, and Michael Clarizio. 2015. "The Highs and Lows of Medical Marijuana Regulation in Canada." *Criminal Law Quarterly* 62 (4): 536–61.

Stein, David Lewis. 1964. "How I Worked My Way through College Selling Pot." *Maclean's*, January 4.

Stevenson, George H. 1956. *Drug Addiction in British Columbia.* Vancouver: UBC.

Stop the Violence. "About Us." http://stoptheviolencebc.org/.

Trudeau, Margaret. 1979. *Margaret Trudeau: Beyond Reason.* New York: Paddington Press.

UNICEF. 2013. *Child Well-Being in Rich Countries: A Comparative Overview.* UNICEF Office of Research, Innocenti Report Card 11. https://www.unicef.ca/sites/default/files/legacy/imce_uploads/DISCOVER/OUR%20WORK/ADVOCACY/DOMESTIC/POLICY%20ADVOCACY/DOCS/unicef_report_card_11.pdf.

Vancouver Sun. 1988. "Parents Advised to Look for Clues of Drug Use by Kids." May 31.

Victoria Colonist. 1996. "'Century Belongs to Canada': Thousand Throng to Parliament." July 2.

Waddell, Ray. 2004. "The Dead Still Live for the Road." *Billboard*, July 3. https://books.google.ca/books?id=OhAEAAAAMBAJ&pg=PA18&redir_esc=y#v=onepage&q&f=false.

West, Steven L., and Keri O'Neal. 2004. "Project D.A.R.E Outcome Effectiveness Revisited." *American Journal of Public Health* 94 (6): 1027–29.

Whitaker, Reginald. 1969. *Drugs and the Law: The Canadian Scene.* Toronto: Methuen.

Wortley, Scot, and Julian Tanner. 2005. "Inflammatory Rhetoric? Baseless Accusations? A Response to Gabor's Critique of Racial Profiling Research in Canada." *Canadian Journal of Criminology and Criminal Justice* 47 (3): 581–609.

2

Cannabis-Policy Integration and Alignment
Missed Opportunities and Obstacles to Collaborative Governance
JARED J. WESLEY

When confronted with a common policy challenge, subnational levels of government in federations such as Canada must choose whether to align their responses or proceed with their separate approaches. Despite the many benefits of collaboration, policy makers often opt to go it alone. Using the legalization of cannabis in Canada as a case study, this chapter probes the reasons behind this tendency, finding that the central government's initial approach to intergovernmental policy-making and its framing of acceptable regulatory options are central determining factors.

The Government of Canada's decision to legalize cannabis created an opportunity for its provincial and territorial counterparts to align their policy frameworks across respective jurisdictions to establish an integrated, pan-Canadian approach to regulating recreational cannabis. Indeed, cross-government alignment was a stated objective of the federal government's approach, and there was widespread agreement on the high-level policy objectives among provincial and territorial (PT) governments. Yet, PTs opted not to pursue this route; they instead replicated their own existing policy frameworks around alcohol and tobacco to suit the regulation of cannabis. The resulting patchwork of laws, regulations, and markets not only raises concerns about the federal government's ability to achieve its high-level policy objectives concerning public health and public safety, it also raises the question: Why did PT governments reject a more coordinated approach, and what could be done to encourage policy alignment in similar situations in the future?

This chapter draws on interviews with key policy officials to determine the extent to which governments collaborated, versus turning inward, in designing the new Canadian cannabis regime. This study is based on a combination of elite interviews and qualitative document analysis of government sources, including task force reports and all major cannabis-policy framework releases. A total of seven semi-structured interviews involving PT justice, finance, and intergovernmental officials were conducted between February and April 2018 (see Appendix 1). All federal, provincial, and territorial governments were invited to participate in the study. A total of six PT governments responded, including representatives in each of the major regions of the country. Repeated requests for federal government participation went unanswered. Respondents were provided with the opportunity to provide feedback on an earlier draft of this chapter.

Findings suggest that PT governments' collective choice against policy alignment had less to do with the stringent timelines imposed by their federal counterpart than with the federal government's decision to lay the groundwork for legalization on its own. Specifically, the choice to strike its own task force in favour of a fully collaborative federal-provincial-territorial model removed the opportunity and impetus for PT governments to align their operational policies early in the legalization process. It also precluded provinces and territories from buying into the new system, which would have helped offset the perceived costs of collaboration. Without this opportunity and incentive, PTs succumbed to the powerful forces of path dependence, which tended to lock them into separate, existing policy frameworks and approaches. Lessons from this study may be used to inform federal government strategies in the future, in particular the importance of developing policy in partnership (rather than consultation) with PT partners.

Levels of Policy

As with many areas of public policy in Canada, the legalization of cannabis required a high level of cross-jurisdictional coordination. It meant more than simply amending the Criminal Code of Canada and the Controlled Substances Act, both of which fall under federal jurisdiction. To shift the country away from prohibition to a system of highly regulated production, distribution, retail, possession, and consumption would involve hundreds of legislative changes at the provincial and territorial levels. This does not include the host of bylaws and policy changes required at the municipal level and within quasi-public bodies, such as universities, or private organizations and workplaces. The federal government had the option to force other governments and organizations to undertake these reforms in a uniform fashion. Instead, the Government of Canada took a more decentralized approach that allowed these bodies considerable flexibility in defining their own approaches to legalization.

The federal government has nearly exclusive authority over the production of cannabis in Canada (see Table 2.1). The provincial governments in Manitoba and Quebec challenged the provision allowing for home growing, resulting in court challenges in the post-legalization era. By defining zones

TABLE 2.1
Cannabis legalization in Canada: Areas of jurisdiction

Policy area		Federal	Provincial	Municipal
Production	Commercial cultivation	×		
	Processing	×		
	Packaging/labelling	×		
	Seed-to-sale tracking	×		
	Home cultivation	×	×	
	Land use/zoning			×
Distribution	Trafficking	×		
	Distribution		×	
	Wholesaling		×	
Retail	Medical cannabis system	×		
	Retail model		×	
	Advertising		×	
	Retail locations		×	×
	Taxation	×	×	×
	Zoning			×
Possession	Amounts	×	×	
	Age limit	×	×	
Consumption	Impaired driving	×	×	
	Public health	×	×	
	Public education	×	×	
	Workplace safety		×	
	Public consumption		×	×

Source: Adapted from Alberta 2017, 3.

for industrial and agricultural activity, municipal governments also have a role to play in defining the parameters of production. Once commercially produced, authority passes largely to provincial/territorial governments to oversee the distribution and sale of cannabis. PTs have all handed distribution authority over to their respective liquor control commissions but have taken a wide range of retail approaches. The medical cannabis system remains under the purview of the federal government, and municipalities have a say when it comes to where cannabis shops are located. Rules around possession and consumption feature a combination of federal guidelines and provincial laws.

The federal government opted to set a minimum age (eighteen) and maximum amount (thirty grams) for cannabis possession, rather than dictating precise parameters in absolute terms across the country. This has resulted in a patchwork of different regimes across the country, not unlike regulations for the sale of alcohol, resulting in a complex system of rules and a high level of interdependency. In federations such as Canada, divided sovereignty ensures that decisions by one order of government exert an influence on other levels of government even without their consultation or consent (Smith 2010). When the federal government decided to legalize cannabis, for instance, there were foreseeable downstream effects on provincial and territorial governments, including changes to public health and policing.

Likewise, the federal government can expect to feel upstream effects resulting from the choices PTs make when implementing this policy imperative. Looked at another way, the federal government is often highly dependent on PT governments to act – or, in some cases, not to act – to achieve its overarching policy objectives in areas such as public health and public safety (Atkinson et al. 2013, 2–14). And certain PT governments may be at odds with the overall policy objectives of the federal government, forcing them to choose whether or how best to implement policies with which they disagree (MacNeil and Paterson 2018, 380–81).

In this vein, it is useful to conceive policy-making on three levels: directional, strategic, and operational. As I've defined elsewhere:

> *Directional policy* establishes a government's high-level objective as it pertains to a specific issue. This could involve preserving the status quo either through action or inaction, or it could entail a change in approach, in any number of different directions ...

Strategic policy establishes mid-level plans to achieve these directional objectives. Such actions respond to core questions about how to fund and organize the state's approach to meeting the directional policy, including the pace and sequencing of reform ...

Operational policy breaks strategic policy objectives outcomes into narrower, shorter-term activities and outputs. Operational decisions are often focused around which specific program or service to employ to achieve the strategy. (Wesley 2021, 139–40)

The federal government had uncontested control when it came to defining the directional policy of legalizing cannabis. Provincial and territorial governments took issue with the time and funding the federal government provided them to implement this policy at the strategic level, however. And they took significantly different approaches to defining policy at the operational level.

Policy Alignment versus Path Dependence

How do federated governments create nationwide policy frameworks within a context of considerable jurisdictional complexity? Part of the explanation lies in fundamental processes such as policy diffusion and transfer or uptake (Evans and Davies 1999; Knill 2005; Cairney 2012; Berry and Berry 2018). Central governments may impose their policy direction on subnational governments through legislation or funding mechanisms, for example, inducing or coercing them into alignment. Alignment may also emerge from the bottom up, with provincial and territorial governments agreeing on a common policy approach, whether through competition, harmonization, imitation, the adaptation of best practices, or other processes. In some cases, these two processes coincide. The Canadian social assistance and health care systems emerged from a combination of federal laws (coercive) and conditional funding programs (incentive), on the one hand, and provincial experimentation (transfer), on the other (Boychuk 1998, 2008).

Less is known about why efforts at nationwide policy coordination fail, or why governments choose policy diversity over unity. Faced with the fiscal benefits of aligning with the central government's approach or adopting a similar policy framework, subnational governments nonetheless more often choose to pursue their own policy pathways. The pathway metaphor is a prominent one in neoinstitutionalist approaches to political science. Neoinstitutionalism holds that political actors are both bound by and help shape the rules and structures that constrain their behaviour (Hall and

Taylor 1996; Immergut 1998; Peters 1999). A particular brand of neo-institutionalism, termed historical institutionalism (HI), emphasizes the importance of historical trajectories and critical junctures in explaining how current structures have developed over time (Thelen 1999; Broschek 2008). The HI emphasis helps to explain why relatively less efficient, or otherwise irrational, outcomes may arise despite conditions that seem conducive to better results (Pierson 2000). And by identifying key moments at which interventions could be most effective, HI may highlight alternative solutions to avoid or mitigate such outcomes in analogous situations in the future (Capoccia and Kelemen 2007).

The concept of path dependence lies at the heart of the HI approach (Pierson 2004; Sydow and Schreyögg 2015). Brian Arthur (1994) describes how a combination of costs related to setting up, learning, coordinating, and adapting to a new regime will deter decision makers from choosing it over maintaining or expanding the status quo. Costs, in this context, may refer to fiscal, time, human, or other resources that are required to overcome the preservative forces that make policy replication (as opposed to alignment) so attractive (Wesley 2021). These costs increase as time draws on, making investments in new systems more expensive the longer existing systems persist. The lack of alignment among PT cannabis regulatory frameworks in Canada suggests that the forces of lock-in are more powerful than those encouraging provincial and territorial governments to collaborate with one another.

Impediments to Policy Integration and Alignment

What sorts of institutional solutions are available to overcome resistance to creating a more fully integrated regulatory system across Canada? The lack of integration introduces inefficiencies, unnecessary confusion, and related costs, suggesting that the story of cannabis legalization in Canada is one of missed opportunities. The first critical juncture came following the 2015 federal Speech from the Throne, when the Government of Canada opted to develop its policy framework in relative isolation through its own task force. Treating PT governments as stakeholders rather than full partners contributed to the ensuing decentralization of cannabis policy at the operational level. A second pivotal moment came with the federal government's framing of its preferred regulatory options. Through its initial discussion paper, the task force encouraged PTs to consider replicating their existing approaches to alcohol and tobacco, thus going their own separate ways on cannabis. A third but surprisingly less impactful moment arose when the federal government announced its tight eighteen-month timeline for legalization.

The federal government's main objective in legalizing recreational cannabis was to enhance both public health and public safety through the creation of a national regulatory system governing everything from production and distribution to sale and consumption. While terminology gradually shifted from *marijuana* to *cannabis* from 2015 to 2017, federal messaging remained consistent when it came to its desire to create a single "regulatory framework" or "system" to govern the legalization process. The federal government could have achieved this goal through policy coercion, attempting to legislate all aspects of the cannabis system and constraining the ability of PT governments to develop separate regulatory regimes. Alternatively, the federal government could have pursued policy coordination, bringing PTs together to encourage policy harmonization or disincentivize dealignment. In the end, the Government of Canada chose neither route, largely abandoning the field of operational policy implementation to provincial and territorial governments. If it did not encourage PTs to diversify their approaches, the federal government did little to dissuade them.

The federal government's initial policy statement emerged during the 2015 federal election, when the following plank appeared in the Liberal Party's platform:

> We will legalize, regulate, and restrict access to marijuana. Canada's current system of marijuana prohibition does not work. It does not prevent young people from using marijuana and too many Canadians end up with criminal records for possessing small amounts of the drug. Arresting and prosecuting these offenses is expensive for our criminal justice system. It traps too many Canadians in the criminal justice system for minor, non-violent offenses. At the same time, the proceeds from the illegal drug trade support organized crime and greater threats to public safety, like human trafficking and hard drugs. To ensure that we keep marijuana out of the hands of children, and the profits out of the hands of criminals, we will legalize, regulate, and restrict access to marijuana. We will remove marijuana consumption and incidental possession from the Criminal Code, and create new, stronger laws to punish more severely those who provide it to minors, those who operate a motor vehicle while under its influence, and those who sell it outside of the new regulatory framework. We will create a federal/provincial/territorial task force, and with input from experts in public health, substance abuse, and law enforcement, will design a new system of

strict marijuana sales and distribution, with appropriate federal and provincial excise taxes applied. (Liberal Party of Canada 2015, 55)

The Liberals did not establish a timeline for fulfilling their pledge, although it is reasonable to assume they wished to see an implementation strategy in place in advance of the next federal election (i.e., by fall 2019). Few PT officials interviewed indicated they expected the federal government to request full implementation within that timeframe. Given the complexity of the issue and the federal government's pledge to work collaboratively with PT governments, they anticipated an implementation plan being assembled over the next few years, with legalization occurring sometime after 2020. This extended timeline would not come to pass.

On election, the Liberal government struck a Task Force on Marijuana Legalization and Regulation, led by former deputy prime minister and attorney general Anne McLellan. The task force released a discussion paper to focus its engagement with the public, experts, Indigenous people and communities, and PT governments (Task Force on Marijuana Legalization and Regulation 2016). Through it, the federal government signalled its nine primary policy objectives in establishing the new regime for legalized access to cannabis. These fell under two broad categories: preserving public safety (keeping profits out of the hands of organized crime, reducing the impact of simple possession charges on Canadians and police forces, strengthening laws and penalties around trafficking and drug-impaired driving) and protecting public health (limiting access to cannabis among youth, enhancing public education on the risks of cannabis use, ensuring high standards of product quality and safety, and providing continued access to medical marijuana). These objectives formed the foundation of the task force's final report, which was publicly released in November 2016 (Task Force on Cannabis Legalization and Regulation 2016). (Following the public consultations, the task force changed its name from "Marijuana" to "Cannabis" and dropped the phrase *restriction of access to marijuana* from the title of its report.)

The original discussion paper also framed the regulatory options in a specific and narrow way, pointing to tobacco and alcohol as model policy fields for handling cannabis. This priming helped set the stage for the policy replication that would take place in PTs over the next two years. According to the task force discussion paper:

> One of the central issues to consider in the design of a legal and regulatory framework for legal access to marijuana is to identify those system features

that will best reduce the risks of health and social harms associated with use. When considering how best to minimize harms associated with marijuana use, it is helpful to consider the two different approaches taken in controlling tobacco and alcohol use. In the case of tobacco, the overall objective is to reduce or even eliminate use for all Canadians. In contrast, the overall objective with respect to alcohol is to promote responsible use amongst adults, and to prohibit use amongst youth ... Given that the majority of harms related to marijuana use appear to occur in select high-risk users (e.g., youth) or in conjunction with high-risk use practices (e.g., frequent use; highly potent products; impaired driving), an approach that draws lessons from both tobacco and alcohol control should be examined. Both approaches rely on a comprehensive suite of actions aimed at those users at highest risk for harms through active prevention, education and treatment, as well as policy and legislative interventions. (Task Force on Marijuana Legalization and Regulation 2016, 11)

While the McLellan Report did reflect expert input and public submissions, the initiative was not the collaborative FPT effort promised in the Liberals' 2015 campaign platform. Rather than being invited to assemble or constitute the body, provincial and territorial governments were invited to provide testimony or submit documents to the federal task force as part of the consultation process. PTs were not meaningfully engaged in the formation of the task force or its mandate. Notwithstanding this exclusion, the federal task force delved into all areas of cannabis legalization, including those under provincial and territorial jurisdiction. It touched on federal responsibility for production and criminal enforcement but also provided findings and recommendations related to workplace safety, distribution, and retail.

Fortunately, in terms of aligning the federal government's strategic policy aims with PT operational policy decisions, PTs were generally receptive to the McLellan Report. As reflected in their own cannabis legalization policy framework documents at the time of legalization (Appendix 2), PTs were in general agreement with the federal task force when it came to the dual focus on public health and public safety and its suggestion to draw parallels with alcohol and tobacco regulation. Moreover, all jurisdictions except Quebec and Yukon provided submissions to the federal task force. Yet PTs did not have the same level of buy-in as might have been expected if they had co-created the task force. They also lacked an important early venue for strategic and operational policy discussions, thus delaying their own collaboration while waiting for the federal report to be completed. The federal government increased the time pressures when it released the task force report, setting July 2018 as the target date for full legalization (with the exception of edibles).

In the meantime, and in the absence of federal leadership to pull jurisdictions together at the political level, PT premiers struck their own Provincial-Territorial Working Group on Cannabis Legalization in July 2017. Led by their respective health and justice ministers, the working group was tasked with producing a report for premiers by November 1, 2017, identifying "common considerations and best practices to cannabis legalization and regulation, guided by the objectives of reducing harm, protecting public safety, and reducing illicit activity" (Council of the Federation 2017a). The working group's mandate was broad enough to allow some room for PT collaboration and policy alignment but did not require it.

The PT working group released its report on schedule. Through it, premiers reaffirmed their commitment to the high-level objectives of "protecting public health and safety, preventing access to cannabis by young persons, and reducing illicit activity" but explicitly ruled out widespread policy collaboration at the operational level (Council of the Federation 2017b, 5). Premiers explained their decision to pursue their own separate policy paths for the distribution, sale, possession, and consumption of cannabis in the PT working group report: "Provinces and territories are in the process of addressing a common set of policy issues that fall within their jurisdiction. In general, they are guided by shared considerations, though some variation in approach to account for provincial and territorial circumstances and priorities can be expected. *Extensive collaboration on particular issues is challenging given the timelines associated with implementation*" (Council of the Federation 2017b, 6, emphasis added). In short, premiers cited the federal government's July 2018 deadline as the primary reason for the lack of policy alignment on cannabis regulation.

In the ensuing months, provincial and territorial governments initiated their own, separate public consultation processes, resulting in a set of thirteen unique policy frameworks for the regulation of cannabis (see Table 2.2). Overwhelmingly, in designing their cannabis rules, PTs replicated their regulatory regimes for the distribution, sale, and possession of liquor and their approaches to consumption of tobacco.

Regulations for growing cannabis at home varied widely across the country, for instance, ranging from a relatively loose set of regulations in Ontario to complete prohibition in Manitoba and Quebec. Retail models

TABLE 2.2
PT approaches to selected operational policy areas, c. May 2019

	Home production	Retail	Age of possession	Consumption (i.e., smoking)
BC	Yes, if out of public sight	Public plus[a]	19	Not in cars, child spaces, or where tobacco prohibited
AB	Yes, with landlord restrictions	Hybrid[b]	18	Not in cars, child spaces, or where tobacco prohibited
SK	Yes, with landlord restrictions	Private	19	Only in private spaces where minors are not present
MB	Not permitted	Private	19[d]	Only in private spaces
ON	Yes	Hybrid[b]	19	Only in private spaces, plus landlord restrictions
QC	Not permitted	Public	18[e]	Only where tobacco smoking permitted, except CEGEP and postsecondary campuses
NB	Yes	Public	19	Only in private spaces
NS	Yes	Public	19	Only where tobacco smoking permitted, plus landlord restrictions
PE	Yes, if not accessible to minors	Public	19	Only in private residences, with some exceptions for public spaces
NL	Yes	Hybrid[b]	19	Only in private spaces
YT	Yes, if out of public sight	Public	19	Only in private spaces, plus landlord restrictions
NT	Yes	Hybrid[b]	19	Only in private spaces, with some exceptions for public spaces
NU	Yes	Public[c]	19	Only where tobacco smoking permitted

Notes:
a Private storefronts, public stores and online.
b Private stores, public online.
c No storefronts, only public online.
d Does not align with provincial liquor possession age (eighteen).
e The Quebec government has since increased the age to twenty-one.

also differed, with some provinces opting for fully public systems (Quebec and the Maritimes), others fully private (Saskatchewan and Manitoba), and the remainder employing some combination of the two. Legal age of possession was more uniform across the country, with every jurisdiction but Alberta and Quebec opting to impose a minimum age of nineteen. This relative consistency was due less to proactive collaboration, however, than to the fact that minimum drinking ages follow a similar pattern. Consumption rules were perhaps the most disparate across the country, subject to many different types of restrictions. Moreover, variation in the use of terms, except minimum age, was evident *within* each jurisdiction, as PT governments handed significant policy-making control to municipalities.

These differences notwithstanding, the highest barriers to a pan-Canadian approach to cannabis regulation were erected in relation to distribution. Hopes for a nationwide cannabis market were dashed when PTs decided to adopt a protectionist approach to their respective industries, establishing tight controls over what products could be imported and sold in their jurisdictions. As early as November 2017, the PT working group report noted that most jurisdictions were "considering the use of their already existing entities that are currently charged with distribution and oversight of liquor, or exploring ways to otherwise leverage existing structures and experience in order to establish a functioning distribution and regulatory system in advance of implementation given the limited timeframe" (Council of the Federation 2017b, 15).

The question remains, however: Even if they were provided with more time to share information and develop common approaches, would PTs have developed an aligned policy framework from the bottom up? Was time the only thing standing in their way? Interviews with PT officials suggest the chances were limited given the high costs associated with collaboration and the relatively lower costs associated with taking the federal task force's advice to replicate their existing approaches to alcohol and tobacco regulation. While extending the legalization timeline would have facilitated PT collaboration, it would have taken additional proactive steps by the federal government to alter this cost-benefit balance.

Costs of Replication versus Alignment

In line with Arthur's (1994) model, PT officials were deterred by a series of set-up, learning, coordination, and adaptive expectation costs associated with taking a novel and collaborative approach to cannabis regulation.

Set-Up Costs
Significant investment would be required to establish entirely new regulatory regimes for cannabis, outside of existing liquor and tobacco regimes. This explains why the federal government chose to expand Health Canada's existing licensing program from medicinal to nonmedicinal cannabis producers, as opposed to setting up an entirely new or parallel system. PTs' collective decision to rely on their respective alcohol distribution and retail models, versus investing in the creation of an entirely new pan-Canadian system, is also understandable through this lens. Innovation in either of these examples would have required each government to make a multitude of complex legislative and regulatory changes, drawing valuable legislative resources (e.g., workforce, cabinet time) away from other priorities. Setting up a cannabis-only system would have meant creating new agencies with additional staff. Some governments proved willing to take on these costs on the retail side, founding new publicly owned online and brick-and-mortar stores on the promise of generating offsetting sales revenue. In most cases, however, these new Crown corporations exist as subsidiaries of existing public liquor retailers. (The one exception is Alberta, where no public liquor retailer existed. Online sales are administered by the Alberta Gaming, Liquor and Cannabis.)

Learning Costs
When it comes to informing and educating key players of the rules of the game, designing a new regulatory system imparts real costs on policy makers, policy enforcers, and policy targets. Whatever its complexity, the cost of learning the new system tends to favour replicating a familiar policy framework. PT-based alcohol and tobacco regimes are attractive because they are familiar to bureaucrats, enforcement agents, businesses, consumers, parents, and other stakeholders in the cannabis field. There is real value in this awareness; having a common understanding among all players is the first step in achieving regulatory compliance. If the rules for the consumption of cannabis are different from alcohol or tobacco, new regulations are confusing for both users and nonusers. Confusion about rules creates conditions that lead to inadvertent law breaking, shirking, and loss of trust in the system. At the same time, creating identical regulations can be detrimental to achieving the new policy's objectives. This is one of the impetuses behind the push for zero-tolerance policies with regard to drug-impaired driving, as opposed to rolling cannabis-related offences under the broader definition of impaired driving. Overall, however, the disincentives to implementing an

intelligible pan-Canadian cannabis regime largely favoured sticking to more familiar sets of rules.

Coordinating Costs

Intuitively, it is less costly to integrate a new policy area into an existing regulatory network than it is to set up a separate system. Creating a different set of rules for cannabis smoking and tobacco smoking, for instance, would have required the development of entirely new landlord-tenant arrangements, bylaws, and signage. The same applies for establishing retail buffer zones around schools, community centres, and other places that youth frequent, or workplace-safety regulations. In assigning cannabis regulation to their respective liquor control commissions, most provincial and territorial governments ensured a tight connection between cannabis and alcohol rules. By licensing liquor retailers to sell cannabis (in separate storefronts), some PTs effectively expanded the alcohol policy network to include cannabis. Making such moves lessens the burden on stakeholders throughout the system.

Adaptive Expectation Costs

Lastly, governments' own expectations, grounded in experience in similar policy fields, can have a chilling effect on the development of new, collaborative policy frameworks. In short, a combination of uncertainty and fear of unknown consequences often leads policy makers to choose familiar safeguards over something new – per the old adage, it's better to go with the devil you know than the devil you don't. This helps us to understand the reluctance on the part of most governments to experiment with new retail models, for example, or to risk political capital on increasing the age of consumption above the age of majority.

Absorbing the costs of new policy frameworks can be achieved by governments reallocating funds from other priorities or seeking to offset new expenditures through revenue generation. Indeed, by establishing their own taxation levels and negotiating for a greater share of the federal excise tax, provinces were seeking ways to pay for higher anticipated costs. By banding together to attract commercial production to their region, Atlantic premiers adopted an aggressive approach that sought to generate revenue through increased economic activity. Embracing a competitive dynamic is one avenue for pursuing PT policy alignment within regions.

However, lack of funding appears to be less of a deterrent than lack of time and political will. Even if it were possible to fund the new regime, the costs of starting up, learning, coordinating, and adapting a new system for cannabis regulation *within* a single province or territory are still too high. As Paul Cairney (2012, 255) put it, "the more an importing [jurisdiction] feels compelled to act quickly, then the more bounded its decision-making process." Even if more time had been provided by the federal government, very few PTs appear willing to invest the political capital required to develop an entirely new approach to cannabis regulation.

PT officials made it clear during interviews that their respective ministers considered cannabis legalization to be a federal priority and responsibility. When asked whether their own governments had established metrics for the success of legalization, it was asserted that such assessments would (and, according to some, should) rest solely with the Government of Canada. Instead of being invested in the political success of legalization, PTs remained focused on ensuring smooth implementation and avoiding major mistakes that could cost them politically. From this perspective, few PT governments would be willing to risk incurring the costs associated with the potential failure of an innovative approach.

The federal government's decision to strike a federally mandated task force as opposed to the FPT body once envisaged has been costly. Generating a deeper commitment to the legalization project and securing early buy-in from PT governments would have created common ownership over cannabis legalization, incentivizing them to increase their political investment over time (Meer 2017; Stein 2017). These sorts of positive effects were achieved by Prime Minister Brian Mulroney in the 1980s, when he successfully negotiated two constitutional accords with all ten provincial premiers (Monahan 1991; McRoberts and Monahan 1993).

Would more commitment to FPT collaboration have produced a more aligned cannabis regulation regime? Committing to a full FPT process would most certainly have prolonged the legalization timeline, quite possibly resulting in a deadlock or more compromise than the federal government was willing to accept. Like the mega-constitutional accords, a more focused FPT effort may have ultimately foundered because of external forces, like changes in government or public opposition. Yet, a full FPT partnership could have just as easily given PTs the time they needed to overcome the various perceived costs of collaboration and provided a new set of political incentives to realize a better-integrated policy framework.

Canada's experience with legalizing cannabis, and the related costs of not pursuing integration, holds lessons for students of intergovernmental policy-making. First, the outcomes of the process are highly unpredictable and difficult to engineer. Best-laid plans for policy alignment are just plans, which are subject to the disproportionate power of small choices. Shifting from an FPT to a federal-only task force may have seemed like a minor change, intended to expedite the legalization process and centralize control over the policy-making process in the hands of the Government of Canada. Likewise, framing cannabis in the context of alcohol and tobacco regulation may have seemed like a small element of its discussion paper. Yet, however insignificant they may seem at the time, small events can have a major impact later on in the policy-making process.

Once a policy path is established, it becomes increasingly difficult to change course. The PT's unique approaches to alcohol and tobacco regulation were well-worn paths to travel. Sending cannabis down them only served to institute a decentralized approach. Now that a patchwork of regulatory regimes has been established, governments are highly unlikely to pursue, let alone achieve, greater policy alignment in the future. As Paul Pierson (2000, 252) put it: "In an increasing returns process, the probability of further steps along the same path increases with each move down that path. This is because the *relative* benefits of the current activity compared with other possible options increase over time. To put it a different way, the costs of exit – of switching to some previously plausible alternative – rise." This means efforts at creating a single cannabis market, with common pricing and rules for distribution and sale, are unlikely to come to fruition. Even 2017 commitments to include cannabis under the Canadian Free Trade Agreement (Article 1206), thus eliminating jurisdictional controls over what is sold by whom, have proved to be unrealistic given the power of path dependence. This is particularly true given that the Supreme Court of Canada bolstered PTs in their position, releasing a landmark ruling in April 2018, *R v Comeau*, which confirmed the constitutionality of internal trade barriers for the distribution and sale of alcohol.

There is no guarantee that the established policy paths will lead to the intended policy outcomes. The objectives of improving public health and safety, for example, are unlikely to be met by replication of imperfect alcohol and tobacco policies for cannabis. Yet the tendency, as noted, is to adopt familiar frameworks. Would a one-size-fits-all national policy be better equipped to improve health and safety? Proponents – including medical, police, and industry associations – see the most value in setting common standards for age of consumption, impaired-driving penalties, and cross-border distribution and sales. On the other hand, there are potential advantages to taking a decentralized approach to policy-making. Provincially and territorially defined rules are likely to be more responsive to the unique needs and sensitive to the desires of local populations. Increased PT control over taxation levels allows each government to set prices that best fit local supply and demand, for instance, thus limiting the attractiveness of the illicit market. Moreover, allowing different subnational governments to experiment with different policy frameworks could result in the sort of competition and learning lauded by proponents of the "laboratory" approach to policy-making (Atkinson et al. 2013, 52–53; Boyd and Olive 2021). With time, these processes could even lead to policy alignment, through diffusion and transfer of best practices.

Although an unaligned approach is more unpredictable, policy alignment is not an end unto itself. But when governments in a federation agree on an ambitious policy change, some amount of policy coordination is required to ensure smooth implementation. In the case of cannabis legalization in Canada, the federal government's choice to launch policy development independently, and the aggressive timelines it imposed, made this sort of policy coordination difficult and unattractive. Provincial and territorial governments calculated that it was simply easier to replicate their own existing alcohol and tobacco policy frameworks. Policy makers, citizens, businesses, and other stakeholders are now witnessing the impacts of the resulting misalignment of cannabis regulatory policies across Canada.

Interjurisdictional alignment and policy innovation are by no means default settings for policy-making in federations such as Canada. This makes it important to understand why subnational governments choose to "go it alone" and pursue incremental reforms when addressing complex policy issues like cannabis legalization. Whereas federal, provincial, and territorial governments agreed on the high-level policy objectives behind the legalization process, disagreements over how to implement them have resulted in a patchwork of regulatory regimes across Canada. The resulting regime lacks the degree of pan-Canadian policy alignment originally sought by the federal government. This disjunction is a product of path dependence, with individual governments choosing their own paths based on the perceived costs of aligning their approaches with other governments. The federal government's strategic decisions concerning who to involve in policy development, its narrow framing of regulatory options, and the tight timeline for implementation were all critical factors contributing to the PTs' decisions to pursue their own policy pathways. Ottawa's "go it alone" approach to legalizing cannabis had a significant, if not predictable, impact on provincial and territorial responses in kind. Would-be architects of future regulatory measures, and future planners of collaborative pan-Canadian policy regimes, are wise to keep these lessons in mind.

Appendix 1: Schedule of interviews conducted in person and by telephone*

A Senior provincial government justice official from western Canada (2018–02–23)
B Provincial government justice official from western Canada (2018–03–06)
C Senior territorial government justice official from northern Canada (2018–03–12)
D Senior provincial government justice official from western Canada (2018–03–12)
E Senior territorial government finance official from northern Canada (18–03–27)
F Senior provincial government justice official from central Canada (18–03–27)
G Senior provincial government justice official from Atlantic Canada (18–04–17).

* Some of the interviewees continue to work in government. Their names, precise positions, and jurisdictions have been withheld at their request and per the ethics protocol approved by the University of Alberta Research Ethics Board. The roles identified are those most pertinent to the research focus.

Appendix 2: List of FPT cannabis-policy frameworks, circa May 2019

Alberta. 2017. *Alberta Cannabis Framework.* https://open.alberta.ca/dataset/f86ce345-e194-4277-ae62-774630830f37/resource/7f8a1d7b-c4e6-4d6f-a439-9719fb0fdb40/download/alberta-cannabis-framework.pdf.
British Columbia. 2018. "Cannabis." https://www2.gov.bc.ca/gov/content/safety/public-safety/cannabis.
Canada. 2016. *A Framework for the Legalization and Regulation of Cannabis: The Final Report of the Task Force on Cannabis Legalization and Regulation.* https://www.canada.ca/content/dam/hc-sc/healthy-canadians/migration/task-force-marijuana-groupe-etude/framework-cadre/alt/framework-cadre-eng.pdf.
Council of the Federation. 2017. *Report on Cannabis Legalization and Regulation.* http://www.canadaspremiers.ca/wp-content/uploads/2017/12/COF_Report_on_Cannabis_Legalization_and_Regulation-Final.pdf.
New Brunswick. 2017. *Legislative Framework concerning Cannabis Introduced.* http://www2.gnb.ca/content/gnb/en/news/news_release.2017.11.1445.html.
Newfoundland and Labrador. 2017. *Provincial Government Releases First Details on Cannabis Legalization in Newfoundland and Labrador.* http://www.releases.gov.nl.ca/releases/2017/exec/1123n01.aspx.
Northwest Territories. 2017. *Cannabis Legalization in the Northwest Territories: The Way Forward.* https://www.eia.gov.nt.ca/sites/eia/files/the_way_forward_-_nov_20_final.pdf.
Nova Scotia. 2018. "Cannabis Legalization." https://novascotia.ca/cannabis/.
Ontario. 2017. *Ontario's Plan to Regulate Legalized Cannabis.* https://news.ontario.ca/mag/en/2017/09/ontario-releases-safe-and-sensible-framework-to-manage-federal-legalization-of-cannabis.html.

Prince Edward Island. 2018. *Cannabis Legalization: A Policy and Legislative Framework for Prince Edward Island.* https://www.princeedwardisland.ca/sites/default/files/publications/cannabis_policy_framework_4.pdf.
Quebec. 2017. *Regulation of Cannabis in Quebec: 2017 Consultation Document.* http://publications.msss.gouv.qc.ca/msss/fichiers/2017/17-236-12A.pdf.
Saskatchewan. 2018. *Saskatchewan's Cannabis Framework and Survey Results.* http://publications.gov.sk.ca/documents/13/106026-SK-Cannabis-Framework.pdf.
Yukon. 2017. *Yukon's Proposed Framework for Legalized Cannabis.* https://www.gov.yk.ca/pdf/Cannabis_Framework_Legal_web.pdf.

Acknowledgments
An earlier version of this chapter was presented as "Huddling or Muddling: Cannabis Legalization, Policy Alignment, and Intergovernmental Relations" at the Annual Research Conference in Public Administration, Policy, and Management, Canadian Association of Programs in Public Administration, University of Regina, Saskatchewan, May 31, 2018. The author thanks Malcolm Bird and participants on the panel for constructive feedback on the earlier draft.

Works Cited
Alberta. 2017. *Alberta Cannabis Framework.* Edited by Justice and Solicitor General. Edmonton: Government of Alberta.
Arthur, W. Brian. 1994. *Increasing Returns and Path Dependence in the Economy.* Ann Arbor: University of Michigan Press.
Atkinson, Michael M., Daniel Beland, Gregory P. Marchildon, Kathleen McNutt, Peter W.B. Phillips, and Ken Rasmussen. 2013. *Governance and Public Policy in Canada: A View from the Provinces.* Toronto: University of Toronto Press.
Berry, Frances Stokes, and William D. Berry. 2018. "Innovation and Diffusion Models in Policy Research." In *Theories of the Policy Process,* edited by Christopher M. Weible and Paul A. Sabatier, 253–300. New York: Westview Press.
Boychuk, Gerard William. 1998. *Patchworks of Purpose: The Development of Provincial Social Assistance Regimes in Canada.* Kingston/Montreal: McGill-Queen's University Press.
–. 2008. *National Health Insurance in the United States and Canada: Race, Territory, and the Roots of Difference.* Washington, DC: Georgetown University Press.
Boyd, Brendan, and Andrea Olive, eds. 2021. *Provincial Policy Laboratories: Policy Diffusion and Transfer in Canada's Federal System.* Toronto: University of Toronto Press.
Broschek, Jorg. 2008. "Historical Institutionalism and Canadian Social Policy: Assessing Two Models of Policy Change." Paper presented at the annual meeting of the Canadian Political Science Association, University of British Columbia, Vancouver, June 4.
Cairney, Paul. 2012. *Understanding Public Policy: Theories and Issues.* New York: Palgrave Macmillan.
Capoccia, Giovanni, and R. Daniel Kelemen. 2007. "The Study of Critical Junctures: Theory, Narrative, and Counterfactuals in Historical Institutionalism." *World Politics* 59 (3): 341–69. https://doi.org.10.1017/S0043887100020852.

Council of the Federation. 2017a. *Premiers Highlight Key Justice and Social Issues*. Edmonton: Council of the Federation.

—. 2017b. *Report on Cannabis Legalization and Regulation*. Edited by Working Group on Cannabis Legalization and Regulation. Ottawa: Council of the Federation Secretariat.

Evans, Mark, and Jonathan Davies. 1999. "Understanding Policy Transfer: A Multilevel, Multi-disciplinary Perspective." *Public Administration* 77 (2): 361–85.

Green, Melyvn, and Ralph D. Miller. "Cannabis Use in Canada." In *Cannabis and Culture*. Edited by Vera Rubin, 497–520. The Hague: Mouton, 1975.

Hall, Peter A., and Rosemary C.R. Taylor. 1996. "Political Science and the Three New Institutionalisms." *Political Studies* 44: 936–57.

Immergut, Ellen M. 1998. "The Theoretical Core of the New Institutionalism." *Politics and Society* 26 (1): 5–34.

Knill, Christoph. 2005. "Introduction: Cross-National Policy Convergence: Concepts, Approaches and Explanatory Factors." *Journal of European Public Policy* 12 (5): 764–74.

Liberal Party of Canada. 2015. "Real Change: A New Plan for a Strong Middle Class." https://www.liberal.ca/wp-content/uploads/2015/10/New-plan-for-a-strong-middle-class.pdf.

MacNeil, Robert, and Matthew Paterson. 2018. "Trudeau's Canada and the Challenge of Decarbonisation." *Environmental Politics* 27 (2): 379–84.

McRoberts, Kenneth, and Patrick Monahan. 1993. *The Charlottetown Accord, the Referendum, and the Future of Canada*. Toronto: University of Toronto Press.

Meer, Nasar. 2017. "What Will Happen to Race Equality Policy on the Brexit Archipelago? Multi-level Governance, 'Sunk Costs' and the 'Mischief of Faction.'" *Journal of Social Policy* 46 (4): 657–74. https://doi.org.10.1017/S0047279417000319.

Monahan, Patrick. 1991. *Meech Lake: The Inside Story*. Toronto: University of Toronto Press.

Peters, Guy. 1999. *Institutional Theory in Political Science: The New Institutionalism*. New York: Continuum.

Pierson, Paul. 2000. "Increasing Returns, Path Dependence, and the Study of Politics." *American Political Science Review* 94 (2): 251–67.

Pierson, Paul. 2004. *Politics in Time: History, Institutions, and Social Analysis*. Princeton, NJ: Princeton University Press.

Smith, David E. 2010. *Federalism and the Constitution of Canada*. Toronto: University of Toronto Press.

Stein, Janice Gross. 2017. "The Micro-foundations of International Relations Theory: Psychology and Behavioral Economics." *International Organization* 71 (1): S249–S263. https://doi.org.10.1017/S0020818316000436.

Sydow, Jörg, and Georg Schreyögg. 2015. "Organizational Path Dependence." *International Encyclopedia of Social and Behavioral Sciences* 2: 385–89.

Task Force on Cannabis Legalization and Regulation. 2016. *A Framework for the Legalization and Regulation of Cannabis in Canada: The Final Report of the Task Force on Cannabis Legalization and Regulation*. Edited by Health Canada. Ottawa: Minister of Health.

Task Force on Marijuana Legalization and Regulation. 2016. "Toward the Legalization, Regulation, and Restriction of Access to Marijuana: Discussion Paper." Edited by Government of Canada. Ottawa: Government of Canada.

Thelen, Kathleen. 1999. "Historical Institutionalism in Comparative Politics." *Annual Review of Political Science* 2: 369–404.

Wesley, Jared J. 2021. "Policy Replication: Cannabis Legalization in Canada." In *Provincial Policy Laboratories: Policy Diffusion and Transfer in Canada's Federal System*. Edited by Brendan Boyd and Andrea Olive, 138–53. Toronto: University of Toronto Press.

3

Displacing the Illicit Cannabis Market
Challenges and Trade-Offs
JASON CHILDS and GEORGE HARTNER

When Canada became the second and largest country to legalize cannabis for recreational purposes, the rationale was simple: a century worth of prohibition had failed to eradicate a booming illicit market for cannabis, leaving government regulation of a legal market a more promising alternative to reduce the social costs associated with cannabis use. The relative success of government regulation in ensuring the safety of alcohol and tobacco while limiting access to these products by youth suggests that a similar approach to cannabis could reduce the harms currently associated with cannabis distribution and consumption. Making legalization even more attractive was the promise of increased tax revenues and economic activity and the freeing of resources devoted to policing and enforcing penalties associated with prohibition. With the prior legalization of cannabis for medical purposes eroding the moral objection to allowing a product like cannabis into the legal market, the promise of regulation to enforce a minimum age, ensure the safety of the product, and reduce illegal activity associated with the illicit market became a strong argument for legalization.

The stated rationale and argument for legalization in 2017, despite provinces requesting more time, was the promise that legalizing cannabis would enhance public safety by providing a safe supply of legal cannabis and establishing a minimum consumption age of eighteen to protect youth. The problem facing policy makers is that none of these objectives (reducing youth access, ensuring a safe supply, reducing law-enforcement costs, or generating tax revenues) can be achieved if the illicit market continues to attract consumers and provide youth access to cannabis. In short, if the illicit cannabis market is not significantly reduced in size and scope, legalization will be a failed policy and could have the unintended consequence of further entrenching the illicit market, risking the effectiveness of future policy.

Although legalization and the new legal market are still in their infancy, the results of this public policy experiment show that the process undertaken by the government has failed to achieve its stated aims, at least in the short run. However, establishing a highly regulated or government-run legal market that can compete with a well-developed unregulated illicit market is a lofty ambition. Fortunately for public policy enthusiasts, the federal government's decision to regulate production but allow each province to establish its own approach to the regulation of retail and distribution of cannabis has delivered a wide variety of different approaches to evaluate and critique. It may well be the case that the federal government's approach to regulating production will prove to have the greatest impact on the success of legalization.

The legislation (Bill C-45) divided responsibility for the nascent cannabis industry between the federal government and the provincial governments. The federal government regulates the production of cannabis through the same Health Canada framework that governed the production of medicinal cannabis. This process entails lengthy application processes and substantial barriers to entry. On the other hand, the structures and regulatory framework for retail and distribution had to be designed from scratch by provincial governments, although there was some information from other countries and specific US states that had already established recreational cannabis markets. The variety of approaches taken by provincial governments provides a remarkable opportunity to examine the impact of different distribution and retail models on the ability of the legal cannabis market to compete with the illicit market. It also allows for an evaluation of how the federal government's approach to production either supported or hindered the provinces in achieving objectives.

Both the structure of legalization and the data currently available make a balanced-scorecard approach to assessing the effectiveness of different policy choices an appropriate method of analysis. As stated, the effectiveness of legalization in achieving its policy objectives hinges on the ability of the illicit market to compete with the legal market. Consequently, the scorecard will include metrics identified by the National Cannabis Survey (Statistics Canada 2021a) as major considerations for consumers when purchasing cannabis: quality, price, access, and variety. We aggregate these elements of the balanced scorecard to facilitate a comparison of how successful different provincial markets have been in displacing the illicit market. These findings are supported by comparing the value of cannabis sales in each province, as reported by Statistics Canada (2021b), to estimates of the value of the illicit market prior to legalization as a metric of illicit market capture.

While it is very early in the process of legalization and the data should be considered preliminary, the initial results are not encouraging. The first six months of the legal market were plagued with supply shortages, slow processing of government permits, delayed openings of retail stores, and prices significantly higher than the illicit market. The legal market has displaced little of the illicit market, with legal sales accounting for less than 10 percent of the estimated pre-legalization quantity of cannabis consumed and less than 15 percent of the total value of the market. Within the context of this poor nationwide showing, there was significant variation in the performance of the legal market among provinces.

The Evolution of Federal and Provincial Regulation

Federal Regulation

Each province opted for a slightly different approach to regulating the retail and distribution portions of the legal recreational cannabis market. Some of the differences can be attributed to the histories the provinces have with alcohol, and some of the differences can be attributed to the ideologies of governments left with the responsibility for overseeing the implementation of recreational cannabis legalization. The approaches ranged from an aggressive and highly government-controlled approach in New Brunswick to the reluctant, and hands-off attitude taken by Saskatchewan. The other provinces opted for something in between. The legal and historical background of legalization played an important role in the regulatory decisions made by both the federal and provincial governments.

Although cannabis for recreational use was legalized in Canada in 2018, the process toward legalization began in 2001, when the Ontario Court of Appeal held that prohibiting individual possession of cannabis for medical use was unconstitutional (Health Canada 2016). As a result, Health Canada established the Marihuana Medical Access Regulations (MMAR).[1] This Act allowed licensed physicians to prescribe cannabis for medical purposes and allowed patients to grow cannabis themselves, designate another person to grow for them, or purchase cannabis directly from a Health Canada–authorized producer. Initially, Prairie Plant Systems (later CanniMed, now part of Aurora Cannabis) was the sole Health Canada–authorized producer.

Regulation and policy governing medicinal cannabis in Canada went through two further iterations before recreational cannabis was legalized in 2018. In 2013, the federal government replaced MMAR with Marihuana for Medical Purposes Regulations (MMPR). A major change was the elimination of the right of patients to grow their own cannabis or designate another individual to grow on their behalf. Up until then, patients could only buy from a Health Canada–authorized producer. At this point, the number of authorized producers rose to six, including Prairie Plant Systems.

Patients challenged the requirement to source medicinal cannabis only from an authorized producer. These patients ultimately won their challenge: the Federal Court of Canada ruling in 2016 that such restrictions were a violation of the Charter of Rights and Freedoms. As a result of the court ruling, the MMPR was replaced with the Access to Cannabis for Medical Purposes Regulations (ACMPR), which reverted to the original language, allowing patients to grow their own cannabis or to designate someone to grow on their behalf (Health Canada 2016). By the end of 2016, the number of authorized producers had risen to thirty-seven.

In April 2017, the federal government announced it would legalize possession and consumption of cannabis for those without a prescription (recreational users) (Health Canada 2017). Bill C-45 (the Cannabis Act), which legalized cannabis use for recreational purposes, became law on June 21, 2018 (Senate of Canada 2018). This legislation divided responsibility for recreational cannabis regulation between the federal government and the provinces. The federal government licenses producers and sets minimum standards in record keeping, minimum age requirements, standards for household production, and personal possession limits. Responsibility for the oversight of retail and distribution was allocated to the provinces.

Although the Act called for implementation by July 1, 2018, legalization was delayed until October 17, 2018, to allow provinces more time to prepare regulations covering distribution and retail (Scotti 2018). With the announcement and ultimate proclamation of the Cannabis Act, the number of authorized producers increased radically: there were a total of 84 by the end of 2017, 143 by the end of 2018, and 164 by March 2019 (see Figure 3.1).[2]

Displacing the Illicit Cannabis Market

FIGURE 3.1
Number of federal licence holders in Canada, 2013–19

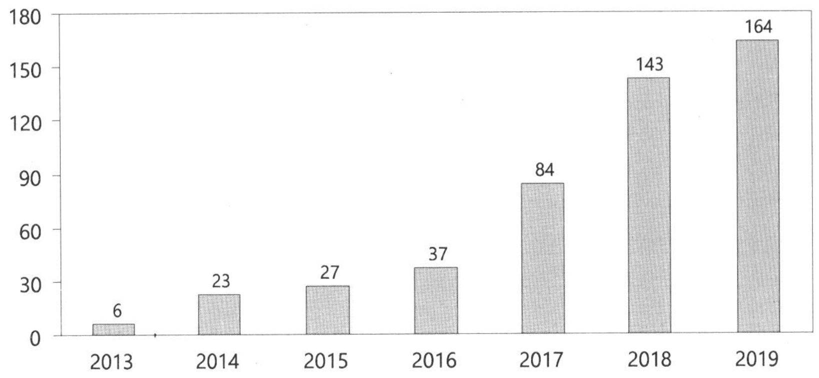

Year	Licence holders
2013	6
2014	23
2015	27
2016	37
2017	84
2018	143
2019	164

Source: Health Canada, n.d.

Provincial Regulation

Although the federal government devolved responsibility to regulate retail and distribution to the provinces, it did provide three core objectives for provincial regulators: protect public safety (quality-controlled cannabis), restrict access to cannabis by youth, and displace the illicit market. Clearly, the first and second objectives are dependent on achieving the third. If the illicit market continues to thrive, the quality of cannabis cannot be assured, and youth will continue to have high levels of access.

Given just over a year to design and implement regulatory frameworks for the retailing and distribution of cannabis, combined with the possibility of millions of consumers switching overnight from the illicit to the legal market, the provinces did not have the opportunity to allow policy to evolve. Further, with no established best practices to emulate – other than alcohol and tobacco regulation, which had evolved slowly over time and only shared some similarities with cannabis – each province had to make its own choices concerning the basic framework for distribution and retail markets. It is important to note that at the time of legalization, several US states had legalized cannabis for recreational purposes. However, a major difference between these examples and the policy challenges facing provinces was that the US states also had control over how to regulate production, something provincial governments had no influence over in Canada. While all provincial governments had frameworks in place for the distribution and retail sale of alcohol, all provinces except Nova Scotia took the opportunity to establish a separate or parallel system for cannabis.

In establishing these parallel frameworks, each province had to determine the number of brick-and-mortar retail locations, their ownership, the availability of online sales, the number and nature of distribution channels, and processes for choosing and allocating permits where private options were chosen. Each decision had important implications for the final makeup of provincial cannabis markets. Furthermore, the choices facing policy makers had important trade-offs when it came to balancing the objectives of competing with the illicit market, minimizing political risk, supporting economic growth, and minimizing the social costs of cannabis use – particularly those related to public health. At the forefront of these decisions was the need to balance supporting maximum access to a legal market (to compete with the illicit market) and ensuring a safe legal supply of cannabis and limiting youth access. All this came with the potential political risk of the public perceiving the government as supporting and regulating a previously banned drug, of them creating a system with the potential for abuse.

Under the Cannabis Act, provinces have the authority to restrict the total number of retail outlets. With respect to the number of retail outlets, policy makers faced a trade-off between ensuring there were enough stores to support access and compete with the illicit market and limiting access to minimize increases in consumption and potential risk associated with having a cannabis store on every corner. Eight of the ten provinces decided to set a maximum number of retail outlets. Only Alberta and British Columbia opted not to limit the number of retail outlets. For those provinces that have limited the number of stores, they range from a low of four in Prince Edward Island to a high of fifty-one in Saskatchewan. Quebec opted for a small number of retail outlets relative to its population, allowing just twenty across the entire province.

In addition to selecting the number of retail outlets, provinces had to determine whether retail outlets would be publicly owned (government-owned), privately owned, or mixed. The primary benefits of public ownership are derived from the government's access to financial resources, increased compliance in government-run stores, and policy makers' direct control over operations and ability to implement policies rapidly. Substantial financial resources give publicly owned stores the ability to navigate market disruptions (shortages) while maintaining set prices and operations, stock, and variety without the pressure of earning profits. With respect to compliance, public employees and managers without profit motives are less likely to sell to youth, engage with the illicit market for cheaper or better supply, or engage in tax avoidance or other forms of noncompliance. Public ownership also ensures that any profit stemming from the industry goes directly to the government. Finally, government-run retail stores generate significant buying power, as the government can buy on behalf of all stores within the province. This is especially important given the concentration and market power in the production market.

On the other hand, the lack of a profit motive reduces incentives to compete with the illicit market in terms of price and variety. In addition, public ownership reduces incentives to seek out new products and support innovation within the cannabis market. Public ownership also exposes the government to political risk because it may be viewed as selling and profiting from the use of a previously controlled substance. Finally, the government also faces political risk if the public or consumers hold it responsible for market failures within the industry (supply shortages, recalls, and so on).

Although private ownership absolves the provincial government of the risks associated with operating retail cannabis stores, a private-ownership model increases the risk of noncompliance with provincial regulation. Private stores have incentives to both sell to youth and access supply from the illicit market. However, effective monitoring and enforcement of inventory tracking and sourcing by regulators can, to some extent, mitigate the likelihood of illegal cannabis entering the legal supply chain. In addition, regulators can use similar methods to those applied to alcohol and tobacco to enforce minimum age requirements.

From a theoretical perspective, privately owned stores are more likely to compete successfully with the illicit market. They have a strong profit incentive to seek out the widest variety and the highest-quality but lowest-cost supply to entice consumers served by the illicit market. Furthermore, private operators have stronger incentives to monitor market conditions and changing consumer preferences, to adapt to changing market conditions and ensure profitability. This is of particular importance since there is strong demand for cannabis in Canada and a great deal of uncertainty surrounding consumer preferences and avenues for new product development and innovation.

A third option is to use a mix of public and private ownership, with private and publicly owned stores competing with each other and the illicit market. It remains to be seen whether this hybrid option offers the best or worst of both worlds. One potential benefit of a mix of private and public stores might be the ability of the publicly owned stores to provide

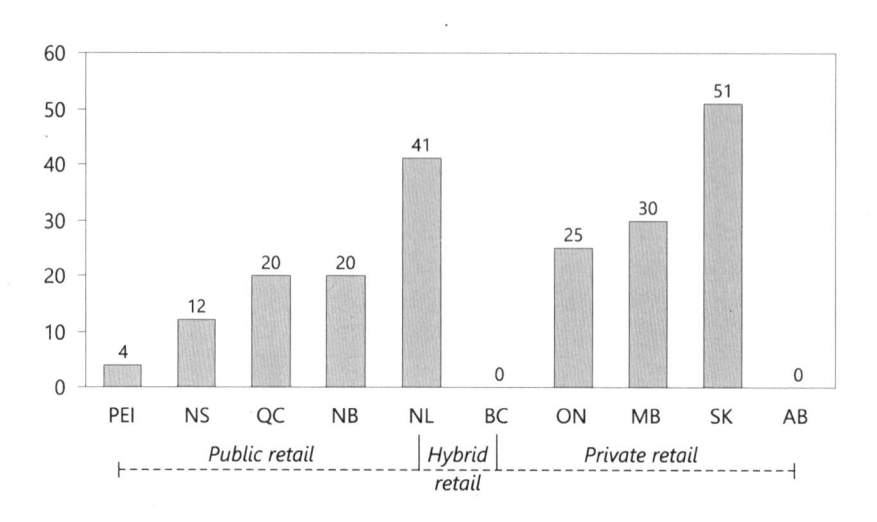

FIGURE 3.2
Maximum number of retail outlets, by province and ownership model

Province	Value	Category
PEI	4	Public retail
NS	12	Public retail
QC	20	Public retail
NB	20	Public retail
NL	41	Hybrid retail
BC	0	Hybrid retail
ON	25	Private retail
MB	30	Private retail
SK	51	Private retail
AB	0	Private retail

Sources: Alberta Liquor and Gaming, n.d.; Alcohol and Gaming Commision of Ontario, n.d.; British Columbia Liquor and Cannabis Licensing, n.d.; Cannabis New Brunswick, n.d.; Government of Newfound and Labrador, n.d.; Liquor, Gaming and Cannabis Authority of Manitoba, n.d.; Nova Scotia Liquor Commision, n.d.; PEI Cannabis, n.d.; Saskatchewan Liquor and Gaming Authority, n.d.; Société québécoise du cannabis, n.d.

legal-market access during periods of market disruptions. For example, many privately run stores faced significant delays in opening due to regulatory requirements, blocked access to supply, and implementation issues. Public stores with access to government resources can provide a legal access point for consumers during this transition phase.

The maximum number of retail outlets by province and ownership model is shown in Figure 3.2. At the time of writing, Alberta, Saskatchewan, Manitoba, and Ontario have opted for complete private ownership of retail cannabis outlets (see Figure 3.2). Ontario had originally decided on public ownership, but a change in the provincial government saw that decision reversed. Four provinces (Prince Edward Island, Nova Scotia, New Brunswick, and Quebec) have opted for a publicly owned monopoly for retail cannabis. Of these, only Nova Scotia has chosen to colocate cannabis retailing within its pre-existing alcohol stores. The remaining provinces, British Columbia and Newfoundland and Labrador, have opted for a hybrid system with both private and publically owned retail outlets.

All provinces have allowed online sales of cannabis and home delivery. In eight of the ten provinces, online purchases must be made from a publicly

Displacing the Illicit Cannabis Market

TABLE 3.1
Retail and distribution regulatory framework, by province

Province	Number of retail outlets	Ownership of retail outlets	Online sales	Distribution
British Columbia	Unlimited	Mixed	Government	Government
Alberta	Unlimited	Private	Government	Government
Saskatchewan	51	Private	Private	Private
Manitoba	30	Private	Private	Government
Ontario	25	Private	Government	Government
Quebec	20	Government	Government	Government
New Brunswick	20	Government	Government	Government
Nova Scotia	12	Government	Government	Government
Prince Edward Island	4	Government	Government	Government
Newfoundland and Labrador	41	Hybrid	Government	Government

Sources: Alberta Liquor and Gaming, n.d.; Alcohol and Gaming Commission of Ontario, n.d.; British Columbia Liquor and Cannabis Licensing, n.d.; Cannabis New Brunswick, n.d.; Government of Newfoundland and Labrador, n.d.; Liquor, Gaming and Cannabis Authority of Manitoba, n.d.; Nova Scotia Liquor Commision, n.d.; PEI Cannabis, n.d.; Saskatchewan Liquor and Gaming Authority, n.d.; Société québécoise du cannabis, n.d.

owned entity. Only in Saskatchewan and Manitoba are private retailers allowed to sell online. The benefits of private versus public online delivery are the same as the benefits and costs for private versus public retail. However, publicly run online retail vendors do provide a single source, which reduces the transaction costs for consumers in comparing and searching multiple sites for lower prices and better varieties.

Distribution is the final point of regulatory difference between the provinces (see Table 3.1). In all provinces except Saskatchewan, distribution is controlled directly by the provincial government. Saskatchewan alone allows for private distribution companies, including distribution directly from federally licensed producers to retail outlets. This may prove a challenge for the legal cannabis market in Saskatchewan, as the market power of producers has no countervailing market power at the distribution or retail level. In all other provinces, the market power of producers is offset by the monopsony (a market in which there is only one buyer) power of the provincially owned distributor. In addition, with multiple distributors, few if any distributors can achieve the minimum efficient scale that leads to potentially higher prices. Another benefit of a single distributor is that the single buyer can act as a central stabilizing agent in the industry to facilitate policy and allow for intervention at a single key point in the industry. Finally, multiple distribution channels increase the complexity and cost associated with monitoring and enforcing regulations.

Direct sales from producers to retailers could allow larger retailers, retailers with strong relationships with producers, or retailers owned by producers (Saskatchewan and Newfoundland allow producers to own retail stores) to have an advantage in terms of pricing and variety over smaller retailers. These risks are mitigated by a single publicly owned distributor. Another option for policy makers would be licensing a single privately owned monopoly for distribution. With effective regulation, especially over markups, a private monopoly could be at an advantage with respect to purchasing power, reduced costs from potential economies of scale, central coordination, and strong incentives to ensure competition with the illicit market and support innovation.

The Elements of the Score Card
The success of the policies and regulations implemented in support of legalization is dependent on inducing people currently consuming illicit-market cannabis to switch to legal products. Understanding consumer choice is not simple even when the product in question is entirely legal and massive amounts of direct observation data are available. The factors in the scorecard we adopted are based on the results of the National Cannabis Survey (Statistics Canada 2021a). The findings are that cannabis consumers are driven by four primary factors when choosing where to buy cannabis: quality and price (see Table 3.2), accessibility (see Table 3.3), and variety (see Table 3.4).[3]

Quality
Although not yet verified through observable decisions, product quality and safety are the primary concerns for consumers when deciding where to purchase cannabis.

The quality of cannabis products available in the illicit market is difficult to assess because of a lack of random testing. Illicit cannabis products seized by law enforcement in Canada and the United States are regularly found to have a wide array of contaminants, ranging from yeast, mould, and bacterial pathogens to pesticides (Robertson and McArthur 2016). The same is true of other contraband substances. Testing of illicit-market tobacco carried out

Displacing the Illicit Cannabis Market 83

by the Royal Canadian Mounted Police found similar issues of contamination (Irvine and Sims 2014; see also Sen 2017).

Despite legitimate concerns about adulterated cannabis, which may warrant higher prices for a regulated product, the legal market is not without its own challenges in terms of product quality and safety. The quality of legal-market cannabis is the element over which provincial agencies have the least control because of the federal government retaining control over the production segment of the newly legal industry. Canadian recalls of legal cannabis have not yet been nationwide; instead, they've affected only one or a few provinces at a time. Whether the provincial government is responsible or not, recalls have an impact on public perception of the quality and safety of legal cannabis in that province. Using the most recent Health Canada recall notices available from 2018 to 2019, we assigned scores to assess the impact of recalls on the safety and quality of legal cannabis available in each jurisdiction.

The province that experienced the most recalls (twelve) was Saskatchewan, the only province to have opted for a private distribution system. However, Manitoba had a similar number of recalls (ten) despite its publicly owned distribution system. This suggests that the number of recalls was likely supply-related or caused by factors other than the province's

TABLE 3.2
Legal cannabis product recalls and ratio of legal to illicit price, by province, 2018–19

Province	No. of recalls	Score	Ratio of legal to illicit price	Score
Newfoundland and Labrador	1	Excellent	1.414	Poor
Prince Edward Island	1	Excellent	1.345	Poor to good
Nova Scotia	1	Excellent	1.743	Needs improvement
New Brunswick	2	Excellent	1.466	Poor
Quebec	3	Excellent	1.071	Good
Ontario	2	Excellent	1.526	Poor
Manitoba	10	Good	1.876	Needs improvement
Saskatchewan	12	Good	1.868	Needs improvement
Alberta	4	Excellent	1.548	Poor
British Columbia	2	Excellent	1.511	Poor

Sources: Health Canada 2019; Statistics Canada 2019.

choice of public or private distribution. The remaining provinces all had relatively few cannabis product recalls since legalization, suggesting either that the legal market had high levels of quality control or that an insufficient amount of product was being tested by third parties.

Price
The National Cannabis Survey identified price as the second most important determinant of sourcing decisions for cannabis consumers. A growing body of literature has assessed the relationship between prices and cannabis users' consumption decisions. Users view legal and illicit cannabis as substitutes for each other and are willing to switch between legal and illicit sources, depending on prices (Amlung et al. 2019; Amlung and MacKillop 2019). As with all goods, a higher price reduces the quantity of a product available. This is the logic behind all Pigovian (sin) taxes, price-based environmental policies such as the carbon tax, and even the justification for subsidies to education. It is the same logic used to justify many of the proposed taxes on the legal cannabis industry, including the current federal policy of taxing retail cannabis at 10 percent of value or one dollar per gram, whichever is greater.

However, the illicit market offers an easy outlet for consumers facing inflated legal-market prices. Jason Childs and J. Stevens (2019) show that under a wide variety of circumstances and policy objectives, the optimal price of legal cannabis is lower than the illicit-market price. As a result, the ratio of the price of cannabis in the legal market to the price of cannabis in the illicit market is used to indicate the performance of the provincial legal markets.

These simple price indexes show that the legal market price is higher than the illicit-market price in all provinces. Quebec has the most competitive prices of all the provinces by far, charging just 7.1 percent more than the illicit market. The highest legal prices relative to the illicit market (87.6 percent higher in the legal market than the illicit market) were in Manitoba. This is to be expected in a market populated with private profit-motivated firms facing inadequate supply. To be clear, legal prices in excess of illicit prices are likely to lead some consumers back to the illicit market.

Accessibility
As of August 2018, about two-thirds of Canadians (65.3 percent) lived more than ten kilometres from a planned legal cannabis retail outlet; 4.1 percent lived within one kilometre (Statistics Canada 2018). To put this finding in

Displacing the Illicit Cannabis Market

TABLE 3.3
Accessibility to legal cannabis retail outlets, by province, 2018

Province	Outlets (per 100,000 people)	Population living within 10 km (%)	Score
Newfoundland and Labrador	4.77	64.8	Excellent
Prince Edward Island	2.58	57.8	Good
Nova Scotia	1.24	55.4	Good
New Brunswick	2.59	55.4	Good
Quebec	0.23	10.4	Needs improvement
Ontario	0	0*	Needs improvement
Manitoba	1.47	64.7	Excellent
Saskatchewan	1.80	66.3	Excellent
Alberta	1.73	63.8	Excellent
British Columbia	0.30	72.8	Excellent

* After a provincial election Ontario transitioned from a fully government-run retail model to a private retail model, which delayed retail storefronts for nearly a year.
Source: Statistics Canada 2018.

perspective, more than 90 percent of Canadians live within ten kilometres of a legal liquor retail outlet.

The accessibility of alcohol and cannabis is associated with both demand for the product and age of first use (Palali and van Ours 2015; Marie 2017). The effort associated with access to a product contributes to the cost of consumption. So, just as the risk of criminal prosecution adds to the total cost of consuming illicit cannabis, travel costs and waiting for delivery from the legal market add to the cost of legal cannabis. The greater the total cost to consumers of the legal market, the more likely they are to participate in the illicit market.

Variety

The National Cannabis Survey (Statistics Canada 2021a) identifies variety (with respect to CBD and THC content) as being a key factor in determining which source cannabis consumers use. Despite the generic designation of "weed" among nonusers, cannabis is not a homogeneous product. In addition to their CBD and THC content, cannabis products contain other chemicals, such as terpenes, which may influence the flavour and physiological

TABLE 3.4
Number of products and producers, by province, 2018–19

Province	No. of products	No. of producers	Score
Newfoundland and Labrador	54	16	Good
Prince Edward Island	79	26	Excellent
Nova Scotia	97	31	Good
New Brunswick	55	15	Good
Quebec	59	13	Good
Ontario	76	31	Good
Manitoba	31	12	Poor
Saskatchewan	70	20	Good
Alberta	39	19	Poor
British Columbia	154	43	Excellent

Sources: Alberta Liquor and Gaming, n.d.; Alcohol and Gaming Commission of Ontario, n.d.; British Columbia Liquor and Cannabis Licensing, n.d.; Cannabis New Brunswick, n.d.; Government of Newfoundland and Labrador, n.d.; Liquor, Gaming and Cannabis Authority of Manitoba, n.d.; Nova Scotia Liquor Commision, n.d.; PEI Cannabis, n.d.; Saskatchewan Liquor and Gaming Authority, n.d.; Société québécoise du cannabis, n.d.

effects. Users – particularly committed users, who account for the majority of cannabis consumed – are likely to have preferences for specific strains. Efforts by producers to differentiate their products range from associating them with celebrities (such as Snoop Dogg and The Tragically Hip) to labelling them "organic," among other things.

Natural and created product differentiation increases the likelihood that consumers will be loyal to specific strains, varieties, and brands. A legal market that cannot provide the precise product a consumer wants will face additional competition from the illicit market. Although there is no meaningful way to identify the most desired brands in illicit markets, making a wide variety of products from a wide variety of producers available should increase displacement of illegal sales.

From Score Card to Actual Performance

While forward-looking analysis is important, it cannot replace data on actual decisions made by consumers spending their own money. Nationally, the first three months of legalization, from October 2018 to December 2018, were not a resounding success. Sales of dry flower cannabis totalled fifteen tonnes (15,060 kg) over this period. Sales of cannabis oil totalled 5,408 litres. Thus, the legal market sold a dry flower equivalent of 15,733 kilograms.[4]

TABLE 3.5
Provincial legal cannabis sales and Parliamentary Budget Office illicit-market estimates (thousands), October 2018 to February 2019

Province	Total ($)	Annual ($)	PBO estimate ($)	Illicit market captured (%)
Newfoundland and Labrador	3,712	10,111	112,883	8.96
Prince Edward Island	1,006	2,741	31,628	8.67
Nova Scotia	6,624	18,043	191,480	9.42
New Brunswick	5,420	14,763	140,478	10.51
Quebec	54,456	148,332	1,008,780	14.70
Ontario	94,438	257,239	2,194,560	11.72
Manitoba	8,684	23,654	200,435	11.80
Saskatchewan	7,978	21,732	179,409	12.11
Alberta	33,816	92,111	672,210	13.70
British Columbia	35,971	97,982	700,700	13.98

Sources: Statistics Canada 2019; Parliamentary Budget Office 2016.

In 2016, the Parliamentary Budget Officer (PBO) forecast demand for cannabis in 2018. The (likely conservative) estimate of demand ranged from 378,000 kilograms up to 1,017,000 kilograms. Even in the best-case scenario, in which total demand would be 378,000 kilograms, the legal market for cannabis would account for only 16.6 percent, leaving 83.4 percent of demand to be served by the illicit market. At the top end of the PBO's estimates for demand, the legal market accounted for just 6.2 percent of the total demand.

Province-level data on the quantity of cannabis sold was not available at the time of writing. Instead, we use the value of sales reported by Statistics Canada (2021b) to assess the size of the legal cannabis market. To estimate the size of the illicit market, we use the two components of demand estimated by the PBO (quantity demanded and price) to establish the value of the total market for cannabis (Table 3.5).

This approach likely overstates the success of the legal market. If the PBO estimated the quantity of cannabis demanded to be twenty tonnes in a province and the price to be ten dollars per gram, for example, the value of the market would be $200 million. Thus, if the estimated value of the legal market is $100 million, it can be concluded that the legal market captured 50 percent of the total market for cannabis ($200 million).

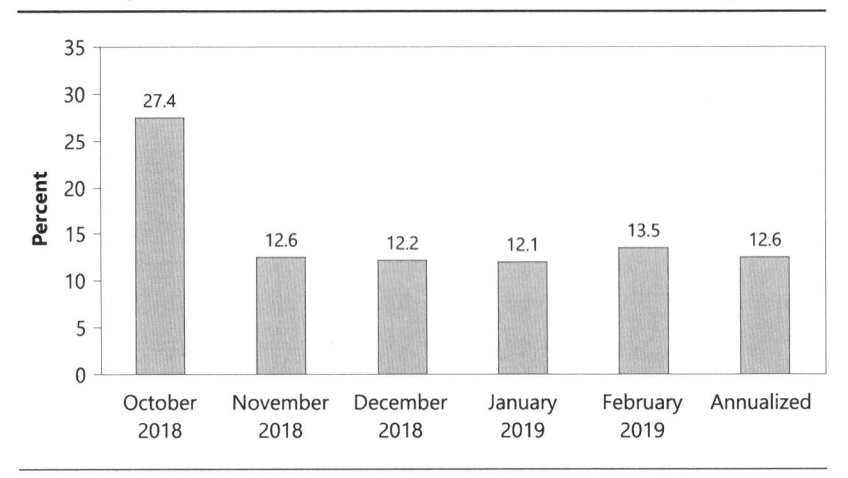

FIGURE 3.3
National legal sales as a share of total market, October 2018 to February 2019

Month	Percent
October 2018	27.4
November 2018	12.6
December 2018	12.2
January 2019	12.1
February 2019	13.5
Annualized	12.6

Source: Health Canada 2021; Parliamentary Budget Office 2016.

Because the PBO aggregated its demand estimates for two regions – the Prairies (Saskatchewan and Manitoba) and the Atlantic region (Newfoundland and Labrador, Nova Scotia, Prince Edward Island, and New Brunswick) – these estimates were decomposed by population weights for each province (each of which has a different retail or distribution model). The portion of the total cannabis market captured by legal markets nationally for each month (the PBO's annual estimate by the portion of a year's days in that month) is shown in Figure 3.3.

The two weeks of legalization in October were characterized by a great deal of excitement and lineups reminiscent of American "Black Friday" sales. The October sales data reflect the excitement and novelty of being able to purchase cannabis legally. The remaining months were plagued by supply issues, and some retail outlets were essentially out of stock.

Nationally, the legal market captured just 12.6 percent of the total estimated value of the market for cannabis. No province was on pace to capture more than 15 percent of the 2018 illicit-market demand estimated by the Parliamentary Budget Office in 2016. By these estimates, the worst performers were the four Atlantic provinces, with Prince Edward Island faring the worst, capturing just 8.67 percent of the market (see Figure 3.4).

Although the estimates derived should be treated with some caution, the top performers in displacing the illicit market were Quebec, British Columbia, and Alberta, which captured around 14 percent of their respective

Displacing the Illicit Cannabis Market

FIGURE 3.4
Percentage of the cannabis market captured by the legal market, by province and retail ownership model, 2018–19

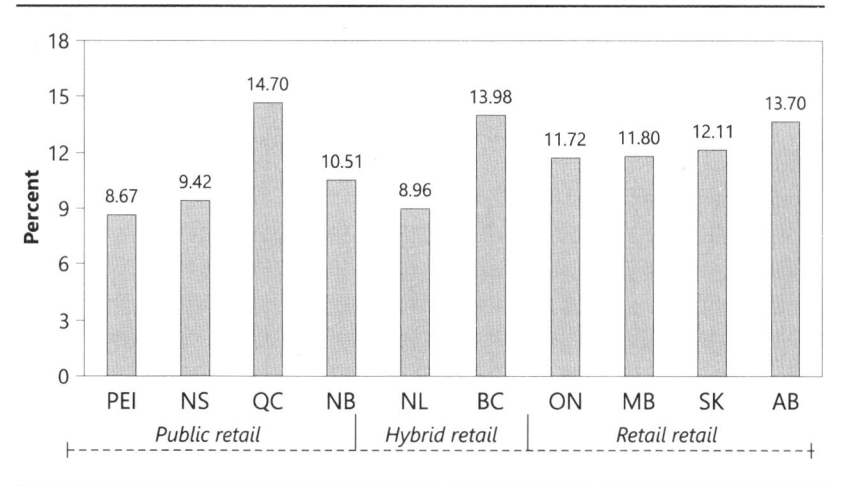

Province	Percent	Model
PEI	8.67	Public retail
NS	9.42	Public retail
QC	14.70	Public retail
NB	10.51	Public retail
NL	8.96	Hybrid retail
BC	13.98	Hybrid retail
ON	11.72	Retail retail
MB	11.80	Retail retail
SK	12.11	Retail retail
AB	13.70	Retail retail

Sources: Statistics Canada 2019; Parliamentary Budget Office 2016.

markets. Each province's performance is considered next in terms of the four elements of the scorecard – quality and price (see Table 3.6) and accessibility and variety (see Table 3.7).

Quality and Price

Assuming recalls are an accurate indicator of the quality and safety of products in the legal market, there were few differences across eight of the ten provinces. Although the fewest recalls were in provinces that captured the smallest portion of the illicit market, the number of recalls was not strongly correlated with displacement of the illicit market. With respect to price, the lower the prices in the legal market, the better able it will be to displace the illicit market. While no provinces were pursuing socially optimal pricing (Childs and Stevens 2019), some offered more competitive legal market prices.

The province with the lowest legal prices, Quebec, saw its legal market capture the highest portion of the total cannabis market. This competitive legal price almost certainly played a role in Quebec's relative success. At the same time, Manitoba's and Saskatchewan's high prices did not cause its legal sellers to capture the smallest portion of the total cannabis market. Relatively low prices in Prince Edward Island and Newfoundland and Labrador were

TABLE 3.6
Number of recalls* and legal price competitiveness** in relation to market performance, by province, 2018–19

No. of outlets	No. of recalls	Legal to illicit price ratio	Illicit market captured (%)
NL (Mixed) 41	1	1.414	8.96
PE (Public) 4	1	1.345	8.67
NS (Public) 12	1	1.743	9.42
NB (Public) 20	2	1.466	10.51
ON (Private) 25	2	1.526	11.72
BC (Hybrid) Unlimited	2	1.511	13.98
QC (Private) 20	3	1.071	14.70
AB (Private) Unlimited	4	1.548	13.70
MB (Private) 30	10	1.876	11.80
SK (Private) 51	12	1.868	12.11

Notes:
* Simple correlation coefficient 0.2961.
** Simple correlation coefficient −0.1542.
Sources: Health Canada 2019; Statistics Canada 2019; Parliamentary Budget Office 2016.

not linked to success either. Clearly, pricing alone was not the sole driver of early legal-market success or failure.

Accessibility and Variety

The degree of access to legal brick-and-mortar retail outlets is one of the largest differences between the provinces. Accessibility was assessed using two different measures: outlets per 100,000 people and percentage of the population living within ten kilometres of a store. Ontario, because of a change in government, had no legal physical outlets during the early portion of legalization and was only beginning to license retail outlets as of May 2019.

During this period, Ontario's legal cannabis market was limited to e-commerce. Similarly, Quebec focused on online sales and captured the largest share of the market. Saskatchewan (ranking fourth behind Alberta and British Columbia) did not have a single e-portal for legal cannabis but instead allowed each private retail outlet to operate its own. Thus, there is no straightforward relationship between distribution models and relative performance on the portion of the market being captured by the provinces.

TABLE 3.7
Accessibility in relation to legal market performance, by province, 2018–19

Province	Outlets (per 100,000 people)	Population living within 10 km of an outlet (%)	Illicit market captured (%)
Ontario	0	0	11.72
Quebec	0.23	10.40	14.70
British Columbia	0.30	72.80	13.98
Nova Scotia	1.24	55.40	9.42
Manitoba	1.47	64.70	11.80
Alberta	1.73	63.80	13.70
Saskatchewan	1.80	66.30	12.11
New Brunswick	2.59	55.40	10.51
Newfoundland and Labrador	4.77	64.80	8.96
Prince Edward Island			8.67

Note: Simple correlation coefficient between outlets per 100,000 and performance is −0.6792 and between portion of the population within ten kilometres and performance is −0.2356.

Sources: Alberta Liquor and Gaming, n.d.; Alcohol and Gaming Commission of Ontario, n.d.; British Columbia Liquor and Cannabis Licensing, n.d.; Cannabis New Brunswick, n.d.; Government of Newfoundland and Labrador, n.d.; Liquor, Gaming and Cannabis Authority of Manitoba, n.d.; Nova Scotia Liquor Commision, n.d.; PEI Cannabis, n.d.; Saskatchewan Liquor and Gaming Authority, n.d.; Société québécoise du cannabis, n.d.; Statistics Canada 2019.

One of the major concerns for any retail operation is ensuring it stocks the products that consumers want. The legal cannabis market is no different and has literally thousands of different potential products. Consumers with a strong preference for a specific combination of qualities (THC and/or CBD content, for example) are more likely to return to the illicit market if their preferred variety is not legally available. We assessed variety on two dimensions: the number of different strains available and the number of different producers represented (see Table 3.8).

Although variety increases the likelihood of having the specific product that consumers want, it does not guarantee higher sales. While British Columbia, for example, has greater variety – ranking second in its portion of the illicit market captured – Quebec captured more of the illicit market than British Columbia, with just a third of the variety. The value of the legal market relative to the estimated value of the illicit market is much less than the National Cannabis Survey suggests.

TABLE 3.8
Variety in relation to legal-market performance, by province, 2018–19

Province	No. of products	No. of producers	Illicit market captured (%)
Ontario	76	31	11.72
Quebec	59	13	14.70
British Columbia	154	43	13.98
Nova Scotia	97	31	9.42
Manitoba	31	12	11.80
Alberta	39	19	13.70
Saskatchewan	70	20	12.11
New Brunswick	55	15	10.51
Newfoundland and Labrador	54	16	8.96
Prince Edward Island	79	26	8.67

Note: Simple correlation coefficient between number of products and performance is 0.1005 and between number of producers and performance is 0.0326.

Sources: Alberta Liquor and Gaming, n.d.; Alcohol and Gaming Commission of Ontario, n.d.; British Columbia Liquor and Cannabis Licensing, n.d.; Cannabis New Brunswick, n.d.; Government of Newfoundland and Labrador, n.d.; Liquor, Gaming and Cannabis Authority of Manitoba, n.d.; Nova Scotia Liquor Commision, n.d.; PEI Cannabis, n.d.; Saskatchewan Liquor and Gaming Authority, n.d,; Société québécoise du cannabis, n.d.

The first-quarter 2019 iteration of the survey reports that 47.4 percent of users accessed cannabis through the legal market (Statistics Canada 2021a, 5262). However, even if almost half of users sourced at least some of their cannabis legally, it does not mean that the illicit market was reduced by half. If legalization induced demand for cannabis among law-abiding citizens, these new users added to the legal market without reducing the illicit market. The first-quarter 2019 survey found that 646,000 people tried cannabis for the first time, almost double the number of new users in the first quarter of 2018.

The number of users alone does not account for the quantity or frequency of use. The survey reported that the number of daily or almost daily users was stable at 1.8 million or 34.6 percent of users. If daily or near-daily users continue to obtain their cannabis from the illicit market and all other users buy cannabis legally, the illicit market will continue to capture the lion's share of the market by value. Accordingly, displacing the illicit market will require incentivizing daily and near-daily users, who account for the majority of cannabis consumed, to switch to legal-market products.

Evaluating the legal market's success in displacing the illicit market requires a multifaceted approach. The categories of the scorecard presented here (quality, price, accessibility, and variety) are based on the determinants of purchasing decisions reported in the National Cannabis Survey. The performance of each province's combined retail and distribution systems was scored on these four dimensions. Notwithstanding limitations due to confounds introduced at the production level – supply failed to meet demand – the analysis provides a better understanding of the relative performance of different distribution models.

The distribution and retail system in all ten provinces led to few recalls. While Saskatchewan and Manitoba saw the most recalls (twelve and ten, respectively), the other provinces had negligible recall rates, suggesting there were few concerns with quality and safety. Although quality and safety concerns were found to be a key consideration for 76 percent of users, it can be concluded that either illicit cannabis was deemed on par in terms of quality and safety with legal cannabis or that these concerns were overstated by National Cannabis Survey respondents.

Pricing was cited as a leading consideration for 38 percent of cannabis users. Although the optimal price of legal cannabis is lower than the illicit-market price (Childs and Stevens 2019), every province set the price above this level, in part because of taxes levied by the federal government. The most competitive on this score was Quebec, which nonetheless succeeded in displacing a mere 15 percent of the total market value. Whereas a portion of consumers was relatively price-insensitive and willing to pay higher legal-market prices, poor sales suggest that the majority of users are not prepared to pay a substantially higher price for legal cannabis.

Accessibility was cited by 28 percent of users as a primary concern. Quebec's pricing strategy was likely partly offset by its decision to limit the number of initial retail outlets to just twenty. Ontario's decision to switch from public stores to private retail outlets following a change in government restricted the analysis here to online sales. Newfoundland and Labrador, the province with the highest legal retail coverage for its small (largely "rural") population, fared poorly, capturing just 9 percent of the value of the cannabis market.

The variety of products available was rated as equally important as accessibility (by 28 percent of the survey respondents). British Columbia, which offered more than 150 varieties from 43 different producers had more than twice the selection of any other legal retailer and captured 14 percent of the value of the cannabis market. However, Nova Scotia, which offered the second-best selection, captured only 9 percent of the market value, faring worse than Manitoba (12 percent), which had fewer cannabis products available. Alberta's low selection likewise did not prevent it from capturing a higher market share. Another variable that confounds a more nuanced interpretation is that provinces performing better on displacement may also have done a better job of stocking popular varieties.

In conclusion, this analysis of "best practices" for legalizing cannabis reveals that the provinces and federal government have far to go to meet the objective of displacing the illicit cannabis market. Effective policy implementation will require more research to identify measures for evaluating cannabis-policy "success" and more evidence-based adaptations and decisions based on this data.

Notes

1 The original Act included the *Marihuana* spelling. The Government of Canada opted for the more conventional spelling in 2014.
2 March is the last month, at the time of writing, for which data on federal licence holders was available from Statistics Canada's Cannabis Stats Hub (Statistics Canada 2019).
3 Statistics Canada identifies five factors: quality and safety, lowest price, accessibility, location, and preferred potencies/formulations. We collapsed accessibility and location into a single category, "accessibility."
4 We use the same method to convert litres of cannabis oil to the dry flower equivalent that Canopy Growth Corporation uses to calculate its inventory and sales: 2,650 litres = 330 kilograms (Canopy Growth Corporation 2018).

Works Cited

Alberta Liquor and Gaming. n.d. *Cannabis.* https://aglc.ca/cannabis.
Alcohol and Gaming Commission of Ontario. n.d. *Cannabis.* https://www.agco.ca/cannabis/general-information.
Amlung, Michael, and James MacKillop. 2019. "Availability of Legalized Cannabis Reduces Demand for Illegal Cannabis among Canadian Cannabis Users: Evidence from a Behavioural Economic Substitution Paradigm." *Canadian Journal of Public Health* 110 (2): 216–21.
Amlung, Michael, Derek D. Reed, Vanessa Morris, Elizabeth R. Aston, Jane Metrik, and James MacKillop. 2019. "Price Elasticity of Illegal versus Legal Cannabis: A Behavioral Economic Substitutability Analysis." *Addiction* 114 (1): 112–18.
British Columbia Liquor and Cannabis Licensing. n.d. *Application Statistics.*
Cannabis New Brunswick. n.d. https://www.cannabis-nb.com/.

Canopy Growth Corporation. 2018. "Management's discussion and Analysis of the Financial Condition and Results of Operations, for the Three Months Ended June 30, 2018." https://www.canopygrowth.com/wp-content/uploads/2020/06/Canopy-Growth-Corporation_Q1_FY_2019_MDA_FINAL.pdf.

Childs, Jason, and J. Stevens. 2019. "The State Must Compete: Optimal Pricing in the Legal Cannabis Market." *Canadian Public Administration* 62 (4): 656–73.

Government of Newfound and Labrador. n.d. *Cannabis in Newfoundland and Labrador.* https://www.gov.nl.ca/cannabis/.

Health Canada. n.d. *Licensed Cultivators, Processors and Sellers of Cannabis under the* Cannabis Act. https://www.canada.ca/en/health-canada/services/drugs-medication/cannabis/industry-licensees-applicants/licensed-cultivators-processors-sellers.html#a1.

—. 2016. *Understanding the New Access to Cannabis for Medical Purposes Regulations.* August. https://www.canada.ca/en/health-canada/services/publications/drugs-health-products/understanding-new-access-to-cannabis-for-medical-purposes-regulations.html.

—. 2017. *Proposed Approach to the Regulation of Cannabis.* Ottawa: Government of Canada.

—. 2019. *Cannabis Recalls, Adverse Reactions and Reporting.* October 2. https://www.canada.ca/en/health-canada/services/drugs-medication/cannabis/recalls-adverse-reactions-reporting.html.

—. 2021. *Dried Cannabis Market Data.* June 15. https://www.canada.ca/en/health-canada/services/drugs-medication/cannabis/research-data/market/dried.html.

Irvine, Ian, and William Sims. 2014. "The Simple Analytics of Tobacco Taxation with Illegal Supply." *Canadian Journal of Economics* 47 (4): 1153–72.

Liquor, Gaming and Cannabis Authority of Manitoba. n.d. *Cannabis.* https://lgcamb.ca/cannabis/.

Marie, Olivier, and Ulf Zölitz. 2017. "'High' Achievers? Cannabis Access and Academic Performance." *Review of Economic Studies* 84 (3): 1210–37.

Nova Scotia Liquor Commision. n.d. *Cannabis.* https://cannabis.mynslc.com/en.

Palali, Ali, and Jan C. van Ours. 2015. "Distance to Cannabis Shops and Age of Onset of Cannabis Use." *Health Economics* 24 (11): 1483–1501.

Parliamentary Budget Office. 2016. *Legalized Cannabis: Fiscal Considerations.* Ottawa: Government of Canada.

PEI Cannabis. n.d. https://peicannabiscorp.com/?.

Robertson, Grant, and Greg McArthur. 2016. "Globe Investigation: What's in Your Weed? We Tested Dispensary Marijuana to Find Out." *Globe and Mail,* July 27.

Saskatchewan Liquor and Gaming Authority. n.d. *Cannabis Retailers.* https://www.slga.com/permits-and-licences/cannabis-permits/cannabis-retailing/cannabis-retailers-in-saskatchewan.

Scotti, Monique. 2018. "Marijuana Won't Be Legal on July 1, and Here's Why." *Global News,* June 13. https://globalnews.ca/news/4271668/marijuana-legal-delay-july-1-why/.

Sen, Anindya. 2017. "Smokes, Smugglers, and Lost Revenues: How Governments Should Respond." Working paper. Toronto: C.D. Howe Institute.

Senate of Canada. 2018. "The Cannabis Act in the Senate." Senate of Canada, October 17. https://www.sencanada.ca/en/sencaplus/news/cannabis-act/.

Société québécoise du cannabis. n.d. Retrieved from https://www.sqdc.ca/en-CA/.

Statistics Canada. 2018. *Access by Canadians to Regulated Liquor and Cannabis Retail Outlets.* Ottawa: Government of Canada. https://www150.statcan.gc.ca/n1/daily-quotidien/181010/dq181010d-eng.htm.

—. 2019. *Cannabis Statistics Hub.* https://www150.statcan.gc.ca/n1/pub/13-610-x/cannabis-eng.htm.

—. 2021a. National Cannabis Survey. https://www23.statcan.gc.ca/imdb/p2SV.pl?Function=getSurvey&Id=1289011.

—. 2021b. "Retail Trade Sales by Industry (x 1,0000)." Table 20–10–0008–02. https://www150.statcan.gc.ca/t1/tbl1/en/tv.action?pid=2010000802.

4

Medical Cannabis Dispensaries

A Conduit for Change?

JENNA VALLERIANI

In 2016, the Liberal Party formed a majority government in what was the largest seat increase by a party in a single election (BBC News 2015), winning on a platform that included a promise to legalize cannabis for non-medical use. While the landscape changed under legalization and for the former medical cannabis program, the Access to Cannabis for Medical Purposes Regulations (ACMPR) (now the Cannabis Act), medical cannabis dispensaries (MCDs) in Canada continued to be a primary source of access to cannabis-based medicines, alongside licensed sellers – who were legally permitted to sell only by mail order. Local police and municipalities adopted a variety of different responses to MCDs as legalization has increased budgets in many major cities. In the lead up to legalization and shortly after, many MCDs moved online to minimize the risk of detection and enforcement, which has only increased as legalization continues to settle.

On April 13, 2017, the Liberal government tabled legislation to "create a strict legal framework for controlling the production, distribution, sale and possession of cannabis in Canada" (Canada 2017). Bill C-45, An Act respecting cannabis and to amend the Controlled Drugs and Substances Act, the Criminal Code and other Acts, was introduced after extensive consultation by a government-appointed task force. Accompanying legislation – Bill C-46: An act to amend the Criminal Code – was also introduced to expand police powers in the detection of drug-impaired driving.

Bill C-45, or the Cannabis Act, removes cannabis from the Controlled Drugs and Substances Act (CDSA), placing the ACMPR under its own jurisdiction. Separating nonmedical and medical markets and access, the new medical program permits a broader range of products and access to more licensed producers and sellers (Canada Gazette 2018). In anticipation of legalization, different jurisdictions took differing approaches to address the abundance of illicit MCDs. Kimberly, British Columbia, was the first city in Canada to regulate MCDs at the local level through business-licensing agreements. As early as 2015, Vancouver also took steps to regulate dispensaries by licensing those in compliance to stem the proliferation of these stores.

At the time, the Conservative federal health minister, Rona Ambrose, expressed her "deep concern" with the intention of Vision Vancouver – the municipal party in power – to regulate MCDs. In an open letter to Mayor Gregor Robertson, she asserted that legitimizing the commercial sale of cannabis was outside local jurisdiction and that "the law is clear: they are illegal" (Minister of Health 2015). The mayor responded by calling the Conservative government "tone deaf" on the need for regulating MCDs (Hagar 2015).

In September 2015, the RCMP issued thirteen letters to MCDs after Health Canada announced it would be monitoring "all forms of marijuana advertising and promotion" (Health Canada 2015). The letter stated that the MCDs were violating both the Controlled Drugs and Substances Act and the Food and Drugs Act and gave these businesses until September 21 to comply with the law (Lowrie 2015). All stayed open. Nothing happened. The RCMP's inaction signalled an evident lack of guidance and cooperation between local and federal levels of enforcement. The heavy-handed approach of the federal government only served to galvanize support among city officials.

Support for regulating MCDs included at least twelve other municipalities outside Vancouver in British Columbia alone – e.g., Victoria, Port Alberni, Cumberland, Nelson, Grand Forks, Squamish, Rossland, Penticton, Invermere, Kimberly, Nanaimo, Abbotsford, and West Kelowna (Village of Cumberland 2016; Druzin 2017). Other jurisdictions across Canada have opted to ramp up enforcement instead. As many Canadian cities continue with campaigns to close down cannabis dispensaries, this chapter explores the history of MCDs in North America to preface their evolution in the legalization era.

Origins and Overview of Canadian Experience

The medical marijuana movement in North America is often traced to the HIV/AIDS epidemic (see Werner 2001). As early as the late 1970s, AIDS emerged with little guidance and no treatment options available. With the illness spreading quickly among gay men, San Francisco was the epicentre of the underground movement for access to medical cannabis (Feldman and Mandel 1998; Sidney 2001; Reiman 2014). In the 1990s, well-known activist Dennis Peron fought to pass Proposition P, a resolution declaring support for medical cannabis, and to make enforcement a lower priority. Later he helped draft and pass Proposition 215 (1996) in California. It granted access to cannabis for medical purposes.

Peron is credited with opening the first MCD, the Cannabis Buyer's Club (CBC) in 1991. It had over 10,000 members by the late 1990s (Werner 2001). Modelled after the AIDS Buyer's Club, which provided members with access to medications not yet approved in the United States, Peron's cannabis "social club" offered access to cannabis and a safe space to socialize (Grinspoon 2004; Reiman 2014). The CBC had the support of the mayor of San Francisco, the Department of Health, and the police (Feldman and Mandel 1998). As the CBC expanded, from serving AIDS and cancer patients to those with other ailments, other MCDs followed. By 1997, there were seventeen more in California (Reiman 2014) operating under an array of service models.

In 1997, an MCD in San Jose, the Santa Clara Medical Cannabis Center, was the first in North America licensed by a municipality (Reiman 2014). Departing from the social club model, this adaptation laid the groundwork for Canada's emerging approach to medical cannabis distribution. With Canada facing its own resurging HIV epidemic in the late 1990s (Public Health Agency of Canada 2018), federal prohibition of cannabis weakened with the rising demand for medical cannabis. The growing demand spawned a handful of "compassion clubs," nonprofit MCD organizations that provide access with a doctor's approval. Despite MCDs' illegality, municipal authorities in Toronto, Vancouver, and other cities were historically tolerant of well-established ones that enforced strict policies, granting membership to only those with verified medical conditions (Hathaway and Rossiter 2007).

Legal Challenges and the Development of Medical Cannabis Access

The history of access to medical cannabis has been shaped by a number of significant court challenges. Jim Wakeford, who used cannabis to cope with

AIDS, sparked the first case to produce a ruling that permitted exemptions for medical use, under section 56 of the CDSA (*Wakeford v The Queen* 1999). In 2000, Terry Parker, who used cannabis to manage his epileptic seizures, challenged charges of possession and cultivation on the grounds that the section 56 exemption did not provide medical users with a legal avenue of access (*Parker v The Queen* 2000). When the case was brought to the Ontario Court of Appeal, the judge struck down the section 56 exemption as an insufficient remedy, instructing the federal government to create a program for Canadians requiring access to cannabis for medical purposes (Lucas 2009).

The use of cannabis as medicine was exempted from the CDSA in 2001 with the introduction of the first federal medical cannabis access program, the Marihuana Medical Access Regulations (MMAR). In the decade that followed, court challenges continued to demonstrate the medical cannabis access system's failure to meet patients' needs (*R v J.P.* 2003; *Hitzig v The Queen* 2003; *Hitzig v Canada* 2005; *R v Long* 2007; *R v Bodner/Hall/Spasic* 2007; *Sfetkopoulos v Canada* 2008; *R v Beren* 2009; *R v Mernagh* 2011). Until 2003, the MMAR program did not include access to a legal supply of cannabis (*Hitzig v The Queen* 2003). Eventually, authorized patients were able to 1) purchase from a sole producer authorized by Health Canada, 2) cultivate their own cannabis, or 3) designate a third party to grow for them (Lucas 2009).

Canada became the second country in the world, after Israel, to establish a centralized medical cannabis program. The first contract to grow cannabis for the federal government was awarded to Prairie Plant Systems in 2000. Delays in production and bureaucracy meant that authorized medical users could not access this supply until 2003 (Capler 2008). In addition to patients' problems gaining access and supply, few doctors were willing to risk their reputation by supporting applications through the MMAR process (Jones and Hathaway 2008). Quality and variety were notoriously poor, with just one-tenth of registered medical users buying from the government (Boyd and Carter 2014). As compared to seven hundred federal exemptees at the time, Vancouver's largest MCD had over three thousand members (Capler 2008).

The MMAR was criticized publicly by antidrug proponents such as MCDs, cannabis activists, and patients. The program was held responsible for the easy diversion of cannabis into the illicit market through home production, lack of monitoring, and inadequate controls (Borden Ladner Gervais LLP 2016). Against a backdrop of legal challenges and grassroots activism since the 1990s, a growing need had been identified, and MCDs responded by building a community. The "first" dispensary in Canada is generally agreed to be Vancouver's British Columbia Compassionate Club Society (BCCCS), opened by Hilary Black. Although other sellers were unquestionably distributing cannabis to medical users by 1997, the BCCCS was the first MCD in Canada to use the storefront model, register as a non-profit society, and require proof of diagnosis or recommendation from a doctor for record-keeping purposes. As the first "above ground" operation of its kind in Canada, the BCCCS continues to operate outside federal legal regulation, now serving well over six thousand members.

Outside of Vancouver and Victoria on the West Coast, MCDs emerged in cities such as Toronto, albeit often more underground out of necessity and for survival. The Cannabis Compassion Club in London, Ontario, run by Lynn and Mike Harichy, served about six hundred patients in the mid- to late 1990s (*London Free Press* 1998, 2003; Larson 2015); it was eventually raided and shut down by police. By 1998, efforts were underway to create the Medical Marijuana Buyer's Clubs of Ontario, with the help of lawyer Alan Young (Freed 1998). It failed to fully materialize and soon became inactive.

In Toronto, Cannabis As Living Medicine (CALM) opened briefly in 1996 but closed five months later and reopened again the following year (Freed 1998). By 1997, the Medical Marijuana Resource Centre (MMRC) was also operating in Toronto (Mernagh 2002). Three years before *R v Parker*, one could apply for medical access to cannabis by completing a physician-supported application at the Toronto Hemp Company, a downtown "head shop" open since 1994 (Nance 2009). Before opening an actual dispensary, like many other origin stories, it all began with home delivery to a few dozen clients who became part of a larger community.

The MMRC faced many challenges in its early days, including a violent robbery and a raid by police, which eventually led to a Supreme Court challenge that upheld the rights of patients to have access to a safe, legal supply of cannabis (*Hitzig v The Queen* 2003; see also Sumach 1998; Mernagh 2002). These early efforts evolved into the Toronto Compassion Club (TCC), a long-standing MCD in a city that saw the number of MCDs expand from one or two in the late 1990s to a dozen by 2013. Unlike the West Coast MCDs, those in Toronto (and many other cities) did not have municipal support. The services often remained hidden in communities, known largely only to members, and unable to operate in the open because of fear of prosecution.

Introducing a Legal Medical Cannabis Market

In 2014, under the Conservative federal government, the MMAR was replaced with the Marihuana for Medical Purposes Regulations (MMPR). The MMPR opened up the production and distribution of cannabis to a free-market model, wherein licensed producers (LPs), approved by Health Canada, were the only ones permitted to legally produce and distribute (by mail to authorized users) regulated cannabis and cannabis products. Existing personal production licences were repealed under the new system, which might have, arguably, allowed for the inclusion of MCDs. However, MCDs were excluded. Additionally, the Canadian Association of Medical Cannabis Dispensaies (CAMCD), now the Association of Canadian Cannabis Retailers (ACCRES), was established in 2011 to ensure best practices across MCDs.

The CAMCD, like other independent trade or industry associations, served a "legitimating function" in the absence of regulation and raised confidence in and among association members (Sine, David, and Mitsuhashi 2007; King, Clemons, and Fry 2011). While the MMPR was expected to allow access to better-quality cannabis, a diversity of strains, and production under regulated and secure conditions, MCDs continued to fill gaps in the supply, including access to a variety of products such as food-infused products and higher-dose oils not available at the time through legal channels (Robertson and McArthur 2017).

In *Allard v Canada* (2014) the Federal Court agreed that the MMPR infringed the section 7 Charter right to freedom and liberty. It ruled that LPs did not provide all medical users "reasonable access," having barred exemptees from growing their own cannabis. The court suspended its ruling for six months to give the federal government time to revise or replace the MMPR. In response, the government introduced the ACMPR, which was, in fact, almost identical to the MMPR but allowed those authorized to apply to grow their own cannabis. More permissive regulations in the legalization era have spurred increased investment in this billion-dollar sector, as medical cannabis access has grown nearly ten-fold in the interim, from 40,000 authorizations to over 350,000 client registrations with federally licensed sellers by the end of December 2018 (Health Canada 2019).

A Legal Medical Cannabis Market alongside Medical Cannabis Dispensaries

The proliferation of MCDs began in Vancouver and Toronto as "business as usual" continued in the shadow of a looming legal medical cannabis industry.

MCDs were criticized as "out of control" in the media, "barely even pretending to cater to patients" (Friscolanti 2016). In 2014–16, over 100 MCDs opened in Toronto alone, doubling to 200 by 2017 (Toronto 2016, 2017). New MCDs adopted bolder tactics, being more open, announcing their locations and advertising, and welcoming "walk-ins" without doctor referrals.

Departing from accepted practices at older MCDs, the newer ones were criticized for their relaxed procedures. Prior to their proliferation, MCDs were left alone. That changed when cities such as Toronto began to take action. In May 2016, Toronto Police Services targeted forty-six MCDs, arresting more than ninety people and laying over 250 charges (Shum 2016). These raids continued through the summer and into 2017, resulting in a total of 611 charges against employees and business owners and the closure of 139 storefronts. Other tactics for closure included zoning, licensing, and obstruction charges against employees, business owners, and property owners. One year later, an estimated sixty MCDs continued to operate in the city (Toronto 2017), including the long-standing, more resilient MCDs that continued to operate while staying relatively hidden and discreet.

Leading up to "Project Claudia," the May 2016 raid that was the largest ever executed on MCDs in Canada, the Toronto mayor had called for "urgent action" by police, and there was little to no council support for the city's dispensaries (Gray 2016). Even the relatively progressive Toronto Drug Strategy committee claimed to be waiting on the federal government for direction (Valleriani 2017). Municipal deferral to the federal government (denying that MCDs were Toronto's responsibility while identifying them as a problem needing action) was perhaps the biggest difference between Toronto's and Vancouver's adaptation to the growth of MCDs.

Toronto's raids were ineffective at preventing a new wave of dispensaries from opening to stake their claim in the expanding legal market. Reaction to police raids in local media was critical (see Delamont 2017; Jeffords 2016), and public opinion was mixed (Forum Research 2016), as activists continued to condemn stepped-up enforcement and called for more inclusive regulatory strategies (Akin 2016).

In early 2017, Toronto Police Services and the RCMP coordinated a Canada-wide raid on recreational dispensaries, targeting the Cannabis Culture franchises in Toronto, Ottawa, and Hamilton and the main office in Vancouver (which did not dispense cannabis on-site). The shops' owners in Toronto and Hamilton were arrested as part of a wider criminal investigation that had them facing up to twenty years in prison for their alleged ties to organized crime. In late 2017, Toronto police raided and shut down twelve more MCDs operating in the city (Levy 2017).

At the time of writing in 2018, police raids and closures continued in Canadian cities, including Toronto, Ottawa, London, Hamilton, Montreal, Quebec City, St. Johns, Calgary, Halifax, and some small municipalities in British Columbia, such as Nanaimo, Chilliwack, and Campbell River (all places where the RCMP, rather than a localized unit, provides policing services). As a national, federal, provincial, and municipal policing body that ran Canada's first drug squads and has long played a central role in implementing prohibition, the RCMP perhaps exercises less discretion when it comes to enforcement than local police.

Why Is More Equitable Access Still Needed in the Legalization Era?

Since the Cannabis Act came into force in October 2018, new regulations have replaced the ACMPR (see Canada 2019, 2021). Despite the gains made in developing a viable medical cannabis access program for Canadians, gaps remain that explain the remarkable resilience of MCDs early in Canada's post-legalization era and legal access remains challenging for equity-deserving populations (Valleriani et al. 2020). Research shows that these providers have long been valued by their members for the wide array of services and benefits they offer (Capler et al. 2017; Hathaway and Rossiter 2007). The key factors and advantages identified in this literature include affordability, access, product quality, and education.

Affordability

Cannabis does not have a drug identification number (DIN) in Canada, so most insurance companies do not cover it as a medicine. Affordability remains a significant barrier, particularly in vulnerable and lower-income communities. Although some insurers are beginning to include medical cannabis as an option in their formularies, prices on the legal medical cannabis market range from four to twenty-five dollars per gram (plus shipping charges and the requirement of making minimum orders), as well as the addition of an excise tax, on top of sales tax, on medical cannabis since legalization was enacted. This is unusual in Canada where other medications are not subject to sales or excise tax.

Those with limited incomes and financial resources who are on disability or social assistance because of chronic and debilitating health conditions do not have equal access. At MCDs, cannabis is available in smaller quantities, members can make multiple visits per week, and they do not have to wait for products to be shipped to an address. This level of access and service is unavailable through legal channels, where cannabis is prepackaged and comes in increments of at least one gram.

Access

Legal access to medical cannabis in Canada is available by mail order only. This means that authorized patients cannot go to a pharmacy or storefront to purchase and pick up cannabis – the one exception is Shoppers Drug Mart, which was authorized to create an online e-commerce portal for medical cannabis access (Canadian Press 2018). Instead, their orders must be processed by the LP, typically with little assistance from a pharmacist or health care provider concerning contraindications or advice for novice users.

On-site dispensing may facilitate proper care and education, especially for those with no fixed address or credit card who are unable to order online. Experienced users often prefer to see and smell the product first. The proliferation of MCDs, accordingly, could have been mitigated by providing a comparable legal on-site sale option for medical access, such as pharmacies.

Consistency, Product Diversity, and Quality

Some patients cannot access the cannabis cultivars they require through their LPs. Finding out "what works" often takes time and depends on having access to a sufficient variety of products. Cannabis affects people differently. In addition to the cultivar (see Russo 2018), other factors include the frequency of use and method of administration (e.g., infused food products, and vaping versus smoking). The elderly and children (who may use cannabis to control seizures, for example) are highly sensitive to changes in varieties and doses. Consistency of access to the right products is essential.

This is clearly not a "shortage of supply issue," considering that in April 2019 there were approximately 150,000 kilograms of cannabis being stored by over 150 licensed producers (Health Canada 2019). Rather it is a shortage of particular cannabis products and cultivars in particularly high demand. In 2018, there was limited variety, with no food-infused products, extracts, edibles, or oils with concentrations above 30 mg/ml of THC. Despite the anticipated introduction of new products in 2019, the quality of cannabis available through legal channels was variable considering the price. Since

2019, however, the legal market has made some vast leaps with product quality, consistency, and bulk price offerings.

Education for Health Care Practitioners and Patients

Educational opportunities for health care practitioners and patients have expanded over the last five years in Canada, but important barriers remain. The science of medical cannabis is seldom included in medical training, leaving it to health care providers, cannabis-industry participants, and patient organizations to try to fill the gaps. Although research has lagged behind other medicines in Canada, clinical trials are examining the use of cannabis to treat epilepsy in children, post-traumatic stress disorder, wound care, palliative care, among many other conditions and symptoms (Cannabis-med.org n.d.). In addition to more guidance being offered to physicians (Canadian Medical Protective Association 2019), there have been substantial gains in training, including newly accredited physician education and calls to include cannabis in medical training and curricula.

※

Legalization continues to erect barriers to medical cannabis patients. For hopeful licensed sellers, the licensing system is not only bureaucratic and complex, it is a lengthy process that requires initial capital and business acumen to meet licensing and security regulations. Although few MCDs have successfully transitioned to the legal marketplace, others have not and will not be "going legal" any time soon. They have had to be resilient in Canada, surviving under total prohibition for two decades without legal or mainstream public support. As the model grew and diversified, MCDs 'adapted to a changing market, providing needed access to cannabis to patients who otherwise would not have their choice of medicine.

The challenge in a post-legal world is creating space for more inclusive regulations that support a shift from illicit to legal status. Instead, it is more likely that illegal MCDs will continue to thwart the regulations – mostly through online channels. The recently discovered profitability of the industry makes it highly likely that nonmedical and medical cannabis production and distribution will be controlled by a handful of large corporations. While some well-known MCD pioneers and activists have found employment in the industry, many others have been systematically excluded. The Cannabis Act in Canada, more generally, continues to inflict injustices on those who suffered under prohibition – and are not likely to see much benefit from cannabis legalization.

Works Cited

BBC News. 2015. "Canada Election: Liberals Sweep to Power." October 20. https://www.bbc.com/news/world-us-canada-34578213.

Borden Ladner Gervais, LLP. 2016. "The Hazy State of Marihuana Regulations." https://www.blg.com/en/insights/2016/02/the-hazy-state-of-marihuana-regulation-in-canada.

Boyd, Susan, and Connie Carter. 2014. *Killer Weed: Marijuana Grow Ops, Media and Justice.* Toronto: University of Toronto Press.

Canada. 2017. "Legalizing and Strictly Regulating Cannabis: The Facts." https://www.canada.ca/en/services/health/campaigns/legalizing-strictly-regulating-cannabis-facts.html.

—. 2019. "Regulations under the Cannabis Act." https://www.canada.ca/en/health-canada/services/drugs-medication/cannabis/laws-regulations/regulations-support-cannabis-act.html.

—. 2021. "Cannabis for Medical Purposes under the Cannabis Act: Information and Improvements." https://www.canada.ca/en/health-canada/services/drugs-medication/cannabis/medical-use-cannabis.html.

Canada Gazette. 2018. "Order Fixing October 17, 2018 as the Day on which Certain Provisions of the Act Come into Force: SI/2018–52." Part 2, 152 (14). http://www.gazette.gc.ca/rp-pr/p2/2018/2018-07-11/html/si-tr52-eng.html.

Canadian Medical Protective Association. 2019. https://www.cmpa-acpm.ca/en/advice-publications/browse-articles/2019/cannabis-legalization-in-canada-one-year-later.

Canadian Press. 2018. "Shoppers Drug Mart Granted License to Sell Medical Marijuana Online." *CBC News.* https://www.cbc.ca/news/canada/toronto/shoppers-medical-cannabis-1.4938506.

Cannabis-med.org. n.d. "Clinical Studies and Case Reports." https://www.cannabis-med.org/studies/study.php.

Capler, Rielle. 2007. *A Review of the Cannabis Cultivation Contract between Health Canada and Prairie Plant Systems.* Prepared for Safe Access, October. http://safeaccess.ca/research/pdf/hc_pps_contract_report.pdf.

Capler, Rielle, Zach Walsh, Kim Crosby, Lynne Belle-Isle, Susan Holtzman, Philippe Lucas, and Robert Callaway. 2017. "Are Dispensaries Indispensable? Patient Experiences of Access to Cannabis from Medical Cannabis Dispensaries in Canada." *International Journal of Drug Policy* 47: 1–8.

Delamont, Kieran. 2017. "It's Time to Stop the Raids." *The Torontoist,* March 9. http://torontoist.com/2017/03/time-stop-raids/.

Druzin, Randi. 2017. "Canadian Dispensaries: Why Vancouver Allows Them and Toronto Doesn't." *Leafly,* February 21. https://www.leafly.com/news/canada/canadian-dispensaries-vancouver-allows-toronto-doesn't.

Feldman, Harvey, and Jerry W. Mandel. 1998. "Providing Medical Marijuana: The Importance of Cannabis Clubs." *Journal of Psychoactive Drugs* 30 (2): 179–86.

Forum Research. 2016. "Majority Think Marijuana Dispensaries Should Be Legal in Toronto." *The Forum Poll,* March 24. Accessed June 5, 2017. http://poll.forumresearch.com/post/2485/one-tenth-have-dispensary-in-the-neighbourhood/.

Freed, Dale Anne. 1998, "Medical Pot Users to Form Buyer Network." *Toronto Star*, February 14.
Friscolanti, Michael. 2016. "Why Buying Pot Has Never Been Easier: Inside Canada's Completely Out of Control Marijuana Business." *Maclean's*, April 20. http://www.macleans.ca/news/canada/canadas-completely-out-of-control-marijuana-business/.
Gray, Jeff. 2016. "Pot Activists Angry as Toronto Defers Debate on Dispensaries." *Globe and Mail*, June 27. https://www.theglobeandmail.com/news/toronto/toronto-city-council-committee-turns-away-marijuana-advocates/article 30627296/.
Grinspoon, Lester. 2004. "Medical Marihuana in a Time of Prohibition." *International Journal of Drug Policy* 10 (2): 145–56.
Hagar, Mike. 2015. "Vancouver Becomes First City to Regulate Dispensaries in Canada." *Globe and Mail*, June 15. https://www.theglobeandmail.com/news/british-columbia/vancouver-regulates-medical-marijuana-dispensaries/article 25093608/.
Hathaway, Andrew D., and Kate Rossiter. 2007. "Medical Marijuana, Community Building and Canada's Compassionate Societies." *Contemporary Justice Review* 10 (3): 283–96.
Health Canada. 2015. "Government of Canada to Take Proactive Approach to Marijuana Advertising Enforcement." News release, August 1. https://www.canada.ca/en/news/archive/2015/08/government-canada-take-proactive-approach-marijuana-advertising-enforcement.html?=undefined&wbdisable=true.
—. 2019. "Authorized Licensed Producers of Cannabis for Medical Purposes." Accessed January 5, 2019. https://www.canada.ca/en/health-canada/services/drugs-health-products/medical-use-marijuana/licensed-producers/authorized-licensed-producers-medical-purposes.html.
Jeffords, Shawn. 2016. "Advocates Say Pot Shop Crackdown 'Waste of Resources.'" *Toronto Sun*, May 26. http://www.torontosun.com/2016/05/26/advocates-say-pot-shop-crackdown-waste-of-taxpayers-resources.
Jones, Craig, and Andrew D. Hathaway. 2008. "Marijuana Medicine and Canadian Physicians: Challenges to Meaningful Drug Policy Reform." *Contemporary Justice Review* 11 (2): 165–75.
King, Brayden G., Elisabeth S. Clemens, and Melissa Fry. 2011. "Identity Realization and Organizational Forms: Differentiation and Consolidation of Identities among Arizona's Charter Schools." *Organization Science* 22 (3): 554–72.
Larson, Dana. 2015. *Cannabis in Canada: An Illustrated History*. Vancouver: Hairy Pothead Books.
Levy, Sue-Ann. 2017. "Cops Swoop Down on Toronto Pot Shops." *Toronto Sun*, June 22. https://torontosun.com/2017/06/22/cops-swoop-down-on-toronto-pot-shops.
Lindores, Sharon. 2016. "Five Things You Need to Know before You Start Your Work Day on Oct. 17." *National Post*, October 17. https://financialpost.com/executive/executive-summaryfive-things-you-need-to-know-before-you-start-your-work-day-on-oct-17.

London Free Press. 1998. "Pot 'Club' to Open Here." *London Free Press*, February 14. http://www.mapinc.org/drugnews/v98/n103/a07.html.

—. 2003. "Crusader for Pot Dies after MS Fight." *London Free Press*, December 29. http://www.mapinc.org/drugnews/v03/n2000/a03.html?2399.

Lowrie, M. 2015. "Health Canada to Crack Down on Marijuana Advertising." *Globe and Mail*, August 1. https://www.theglobeandmail.com/news/national/health-canada-will-actively-monitor-for-marijuana-advertising-violators/article25811557/.

Lucas, Philippe. 2009. "Moral Regulation and the Presumption of Guilt in Health Canada's Medical Cannabis Policy and Practice." *International Journal of Drug Policy* 20: 296–303.

Mernagh, Matt. 2002. "Reefer Sadness." *Now Magazine*, August 22. https://nowtoronto.com/news/features/reefer-sadness/.

Minister of Health. 2015. Letter to Vancouver Mayor Gregor Robertson, April 23. http://docs.openinfo.gov.bc.ca/response_package_hth-2015-51132.pdf.

Nance, Chad. 2009. "Dom Cramer: The Business of Compassion." *Skunk Magazine*, August 25. http://skunkmagazine.com/dom-kramer-the-business-of-compassion/.

Public Health Agency of Canada. 2018. "Estimates of HIV Incidence, Prevalence and Canada's Progress on Meeting the 90–90–90 HIV Targets." https://www.canada.ca/en/public-health/services/publications/diseases-conditions/summary-estimates-hiv-incidence-prevalence-canadas-progress-90-90-90.html.

Reiman, Amanda. 2014. "Cannabis Distribution: Coffee Shops to Dispensaries." In *The Handbook of Cannabis*, edited by Roger G. Pertwee, 339–56. London: Oxford University Press.

Robertson, G., and G. McArthur. 2016. "What's in Your Weed?" *Globe and Mail*, July 27. https://www.theglobeandmail.com/cannabis/article-globe-investigation-whats-in-your-weed-we-tested-dispensary/.

Russo, Ethan Budd. 2018. "The Case for the Entourage Effect and Conventional Breeding of Clinical Cannabis: No 'Strain,' No Gain." *Frontiers in Plant Science* 9: 1969.

Shum, David. 2016. "90 Arrests, 257 Charges Laid in Toronto Marijuana Dispensary Raids." *Global News*, May 27. http://globalnews.ca/news/2725256/charges-and-seizure-details-to-be-released-in-toronto-marijuana-dispensary-raids/.

Sidney, Stephen. 2001. "Marijuana Use in HIV-Positive and AIDS Patients: Results of an Anonymous Mail Survey." *Journal of Cannabis Therapeutics* 1 (3/4): 35–41.

Sine, Wesley D., Robert J. David, and Hitoshi Mitsuhashi. 2007. "From Plan to Plant: Effects of Certification on Operational Start-Up in the Emergent Independent Power Sector." *Organization Science* 18 (4): 578–94.

Sumach, Alexander. 1998. "The Inside Scoop on Ontario's Thriving Pot Clubs." *Cannabis Culture Magazine*, November 1. Accessed June 5, 2017. http://www.yongesterdam.com/news/news159.htm.

Toronto. 2016. "Review of Regulations Governing Marihuana for Medical Purposes: Municipal Licensing and Standards." https://www.toronto.ca/legdocs/mmis/2016/ls/bgrd/backgroundfile-94518.pdf.

–. 2017. "City of Toronto Recommendations for Cannabis Legalization." http://www.toronto.ca/legdocs/mmis/2017/ls/bgrd/backgroundfile-106876.pdf.

Valleriani, Jenna. 2017. "Staking a Claim: Legal and Illegal Cannabis Dispensaries in Canada." Toronto: University of Toronto Press.

Valleriani, Jenna, Rebecca Haines-Saah, Rielle Capler, Ricky Bluthenthal, M. Eugenia Socias, M.J. Milloy, Thomas Kerr, and Ryan McNeil. 2020. "The Emergence of Innovative Cannabis Distribution Projects in the Downtown Eastside of Vancouver, Canada." *International Journal of Drug Policy*, 79. https://doi.org/10.1016/j.drugpo.2020.102737

Village of Cumberland. 2016. "Council Report: Medical Marijuana Dispensaries." Accessed May 5, 2017. https://cumberland.ca/wp-content/uploads/2016/06/Medical-Marijuana-Dispensaries-rpt.pdf.

Werner, Clinton A. 2001. "Medical Marijuana and the AIDS Crisis." *Cannabis Therapeutics in HIV/AIDS* 1 (3/4): 17–33.

PART 2

CANNABIS AND PUBLIC HEALTH

A MULTIDISCIPLINARY VIEW

5

Cannabis Legalization

Déjà Vu All over Again?

MICHAEL DEVILLAER

The legalization of cannabis in Canada represented a historic change in public policy that was greeted with both accolades and concerns. Cannabis users found some relief from the risks under prohibition, and social justice advocates felt a sense of victory. Others saw an opportunity for commercial enterprise. There were also concerns about the impact on public health and safety, particularly for young people, for those with pre-existing drug and mental health problems, and for those who might use the drug excessively or carelessly. Such concerns prompted the Canadian government to prescribe a variety of safeguards to ensure that the health and safety of its citizens would not be imperilled (Task Force on Cannabis Legalization and Regulation 2016). The intended safeguards can be summarized as follows:

- the legislation would be informed by input from experts and the public and would be based on a public health approach
- the cannabis industry would be strictly regulated like other drug industries
- a legal cannabis industry, operating under a law-abiding framework, would replace a dangerous criminal trade that imperilled cannabis users
- cannabis revenues would be directed toward the legal economy rather than supporting criminal organizations and their harmful and exploitive unlawful activities. (Task Force on Cannabis Legalization and Regulation 2016)

To assess the effectiveness of the above measures for protecting health and safety, this chapter focuses on the legalization of cannabis in Canada for recreational use. However, the Canadian government's choice of commercial legalization as the operational model for the cannabis trade invokes a multifaceted context that necessarily includes consideration of other legal commercial drug industries, commercial legalization of cannabis for medical and recreational use in the United States, and commercial legalization of cannabis for medical use in Canada.

Other Commercial Drug Industries: A Viable Model?

There is a long-established tradition of a legal, government-regulated, private-industry commercial model for providing drug products. This includes both recreational drug products (alcohol and tobacco) and medicinal drug products (pharmaceuticals). The model is familiar to governments and appears to be generally accepted as an immutable norm. The wisdom of this resignation is questionable, however, when we consider the level of harm associated with the products of each of the long-established drug industries in Canada.

The alcohol and tobacco industries are legal, government-regulated, commercial drug industries. The profound levels of harm and economic cost from the products of these industries were well documented at the time that the Canadian government was implementing a plan to commercialize a new drug industry with cannabis. The most recent data available at that time from the Canadian Substance Use Costs and Harms Scientific Working Group (CSUCH), showed that, in 2014, annual hospitalizations across the country numbered 87,911 for alcohol and 145,801 for tobacco. Workplace absenteeism was connected to alcohol misuse for 35,777 workers and use of tobacco for 39,727 workers. There were 14,827 alcohol-related premature deaths, accounting for 244,144 years of lost life. The respective figures for tobacco were 47,562 deaths and 326,870 years of lost life. The economic costs totalled $14.6 billion for alcohol and $12.0 billion for tobacco (Canadian Substance Use Costs and Harms Scientific Working Group 2018). A subsequent report from CSUCH, including data up to 2017 (Canadian Substance Use Costs and Harms Scientific Working Group 2020), showed that, as in the previous report, the levels of harm are increasing. Earlier reports (Rehm et al. 2006; Single et al. 1996) have documented similarly compelling levels of harm and costs going back to 1992. Such levels of harm likely occurred for many years before they were systematically documented.

Currently, there is no cause for optimism that the prevalence of these problems will diminish in the future.

The pharmaceutical industry is another legal, government-regulated, commercial drug industry. At the time of this writing, much of the Western world was currently in the third decade of an epidemic of opioid-related deaths that had its genesis in aggressive, misleading, illegal marketing campaigns for opioid medications by the pharmaceutical industry. Data available at the time of cannabis legalization from the Public Health Agency of Canada (PHAC) reported apparent opioid-related deaths at 2,946 for 2016, and at least 2,923 for January through September in 2017 (Canada 2018). Ginette Petitpas-Taylor was the third consecutive Canadian minister of health to acknowledge opioid overdose deaths as a public health crisis in this country (Wells 2017). Subsequent data reported by PHAC has demonstrated that the carnage continues (Special Advisory Committee on the Epidemic of Opioid Overdoses 2021). The opioid crisis is not restricted to Canada; it reached epidemic proportions in the United States and parts of Europe as well. Nor is the problem restricted to opioids. As early as 2013, Canada's National Advisory Committee on Prescription Drug Misuse noted that for prescribed opioids, sedative-hypnotics, and stimulants "the associated harms have become a leading public health and safety concern" (National Advisory Committee on Prescription Drug Misuse 2013, 1).

To summarize, the developed world already has three legal, government-regulated, commercial drug industries, each of which is linked to international health crises. It cannot be proven that the model of a legal, government-regulated, commercial industry is solely responsible for the harms and costs observed. However, data available from the Canadian Substance Use Costs and Harms Scientific Working Group (2018) at the time of cannabis legalization had shown that the costs and harms observed for alcohol and tobacco exceeded those attributable to all illegal drugs combined. A subsequent report from CSUCH including data up to 2017 reported the same (Canadian Substance Use Costs and Harms Scientific Working Group 2020). At minimum, these and earlier reports compel us to be wary of potential contributions of commercial drug industries to the epidemic of drug harm and costs. The data on harms from alcohol and tobacco, relative to illegal drugs, might also prompt us to wonder what the *war on drugs* was all about.

Within the orthodoxy of drug policy, legal drug industries (as we have for alcohol, tobacco, and pharmaceuticals) are generally held in high esteem as a desirable alternative to the illegal trade in drugs. Providing safer products within a legal framework is reasonably assumed to be superior to organized crime and criminal activity. Yet there is reasonable cause to question these long-held assumptions. It is well documented that quality control of legal recreational and medical drug products can be substandard and sometimes shows wilful neglect in manufacturing (DeVillaer 2017, 41–56).

Criminality and serious breaches of ethical business practices are commonplace in our legal drug industries. In many cases, these practices pose a serious risk and actual adverse consequences to public welfare. Government regulatory interventions have repeatedly failed to deter and reform such conduct, which has continued unabated decade after decade. The historically perilous conduct of legal drug industries suggests that transgressions in the emerging legal cannabis industry are not anomalies (DeVillaer 2019). They should have been predicted given that the warnings were in plain sight.

Legalization meant a dramatic transition of the cannabis trade from an illegal, demonized, prohibition framework to a legal one, first as a contentious medical treatment and then as a commodity for recreational consumption. Historic evidence of harm from the legal drug industry, corporate malfeasance, and regulatory failure was not enough to compel legislators to consider adopting an alternative to the commercial model. An evidence-based review on cannabis law reform by the RAND Corporation in the United States (Caulkins et al. 2015) stopped short of recommending a particular model. However, RAND strongly recommended that jurisdictions avoid moving, by default, from prohibition to commercial legalization – a recommendation that has not been heeded.

Legalization for Medical and Recreational Use in the United States

State-level cannabis legalization in the United States provides important insight into challenges in the commercial cannabis industry that are transferable to Canada. These challenges include lessons learned about the difficulty of guaranteeing product quality and safety and ethical business practices in the commercial industry.

Product Quality and Safety

A strong argument for legalization has always been the long-held belief that illegal cannabis products are of unknown potency and often contaminated and that legalization would introduce regulations to ensure the integrity of the product. However, there were clear and largely ignored warnings about the safety of the legal product in the United States, particularly regarding pesticide contamination. As early as 2014, reports were emerging from both Maine and California of illegal pesticides being detected on cannabis products sold in legal medical cannabis dispensaries (Stone 2014).

Analyses of medical cannabis samples have also shown inconsistent product strength, which has resulted in insufficient or dangerously high dosing. Edible products, in particular, were commonly mislabelled (Thomas and ElSohly 2015).

Colorado was the first state jurisdiction in the United States to legalize the sale of cannabis for recreational use. Substandard product integrity was apparent from the beginning. Problems of underreported THC levels and high levels of pesticides added to concerns about introducing edibles for retail, which are often sold as products like candy and cookies that are particularly enticing to children and linked to increased hospitalization for treatment of toxic reactions from inadvertent ingestion (Rocky Mountain High Intensity Drug Trafficking Area 2014; Wang et al. 2016).

Industry Conduct

The legal cannabis industry in the United States has, on occasion, been profoundly indifferent to public health concerns. The industry in Colorado successfully manipulated the political system to sabotage Ballot Initiative 139, a grassroots-initiated attempt to introduce child-proof packaging with health warnings and lower product potency. Having failed to use the courts to block these changes, the cannabis industry paid all signature collection companies in the state not to work on collecting signatures to support the initiative.

When the Initiative 139 sponsors attempted to hire a company from Arizona, the industry paid off that company as well. This effectively sabotaged the democratic process of documenting public support for the initiative (*The Gazette* 2016), showing the industry's contempt for law and public health protection. In pursuit of revenue maximization, the industry will be inclined to exploit whatever regulatory vulnerabilities or legislative loopholes might exist in a given jurisdiction.

Outright disregard for the rule of law has been documented elsewhere in the US cannabis industry. Tax evasion by regulated medical cannabis retail outlets in Washington State, for example, is so common that reported sales of legal cannabis for tax purposes are estimated to represent only one-fifth of actual sales (Kleiman et al. 2015).

Legalization for Medical Use in Canada

In the year 2000, the Supreme Court of Canada ruled that the government could not deny people their medicine and had a duty of care to provide a legal mechanism by which Canadians could access cannabis for therapeutic use. In response, the Liberal government passed the Marihuana Medical Access Regulations in 2001, and a legal cannabis supply was formally born in Canada. Few Canadians would challenge the principle of people having access to medicine. However, there is a question about the extent to which, in the year 2000, cannabis could have been legitimately considered a medicine.

Evidence for Therapeutic Effectiveness

In the year 2000, there was no clinical trial evidence (the gold standard for establishing a drug's effectiveness) demonstrating that cannabis was therapeutically effective for any of its alleged and practised applications. Some portion of cannabis users may have benefitted therapeutically from their use of cannabis. But no medicine produced by a pharmaceutical company could ever be brought to market without convincing clinical trials. Thus, it may be that the Supreme Court overstepped its jurisdiction and responsibilities. At minimum, the Liberal government failed to assign sufficient importance to the usual requirements of approving medicine for use.

However, it was the Progressive Conservative Party, which on achieving a majority in the 2011 election, replaced the MMAR with the Marihuana for Medical Purposes Regulations (MMPR) in 2013. The MMPR established a licensing system for commercial growers who could sell to authorized users by a mail order system.

The creation of a new legal industry for a single drug with no clinical trial support seems to have been an example of legislative overreach. Perhaps as damage control or as mitigation of legal liability, Health Canada's website, as of September 2021, still stated: "Cannabis is not an approved therapeutic product and the provision of this information should not be interpreted as an endorsement of the use of cannabis for therapeutic purposes, or of marijuana generally, by Health Canada" (Canada 2016a). Health Canada has still not assigned a drug identification number (DIN) to cannabis flower products – a requirement for all drugs before they can be marketed in Canada. By 2015, some clinical trials had been conducted, some of which showed some modest benefit of some formulations of cannabis, for some conditions, for some people. However, meta-analysis of clinical trials found mixed results and recommended caution on the part of prescribers (Whiting et al. 2015; Allan et al. 2018).

The premature legalization of a drug for medical use remains an anomaly in Canadian law and health policy. With such a clear need for more evidence, the government would have reasonably been expected to establish a funding stream for research to examine the therapeutic effectiveness of cannabis. A decade and a half later, medical researchers and professional practitioners still lament a lack of compelling evidence to guide prescribers (Whiting et al. 2015; Allan et al. 2018).

Product Quality and Safety
The lack of quality control over unregulated cannabis (Robertson and McArthur 2016a, 2016b) gives the legal industry a significant opportunity for improvement. And this has been a prominent rationale for legalization (Centre for Addiction and Mental Health 2014). However, as in the United States, pesticide contamination is a concern for legal cannabis in Canada. As early as 2014, Health Canada required recalls of cannabis products for bacteria (Canada 2014a) and mould (Canada 2014b). In these and another recall because of unspecified "issues with the company's production practices" (Canada 2014c) the licensed producer's patients were advised "to immediately discontinue use." There have also been recalls for inaccurate labelling of the potency of products (Canada 2015, 2017a).

By the end of 2016, several recalls had also been issued because of the presence of unauthorized pesticides on flower product (Canada 2017b). *Globe and Mail* reports (Robertson 2016, 2017) on the use of pesticides by one company, Mettrum, found there was

- reluctance on the part of Mettrum in the disclosure of the full extent of contamination to its patients and to investigative reporters;
- discrepancy between Health Canada's alleged "zero-tolerance" policy for use of banned pesticides and its lenient treatment of the producer; and,
- apparent collusion between the producer and Health Canada to minimize public awareness of the problem.

Health Canada continued to issue cannabis product recalls for a variety of contamination and mislabelling infractions during the period leading up to legalization for recreational use in October 2018 (Canada 2021).

Product-Promotion Practices

Non-compliance by licensed producers goes beyond failing to ensure product integrity. The Marihuana for Medical Purposes Regulations (the precursor to the current Access to Cannabis for Medical Purposes Regulations) specifically prohibits the advertising of cannabis for medical use. In November 2014, Health Canada issued citations to twenty separate licensed producers for continuing illegal advertising practices, after an advertising standards bulletin had been sent to all producers five months earlier (Canada 2014d). Health Canada did not release the names of violators. However, one prominent producer, Aphria, was known for its blatant, illegal sponsorship of race car driving (Betting Bruiser 2018).

Without the benefits of conventional advertising, licensed cannabis producers rely on their websites as their primary means of interacting with patients. Two such companies, Aphria and MedReleaf, used websites to exploit a Veterans Affairs Canada program that covered the cost of therapeutic cannabis for veterans. The companies set up separate websites, specifically for veterans, which charged higher prices and excluded less expensive products from their menus (Ling 2016). In 2013, there were 112 Canadian veterans on the program at a total cost of $400,000. By 2016, there were 1,762 at a cost to the program of $20,000,000 (Ling 2016). A three-fold increase in the cost per veteran was a windfall for medical cannabis companies at the expense of the publicly funded care system. In the meantime, other companies set their sights on larger markets that were anticipated because of the forthcoming legalization of cannabis for recreational use.

In early 2016, licensed cannabis producer Tweed announced a partnership with US entertainer Snoop Dogg to promote each other's commercial interests. As a "key icon advisor," Snoop was to play a role in ushering in Tweed's transition from the medical market to the recreational market (Foote 2016) under the branding banner "Leafs by Snoop."

Tweed's decision to capitalize on its association with a famous entertainer – with a lengthy criminal record and recordings celebrating criminality and violence (Giovacchini 1999) – as a branding strategy is certainly ironic, considering that the government's often-stated primary purpose for legalizing cannabis was to protect users, especially children, from exposure to criminal involvement.

Such a blatant violation of product-promotion provisions in the ACMPR, after repeated warnings to licensed producers by Health Canada, reflects a sense of entitlement at a time when good judgment and business ethics called for showing some restraint. These varied and serious improprieties occurred within legal, government-regulated, commercial regimes for medical use in Canada and medical and recreational use in the United States. And they provided a warning of greater improprieties to come in Canada.

Securities Practices
Start-up businesses often lack the financial reserves to enter an expensive enterprise such as cannabis production, so they must attract investors. It is the job of securities regulators to ensure that the strategies employed conform to the legal requirements and to prevent offending companies from entering the industry. Canadian securities regulators found that twenty-five newly registered medical cannabis companies were misleading investors with disclosures that raised major investor protection issues (Reuters 2015). One application for licensing was so seriously riddled with misrepresentations that Canada's health minister twice referred the matter to the RCMP for investigation (Robertson 2015).

Organized Crime as Licensed Producers
One of the pillars of the Liberal Party's legalization campaign was to significantly reduce and perhaps even eliminate the role of organized crime in the cannabis trade. This role was shown to be highly exaggerated by the government (see Capler, Boyd, and MacPherson 2016; Solecki, Burnett, and Li 2011). However, organized criminal activity in the cannabis trade became more evident following the establishment of the legal cannabis industry – which involved the diversion of personal medical cannabis cultivation licences issued by Health Canada to criminal organizations (Pfeffer and Dumont 2017) – the exact opposite of what legalization was supposed to accomplish.

In sum, the legislative and regulatory quagmire resulting from the legalization of medical cannabis did not provide an attractive template for the development of sound public policy for the recreational use of the drug. An industry emerged with high ambitions for expansion beyond the much smaller medical market. The threat to public health posed by the expansion of the market was largely overlooked on the road to legalization for recreational use. The Liberal Party's promised public health approach has so far failed to deliver, as is established below.

Legalization for Recreational Use
The Liberal Party's strategy for the legalization of cannabis for recreational use was born during its tenure as the official Opposition prior to forming

a government in the 2015 federal election. The strategy consisted of first generating fear of the illegal cannabis trade as being controlled by "gun-runners" and "street gangs" selling unsafe, contaminated cannabis and other dangerous drugs. The Liberal Party's narrative thus amounted to Reefer Madness–like claims but repurposed for the modern era. The research told a different story in that the illegal cannabis trade looked more like a disconnected cottage industry of otherwise law-abiding citizens earning modest incomes that were contributing to the local legal economy (DeVillaer 2017).

The second objective of the party's strategy was to foster confidence in and support for legalization by extolling the virtues of a legal, government-regulated cannabis industry over an unregulated, dangerous, illegal trade. The Liberal Party's pitch for cannabis legalization also bore little resemblance to the real world of existing legal drug trades. Its commitment to a *public health approach* – one that prioritized protecting children, fighting organized crime, and strengthening the economy – was little more than promises dominated by pretense.

So Was It All an Inside Job?
In 2003, the Liberal Party proposed legislation to decriminalize cannabis. This did not mean commercial legalization; instead, possession of small amounts of cannabis, though still illegal, would not result in a criminal record (only confiscation and a modest fine). The decriminalization legislation proposed was never passed (Erickson and Hyshka 2010), and the issue lay dormant for almost a decade.

In 2011, Chuck Rifici, cofounder of Tweed, Canada's largest cannabis producer at the time, was appointed to the executive ranks of the federal Liberal Party as chief financial officer (Kirkup 2015). At the opening of the party's Ottawa convention in January 2012, Justin Trudeau's perspective on legalization was highly reticent. He stated: "I don't know that it's entirely consistent with the kind of society we're trying to build" (Di Fiore 2017). Trudeau's stance is understandable considering, at the time, only the Green Party was on record supporting legalization (Cormier 2015).

But the direction of the Liberal Party suddenly changed at its 2012 convention when it began to forge a platform for the 2015 federal election. It was later revealed that in 2011, the same year that Rifici joined the Liberal Party executive, a communications firm was hired to promote the idea of cannabis legalization among the delegates to the Liberal Party's convention. The firm's team leader, James Di Fiore, tells the story:

In 2011, I was hired by the Liberal Party of Canada's upper brass to pressure their delegates to vote yes on a policy initiative that would push for legalization. For three months, my team approached marijuana advocacy groups and rallied their members to bombard LPC delegates via email, tweets, and Facebook messages. The plan was to put enough pressure on delegates until they voted for a Canada who would shed its draconian views on weed. When we started, just 30 percent of delegates were in our camp. After the votes were tallied at the Liberals' 2012 convention, more than 75 percent of delegates voted yes. (Di Fiore 2017)

Cannabis legalization was included as a formal part of the party's platform in the following federal election.

As newly elected party leader (and now sporting a different attitude about legalization), Trudeau campaigned enthusiastically for legalization throughout his 2013–15 run for prime minister. On forming a government, the Liberals reaffirmed the commitment and in mid-2016 announced they would strike a task force to study and make recommendations, with the objective of introducing legislation in spring 2017. In response to pressure from the NDP to decriminalize cannabis possession immediately while forging the new legislation, the government declared that "decriminalization does not meet any of our objectives" (CBC News 2016).

Chuck Rifici left Tweed in September 2014 to pursue a variety of other cannabis business interests (which continue into 2021). By October 2016, the Liberal Party's website no longer mentioned Rifici's involvement on the board. It is noteworthy that Rifici's generous contributions to the Liberal Party coincided with a seismic shift in drug policy, a shift that would potentially bring substantial monetary benefits to the business interests of Rifici and other major players in the Canadian cannabis industry – a connection that the party and Rifici denied (Cannabis Life Network 2015).

Many Liberal Party elites, nonetheless, have publicized connections to the cannabis industry (Sheikh 2016; Campbell 2017; Levesque 2017; DiMatteo 2018) and stood to benefit financially from the potentially enormous windfall of a regulated recreational market. The expansion of a lucrative commercial cannabis industry would also generate an enormous amount of tax revenue for the anticipated Liberal government.

Privileged Access to Policy Makers?
An important role of government in health policy is to ensure that it strikes a reasonable balance between allowing industry to pursue revenue genera-

tion opportunities and protecting public health. The neutrality of the political process to ensure equal opportunity to influence policy outcomes can be subverted, however, by industry influence on policy-making through privileged access. Cannabis is a clear example.

By March 2016, there were already eighty-five incidents of cannabis-industry lobbying entered in the federal registry (Woodward 2016). A subsequent check of the registry revealed that, as of April 17, 2019, lobbying activity on the part of Canada's largest licensed producers at the time, Aurora and Canopy, had continued throughout the pre-legalization period and into at least March 2019. A subsequent check in September of 2021 revealed that both companies had maintained a prominent presence into July 2021 (Office of the Commissioner of Lobbying of Canada 2021). The arena of influence was not restricted to Parliament Hill. Liberal Party "cash-for-access" fundraising events also provided cannabis-industry executives with the opportunity to promote their business interests with members of the government (Fife and Chase 2017). This level of access and policy influence stands in stark contrast to that enjoyed by most non-industry players, including public health authorities, relegated to having only a faint voice in the crowd of public consultations.

Conflicts of Interest

The consultation phase of introducing new legislation began with the appointment of the Task Force on Marijuana Legalization and Regulation (2016), which had a lawyer as chair and a physician as co-chair, representing the pertinent domains of law and health. The task force's membership included representatives from the legal and medical professions, municipal politics, law enforcement, public health, public policy, and academia.

The chair of the task force, Anne McLellan, quite properly declared "indirect financial interests" in her role as a senior adviser with Bennett Jones, a law firm in Edmonton that "represents some clients with interests in the legal marijuana business" (Canada 2016b). Among the business associates of Bennett Jones is Tweed (Bennett Jones 2014), the same producer whose cofounder, Chuck Rifici, served as an executive in the Liberal Party's board of directors. In a *Toronto Star* article, one of the Toronto partners at Bennett Jones spoke of the changing and growing cannabis industry and of Bennett Jones's ambitions for that industry: "We want to be the go-to advisors" (Flavelle 2015).

With its final report submitted directly to cabinet (Task Force on Cannabis Legalization and Regulation 2016), the task force was positioned to have a substantial and unparalleled influence on key decisions that would shape Canada's legal cannabis regime. This included decisions on how the industry would conduct its business and how the government would regulate it. Many of those decisions revolved around potential trade-offs between industry revenue and public health protection. For example, a higher minimum age of twenty-one would better protect public health and safety while a lower age of eighteen would generate more sales and revenue. An online-only system for purchasing cannabis would reduce public normalization and glamorization of cannabis, but allowing highly visible retail outlets (as exist for alcohol) would increase visibility, sales, and revenue. A ban on advertising, versus allowing advertising, would carry the same potential impacts.

Clearly, any interest in the industry by a task force member had the potential to compromise the public's health. The task force had no representatives from the cannabis industry, thus ensuring there were no direct conflicts of interest. McLellan's declaration of indirect interests was intended to prevent or minimize the suggestion of undue influence on the development of legislation. But be it direct or indirect, this declaration by the chair of the task force was far from reassuring. Following the work of the task force, McLellan spoke at cannabis industry meetings where she handed out her law firm's business cards (Hager and Robertson 2017).

The co-chair of the task force, Mark Ware, a physician and renowned cannabis researcher and academic at McGill University in Montreal, also declared indirect financial and intellectual interests (Canada 2016). Before the work of the task force began, Ware had a consulting relationship with at least one licensed cannabis producer, Mettrum (Shaw 2016). That interest intensified two months after the release of the task force report when Canopy Health Innovations (owned by Canopy Growth Corporation, which also owned Tweed and Mettrum) announced it was entering "into a 3-year consulting agreement with EPIC Consulting Inc., the Quebec-based consulting firm of Dr. Mark Ware" (Canopy Growth Corporation 2017).

Ware was soon appointed Canopy's chief medical officer and took a leave from his academic post at McGill (Canopy Growth 2018). One month after the task force released its report, another member, Raf Souccar, a former RCMP deputy commissioner, became the president and CEO of Aleafia Health, a medical cannabis company that was incorporated that month

(Platt 2017). Potential conflicts of interest understandably threaten the confidence that public health advocates have in the integrity of the process of cannabis law reform.

Market Expansion versus Public Health Protection
Legislation should provide comprehensive and clear provisions to serve its stated intentions. The Cannabis Act purportedly reflects a public health approach within a law-abiding framework. Recommendations in the task force's final report were given high priority in determining the Act's provisions. The report acknowledged some of the perils inherent in commercial legalization in addition to the challenge of balancing a myriad of interests, including the interests of those who seek to profit and those who seek to protect public health. It was observed that "as with other industries, this new cannabis industry will seek to increase its profits and expand its market, including through the use of advertising and promotion" (Task Force on Cannabis Legalization and Regulation 2016, 18).

Maximizing financial return requires expansion and capturing as much of the market as possible. However, legal drug products are no ordinary commodity because they pose more of a threat to public health than do most products. This tension compelled the task force to make many recommendations to address known risks, including

- allowing no promotion that would be appealing to children
- prohibiting products with high THC potency
- providing public education and prevention programs
- improving access to treatment
- avoiding criminalizing youth
- preventing impaired driving. (Task Force on Cannabis Legalization and Regulation 2016)

Legislative measures resulting from such recommendations, for the most part, would have little impact on the industry's ambitions for expansion. However, on matters that could impact market expansion, the task force recommendations were more favourable to the interests of the industry than to public health protection. Some examples follow.

Minimum Age
Setting a legal minimum age for cannabis purchase and possession was one of the most divisive issues tackled by the task force. Suggestions ranged from

eighteen to twenty-five years, the most often recommended age being nineteen and twenty-one. The task force recommended the lowest legal minimum age of eighteen. The report acknowledged that "health-care professionals and public health experts tend to favour a minimum age of 21" (Task Force on Cannabis Legalization and Regulation 2016, 17). To justify lowering the age, among other debatable assertions, the task force noted that "many [stakeholders] suggested that 18 was a well-established milestone in Canadian society marking adulthood" (Task Force on Cannabis Legalization and Regulation 2016, 17).

The task force's recommendation of eighteen was adopted, with the proviso that provinces could raise the minimum age. Almost all did, but only to nineteen. Interestingly, although not disclosed in its report, the minimum age recommended by the task force was the lower end of a range recommended by the Cannabis Trade Alliance of Canada (2016, 3). The high prevalence of use among late teens ensured a considerable expansion of market size for the legal cannabis industry. In its rejection of the advice of public health authorities, the task force did not even recommend the midpoint as a compromise but rather gave the industry exactly the minimum age it wanted – as did the Cannabis Act.

Product Promotion Practices

Support for the cannabis industry's ambitions was also evident in the task force's final report recommendations on product promotion. To expand the recreational market for cannabis to a level closer to that of alcohol, aggressive promotion of the product was required.

The adverse impact of alcohol and tobacco advertising on public health is widely documented (Babor 2010; Canadian Public Health Association 2011; Tobacco Control Legal Consortium 2012; Pacula et al. 2014; Public Health Agency of Canada 2016). Accordingly, an outright ban on advertising cannabis products was called for by health policy authorities (Canadian Public Health Association 2016; Centre for Addiction and Mental Health 2016; Chief Medical Officers of Health of Canada and Urban Public Health Network 2016; Canadian Medical Association 2016).

In its final report, the task force acknowledged "the public health perspective that, in order to reduce youth access to cannabis, strict limits should be placed on its promotion" (Task Force on Cannabis Legalization and Regulation 2016, 19). However, the task force's emphasis on threats to youth completely overlooked the impact of advertising on adults as emphasized by health policy organizations. Furthermore, the task force's position misrepresented the "public health perspective," which did not call for "strict limits" but rather a *full ban* on all product promotion. The difference is significant since limits are open to interpretation and manipulation by the industry (Miller 2018a).

The challenges of dealing with ambiguous limits are all too familiar to public health authorities, who have decades of experience dealing with legal drug industries committed to market expansion. But the task force's final report noted that

> the industry representatives from whom we heard, while generally supportive of some promotion restrictions – particularly marketing to children and youth, and restrictions on false or misleading advertising – made the case for allowing branding of products ... [And] it was suggested that brand differentiation would help consumers distinguish between licit and illicit sources of cannabis, helping to drive them to the legal market. (Task Force on Cannabis Legalization and Regulation 2016, 18)

The credibility of the first statement is questionable considering the industry's track record of being unsupportive of advertising regulation.

The second claim was profoundly disconnected from the realities of retail, where distinctions between licit and illicit products are made at the point of purchase – i.e., a legal store or website versus other sources that are known to be illegal – rather than by brand name packaging or advertising. In the end, the task force recommended "plain packaging," which, apart from information related to the product's composition and strength, and warning labels, would allow only the company's name. The Cannabis Act, however, went further, also allowing brand names and logos, and only a few restrictions on the use of colour. These are all features that public health experts recognize as intended not to educate the consumer but to induce purchases and brand loyalty.

But the cannabis industry had far greater ambitions for market expansion and revenue. An ambitious proposal from the industry was subsequently submitted to government for a self-regulated approach to cannabis product promotion (Aphria et al. 2017). The proposal was overt in its adoption of the promotional playbook of the alcohol industry, proposing to advertise cannabis "in all types of media, including print, television, radio, out-of-home, digital, and social media platforms ... where at least 70% of the audience is over 18 years of age or over a province's or territory's legal age for purchase" (Aphria et al. 2017, 3).

Adopting this proposal would allow for advertising on websites, for example, where almost one-third of visitors are underage, which would create appeal to potentially millions of young teens and children. The Cannabis Act did not ultimately grant the industry its full wish list on product advertising but presented, instead, what might be seen as a reasonable compromise. But a compromise is reasonable only if reasonable alternatives are presented by stakeholders on both sides of the issue. Whereas the public health position was evidence-based and intended to protect the public, the industry proposal to market cannabis like alcohol was rooted in financial gain, and a threat to the public's health.

Despite the advice of public health authorities, the task force's recommendation of strict limits rather than a full ban on cannabis promotion was incorporated into the Cannabis Act. The Act restricted advertising to venues not accessible to minors and prohibited content that would appeal to children. Advertising was defined as including marketing, event sponsorship, contests, and celebrity endorsements. These restrictions may seem reasonable. However, they provide substantial opportunities for the industry to manipulate the system to ensure market expansion – at increased risk to public health.

Edibles

Cannabis-infused confections – including candy, baked goods, and beverages – have a broad appeal to all age groups, particularly young and novice cannabis users who do not smoke tobacco. Product innovation, including the sale of edibles, when paired with the allure of lifestyle advertising, is a powerful tool for market expansion and increased revenue.

The task force's final report cited input from observers in Colorado, who advised: "Expect edibles to have a broad appeal. Cannabis products such as brownies, cookies and high-end chocolates are attractive to novice users" (Task Force on Cannabis Legalization and Regulation 2016, 20). And it was acknowledged that public health stakeholders in Canada had advised against the legalization of edibles. The task force, however, again stopped short of recommending a full ban in favour of restrictions.

From a public health perspective, it was recognized that edibles are advantageous as a healthier alternative to smoking. But a complication of allowing them, according to the task force, was "that any discussion about regulating a new cannabis industry quickly leads to an understanding of the complexity of regulating not one but potentially thousands of new cannabis-based products" (Task Force on Cannabis Legalization and Regulation 2016, 20). The task force could have recommended restricting the sale of cannabis edibles to oils that would be consumed by placing drops on the tongue. This would have less marketing appeal and would have made them less attractive to young children than confections. However, the task force recommended provisions for edibles that favoured a more ambitious expansion of the legal market.

Harsh Penalization of the Illegal Trade
For a half century, global efforts at cannabis law reform were driven by a concern that the prohibition of cannabis punished a victimless crime and that, for the great majority of cannabis users, the stigmatizing, marginalizing, and adverse economic impacts of a criminal record were far more harmful than the drug itself. Decriminalization emerged as a popular solution with a well-established, international record of success.

A motion to decriminalize cannabis was introduced in the Canadian House of Commons in June of 2016 by Murray Rankin, NDP justice critic at the time. However, it was opposed by Attorney General Jody Wilson-Raybould and did not receive house support. The record shows that the arguments made in the House against decriminalizing cannabis emphasized the discredited beliefs that decriminalization would continue to support the activities of dangerous criminals who threatened the safety and propriety of cannabis users, including children (Canada, House of Commons 2016).

This was the same hyperbole against the illegal trade that was leveraged to create public support for the legalization of cannabis by invoking parents' fears. The hyperbole also served to justify harsh penalties for unlicensed sellers – with the purpose of reducing competition for the licensed trade. The task force's final report offered nothing to challenge this misrepresentation. Like the Liberal government, its priority appeared to be the development of a lucrative new industry. Of course, it is desirable to replace the unlicensed trade in cannabis with a licensed one. However, this should not be accomplished through the demonization and criminalization of those engaged in a victimless crime. There are better ways.

Product-Quality Control
The most promising strategy for reducing the illegal trade in cannabis is providing a product that is confidently known to be accurately labelled and

uncontaminated. The lack of these assurances in the illegal market is an often-cited rationale for legalizing cannabis. As we have seen, however, lack of quality control is also a well-documented problem in the legal trade. Most of the legal industry has chosen mass production with insufficient emphasis on quality control. Lowering production costs obviously leads to more profits, but this business model may prove to be short-sighted and counterproductive.

Despite evidence of contaminated, mislabelled products from legal cannabis producers and recalls required by Health Canada, the task force's final report noted: "Task Force members had the opportunity to visit some of these producers and were impressed by the sophistication and quality of their work" (Task Force on Cannabis Legalization and Regulation 2016, 9). The government, it recommended, should therefore move to "regulate the production of cannabis and its derivatives (e.g., edibles, concentrates) at the federal level, drawing on the good production practices of the current cannabis for medical purposes system" (Task Force on Cannabis Legalization and Regulation 2016, 33).

Considering the industry's quest for profitability at the expense of product integrity and consumer protection, fair market competition would be better served by the task force recommending some basic measures. These might include unannounced inspections of production facilities with sample selection, not by company employees, but by the inspectors. Penalties for repeat violations should include suspending or revoking licences, and the penalties should be enforced. To inform consumers and encourage more rigorous production standards, there could be requirements that dates of past recalls for a given product must be included on its packaging. The pursuit of best production practices would thereby be rewarded, providing a market advantage to more conscientious producers.

In sum, the ambition for market expansion trumped public health priorities throughout the consultation and legislative process leading to the Cannabis Act. As recreational legalization approached, the Liberal government's track record of enforcing medical cannabis regulations offered little assurance that its promise of a public health approach would be realized.

Moving Forward?

The cannabis industry's performance did not improve following legalization for recreational use in October of 2018. Health Canada continued to list recalls of products from licensed producers. In the first six months, there were eleven alerts involving nine different licensed producers. The most common problem was mislabelling of oil and capsule products, such as reversing the ratio of THC to CBD content and incorrect dosing instructions on labels. In addition to faulty record keeping, mould on flower product was also reported, as was exceeding "some of the microbial and chemical contaminant limits as specified by the Good Production Practices requirements of the Cannabis Regulations." Failures in product integrity continued through July 2021 (Canada 2021).

Production failures in some companies and not others suggest that there is an irregular standard of production in the industry that is not being effectively addressed by regulation. This is a significant concern for regulators, public health authorities, the public, and especially for cannabis users, who are being placated by the promise of a reliable product. If the government is concerned about the quality and safety of illegal products and confident that a legal industry will do better, it should ensure that this is the case.

People will pay more for a legal product if they are assured that the legal products are, in fact, a safer purchase. Consumers require not only government transparency about production failures but also confidence in the measures it will take to address repeated failures beyond recalls.

Securities violations are another ongoing problem in the industry. When legalization for recreational use was enacted in October of 2018, the Canadian Securities Administrators (CSA), an umbrella organization for provincial securities regulators, issued a warning about a higher incidence of "problematic promotional activities." The CSA stopped short of naming names (Lamers 2018), but two high-profile cases attracted considerable business media attention (Ligaya 2018; Swaby 2018; Subramania 2019).

Since legalization, several law firms have been on record as investigating other companies involved for potential class action lawsuits.

The promise of replacing a criminal cannabis trade in Canada with a law-abiding one has been further compromised. In 2019, licensed producer Bonify was found to have been "possessing, distributing and selling product that was purchased from an illegal source" (Froese 2019; Israel 2019). Health Canada suspended Bonify's production licences, which were renewed in less than a year (Gowriluk 2019). No criminal charges were laid. In August 2021, Bonify announced that it was "winding down" its production facility (Stratcann 2021).

In August 2019, revelations surfaced of illegal growing operations by licensed industry leader CannTrust Inc., prompting a joint investigation by the Ontario Securities Commission, the RCMP Financial Crime Program, and the Ontario Provincial Police Anti-rackets Branch (Canadian Press 2019a). Ultimately, CannTrust had its production licences suspended by Health Canada, but reinstated in less than a year. Two of its executives were dismissed by the company (Lamers 2020), and three have been subsequently charged with a variety of financial crimes (Ontario Securities Commission 2021).

Another licensed producer, Agrima Botanicals Corporation, had its licence permanently revoked (Canadian Press, 2019b). In contrast to the considerable amount of disclosure and media attention on the Bonify and CannTrust cases, the details of the Agrima case remain enshrouded as privileged information. In November 2018, CBC News reported evidence of ties between licensed cannabis growers and organized crime (Denis 2018). The government's screening process for granting production licences is such that the identities of investors and applicants are sometimes obscured by trusts with undisclosed beneficiaries. These findings are consistent with an earlier RCMP report that warned that "there is no shortage of organized criminal groups who have applied to produce medical marijuana" (Pfeffer and Dumont 2017).

Product-promotion transgressions by licensed producers also persist, despite repeated warnings from regulators. Over nearly two decades of medical marijuana and then full legalization, not one penalty was imposed for product-promotion transgressions. Furthermore, Health Canada provided lawbreakers not only with immunity but also with the protection of anonymity (Miller 2018a, 2018b). Accordingly, both industry investors and cannabis consumers are left in the dark as to the identities of companies that violate the laws on product promotion.

In light of its permissive treatment by Health Canada, the industry can be expected to continue to seek out even more assertive strategies for market expansion. At the O'Cannabiz 2019 event in Toronto, for example, the schedule (no longer available online) included a panel discussion, moderated by a prominent Canadian lawyer specializing in cannabis law, on "Subtle Sales: How to Brand and Market within the Regs." It included this tempting description for conference-goers: "How do you portray your product in a positive light without glamourizing it? Believe it or not, there is a way to stickhandle the regs and get the word out. Our industry strategists have advice on judicious packaging, branding, copywriting and logo differentiation that will attract attention" (O'Cannabiz Conference and Expo

2019). This suggests that at least some players in the industry do not intend to respect the intent or spirit of the regulations but to keep conjuring new ways to get around them.

※

The day that the Cannabis Act came into force marked the zenith of the spectacle of legalization, generating nothing short of a media frenzy, for which the Liberal Party had crafted a marquee slogan: "Keep Cannabis Out of the Hands of Youth and Profits Out of the Pockets of Criminals." To cement public comfort with the legislation – among Canadians less mesmerized by the pageantry of legalization – the line was frequently repeated. Despite the achievement of this significant milestone, however, legalization has been a rough journey for the government.

The Liberal Party of Canada built much of its case for legalization on its promise to strictly regulate the new cannabis industry to protect public health and safety. Evidence of industry indifference to the law and public health is the predictable result of a tainted process of legislative development that, by design, enabled industry expansion and entitlement. Public health authorities are fighting a losing battle, which has been the story of drug policy for decades in Canada and across continents. Canada, like most Western democracies, has a drug-policy problem – and its government remains in unabashed denial (Keung 2019).

On forming a government in 2015, the Canadian Liberal Party had the opportunity, with its cannabis legalization campaign, to strike a major departure from a chronically failing system of drug policy. Public health authorities and drug-policy academics invested time and effort and resources to provide a solution that the government had no intention of adding to the menu.

The government's devotion to orthodoxy leaves two potential paths for reform. The first is class action lawsuits on the scale we've seen launched against pharmaceutical and tobacco companies, lawsuits that have the potential to ruin companies.

As of September 2021, there were over three thousand class actions listed against Purdue Pharma for its role in the opioid epidemic. That same month, a United States bankruptcy judge conditionally approved a master settlement for USD$4.5 billion (Mulvihill 2021). There has been substantial criticism of the settlement amount given that the company, by its own admission, made $10 billion in sales from the drug. The United States Department of Justice has filed for a stay of the settlement, claiming that the owners of the company, the Sackler family and associates, were abusing the bankruptcy system to avoid meaningful liability (Mann 2021).

In 2019, the Quebec Court of Appeal unanimously upheld a judgment for CDN$17 billion against Canada's three tobacco companies: Imperial Tobacco Canada, JTI-Macdonald, and Rothmans, Benson & Hedges (CTV Montreal 2019). Cannabis companies (and certainly their stockholders) would be wise to watch these legal precedents closely.

A more systemic approach to reform would be to establish national, government-run, not-for-profit monopolies of the kind proposed for cannabis in Canada and abroad by health policy authorities (Caulkins et al. 2015; Spithoff, Emerson, and Spithoff 2015; Chapados et al. 2016; Chief Medical Officers of Health of Canada and Urban Public Health Network 2016; Rolles et al. 2016; and DeVillaer 2017). The reports by Chapados et al. and DeVillaer provide a detailed rationale for not-for-profit approaches and some of the operational logistics. A not-for-profit retail system has been implemented in Quebec, where provincial legislation directs all revenues from the provincial government's cannabis retail monopoly to cover operational costs first and then be allocated for treatment and prevention programs (Quebec Legislature 2018). A more ambitious not-for-profit proposal arose in France, where the Conseil d'analyse économique suggested the creation of a national monopoly on production and distribution of recreational cannabis (Auriol and Geoffard 2019).

The Canadian government, however, has shown no appetite for systemic change in how legal drug products are provided to its people. With the status quo intact, the only avenue available for public health authorities is to wait for opportunities to propose small, incremental changes for small gains, which might stimulate more ambitious reforms in the future. For example, a change in governing party in Quebec brought about a raise in the minimum age for cannabis possession from eighteen to twenty-one (CBC News 2020a) – a move that was recommended by several health policy authorities during the consultation phase of Canada's legalization process. And there have been overtures that a change in government at the federal level could result in other, possibly significant, cannabis reforms (Gilmore 2018).

Health Canada may continue to bring cannabis producers more in line with the laws on product promotion, following up on its modest success with curtailing celebrity product endorsements. While Health Canada continues to issue recalls, the government has yet to publicly acknowledge systemic quality-control problems in the cannabis industry. Perhaps market forces will eventually improve product integrity, as more small craft growers successfully navigate existing barriers to their entry to the legal market.

However, piecemeal changes do not have the same potential to avert harm to public health as would shifting from the prevailing revenue-driven, private-industry paradigm to a national not-for-profit government monopoly for cannabis sales. Such significant reform does not seem imminent, but there is an international, evidence-based, humanitarian discussion underway among drug-policy analysts who are observing developments in Canada and elsewhere.

A final and critical point concerns the importance of learning from the experience of the commercialization of cannabis. There is an emerging narrative in Canada and elsewhere involving the commercialization of other psychedelic drugs such as psilocybin, LSD, and MDMA. Most of this discussion concerns commercialization for therapeutic use, and once again, without compelling clinical trial evidence. Certainly, decriminalization of possession of psychedelics and funding of clinical trials to assess their therapeutic value would be worthwhile policy undertakings. However, there are also overtures on the potential for a commercialized recreational market for psilocybin. This progression of events is a familiar scenario for those who have observed cannabis commercialization. As we have seen, commercialization takes us in a predictable direction and introduces a familiar set of perils. Déjà vu all over again, again?

Works Cited

Allan, G., Caitlin Finley, Joey Ton, Danielle Perry, Jamil Ramji, Karyn Crawford, Adrienne Lindblad, Christina Korownyk, and Michael Kolber. 2018. "Systematic Review of Systematic Reviews for Medical Cannabinoids: Pain, Nausea and Vomiting, Spasticity, and Harms." *Canadian Family Physician/Medecin de famille canadien*. 64. e78–e94. https://www.cfp.ca/content/64/2/e78.

Aphria, Aurora Cannabis, Canadian Medical Cannabis Council, et al. 2017. *Adult Use Cannabis Advertising and Marketing Self-Regulatory Guidelines for Licensed Producers*. November. https://cannabislaw.report/wp-content/uploads/2017/11/GuidelinesforCannabis-EN-Nov6.pdf.

Auriol, Emmanuelle, and Geoffard Pierre-Yves. 2019. "Cannabis: Comment reprendre le contrôle?" [Cannabis: How to resume control?] *Notes du Conseil d'Analyse Économique* 4 (52). https://www.cae-eco.fr/staticfiles/pdf/cae-note052.pdf.

Babor, Thomas F. 2010. "Alcohol: No Ordinary Commodity – A Summary of the Second Edition." *Addiction* 105: 769–79. https://onlinelibrary.wiley.com/doi/10.1111/j.1360-0443.2010.02945.x.

Bennett Jones. 2014. "Bennett Jones Attends the Official Launch of Tweed Inc's Medicinal Marijuana Facility." Announcement, June 18. https://www.bennett jones.com/en/Publications-Section/Announcements/Bennett-Jones-Attends-the-Official-Launch-of-Tweed-Inc,-d-,s-Medicinal-Marijuana-Facility.

Betting Bruiser. 2018. "Wouldn't Someone Like Myself Sponsor an Investigated Podcast." Twitter, December 4, 9:12 a.m. https://twitter.com/BettingBruiser/status/1070002859452915712.

Campbell, Meagan. 2017. "How Public Officials Got into the Weed Game." *Maclean's*, April 13. https://www.macleans.ca/politics/how-public-officials-got-into-the-weed-game/.

Canada. 2014a. *Recall of Marijuana for Medical Purposes – Peace Naturals Project Inc.* May 9. https://www.healthycanadians.gc.ca/recall-alert-rappel-avis/hc-sc/2014/39457a-eng.php.

—. 2014b. *Recall of Marijuana for Medical Purposes – Whistler Medical Marijuana Corp.* August 15. https://www.healthycanadians.gc.ca/recall-alert-rappel-avis/hc-sc/2014/41115a-eng.php.

—. 2014c. *Recall of Marijuana for Medical Purposes – Greenleaf Medicinals.* April 18. https://www.healthycanadians.gc.ca/recall-alert-rappel-avis/hc-sc/2014/39183a-eng.php.

—. 2014d. "Information Update – Marijuana for Medical Purposes – Advertising and Licensed Producers." November 25. http://www.healthycanadians.gc.ca/recall-alert-rappel-avis/hc-sc/2014/42677a-eng.php.

—. 2015. *Recall of Marijuana for Medical Purposes – Peace Naturals Project Inc.* February 10. https://www.healthycanadians.gc.ca/recall-alert-rappel-avis/hc-sc/2015/43677a-eng.php.

—. 2016a. "Consumer Information – Cannabis (Marihuana, marijuana)." August 19. https://www.canada.ca/en/health-canada/services/drugs-medication/cannabis/licensed-producers/consumer-information-cannabis.html.

—. 2016b. "Task Force on Marijuana Legalization and Regulation: Summary of Expertise, Experience, and Affiliations and Interests." June 30. http://healthy canadians.gc.ca/health-system-systeme-sante/consultations/legalization-marijuana-legalisation/affiliations-eng.php.

—. 2017a. *Recall of Cannabis for Medical Purposes – Emblem Cannabis Corp.* April 7. https://www.healthycanadians.gc.ca/recall-alert-rappel-avis/hc-sc/2017/62980r-eng.php.

—. 2017b. *Recall of Cannabis for Medical Purposes – Mettrum Ltd.* February 7. http://www.healthycanadians.gc.ca/recall-alert-rappel-avis/hc-sc/2016/62102r-eng.php.

—. 2018. *National Report: Apparent Opioid-Related Deaths in Canada.* March. https://www.canada.ca/en/public-health/services/publications/healthy-living/national-report-apparent-opioid-related-deaths-released-march-2018.html.

—. 2021. Recalls & Alerts (Search on "Cannabis" OR "marijuana"). Ottawa: Government of Canada. September 12. https://www.healthycanadians.gc.ca/recall-alert-rappel-avis/search-recherche/result-resultat/en?search_text_1=cannabis+OR+marijuana.

Canada, House of Commons. 2016. "Opposition Motion: Decriminalization of Marijuana Possession." *House of Commons Debates*, 42nd Parl, 1st Sess, No 071 (June 13) 4368 (1200–1400) (Hon Geoff Regan). https://www.ourcommons.ca/DocumentViewer/en/42-1/house/sitting-71/hansard.

Canadian Medical Association. 2016. "Legalization, Regulation and Restriction of Access to Marijuana." Submission to Government of Canada Task Force on Marijuana Legalization and Regulation, August 29. https://www.cma.ca/sites/default/files/pdf/News/2016-aug-29-cma-submission-legalization-and-regulation-of-marijuana-e.pdf.

Canadian Press. 2019a. "OSC Launches Investigation into Unlicensed Pot Growing at Canntrust." *Toronto Star*, August 1. https://www.thestar.com/business/2019/08/01/canntrust-says-osc-launches-investigation-into-unlicensed-pot-growing.html.

—. 2019b. "Health Canada Revokes Licences of Pot Producer Agrima Botanicals." *Toronto Star*, July 15. https://www.thestar.com/business/2019/07/15/health-canada-revokes-licences-of-pot-producer-agrima-botanicals.html.

Canadian Public Health Association. 2011. *Too High a Cost: A Public Health Approach to Alcohol Policy in Canada*. Ottawa: Canadian Public Health Association. https://www.cpha.ca/sites/default/files/assets/positions/position-paper-alcohol_e.pdf.

—. 2016. *A Public Health Approach to the Legalization, Regulation and Restriction of Access to Cannabis*. Ottawa: Canadian Public Health Association. https://www.cpha.ca/public-health-approach-legalization-regulation-and-restriction-access-cannabis.

Canadian Substance Use Costs and Harms Scientific Working Group. 2018. *Canadian Substance Use Costs and Harms, 2007–2014*. Ottawa: Canadian Centre on Substance Use and Addiction. https://www.ccsa.ca/sites/default/files/2019-04/CSUCH-Canadian-Substance-Use-Costs-Harms-Report-2018-en.pdf.

—. 2020. *Canadian Substance Use Costs and Harms Visualization Tool, Version 2.0.0* [Online tool]. Ottawa and Victoria: Canadian Centre on Substance Use and Addiction and Canadian Institute for Substance Use Research. https://csuch.ca/.

Cannabis Life Network. 2015. "Liberal CFO Rifici Sees Green from Tweed." *Cannabis Life Network*, October 29. https://cannabislifenetwork.com/liberal-cfo-rifici-sees-green-from-tweed/.

Cannabis Trade Alliance of Canada. 2016. *Public Consultation: Toward the Legalization, Regulation and Restriction of Access to Marijuana*. Vancouver: Cannabis Trade Alliance of Canada. https://issuu.com/sustainablecannabis.ca/docs/consultation_submission__final_.

Canopy Growth. 2018. "Dr. Mark Ware Joins Canopy Growth Corporation as Chief Medical Officer." *Cision*, May 28. https://www.newswire.ca/news-releases/dr-mark-ware-joins-canopy-growth-corporation-as-chief-medical-officer-683849601.html.

Canopy Growth Corporation. 2017. "Canopy Health Innovations Enters into Agreement with Dr. Mark Ware." *Cision*, February 10. https://www.newswire.ca/news-releases/canopy-health-innovations-enters-into-agreement-with-dr-mark-ware-613388233.html.

Capler, Rielle, Neil Boyd, and Donald MacPherson. 2016. "Organized Crime in the Cannabis Market: Evidence and Implications." Submission to the Cannabis Legalization Task Force, August 9. https://www.drugpolicy.ca/wp-content/uploads/2016/11/CDPC_Submission_Cannabis-and-Organized-Crime_Aug9-2016_Full-Final-1.pdf.

Caulkins, Jonathan P., Beau Kilmer, Mark A.R. Kleiman, Robert J. MacCoun, Gregory Midgette, Pat Oglesby, Rosalie Liccardo Pacula, and Peter H. Reuter. 2015. *Considering Marijuana Legalization: Insights for Vermont and Other Jurisdictions.* Santa Monica, CA: Rand. http://www.rand.org/pubs/research_reports/RR864.html.

CBC News. 2016. "Marijuana Task Force to Be Led by Former Deputy PM Anne McLellan." June 30. https://www.cbc.ca/news/politics/liberals-marijuana-task-force-1.3659509.

–. 2020. "Legal Age to Buy Cannabis in Quebec Is Now 21, the Highest in Canada." January 1. https://www.cbc.ca/news/canada/montreal/legal-age-cannabis-edibles-1.5399211.

Centre for Addiction and Mental Health. 2014. *Cannabis Policy Framework.* Toronto: Centre for Addiction and Mental Health. October. https://www.camh.ca/-/media/files/pdfs---public-policy-submissions/camhcannabispolicyframework-pdf.

–. 2016. "Re.: Consultation on the Legalization, Regulation and Restriction of Access to Marijuana in Canada." Submission to the Cannabis Legalization and Regulation Secretariat, August 29. http://www.camh.ca/-/media/files/pdfs---public-policy-submissions/camhsubmission_cannabistaskforce_20160829-pdf.

Chapados, Maude, François Gagnon, Geneviève Lapointe, Sébastien Tessier, Nicole April, Richard C. Fachehoun, and Samuel Onil. 2016. *Legalization of Nonmedical Cannabis: A Public Health Approach to Regulation.* Montreal: Institut National de Santé Publique du Québec. https://www.inspq.qc.ca/sites/default/files/publications/2233_legalization_non_medical_cannabis_0.pdf.

Chief Medical Officers of Health of Canada and Urban Public Health Network. 2016. *Public Health Perspectives on Cannabis Policy and Regulation.* Policy paper, September 26. http://uphn.ca/wp-content/uploads/2016/10/Chief-MOH-UPHN-Cannabis-Perspectives-Final-Sept-26-2016.pdf.

Cormier, Beth. 2015. "Cannabis and the Green Party of Canada: Get Out the Cannabis Vote – Part 4 of 5." *Cannabis Digest,* October 17. https://cannabisdigest.ca/cannabis-and-the-green-party-of-canada/.

CTV Montreal. 2019. "Tobacco Companies Will Pay Out $17B to Smokers after Losing Appeal." March 1. https://montreal.ctvnews.ca/tobacco-companies-will-pay-out-17b-to-smokers-after-losing-appeal-1.4318946.

Denis, Marie-Maude. 2018. "Licensed Cannabis Growers Have Ties to Organized Crime, Enquête Investigation Finds." *CBC News,* November 2. https://www.cbc.ca/amp/1.4887997.

DeVillaer, Michael. 2017. *Cannabis Law Reform in Canada: Pretense and Perils.* Hamilton: McMaster University/Peter Boris Centre for Addictions Research. https://fhs.mcmaster.ca/pbcar/documents/Pretense%20&%20Perils%20FINAL.PDF.

–. 2019. "Cannabis Legalization: Lessons from Alcohol, Tobacco, and Pharmaceutical Industries." In *High Time: The Legalization and Regulation of Cannabis in*

Canada, edited by Andrew Potter and Daniel Weinstock, 182–201. Montreal/Kingston: McGill-Queen's University Press. https://www.mqup.ca/high-time-products-9780773556416.php.

Di Fiore, James. 2017. "I Would Never Have Pushed for Legal Pot If I Knew It'd End This Way." *Huffington Post,* September 14. https://www.huffpost.com/archive/ca/entry/i-would-never-have-pushed-for-legal-pot-if-i-knew-itd-end-this-way_a_23202887.

DiMatteo, Enzo. 2018. "The Ex Cops, Politicians and Friends of Bill Blair Cashing in on Legal Weed." *NOW Toronto,* January 29. https://nowtoronto.com/news/cops-politicians-cashing-in-on-cannabis/.

Erickson, Patricia G., and Elaine Hyshka. 2010. "Four Decades of Cannabis Criminals in Canada, 1970–2010." *Amsterdam Law Forum* 2 (4): 3–4. https://www.researchgate.net/publication/228124186_Four_Decades_of_Cannabis_Criminals_in_Canada_1970–2010.

Fife, Robert, and Steven Chase. 2017. "Trudeau's Lead on Legalizing Marijuana Lobbied during Cash-for-Access Fundraiser." *Globe and Mail,* April 10. http://www.theglobeandmail.com/news/politics/trudeaus-marijuana-czar-lobbied-during-cash-for-access-fundraiser/article33084843/.

Flavelle, Dana. 2015. "Bay St. Law Firms Cash in on Pot Industry." *Toronto Star,* January 8. https://www.thestar.com/business/2015/01/08/bay_st_law_firms_cash_in_on_pot_industry.html.

Foote, Andrew. 2016. "Snoop Dogg Deal Represents Changing Marijuana Industry: Tweed CEO." *CBC News,* February 13. http://www.cbc.ca/news/canada/ottawa/snoop-dogg-tweed-smiths-falls-1.3445854?cmp=rss.

Froese, Ian. 2019. "RCMP Not Investigating Winnipeg Cannabis Producer That Sold Unauthorized Weed." *CBC News,* March 25. https://www.cbc.ca/amp/1.5070578#click=https://t.co/JIgM1IYSt9.

The Gazette. 2016. "Editorial: Big Marijuana Trashes Democratic Process." July 8. http://m.gazette.com/editorial-big-marijuana-trashes-democratic-process/article/1579890?_ga=1.69083667.306833286.1467984685.

Gilmore, Rachel. 2018. "Scheer Won't Commit to Keeping Cannabis Legal If Tories Form Government." *CTV News,* October 19. https://www.ctvnews.ca/politics/scheer-won-t-commit-to-keeping-cannabis-legal-if-tories-form-government-1.4140546.

Giovacchini, Anthony M. 1999. "The Negative Influence of Gangster Rap and What Can Be Done about It." *Poverty and Prejudice: Media and Race,* June 4. https://www.coursehero.com/file/29727933/The-Negative-Influence-of-Gangster-Rap-And-What-Can-Be-Done-About-Itpdf/.

Gowriluk, Caitlyn. 2019. "Winnipeg-based Cannabis Producer Bonify has Licence Reinstated by Health Canada." *CBC News,* October 23. https://www.cbc.ca/news/canada/manitoba/bonify-licence-reinstated-after-health-canada-suspension-1.5332637.

Hager, Mike, and Grant Robertson. 2017. "Questions Raised over Marijuana Task Force Chair's Ties to Industry." *Globe and Mail,* April 13. https://www.the

globeandmail.com/news/national/questions-raised-over-marijuana-task-force-chairs-ties-to-industry/article34694710/.

Israel, Solomon. 2019. "Health Canada Pulls Bonify's Licences for Selling Illegal Weed." *Winnipeg Free Press*, February 5. https://www.winnipegfreepress.com/local/health-canada-pulls-bonifys-licences-for-selling-illegal-weed-505382112.html.

Keung, Nicholas. 2019. "Feds Pleased with 'Orderly' Transition to Pot Legalization, Bill Blair Says." *Toronto Star*, March 6. https://www.thestar.com/news/cannabis/2019/03/06/feds-pleased-with-orderly-transition-to-pot-legalization-bill-blair-says.html.

Kirkup, Kristy. 2015. "Justin Trudeau Prepares to Tackle Pot Politics with Conservative Framework." *Globe and Mail*, October 28. http://www.theglobeandmail.com/news/british-columbia/justin-trudeau-prepares-to-tackle-pot-politics-with-conservative-framework/article27024564/.

Kleiman, Mark A.R., Steven Davenport, Brad Rowe, Jeremy Ziskind, Nate Mladenovic, Clarissa Manning, and Tyler Jones. 2015. *Estimating the Size of the Medical Cannabis Market in Washington State*. Los Angeles: BOTEC Analysis Corporation. https://static1.squarespace.com/static/5e5fc3d054a9e32eaf6411e0/t/5ea1173fcf24b67402f5b936/1587615552578/BOTEC-MMJ-Report+-+2015.pdf.

Lamers, Matt. 2018. "Regulator Warns Canadian Marijuana Firms against 'Problematic Practices.'" *Marijuana Business Daily*, December 6. https://mjbizdaily.com/canadian-cannabis-firm-regulatory-warning/.

–. 2020. "With All Licenses Reinstated, Canntrust Aims for Cannabis Product Relaunch." *Marijuana Business Daily*, August 6. https://mjbizdaily.com/with-all-licenses-reinstated-canntrust-aims-for-cannabis-product-relaunch/.

Levesque, Maurice. 2017. "Knightswood Enters Pot Deal with PanCann for $1M." *Stockwatch*, April 26. https://www.stockwatch.com/News/Item.aspx?bid=Z-C:KWF-2463886&symbol=KWF&region=C.

Ligaya, Armina. 2018. "Aphria Shares Plunge 28 Per Cent after Short Seller Report." *CTV News*, December 3. https://www.ctvnews.ca/business/aphria-shares-plunge-28-per-cent-after-short-seller-report-1.4202897.

Ling, Justin. 2016. "High Prices." *Vice News*, November 16. https://news.vice.com/en_ca/article/9kn95y/veteran-medical-marijuana-benefits-are-costing-canada-a-fortune.

Mann, Brian. 2021. "The DOJ Moves to Block the Purdue Pharma Bankruptcy Deal That Shields the Sacklers." *NPR*, September 16. https://www.npr.org/2021/09/16/1037806819/opioids-purdue-pharma-sackler-settlement-bankruptcy-deal.

Miller, Jacquie. 2018a. "Cannabis Companies Ramp Up Marketing as Health Canada Warns Them Not to Advertise Pot." *Ottawa Citizen*, October 11. https://ottawacitizen.com/news/local-news/warning-on-ads.

–. 2018b. "Trailer Park Buds? Cannabis Companies Devise Catchy Brand Names amid Strict Health Canada Rules." *Ottawa Citizen*, October 15. https://ottawacitizen.com/cannabis/cannabis-business/pot-names.

Mulvihill, Geoff. 2021. "Judge Conditionally Approves Purdue Pharma Opioid Settlement." *PBS News,* September 1. https://www.pbs.org/newshour/economy/judge-conditionally-approves-purdue-pharma-opioid-settlement.

National Advisory Committee on Prescription Drug Misuse. 2013. *First Do No Harm: Responding to Canada's Prescription Drug Crisis.* Ottawa: Canadian Centre on Substance Abuse; March. https://ccsa.ca/sites/default/files/2019-04/Canada-Strategy-Prescription-Drug-Misuse-Report-en.pdf.

O'Cannabiz Conference and Expo. 2019. Schedule. April 25–27.

Office of the Commissioner of Lobbying of Canada. 2021. *Registry of Lobbyists.* https://lobbycanada.gc.ca/app/secure/ocl/lrs/do/advSrch.

Ontario Securities Commission. 2021. "Former Officers and Directors of CannTrust Charged with Securities Act Offences." June 22. https://www.osc.ca/en/news-events/news/former-officers-and-directors-canntrust-charged-securities-act-offences.

Pacula, Rosalie Liccardo, Beau Kilmer, Alexander C. Wagenaar, Frank J. Chaloupka, and Jonathan P. Caulkins. 2014. "Developing Public Health Regulations for Marijuana: Lessons Learned from Alcohol and Tobacco." *American Journal of Public Health* 104 (6): 1021–28. https://www.ncbi.nlm.nih.gov/pmc/articles/PMC4062005/.

Pfeffer, Amanda, and Guillaume Dumont. 2017. "Police Warn Organized Crime, including the Hells Angels, Has Infiltrated the Medical Marijuana Market." *CBC News,* April 13. https://www.cbc.ca/news/canada/ottawa/police-warn-organized-crime-including-the-hells-angels-has-infiltrated-the-medical-marijuana-market-1.4067112.

Platt, Brian. 2017. "Marijuana Task-Force Member's Move to Legal Weed Company Raises Conflict-of-Interest Concerns." *National Post,* September 25. https://nationalpost.com/news/politics/marijuana-task-force-members-move-to-legal-weed-company-raises-conflict-of-interest-concerns.

Public Health Agency of Canada. 2016. *The Chief Public Health Officer's Report on the State of Public Health in Canada 2015: Alcohol Consumption in Canada.* Ottawa: Public Health Agency of Canada. http://healthycanadians.gc.ca/publications/department-ministere/state-public-health-alcohol-2015-etat-sante-publique-alcool/alt/state-phac-alcohol-2015-etat-aspc-alcool-eng.pdf.

Quebec Legislature. 2018. An Act to Constitute the Société québécoise du cannabis, to Enact the Cannabis Regulation Act and to Amend Various Highway Safety-Related Provisions, SQ 2018, c 19. http://www2.publicationsduquebec.gouv.qc.ca/dynamicSearch/telecharge.php?type=5&file=2018C19F.PDF.

Rehm, J., D. Baliunas, S. Brochu, B. Fischer, W. Gnam, J. Patra, S. Popova, A. Sarnocinsk-Hart, and B. Taylor. 2006. "The Cost of Substance Abuse in Canada Technical Report." Ottawa: Canadian Centre on Substance Abuse. https://www.zora.uzh.ch/id/eprint/95508/1/Rehm%2C_Baliunas_et_al_2006_-_The_costs_of_substance_abuse.pdf.

Reuters. 2015. "Canadian Regulators Warn on Medical Marijuana Disclosures." February 23. https://www.reuters.com/article/canada-regulator-marijuanaid CAL1N0VX14220150223.

Robertson, Grant. 2015. "Health Canada Puts Medical Marijuana Firm under Further RCMP Review." *Globe and Mail*, January 30. http://www.theglobeandmail.com/report-on-business/health-canada-puts-medical-marijuana-firm-under-further-rcmp-review/article22716002/.

–. 2016. "Canadians Not Told about Banned Pesticide Found in Medical Pot Supply." *Globe and Mail*, December 29. http://www.theglobeandmail.com/news/national/canadians-not-told-about-banned-pesticide-found-in-medical-marijuana-supply/article33443887/.

–. 2017. "Two Medical Marijuana Companies Face New Rules after Banned Pesticide Use." *Globe and Mail*, February 9. http://www.theglobeandmail.com//news/national/health-canada-adds-new-rules-to-licences-of-two-medical-marijuana-companies/article33976056/?cmpid=rss1&click=sf_globe.

Robertson, Grant, and Greg McArthur. 2016a. "Globe Investigation: Marijuana Edibles Tests Reveal Misleading Claims." *Globe and Mail*, August 12. http://www.theglobeandmail.com/news/investigations/globe-investigation-marijuana-edibles-tests-reveal-misleading-claims/article31198569/.

–. 2016b. "Globe Investigation: What's in Your Weed? We Tested Dispensary Marijuana to Find Out." *Globe and Mail*, July 27. http://www.theglobeandmail.com/news/investigations/globe-investigation-whats-in-your-weed-we-tested-dispensary-marijuana-to-findout/article31144496/.

Rocky Mountain High Intensity Drug Trafficking Area. 2014. *The Legalization of Marijuana in Colorado: The Impact*. Vol. 2. Colorado: Rocky Mountain High Intensity Drug Trafficking Area. https://www.tpchd.org/home/showdocument?id=2425.

Rolles, Steve, Mike Barton, Niamh Eastwood, Tom Lloyd, Fiona Measham, David Nutt, and Harry Sumnall. 2016. *A Framework for a Regulated Market for Cannabis in the UK: Recommendations from an Expert Panel*. London: Liberal Democrats. http://fileserver.idpc.net/library/A_framework_for_a_regulated_market_for_cannabis_in_the_UK.pdf.

Shaw, Barbara. 2016. "Marijuana, Inc: The Buzz behind the Canadian Bud Biz." *NowToronto*, April 13. https://nowtoronto.com/news/marijuana-inc-the-buzz-behind-the-bud-biz-canada/.

Sheikh, Iman. 2016. "These Prominent Canadians Want You to Buy Their Weed." *TVO*, February 25. https://tvo.org/article/current-affairs/the-next-ontario/these-prominent-canadians-want-you-to-buy-their-weed.

Single, E., L. Robson, X. Xie, and J. Rehm. 1996. *The Costs of Substance Abuse in Canada*. Ottawa: Canadian Centre on Substance Abuse.

Solecki, A., K. Burnett, and K. Li. 2011. *Drug Production Cases in Selected Canadian Jurisdictions: A Study of Case File Characteristics, 1997–2005*. Ottawa: Department of Justice. Released under the Access to Information Act.

Special Advisory Committee on the Epidemic of Opioid Overdoses. 2021. *Opioids and Stimulant-related Harms in Canada*. Ottawa: Public Health Agency of Canada; June 23. https://health-infobase.canada.ca/substance-related-harms/opioids-stimulants.

Spithoff, Sheryl, Brian Emerson, and Andrea Spithoff. 2015. "Cannabis Legalization: Adhering to Public Health Best Practice." *Canadian Medical Association Journal* 187 (16): 1211–16. http://www.cmaj.ca/content/187/16/1211.figures-only.

Stone, Dave. 2014. "Cannabis, Pesticides and Conflicting Laws: The Dilemma for Legalized States and Implications for Public Health." *Regulatory Toxicology and Pharmacology* 69 (3): 284–88. https://www.sciencedirect.com/science/article/abs/pii/S027323001400097X.

Stratcann. 2021. "Bonify Is 'Winding Down' Operations in the Coming Weeks." August 13. https://stratcann.com/2021/08/13/bonify-is-winding-down-operations-in-the-coming-weeks/.

Subramaniam, Vanmala. 2019. "Namaste Technologies Plunges 21% after It Fires CEO and Launches Strategic Review." *Financial Post*, February 4. https://financialpost.com/cannabis/cannabis-business/namaste-technologies-plunges-21-after-it-fires-ceo-and-launches-strategic-review.

Swaby, Nickeesha. 2018. "Canadian Cannabis Company Faces Class Action after Damning Research Report Calls US Listing Plan 'Fake.'" *Courthouse News Service*, October 30. https://www.courthousenews.com/canadian-cannabis-company-faces-class-action-after-damning-research-report-calls-u-s-listing-plan-fake/.

Task Force on Cannabis Legalization and Regulation. 2016. *A Framework for the Legalization and Regulation of Cannabis in Canada: Final Report.* Ottawa: Government of Canada, Health Canada. http://healthycanadians.gc.ca/task-force-marijuana-groupe-etude/framework-cadre/alt/framework-cadre-eng.pdf.

Task Force on Marijuana Legalization and Regulation. 2016. *Toward the Legalization, Regulation and Restriction of Access to Marijuana: Discussion Paper.* Ottawa: Government of Canada. http://healthycanadians.gc.ca/health-system-systeme-sante/consultations/legalization-marijuana-legalisation/alt/legalization-marijuana-legalisation-eng.pdf.

Thomas, Brian F., and Mahmoud A. Elsohly. 2015. *The Analytical Chemistry of Cannabis: Quality Assessment, Assurance, and Regulation of Medicinal Marijuana and Cannabinoid Preparations.* Cambridge: Elsevier/RTI Press. https://www.elsevier.com/books/the-analytical-chemistry-of-cannabis/thomas/978-0-12-804646-3.

Tobacco Control Legal Consortium. 2012. *Cause and Effect: Tobacco Marketing Increases Youth Tobacco Use – Findings from the 2012 Surgeon General's Report.* St. Paul, MN: Tobacco Control Legal Consortium. http://publichealthlawcenter.org/sites/default/files/resources/tclc-guide-SGReport-Findings-Youth-Marketing-2012.pdf.

Wang, George Sam, Marie-Claire Le Lait, Sara J. Deakyne, Alvin C. Bronstein, Lalit Bajaj, and Genie Roosevelt. 2016. "Unintentional Pediatric Exposures to Marijuana in Colorado, 2009–2015." *Journal of the American Medical Association Pediatrics* 170 (9): e160971. https://www.ncbi.nlm.nih.gov/pubmed/27454910.

Wells, Paul. 2017. "Canada's New Health Minister Faces the Opioid Crisis." *Maclean's*, September 12. https://www.macleans.ca/politics/ottawa/canadas-new-health-minister-faces-the-opioid-crisis/.

Whiting, Penny F., Robert F. Wolff, Sohan Deshpande, Marcello Di Nisio, Steven Duffy, Adrian V. Hernandez, J. Christiaan Keurentjes, Shona Lang, Kate Misso,

Steve Ryder, Simone Schmidlkofer, Marie Westwood, and Jos Kleijnen. 2015. "Cannabinoids for Medical Use: A Systematic Review and Meta-analysis." *Journal of the American Medical Association* 313 (24): 2456–73. https://www.ncbi.nlm.nih.gov/pubmed/26103030.

Woodward, Jon. 2016. "Political Pot Donations Sign of 'Normalized' Industry: Advocate." *CTV News*, March 22. http://bc.ctvnews.ca/political-pot-donations-sign-of-normalized-industry-advocate-1.2826836.

6

Cannabis Substitution

The Canadian Experience

MICHELLE ST. PIERRE, SARAH DANIELS, and ZACH WALSH

Evidence for the therapeutic use of cannabis dates back millennia, and descriptions of cannabis used to substitute for opioids and other substances were included in the formal medical literature well over a century ago (Mattison 1891). After a brief period of relative latency in the mid-twentieth century (Lee 2012), scholarship on the medical use of cannabis as a substitute for other substances re-emerged in North America in the wake of the patient-led medical cannabis movement on the West Coast (Mikuriya 1970; Lucas 2009).

Clinical scientists and community-based researchers in this movement initiated a wave of substitution studies focused largely on retrospective self-reports by medical cannabis users (Mikuriya 2003; Lucas et al. 2016; Reiman, Welty, and Solomon 2017). This work was bolstered by epidemiological studies demonstrating an inverse relationship between medical cannabis access and opioid overdose fatalities (Bachhuber et al. 2014), alcohol use and traffic accidents (Anderson, Hansen, and Rees 2013; Santaella-Tenorio et al. 2017), and expenditures on medicines for which cannabis might serve as a substitute – such as benzodiazepines and opioids (Bradford and Bradford 2017).

The excerpts from interviews presented in this chapter describe how observations of substitution emerged from early work in dispensaries, gained prominence in the context of the opioid overdose epidemic and liberalization of cannabis regulation, and became the subject of more formal academic study. The interviews covered a variety of topics from the early days of the movement for the provision of medical cannabis as a substitute therapy in Canada, to the development of formal assessments, to more recent attempts to facilitate outreach beyond cannabis dispensaries by initiating direct contact with communities who use opioids.

Six key informants in the area of cannabis substitution research, policy, and practice took part in structured interviews. The participants agreed to be identified by name (see Appendix for contributor biographies). To retain the voices of the interviewees, the excerpts presented are taken verbatim directly from the transcripts.

The Early Days

Cannabis use was restricted in Canada in 1923 under an amendment to the Opium and Narcotics Drug Act. Over the following decades, brave Canadians engaged in civil disobedience to push for the re-legalization of medical cannabis use. In 2000, the Ontario Court of Appeal ruled that cannabis prohibition was unconstitutional after Parker was arrested for possessing cannabis that he was using to treat his epilepsy (*R v Parker*, 2000). The court ruled that limiting the use of medical cannabis was a violation of the right to life, liberty, and security of persons. Following this ruling, dispensaries began to emerge to fill a growing need. Below are the voices of some of those who were active in cannabis dispensaries in Canada.

Rielle Capler

I first heard about cannabis substitution when I was working in Vancouver in the late 1990s and early 2000s at the city's first compassion club. I remember hearing from one of the patients who came in to say: "Thank you so much for being here and providing cannabis. I've been able to wean off my opiates." I was just floored that this was possible with cannabis.

Early on, I prepared a poster presentation for an international harm-reduction conference about our perspectives and observations of cannabis substitution, and over time the research evolved into asking patients questions about substitution in surveys and analyzing the responses. Over time, our observational research and surveys continued to find that this is a real phenomenon. At the British Columbia Centre on Substance Use (BCCSU), where I am currently a postdoctoral fellow, there is an area of research focus around the instrumental use of cannabis to substitute for opioids and other substances, and this stream is now moving into clinical research.

Philippe Lucas
The early customer base in Canada and the United States was people affected by HIV and hepatitis C, many of whom were infected through injection drug use. In my position as a dispensary operator in the early 2000s, I kept hearing interesting stories such as: "My doctor's recommendation for using cannabis was for HIV, AIDS, or hepatitis C, but when I eat a cannabis cookie or smoke cannabis I don't have to go out and look for heroin, or I don't feel the need to go out and smoke crack or crystal meth." I kept hearing these stories again and again, largely from the street-involved population we were working with. These reports seemed to fly in the face of what the government, schools, and health care system were telling us at the time: that cannabis is a gateway drug. According to patient accounts, it seemed to be an exit drug from some substance-use disorders.

There was a physician by the name of Tod Mikuriya who came to cannabis substitution in a similar way; he was prescribing medical cannabis to patients and hearing that it was reducing their use and cravings for alcohol or illicit drugs. Mikuriya was one of the early innovators in this space, doing case studies and gathering data. There was also a researcher named Karen Model who authored a great early paper that looked at retrospective data on the decriminalization of cannabis in the 1970s (Model 1993). She concluded that by decriminalizing cannabis, states had reduced the harms associated with alcohol and illicit substance use. She was suggesting that people who had easier access to cannabis because of a change in the legal regime were using less alcohol and illicit drugs; therefore, cannabis decriminalization had a net benefit to public health.

Adolfo Gonzalez
I went through a really serious snowboarding injury and a terribly long period of recovery where I was prescribed some pretty heavy opiates, and I became addicted. Then I got completely off opiates using a really heavy Kush strain of cannabis. I also realized how complicated it can be for somebody who's sick to get to know the underground cannabis-growing community, so I wanted to help other people with similar conditions. I was in awe of the people that were breaking the law to give people like myself access to clean medicine at a decent price, and I started volunteering at one of the first compassion clubs in Vancouver.

When given the position of research coordinator for a DTES (Downtown Eastside)–based dispensary, I decided to launch an opiate substitution program. I did it without ethics committee approval, so I knew we would never have this project published in a scientific journal. The goal was to help people. I knew that some clients were from the methadone clinic because they would bring their tickets from the methadone clinic so that they could access the dispensary. I believed that they would benefit from having discounted or free cannabis capsules because they were already consuming edibles, mostly for pain. We developed a system where growers would donate specific varieties with standardized terpene and cannabinoid profiles. We started with about thirty-five to forty participants and ended up with nine that actually stuck with the program for the full three months of data collection. Six of them had more than 50 percent reduction in their methadone use and one of them completely stopped going to the methadone clinic. I saw him on the regular and I could tell by his skin and body, this guy was just a different person.

Sarah Blyth
I work in the overdose prevention site, which was created to help people during the overdose crisis in the Downtown Eastside neighbourhood of Vancouver. We were brainstorming how to provide safe access to something – anything – that would be helpful, and my partner mentioned that he knew that people use cannabis for post-traumatic stress disorder, trauma, and injuries. He suggested trying to do a cannabis program here to see if we could help people who were using opioids for some of these same reasons.

Since starting High Hopes Foundation, we have been able to provide free and low-cost access to cannabis to help individuals get safe access and help with recovery, pain, sleep, and trauma. We started High Hopes in order to decrease barriers to accessing cannabis for individuals in the DTES; to provide the opportunity for individuals with access to all sorts of other drugs to make safer choices. The police shut us down, but we've now established a cannabis program for safe access at the overdose prevention site. We are going the legal route, trying to open High Hopes as a research-based, social enterprise.

M.-J. Milloy
My training was in epidemiology, and until around 2013 I was under the mistaken impression that cannabis was not all that important to my work on harm reduction for people who use drugs. That changed when a graduate student encouraged me to explore the idea of cannabis substitution in our large cohort living in the DTES. At that point, we did not ask people if they were using cannabis instead of other substances, but we did have data

regarding how often people used cannabis in the last six months and if they used heroin, et cetera. We were wondering if, for example, there was a correlation between changes in heroin use with changes in cannabis use. We took a couple runs at it, but we realized that we really didn't have the sort of data that we needed to try and explore this properly. The next stage was adding questions to more explicitly ask about the possible substitution effect and more generally about the role of cannabis in their lives. That's really been the foundation of our work over the last couple of years – looking at the links between cannabis and the health and well-being of members of this marginalized and vulnerable group.

More recently, we've added questions around what type of cannabis people are using, what their intentions around cannabis use are, and their sources of cannabis, because we know that with legalization that is an important question. Our work is mainly focused on marginalized and vulnerable people who use drugs. We want to learn more about cannabis use in the hopes that it might be a useful tool to address the public health crisis that we are living through.

Kim Crosby

I was first involved in cannabis substitution research during my master's degree. I heard patients reporting that they were using their prescription medications less by effectively substituting cannabis. I'm a big proponent of harm reduction, and in light of the worsening opioid crisis, it's a public health issue.

In the survey-based studies that were examining substitution among medical cannabis users, we asked basic yes and no questions about whether or not they substituted cannabis for other prescription drugs. I wondered if there were other ways that we could demonstrate that individuals might use cannabis instead of other drugs, and now our research is more nuanced, utilizing more in-depth surveys, interviews, and ecological momentary assessments to track patterns of use and substitution. We are delving into the concepts of behavioural economics and looking at how we can measure substitution using more task-oriented methods to really understand how substitution happens.

Remaining Barriers

The past several decades have witnessed a dramatic increase in interest in the potential for cannabis to be used as a substitute for opioids and other substances. However, as has been the case with therapeutic cannabis use more generally, broad acceptance has faced considerable barriers (Belle-Isle et al. 2014), and obstacles remain to establishing a more complete understanding of how cannabis might substitute for other substances.

The interviews pointed to cost as a key issue in the adoption of cannabis substitution. Affordability is an issue in a context where alternative medications such as opioids and benzodiazepines are subsidized by a health care system that does not subsidize medical cannabis. Lack of support and awareness of the potential of cannabis substitution among health care providers is another barrier, along with lack of education and confidence among providers (Fitzcharles et al. 2014; Ziemianski et al. 2015; Balneaves et al. 2018). Limited storefront access and restrictions on public use were also identified as factors, among others, which might present barriers to the use of cannabis as a substitute.

Rielle Capler
An issue that came up at the compassion club is that we had members that were using cannabis as a substitute for opioids, and they were in recovery programs, and sometimes they would be kicked out if it was found out that they were using cannabis. That was something we would try to advocate on their behalf. They could have been using cannabis for pain or anxiety. However, in some treatment programs, cannabis is seen as an addictive substance, and there is zero tolerance for any such substance. Cannabis can play a positive role in recovery, but there needs to be some education and changing of attitudes.

In the future, I expect concerns related to financial barriers. Affordability is going to be huge. I remember a patient who had been using cannabis edibles as a substitute for opioids, and he was successful but stopped because he couldn't afford the cannabis. He went back onto the opioids, and his whole life degraded. It was very sad. I think if we want to take this seriously, there will have to be a way to bring it into the health care system and have cost coverage. Another barrier I anticipate is in terms of health care providers. Will they support working with herbal cannabis as a plant medicine, or are they going to wait for pharmaceutical products?

Kim Crosby
Overcoming barriers will require more availability and more accessibility. That just hasn't materialized here in British Columbia as of right now. We have few brick-and-mortar stores and none close to the DTES. Ordering online can be difficult for naive users or for those who may not have a stable

residence for mailing. I think that's a practical and perhaps widespread barrier for cannabis substitution. There's a lack of people who can tell you how to do it, and how to use it safely, and teaching people how to find a good balance for themselves.

I think it will be challenging to get key people on board; getting the general public and physicians and health care practitioners willing to take that chance. Because as it stands right now, many physicians are reluctant to prescribe medical cannabis, even though it has been legal in Canada for a long time. One of the challenges will be having that attitude shift toward cannabis – that it may not be as harmful so it may be a good choice for individuals who are struggling with addiction. Some physicians feel like they don't know enough about cannabis to prescribe it or are worried that they may be replacing one addiction with another.

Philippe Lucas
I think a primary structural barrier right now is cost. We are not reaping the potential benefits of substitution effects, certainly when it comes to opioids, because over 90 percent of patients in Canada are still paying out of pocket for cannabis, but in a lot of cases, they are not having to pay for prescription opioids or benzodiazepines. It disincentivizes the use of cannabis, a safer alternative, and emphasizes the use of potentially more dangerous prescription drugs. One of the barriers to maximizing the benefits of substitution is the fact that we are not covering the cost of medical cannabis, but we are covering the cost of other potentially more dangerous substances.

The second barrier would be raising awareness and education around the therapeutic potential of cannabis. If we had more physicians learning about the endocannabinoid system, cannabinoid therapeutic use, and potential therapeutic effects of THC, CBD, and other cannabinoids in medical school, they would have a better understanding. There is an educational component that needs to happen both in the medical school system and through continuing medical education so physicians are aware of the endocannabinoid system, the substitution effect, and the evidence supporting it, and certainly that they are aware that substances like opioids and benzodiazepines are all too often dependence forming in the patient.

M.-J. Milloy
If we're talking about substituting for alcohol, then the primary challenge is probably social. It's easy to socialize with alcohol. That's what we've been socialized to do. Certainly, it's still more easy to socialize with alcohol than

cannabis. So it would be nice if the government took seriously the idea that there might be benefits to promoting cannabis use and in fact allow there to be spaces where people could socialize and use cannabis. It's crazy to me that we have legalized cannabis and yet, if you live in an apartment, there's almost no legal place to use cannabis. You can't use it in your apartment, in the park, in view of a child. So that, I think, is probably the number one sort of social structural barrier, is just the socialization, the fact that the structures around legalization have not permitted those social changes.

I think the barrier for the substitution for opioids is structural in that there's, obviously, a thriving cannabis market in the DTES, but it is in danger because the governments have said that they want to wipe out the illicit cannabis trade, and they have yet to provide any meaningful replacement. If you are the typical person living in the DTES, you're getting cannabis from one or two low-barrier illicit dispensaries, which the city, the police, the province, and federal government have all committed to close. There is not a legal dispensary in the DTES – the City of Vancouver had a bylaw saying that legal cannabis cannot be sold in the DTES – so what are people who use cannabis therapeutically going to do? They're not the kind of people who have credit cards to go online and buy that way. Many of them don't have addresses to receive cannabis through the mail.

Adolfo Gonzalez
The number one block to access has never been laws in this country; the number one block to medicine is price. As long as we can have a wide set of products and a decent price then legalization will be a great thing for opiate harm reduction, but legalization may not actually help us because we have to pay more for a medicine, and we're already people that are at risk. Most of us don't have a lot of money to spend, and Health Canada doesn't want to pay for my medicine. This is a plant that grows in the ground. I've been growing cannabis since 2001; I know the price point for production, if you do it the right way, and it breaks my heart knowing that people are dying unnecessarily.

The Impact of Cannabis Legalization
Canada was among the first nations to develop a federal program for providing medical cannabis to patients and was among the first to legalize adult cannabis use (Lucas 2008). The interviewees were enthusiastic regarding the potential for Canada to be an international leader in research and the application of substitution programs but also noted the need for greater

integration with national, provincial, and local health care systems and a focus on reducing barriers to access. The call for barrier reduction is particularly important among marginalized populations of substance users, whose experience of obstacles to substitution may be maintained or even exacerbated under legalization.

Sarah Blyth
We should be making it easy to access with simple regulation. There are still too many laws and bylaws in place that may make it confusing for people. We need easy access in places where people are using other drugs. In Vancouver, they've basically said that you can't have a dispensary in the DTES, which is stupid because people are going to get drugs down here, so why not make sure that you have access to ones that are less risky and perhaps even helpful.

Canadians have the opportunity to be on the leading edge of helping people by moving beyond the traditional opiate-based approaches. We have the opportunity to be a leader in the way that we see cannabis medically and, through this, help change the trajectory of the opiate crisis. Since cannabis is now legal, we can choose to be real leaders in how we act during this crisis, or we can be conservative about it and just hand it over to big companies to benefit. Let's show people how it can be used in a medical and therapeutic context as opposed to harder chemicals, and make sure people who use drugs and people who use cannabis are a part of the conversation.

M.-J. Milloy
Many of us are hopeful that legalization could make a dent in the overdose crisis. I think it's unfortunate that the government's implementation so far has not delivered low-barrier, legal cannabis to the people who probably need it most, which would be people at risk of opioid overdose – people who do not have a safe or regulated supply of cannabis for various reasons, whether it's not having a credit card or not being able to go online and put an order through the BC Cannabis Store.

The government has emphasized quite strongly a very slow and very conservative approach to legalization in order to put in place structures to minimize possible harms. I hope that the government not only seeks to minimize the harms of cannabis but also to try and maximize the benefits of cannabis for the health and well-being of Canadians. I think alcohol use and cannabis substitution would be a great place to start. In university communities, binge drinking takes a toll; one might hope that, eventually, we will see student unions stop selling booze and start selling cannabis. I think this is, hopefully, an example of what we'll see in the coming years as legal cannabis is normalized and we take a more clear-eyed look at the role different substances play in our health and well-being.

Philippe Lucas
Having a federal medical cannabis program puts Canada in a unique position to develop a deliberate cannabis substitution strategy here by reaching out to the eighteen thousand physicians prescribing cannabis and making them aware that it might be potentially safer than opioids or benzodiazepines. I think that the benefit of the Canadian system is that it's federally recognized and authorized, unlike the US system. This gives us an opportunity to do some serious research around substitution effects and to put in place federally supported strategies that may reduce our dependence on opioids in the treatment of pain and other conditions. The next step is going to be pharmacy-based access, because although we have tracking programs to see how patients are using pharmaceuticals in a number of provinces, cannabis is still not included in that data tracking. That would really give a lot of great information from a public health point of view and could inform both private-payer and public-payer coverage of cannabis. For example, if we compare a pain patient who uses cannabis to a similar pain patient who doesn't use cannabis on health and financial variables – including things like ER visits, doctor visits, and use of opioids – and find less financial and health impact for the patient using cannabis, then that would argue for provinces to cover the cost of medical cannabis in order to have cost savings at the provincial level in health care delivery.

With legalization, there is an opportunity in light of the opioid overdose crisis. We just need better training for doctors to specifically look to use cannabis as a tapering program. When it comes to recreational use, wherever we see cannabis access legalized and regulated, we've seen an impact on both alcohol use overall and more specifically the harm associated with alcohol use. In US states, they have seen reductions in alcohol-related automobile fatalities, in violent crime, in homicides, and with all of these academic papers, researchers are attributing that to cannabis legalization for medical or recreational use. We see alcohol use related to suicides, homicides, violent crime, and domestic violence. There are certainly suggestions that if you can shift even a small percentage of the population on any given day or night using alcohol to using cannabis, at the population level you see net public health benefits, because by reducing the use of alcohol, you'll effectively reduce all of the other alcohol-related harms that were just named.

Kim Crosby

As one of the first countries to legalize recreational cannabis in the world, Canada is a trailblazer in this area. I think we can model for other nations what legalization looks like – a pathway to legalization – and I'm hoping that we can eventually present real concrete data that demonstrates that the harms of addiction, opioid and alcohol use, and abuse is lessened by legalization. I think it will have a big impact on recreational substances, whether that is alcohol or drugs like heroin or other opioids. Legalization can make cannabis more available and accessible for individuals, so they may be more likely to try it as a potential substitute. It also reduces the stigma of cannabis; we have all different demographics and different ages, different income levels of people using cannabis.

I think physicians need to be directed to this area, that this is now a part of the medical system, and it needs to be taken seriously as an opiate alternative. There is a lot of hesitation to use it as a substitute for prescription medication, but I think more knowledge needs to be given to doctors about how it can be an alternative. Even if it causes some anxiety in some people, it's worth the risk to figure that out before giving them something that could cause long-term addiction that can be life-crippling. It may not be a perfect fit for everyone, but it's worth looking into, especially with CBD for pain and anxiety.

Kim Crosby

The Canadian context provides opportunity to lead the way in research, understanding, and acceptance. Canada is very cannabis tolerant, and that is definitely not the case in other places. The other context is that there are still real barriers to access in terms of affordability and cost coverage. Increased funding for research is going to have a huge influence on acceptability of cannabis use by the medical profession and knowledge on how to use cannabis and awareness for people to be using cannabis instrumentally.

Next Steps

Cannabis is a complex medicine with an array of treatment outcomes. Similarly, problematic use of opioids and other substances manifests in multiple ways and can be attributable to distinct combinations of social, psychological, developmental, and environmental risk factors. Determining what works best for whom will be essential for maximizing the potential of cannabis as a substitute.

Potential mechanisms suggested by interviewees included replacing one analgesic for another and the reduction of cravings associated with the more subtle effects of CBD. Substitution for tobacco and alcohol was identified as a promising area for future research, and interviewees agreed that moving beyond cross-sectional surveys to more carefully controlled trials of purposeful substitution was needed to enhance understanding of these issues. Interviewees also highlighted the importance of education for reducing the stigma still experienced by users and facilitating the adoption and further evaluation of cannabis substitution as a form of harm reduction.

Sarah Blyth
Cannabis can be helpful to people who are getting off opiates by helping with some of the symptoms of withdrawal, or working in combination with methadone or suboxone, or reducing pain and anxiety. It's not the end all be all, but it can be a supportive tool when people are trying to get off other substances. We can see that on the front lines, and over time we will have more data and research supporting its effectiveness. When people are in recovery, sometimes they are so sick they just can't handle it, and then they give up. Cannabis can address some of the symptoms of withdrawal. It's a healthier option and not a hard thing to quit. It could be an alternative in recovery to using opiates for pain, mental health, and stress. Easy access is a big thing – making sure people have easy, affordable access on the front lines to cannabis – because it's easier to get five dollars' worth of fentanyl.

Hopefully, health care providers will start prescribing cannabis instead of opiates to begin with, especially CBD. I really hope that the medical community embraces it as an option that is going to be less harmful – I mean at least for people to try or as an alternative for people who have an addiction, even in recovery centres – as a way to get off harder drugs. A lot of people use drugs because they are dealing with other issues, and those issues don't necessarily go away when you quit drugs. It can help in hospitals. Trying cannabis could be helpful even for seniors seeking pain relief. We could use it to help people with terminal illnesses like cancer and HIV. It helps with the pain, anxiety, trauma. You don't want to take more opiates if you don't have to because they are addictive; for most people, the amount you need goes up until you're balancing on lethal doses. Supplementing opiates with cannabis and CBD can lower the dose of opiates, especially when using cannabis edibles because of the way they are digested, how long their effects last, and the way they help the pain.

Philippe Lucas
We need to be able to have a better understanding of exactly how to maximize the potential benefits of substitution effect, and that can only be done through randomized clinical trial studies. I am happy to see that those are starting to move forward, and I think that 2019 will be a year when we start to see announcements of actual clinical trials focused on substitution effect. The patients certainly need more information but, more importantly, the physicians need to be involved in a deliberate strategic way to reduce opioid use. I would like to see a very deliberate public health strategy that would educate physicians about the potential benefits of cannabis in the treatment of a pain and other conditions and then highlight the opportunity where physicians can work with patients on opioid tapering strategies, some of which may involve cannabis as an alternative to opioids.

We need many novel interventions to impact the overdose crisis, and it's not going to be a one-size-fits-all solution. One of the interventions we should be doing is a deliberate substitution strategy. Treatment guidelines for pain indicate that cannabinoids are a third-line treatment option, after over-the-counter medications and then opioids. In light of everything that we know about the potential harms associated with opioid use and overuse and the relative safety of cannabis and cannabinoids, we need to modernize these treatment guidelines and make cannabis and cannabinoids a second-line treatment option.

M.-J. Milloy
It is clear from our research that there are at least some people at risk of overdose who are using cannabis instead and lowering their risk of overdose. If people are using cannabis, they are approximately 50 percent less likely to suffer a nonfatal overdose. That is after you adjust those models for all of the typical risk factors for overdose, including injecting heroin every day, injecting prescription opioids every day, being incarcerated, being homeless, and being younger. Even if you hold those risk factors, using cannabis daily is associated with lower risk of overdose. I think that it's fair to say scientifically – there is probably something there. The challenge is going to be figuring out how to exploit that to save the lives of people who are using drugs.

I also hope people don't jump to equate cannabis substitution only with the overdose crisis. We also have to be aware that one of the biggest substances that contributes to the largest role of morbidity and mortality in our society remains alcohol. In terms of health care costs, policing costs, cost of social assistance, cost of interpersonal violence, and premature death, I mean it is a poison and, unfortunately, in our society, we've largely lost sight of that fact. If we are going to move the needle on alcohol-related harms in our society, it's not going to be by getting people to stop drinking; rather, it's going to be by getting people to use other substances that are less dangerous to themselves and others. I'm hopeful that we see not only evidence of substitution for alcohol but also that the government begins to take this seriously and begins to promote cannabis as a safer, less toxic, less troubling alternative than alcohol.

We're only limited by the creativity of people who use cannabis. The medical cannabis movement and the movement of people who use cannabis has taught science a tremendous amount about the possible benefits of cannabis. I think we have to continue to listen to those people to figure out possible beneficial interventions for cannabis.

The interviews present the perspective of care providers working on the front lines of the opioid-poisoning epidemic, researchers working to determine for whom and when cannabis may be an effective substitute, and participants in the early moments of the current wave of interest in substitution. Despite their diverse backgrounds and experiences, consistent themes emerged. Several contributors highlighted that therapeutic applications of cannabis have been driven by patients and emphasized the critical role of patients in inspiring and contributing to research on cannabis substitution.

Rather than moving from the lab to the community, cannabis substitution emerged from observations of care providers, often operating outside the formal health care system, to become a subject of more formal scientific inquiry. There was consistent emphasis among the interviewees on the importance of rigorous evaluation of substitution effects, including clinical trials, cohort studies, and experimental examination of underlying mechanisms.

The interviewees were largely optimistic about the prospects for the legalization of adult cannabis use in Canada to facilitate research and uptake. But they also expressed concern that ongoing barriers to access such as stigma and lack of physician education might reduce the potential health benefits of substituting cannabis for alcohol and opioids. Affordability was also identified as a prominent barrier to substitution, which should be fully covered by the health care system considering the appreciable cost benefits to be realized by improving access to treatment for addiction. Cannabis lacks comparable levels of health care reimbursement available to many pharmaceuticals, and taxes imposed since the legalization of cannabis may make it even less affordable for those with few resources.

The perspectives of the interviewees have been influenced by contextual factors, including a shared history and location within British Columbia. Moreover, several interviewees collaborated with us on issues related to medical cannabis research and access. Their perspectives may not capture the experiences of those working on issues related to cannabis substitution in other parts of Canada and may, in fact, reflect a rather distinct perspective.

The aim here is not to generalize beyond this small sample but rather to document the insights of those who have first-hand experience of the transformation of research on cannabis substitution from anecdote to formal study. Indeed, although a growing evidence base supports the potential of cannabis substitution, the formal results are often mixed, and there is no clear expert consensus regarding the validity of this form of treatment (Humphreys and Saitz 2019).

Since 2000, Canada has seen the convergence of increasing interest in the therapeutic uses of cannabis followed by the emergence of a spiralling opioid-overdose crisis. These distinct developments have intersected as diverse stakeholders – including patients, front-line health care providers, and community-based and academic researchers – have noted the potential for cannabis to help address the overdose crisis by serving as a substitute for opioids. Based on interviews with key informants with related expertise and research in this area, this chapter traced the development of cannabis substitution in Canada in the context of the opioid overdose epidemic and other widely used substances, most notably alcohol. Growing recognition of the therapeutic potential of cannabis substitution emerged from anecdotal patient reports and observations of front-line workers. More recently, the potential of this form of treatment has become a topic of broader scientific interest as clinicians and investigators have struggled to find new approaches to address a growing health care crisis. The liberalization of cannabis regulations affords new opportunities to facilitate research and for the uptake of cannabis substitution. Barriers remain such as affordability, stigma against people who use drugs, and reluctance by physicians. Thus, needed access to this option remains limited, particularly among marginalized people who use drugs – those most often at high risk of opioid poisoning and among those most likely to benefit from substitution.

Appendix: Contributors

Sarah Blyth is the president of the High Hopes Foundation, which offers affordable and sometimes free access to cannabis products as an alternative to opioids. She is a founding member of the Overdose Prevention Society, which began in 2016 by establishing pop-up overdose prevention sites in Vancouver's Downtown Eastside. This initiative served as a model and inspiration for the establishment of similar sites across Canada. She is also the former chair of the Vancouver Park Board Commission.

Rielle Capler is a postdoctoral fellow at the British Columbia Centre on Substance Use (BCCSU). After receiving a master's degree in health administration, Rielle worked with Canada's first medical cannabis dispensary from 1999 to 2007 to provide cannabis to Canadians in medical need. As a cofounder of the Association of Canadian Cannabis Retailers (formerly CAMCD), she has engaged with dispensaries, patients, government regulators, and other stakeholders to develop national standards and a certification program for dispensaries. She has published and presented widely on topics related to cannabis policy and access and received the Queen Elizabeth II Diamond Jubilee Medal in 2013 for her work in this field.

Kim Crosby is currently working as a psychologist in Alberta in psychosocial oncology. She began her cannabis research as an undergraduate research assistant on studies of medical cannabis access and the development of a regulatory framework for cannabis dispensaries. She was a research coordinator for Canada's first clinical trial of cannabis for a mental health condition. Her SSHRC-funded master's thesis work at the University of British Columbia focused on the interaction between and influence of alcohol and cannabis on domestic violence; her dissertation work examines how price and availability influence decisions related to cannabis substitution. At the time of the interview, Kim Crosby was a PhD candidate in clinical psychology at the University of British Columbia.

Adolfo Gonzalez is a medical cannabis educator and cofounder of CannaReps, an interactive training program for cannabis providers based in Vancouver, British Columbia. He experienced cannabis substitution after becoming dependent on prescribed opioids to treat pain after an injury. This experience, along with the experience of working with medical cannabis patients in similar circumstances, led him to design and manage Canada's first cannabis-based opioid-substitution project. The pilot project provided standardized cannabis capsules to individuals who were on long-term methadone to reduce reliance on opioids.

Philippe Lucas is president of Sabi Mind, a clinic group focused on increasing access to psychedelic-assisted therapy in the treatment of mental health and pain. Philippe is an experienced researcher examining the therapeutic potential of plant medicines in the treatment of pain, trauma and addiction, and was founder and executive director of the Vancouver Island Compassion Society, one of Canada's first medical cannabis dispensaries, and a founding board member of the Multidisciplinary Association of Psychedelic Studies Canada. More recently, Philippe worked as vice-president, global patient research and access at Tilray, where he oversaw a comprehensive international clinical and observational cannabis research program, and he is also acting-CEO of Compassionate Analytics, which produces on-site analytical tools for the cannabis industry. He has provided expert testimony to the BC Supreme Court and has been invited to present his research before the Canadian House of Commons and Senate on a number of occasions, as well as to federal governments and regulatory bodies around the globe. Philippe has received a number of accolades for his work and research, including the Americans for Safe Access Researcher of the Year Award 2021, the Cannabis Council of Canada Lifetime Achievement Award, and the Queen Elizabeth II Diamond Jubilee Medal. At the time of the interview, Philippe Lucas was a PhD candidate at the University of Victoria.

M.-J. Milloy is an epidemiologist and research scientist at the British Columbia Centre on Substance Use (BCCSU), where he leads research that evaluates the use of cannabis by people living with substance-use disorders. He has worked extensively with populations at risk of opioid overdose, including work on the impact of Insite, North America's first legal, medically supervised injection facility, and has led seminal research on cannabis use and HIV outcomes. M.-J. is the first Canopy Growth Professor of Cannabis Science at the University of British Columbia, where he is leading trials to explore diverse aspects of cannabis substitution and the role of cannabis use on compliance with treatments for opioid use disorder.

Works Cited

Anderson, D. Mark, Benjamin Hansen, and Daniel I. Rees. 2013. "Medical Marijuana Laws, Traffic Fatalities, and Alcohol Consumption." *Journal of Law and Economics* 56 (2): 333–69.

Bachhuber, Marcus A., Brendan Saloner, Chinazo O. Cunningham, and Colleen L. Barry. 2014. "Medical Cannabis Laws and Opioid Analgesic Overdose Mortality in the United States, 1999–2010." *JAMA Internal Medicine* 174 (10): 1668–73.

Balneaves, Lynda G., Albeer Alraja, Daniel Ziemianski, Fairleth McCuaig, and Mark Ware. 2018. "National Needs Assessment of Canadian Nurse Practitioners Regarding Cannabis for Therapeutic Purposes." *Cannabis and Cannabinoid Research* 3 (1): 66–73.

Belle-Isle, Lynne, Zach Walsh, Robert Callaway, Philippe Lucas, Rielle Capler, Robert Kay, and Susan Holtzman. 2014. "Barriers to Access for Canadians Who Use Cannabis for Therapeutic Purposes." *International Journal of Drug Policy* 25 (4): 691–99.

Bradford, Ashley C., and W. David Bradford. 2017. "Medical Marijuana Laws May Be Associated with a Decline in the Number of Prescriptions for Medicaid Enrollees." *Health Affairs* 36 (5): 945–51.

Fitzcharles, Mary-Ann, Peter A. Ste-Marie, Daniel J. Clauw, Shahin Jamal, Jacob Karsh, Sharon LeClercq, Jason J. McDougall, Yoram Shir, Kam Shojania, and

Zach Walsh. 2014. "Rheumatologists Lack Confidence in Their Knowledge of Cannabinoids Pertaining to the Management of Rheumatic Complaints." *BMC Musculoskeletal Disorders* 15 (228): 258–63.

Humphreys, Keith, and Richard Saitz. 2019. "Should Physicians Recommend Replacing Opioids with Cannabis?" *Journal of the American Medical Association* 7 (7): 639–40.

Lee, Martin A. 2012. *Smoke Signals: A Social History of Marijuana – Medical, Recreational, and Scientific.* New York: Scribner.

Lucas, Philippe. 2008. "Regulating Compassion: An Overview of Canada's Federal Medical Cannabis Policy and Practice." *Harm Reduction Journal* 5 (5). https://doi.org/10.1186/1477-7517-5-5.

—. 2009. "Moral Regulation and the Presumption of Guilt in Health Canada's Medical Cannabis Policy and Practice." *International Journal of Drug Policy* 20 (4): 296–303.

Lucas, Philippe, Zach Walsh, Kim Crosby, Robert Callaway, Lynne Belle-Isle, Robert Kay, Rielle Capler, and Susan Holtzman. 2016. "Substituting Cannabis for Prescription Drugs, Alcohol and Other Substances among Medical Cannabis Patients: The Impact of Contextual Factors." *Drug and Alcohol Review* 35 (3): 326–33.

Mattison, J. 1891. "The Treatment of the Morphine-Disease." *Indian Medical Gazette* 26 (3): 65–68.

Mikuriya, Tod H. 1970. "Cannabis Substitution: An Adjunctive Therapeutic Tool in the Treatment of Alcoholism." *Medical Times* 98 (4): 187–91.

—. 2003. "Cannabis as a Substitute for Alcohol: A Harm Reduction Approach." *Journal of Cancer Therapy* 4 (1): 79–93.

Model, Karyn E. 1993. "The Effect of Marijuana Decriminalization on Hospital Emergency Drug Episodes: 1975–1978." *Journal of the American Statistical Association* 88 (423): 737–47.

R v Parker, 2000 CanLII 5762 (ON CA). https://canlii.ca/t/1fb95.

Reiman, Amanda, Mark Welty, and Perry Solomon. 2017. "Cannabis as a Substitute for Opioid-Based Pain Medication: Patient Self-Report." *Cannabis and Cannabinoid Research* 2 (1): 160–66.

Santaella-Tenorio, Julian, Christine M. Mauro, Melanie M. Wall, June H. Kim, Magdelana Cerdá, Katherine M. Keyes, Deborah S. Hasin, Sandro Galea, and Silvia S. Martins. 2017. "US Traffic Fatalities, 1985–2014, and Their Relationship to Medical Marijuana Laws." *American Journal of Public Health* 107 (2): 336–42.

Ziemianski, Daniel, Rielle Capler, Rory Tekanoff, Anaïs Lacasse, Francesca Luconi, and Mark A. Ware. 2015. "Cannabis in Medicine: A National Educational Needs Assessment among Canadian Physicians." *BMC Medical Education* 15 (1): 52. https://doi.org/10.1186/s12909-015-0335-0.

7
Cannabis and Mental Health
A Sociological Perspective
ANDREW D. HATHAWAY

The research literature on mental health and substance use is highly biased in its emphasis on the symptoms of disorder. Positive experiences are neglected due to an orientation toward treating mental illness and addiction as comorbid pathological conditions. A balanced view of substance use and mental health requires a more nuanced understanding of drug users' motivations for self-medicating or using drugs for recreation, including positive experiences that contribute to well-being. This chapter overviews the literature on cannabis and mental health, which employs a variety of social scientific methods, to provide a better understanding of the established positive and negative effects of cannabis use from the perspective of the user.

What Information Is Out There?
There is a vast array of information "out there" for Canadians concerned about cannabis use and mental health. Those curious enough to do a Google search will find a wealth of credible, authoritative information about the drug's short-term and long-term effects. At the time of writing, in 2021, the official source of information was the government (the Health Canada website topped the list of first-page hits).

Every time you use cannabis, the Google searcher is advised, it can have the following short-term effects:

- impair your ability to drive safely or operate equipment
- make it harder to learn and remember things
- affect mood and feelings
- affect mental health.

The effects on mental health, as well as mood and feelings, are as adverse and unwanted as the other two effects. The website visitor is informed that cannabis use can cause anxiety or panic and that it can also "trigger a psychotic episode (not knowing what is real, experiencing paranoia, having disorganized thoughts, and in some cases having hallucinations)" (Health Canada n.d.).

The long-term effects of using cannabis regularly (defined as daily or almost daily over several months or years) are that it can

- hurt the lungs and make it harder to breathe
- affect mental health
- make you physically dependent or addicted.

According to the sources cited on the website, about 9 percent of users will become addicted, and the addiction rate is higher among adolescent users. Up to half of users who smoke daily are addicted. Regular continuous users of cannabis are also "more likely to experience anxiety, depression, psychosis, and schizophrenia." Using higher-strength varieties can worsen the mental health effects. But the adverse effects can be improved by stopping or reducing use.

Among the first-page Google hits are official websites resembling Health Canada's based in the United States, the United Kingdom, and Australia. The US National Institute of Health (n.d.) website posts a link to the 2002 clinical research edition of the *British Medical Journal* (*BMJ*). That edition of the *BMJ* includes an article titled "Cannabis and Mental Health: More Evidence Establishes Clear Link between Use of Cannabis and Psychiatric Illness" (Rey and Tennant 2002) and another from Australia. The second article reports: "Frequent cannabis use in teenage girls predicts later depression and anxiety, with daily users carrying the highest risk." The authors conclude: "Given recent increasing levels of cannabis use, measures to reduce frequent and heavy recreational use seem warranted" (Patton et al. 2002, 1195).

Another US website, run by Mental Health America (MHA; n.d.), is among the listed first-page hits. Founded in 1909, MHA is touted as "the nation's leading community-based non-profit dedicated to addressing the needs of those living with mental illness and to promoting the overall mental health of all Americans." On the MHA website is an article titled "Risky Business: Marijuana Use," which has a wealth of information and resources to address the rising tide of problematic use.

"Risky Business" overviews the evidence, gives answers, and provides suggestions under the following headings:

- Availability is increasing. Attitudes are changing.
- Marijuana is widely used.
- Marijuana use is higher among people with mental illnesses.
- When does marijuana use become a problem?
- Can marijuana cause mental illnesses?
- Can marijuana treat mental illnesses?
- Take control of marijuana use.

"Marijuana use becomes a problem," it is noted, "when it interferes with a person's ability to function in their personal and/or professional lives" (Mental Health America n.d.). The DSM-5 criteria for marijuana use disorder (MUD) are provided.[1] Being diagnosed with MUD requires the user to respond yes to two or more of the following questions over the past year:

- Used marijuana in large amounts for longer than intended?
- Wanted to stop using marijuana, but weren't successful in attempts to quit?
- Spent a great deal of time getting, using, or recovering from marijuana?
- Had strong cravings or urges to use?
- Failed to perform work, school, or home duties because of marijuana?
- Continued use despite it causing problems with relationships?
- Stopped participating in activities you used to enjoy because of marijuana use?
- Used marijuana in physically dangerous situations (driving, etc.)?
- Continued using marijuana despite physical or mental health problems that it has caused or made worse?
- Developed a tolerance to marijuana (needed more to get the desired effect)?
- Felt withdrawal symptoms when you stopped using marijuana, possibly using again to relieve your discomfort? (Mental Health America n.d.)

In addition to a list of symptoms, website visitors are provided with an overview of current research evidence in answer to frequently asked questions.

In response to the question "Can Cannabis Cause Mental Illnesses?," the website contends that although more research is still needed, marijuana use may increase the risk of developing psychosis and worsen symptoms in people who already have psychosis. It is also putatively established that marijuana use during adolescence can have lasting effects on the brain (including trouble thinking and remembering), and it can cause symptoms of mental health problems such as psychosis, anxiety, depression, and sleep disorders. It is further noted that adults with MUD have high rates of mental health disorders, including anxiety, depression, PTSD, and ADHD. However, it is hard to know whether MUD appeared before or after the mental health disorder, because many people use drugs to self-medicate.

In response to the question "Can Cannabis Treat Mental Illnesses?," Mental Health America contends that much of the research on medical uses is based on anecdotal evidence or experiments with rats. In some US states, however, it is noted that physicians may be able to prescribe marijuana for mental health problems, at their discretion, if traditional methods of treatment have not been successful.

Users are advised to *take control of marijuana use* by keeping track, taking a break, and identifying triggers. Do not mix marijuana with alcohol or other drugs or use it before activities such as work and school. And get immediate help if you are unable to control your use.

Readers who need help for marijuana use–related problems are invited to complete an online screening test and "Use the results to start a conversation with your health care provider." Or "You can find treatment providers ... using the online SAMHSA [Substance Abuse and Mental Health Services Administration] Treatment Locator" (Mental Health America n.d.). In sum, the MHA provides a comprehensive range of evidence, information, and advice for problem users. None of the information given, like other leading online sources, is concerned with the reasons users give for using marijuana.

The website run by the UK's Royal College of Psychiatrists (RCP) (n.d.) features an article titled "Cannabis and Mental Health: For Young People." The tone is more foreboding yet familiar. The RCP observes (in answer to the question, How does cannabis affect mental health?):

- Using cannabis triggers mental health problems in people who seemed to be well before, or it can worsen any mental health problems you already have.

- Research has shown that people who are already at risk of developing mental health problems are more likely to start showing symptoms of mental illness if they use cannabis regularly. For example if someone in your family has depression or schizophrenia, you are at higher risk of getting these illness when you use cannabis.
- The younger you are when you start using it, the more you may be at risk. This is because your brain is still developing and can be more easily damaged by the active chemicals in cannabis.
- If you stop using cannabis once you have started to show symptoms of mental illness, such as depression, paranoia or hearing voices, these symptoms may go away. However, not everyone will get better just by stopping smoking.
- If you go on using cannabis, the symptoms can get worse. It can also make any treatment that your doctor might prescribe for you, work less well. Your illness may come back more quickly, and more often if you continue to use cannabis once you get well again.
- Some people with mental health problems find that using cannabis makes them feel a bit better for a while. Unfortunately this does not last, and it does nothing to treat the illness. In fact, it may delay you from getting help you need and the illness may get worse in the longer term. (Royal College of Psychiatrists n.d.)

In contrast with the more cautious anticannabis perspective put forward by the RCP, the Google search turned up only one first-page hit providing information that offers a more balanced point of view. In Australia, the National Drug and Alcohol Research Centre's website hosts an article written by Peter Gates (n.d.) for a general audience that asks: "Does cannabis cause mental illness?" The posted commentary explicitly acknowledges the motivations and experiences of people who use cannabis to enjoy the drug's euphoric and relaxing effects. While it is often used to relieve anxiety or stress, it is also recognized that using cannabis can cause some users to feel anxious.

Despite the common finding of a significant relationship between the use of cannabis and depression and anxiety, the association, it is noted, "is complex and involves the individual's reasons for cannabis use and external situations. That is, cannabis may be used to help cope with social problems that were not necessarily caused by cannabis use" (Gates n.d.).

And despite the well-established relationship between cannabis use and developing symptoms of psychosis, this risk is put in context by the author.

Gates (n.d.) observes that "the proportions of individuals with psychosis among the population and among cannabis users are low. Current estimates suggest that if frequent long-term cannabis use was known to cause psychosis, the rates of incidence would increase from seven in 1,000 in non-users to 14 in 1,000 cannabis users."

To summarize, a Google search using the term "cannabis use and mental health" resulted in first-page hits that (not unsurprisingly, perhaps) predominantly concerned the adverse effects of use. Most notably, this emphasis on cannabis use and mental illness, while neglecting the benefits of use for *mental health*, is also found in scientific research. To examine the extent of this bias, I consulted another common search engine available to non-experts, Google Scholar.

Cannabis Pathologies

When cannabis consumption is pathologized, it is characterized as a symptom of a medical or psychological disorder. This association treats non-medical drug use as a comorbidity that occurs along with other mental health disorders such as anxiety, depression, and other pathological conditions requiring treatment.

A Google Scholar search employing the same search term, "cannabis use and mental health," returned a wealth of studies about the adverse effects of use. That focus notwithstanding, many of them cautioned against an overly malignant view of the effects of cannabis. The following assessment by Wayne Hall and Nadia Solowij (1997, 107) seems equally applicable and pertinent today:

> The mental health consequences of the daily or near-daily use of cannabis over years and decades remain uncertain, and are likely to remain so for some time given the difficulties involved in investigating them. Nevertheless, there is sufficient evidence that its effects are neither as benign as proponents of its legalisation often argue, nor as malign as some partisans of continued prohibition claim.

A more recent review of the research literature reported "an increased risk of any psychotic outcome in individuals who had ever used cannabis ... with greatest risk in people who used cannabis most frequently" (Moore et al. 2007, 319). The authors conclude that, despite continuing uncertainty about whether cannabis causes psychosis, there is "sufficient evidence to warn young people that using cannabis could increase their risk of developing a psychotic illness later in life" (Moore et al. 2007, 319). A later study looking at the prevalence of cannabis use and cannabis use disorders among individuals with mental illness found "further evidence of the strong association between cannabis use and a broad range of primary mental illness" (Lev-Ran et al. 2013, 589).

Far more equivocal assessments of the scientific evidence are found in other studies, using other research methods, of the relationship between cannabis use and mental health. Louisa Degenhardt, Wayne Hall, and Michael Lynskey (2003) reviewed studies examining the relationship between cannabis use and depression, finding little evidence of an association between depression and infrequent cannabis use. The research literature reviewed indicated a modest relationship between heavy cannabis use and depression, and between early-onset, regular cannabis use and developing depression later. However, these studies were unable to rule out the role of social, family, and contextual factors that increase the risks of both heavy cannabis use and depression. Thus, they conclude that "cannabis use makes, at most, a modest contribution to the population prevalence of depression" (Degenhardt, Hall, and Lynskey 2003, 1493).

A cohort study of adolescents in Australia also found that there was a relationship between the early onset of cannabis use and mental health disorders in young adulthood. Weekly or more frequent use in teenagers predicted a twofold increase in risk for later depression and anxiety. Frequent cannabis use among young women, more alarmingly, was found to predict later depression and anxiety, with daily users at the highest risk (an over five-fold increase) (Patton et al. 2002).

Another study in Australia reported that "the primary causal direction leads from mental disorder to cannabis use among adolescents and the reverse in early adulthood" (McGee et al. 2000, 491). Smoking cigarettes and drinking alcohol were found to be independently associated with later mental health disorders. Both of the outcome variables (cannabis use and mental disorder) were also found to share "similar pathways of low socio-economic status and history of behavior problems in childhood, and low parental attachment in adolescence" (McGee et al. 2000, 491).

Other research that has longitudinally examined the relationship between cannabis use and mental illness reports similarly modest adverse outcomes and conclusions. A more recent study by Daniel Feingold and his colleagues (2016, 493) looking at relationships between cannabis use and anxiety disorders found no association, although it was observed that "individuals with baseline panic disorder were more prone to initiate cannabis use at follow-up ... possibly as a means of self-medication." They concluded that "cannabis use and CUDs [cannabis use disorders] are not associated with increased incidence of most anxiety disorders and inversely, most anxiety disorders are not associated with increased incidence of cannabis use or CUDs" (Feingold et al. 2016, 494).

Yet another study from Australia examined the relationship between cannabis use, depression, and anxiety among adults. It found that "cannabis use did not appear to be directly related to depression or anxiety when account was taken of other drug use." Of further note, however, the authors concluded that "the association between heavier involvement with cannabis use and affective and anxiety disorders has implications for the treatment of persons with problematic cannabis use" (Degenhardt, Hall, and Lynskey 2001, 219).

A recent study that examined the association between cannabis use and depressive disorders found that women who use regularly scored significantly lower than nonusers on mental health–related quality of life. No statistically significant group difference was found between female nonusers and occasional users, or between male nonusers, occasional users, and regular users (Aspis et al. 2015). Another study using the same measures to examine the relationship between cannabis use and anxiety disorders found that regular (but not occasional) use is associated with significantly lower scores on mental health–related quality of life (Lev-Ran et al. 2012).

In sum, a brief review conducted using Google Scholar on the relationship between cannabis use and mental health suggests that the research literature is predominantly focused on understanding the adverse effects of using cannabis. A more balanced and more nuanced understanding of the complex relationship between cannabis use and mental health requires more research on the benefits of use.

A More Nuanced Point of View

Comparatively little research has been devoted to better understanding the reported benefits of use. Cannabis is widely used for recreational enjoyment and to enhance a wide variety of experiences and activities. As compared to alcohol and other drugs, its low toxicity makes cannabis less hazardous and more functionally adaptive because the rewards outweigh the known risks. This subjective understanding of the costs and benefits to users is more difficult to calculate in medically objective terms than it is for alcohol and many other drugs.

Users' motivations vary widely, ranging from relaxation to enhancing recreational activities to coping with unwanted mental states. Cannabis use patterns and effects transcend the overly simplistic distinctions often made between nonmedical and medical consumption of the drug (Hathaway 2015). Regardless of the users' motives, informal norms support controlled use. Avoiding the development of cannabis use–related problems can be interpreted more broadly as establishing a pattern and level of consumption that is functionally adaptive (Müller and Schumann 2011).

Optimizing the experience of benefits involves a social-learning process in which users must discover how to isolate and exploit the useful properties of cannabis. Users as a group and as individuals must learn the circumstances, times, and places in which use is advantageous and when it may not be. Overly simplistic explanations using language and terms denoting drug dependence, escapism, or impairment neglect the instrumental role of cannabis for users. The controlled user's mental health is neither harmed nor is it helpful to claim that mental illness is a cause of using cannabis.

Functionally adaptive use is far from pathological. When cannabis is viewed as a multipurpose tool with a variety of benefits, users' motivations are more meaningful and nuanced. Concerns about the adverse effects of cannabis do not negate the many benefits and positive experiences for those who use it to achieve a change in mental state. An adaptive orientation to understanding drug use is informed by research and theory that recognizes the combined influence of culture, drug-use settings or environments, and how users' expectations shape experiences of use (Zinberg 1984).

A sociological perspective is developed here to provide a fuller and more balanced understanding of the relationship between cannabis use and mental health. This perspective deviates considerably from more prominent biomedical and psychological explanations, which contribute to the tendency to treat the use of drugs as a trivial indulgence or pathological condition. Such tendencies have fostered remarkable neglect of users' explanations of the benefits of use.

As with alcohol, the use of cannabis for coping can be maladaptive. Quite unlike alcohol, however, its use in moderation as a way to reduce stress has not been widely studied and is not well understood. Its reputation as an illegal drug has hampered scientific and public understanding of its sought-after effects.

People who use cannabis, much like people who use alcohol at moderate-use levels, report few negative effects (Hathaway, Kirst, and Erickson 2013).

Cannabis is also used as a social lubricant for relaxing and enhancing recreational activities. The use of drugs as tools for recreation is often trivialized. That interpretation fails to adequately capture their functionality and meaning as tools used to re-create.

In its subculture, the psychoactive properties of cannabis have long been celebrated as consciousness-expanding. Quite unlike alcohol, narcotics, or sedatives, cannabis use "increases awareness of surroundings and bodily processes" and "serves as a guide to psychic areas which can then be re-entered without it" (Solomon 1966, 443, 446). These reported benefits – but not reported problems – are often described as anecdotal and thus irrelevant to science.

Better understanding cannabis use and mental health requires knowledge of the social circumstances and expectations that determine culturally appropriate behaviour. The classic work of Becker (1963, 1967) explains the process by which users overcome societal controls that discourage substance use. Through participation in a deviant subculture, consisting of a peer group of more experienced users, novices gain access to cannabis in social settings conducive to developing a positive outlook.

The modern history of cannabis in the United States, for Becker (1967), demonstrated why sociologists steadfastly reject uni-causal explanations of complex social behaviour. For example, he observed that the reported incidence of cannabis psychosis paradoxically diminished by the 1950s, at a time when use rates were dramatically increasing. Explaining this phenomenon requires an understanding of the social bases of subjective drug experiences. The social history and cultural experience of drug use are no less central to explaining the subjective drug experience than human physiology and chemical effects.

The Western cultural understanding of marijuana use has long viewed it as an activity engaged in by the mentally disturbed. The link between marijuana and madness was fostered by depictions like the following offered by Canadian magistrate Emily Murphy,[2] who cited the police chief of Los Angeles:

> Persons using marijuana smoke the dried leaves of the plant, which has the effect of driving them completely insane. The addict loses all sense of moral responsibility. Addicts to this drug, while under its influence, are immune to pain, becoming raving maniacs, and are liable to kill or indulge in any form of violence to other persons. (Murphy 1922, 332–33)

Scientific understanding of marijuana's psychopharmacology and its potential link to madness dates to the work of Jacques Moreau (1845), who likened cannabis intoxication to mental processes and symptoms likely to occur in mental patients.

Seeking to gain insight into mental illness, Moreau invited students, friends, and acquaintances (including famous literary figures Charles Baudelaire, Victor Hugo, and Alexandre Dumas) to systematically ingest oral doses of hashish and document their observations. He noted eight symptoms commonly reported by mental patients and observed during hashish intoxication. In order of increasing mental disorganization, the reported symptoms are

- unexplainable feeling of bliss, happiness
- excitement; dissociation of ideas
- errors of time and space appreciation
- development of the sense of hearing; the influence of music
- fixed ideas (delusions)
- damage to the emotions
- irresistible impulses
- illusions; hallucinations. (see Nahas 1992, 345)

The artificial paradise that Baudelaire (c. 1860) described on consuming often massive doses of hashish is a kind of wondrous debauchery that produces an extension of the self and deeper feelings of benevolence. This god-like state, however, invoked a heavy payment in the form of lethargy and discomfort after intoxication ended and a surrender of the will due to intense habituation on failure to achieve the high without the use of drugs (Baudelaire 1971 [c. 1860]; see also Hathaway and Sharpley 2010). States of altered consciousness acquired by using drugs are thereby deemed practically and morally inferior to the more enduring states of mind achieved by mystics and poets through hard work and meditation.

The enduring bias that treats nonmedical drug use as a pathological condition or disorder is derived from the same worldview that deems altered states of consciousness as immoral and thus reasonably prohibited by law. Becker (1967) noted that drug users often take drugs to experience the very same effects that moral-legal-medical authorities consider signs or symptoms of a societal disorder, or the unwanted noxious side effects of taking drugs. Their motivations, expectations, and perceptions are precisely that taking drugs will produce a sought-after deviation from conventional accounts of subjective experience.

The effects of the same drug are different for different people and can vary for the user depending on the time and place. Several perceived effects of drug use have the potential to be singled out by users as desirable or pleasurable, as the reason for taking the drug. Subjective drug experience is partially contingent on users' understanding that a drug's effects are characteristic of their own experiences of use. The meaning of the act is not inherent to the object; rather, it arises in the course of interactions that collectively define the social meaning of the act.

In the scientific literature and media, psychosis is widely understood as an array of symptoms of mental disturbance, ranging from auditory and visual hallucinations to disorganized thinking to behaving in a socially inappropriate manner. Although drug-induced psychoses are relatively rare, symptoms of this nature are quite common for inexperienced users of a wide variety of drugs. Faced with evidence suggesting that one is "going crazy," the inexperienced user, Becker (1967) argues, may experience anxiety or panic, which explains the drug reaction rather than the properties of cannabis itself.

A drug experience is in part physiologically determined. The way that the experience is understood, however, originates in definitions of its meaning that derive from social interaction within drug-using groups. Competing definitions of unsettling mental states emerge through interaction with more experienced users, who offer reassurances based on their own experience that these effects are manageable and only temporary. Frightening experiences are redefined as pleasurable, as opposed to symptoms of mental instability. These shared understandings, acquired through social interaction, counter evidence suggesting that the user has gone crazy.

Over the last half century, as the use of marijuana has transitioned from the margins to the mainstream of society, cultural attitudes have changed (Hathaway 2015). Long before the drug was legalized, the social differences between users and nonusers were observed to have diminished to the point that many people were relatively open about using marijuana. The use of cannabis today reflects quite different expectations than those associated with a deviant subculture closely dependent on the peer group for ideological support.

Use in less clandestine social settings shapes use patterns, motives, and experiences by reflecting different lifestyles. More individual and personal patterns of consumption of cannabis diverge from those connected to the social norms and expectations of the group. Developing a better understanding of the benefits of cannabis consumption for contemporary users is essential to deriving theoretical explanations that reflect the changing social circumstances of drug use.

"Anecdotal Evidence" of Mental Health Effects

Taking the perceptions and experiences of cannabis users seriously means listening to what they have to say. Much so-called anecdotal evidence is, in fact, rigorously empirical because it comes up time and time again. The foregoing observations were a catalyst for the development of my research program over twenty years ago. The first of several studies used exploratory interviews. The insights gained from in-depth interviews informed the conduct and development of surveys more representative of users in the general population, including standard items about cannabis effects.

Asking people why they use and how they use revealed a variety of patterns and experiences with cannabis as a tool for leisure-time and work-related tasks. People also use it to transcend mundane reality in ways described as having benefits for mental health. The reputation of cannabis as a restorative relaxant is complemented by its somewhat paradoxical enhancement of recreational activities as a stimulant that heightens perceptions and awareness of one's immediate surroundings (Hathaway 1997). Its consciousness-expanding characteristics are described as a stimulation of the senses that is superior to alcohol, with fewer unwanted short-term and long-term side effects.

The effects of cannabis, as a relaxant and a stimulant, have reported benefits for work as well as leisure. Some users said using it for work-related tasks enhanced their performance of monotonous activities that required concentration and attention to detail. Gaining an alternative perspective, different outlook, or view of the big picture – elsewhere described as flow experience (Hathaway and Sharpley 2010) – is among the psychoactive properties users credit with improving their mental health.

Studies conducted with medical users have shown that cannabis as a treatment for depression and anxiety, and other chronic mental health conditions, is commonly reported. Such use is likely underestimated given that enhancing psychological well-being is among the therapeutic benefits of cannabis extolled by those who use it to manage pain and other health conditions (Hathaway and Rossiter 2007; Jones and Hathaway 2008). Since many also use for recreational enjoyment, the lines between its use for health and wellness are often blurry.

Used as a relaxant and a stimulant, for calming the body and mind, and for lifting the spirits, cannabis is valued for eliciting in users a sense of fascination with the world and their surroundings (Hathaway 2015). In addition to relief from an array of health conditions, medical consumers credit cannabis with fostering heightened energy, awareness, motivation, inspiration, and spiritual connections that contribute to well-being. Their perceptions and experiences of use for mental health deviate substantially from standard definitions of treatment observed in conventional medicine.

Studies of recreational cannabis consumers consistently report that the perceived benefits of use significantly exceed the reported negative effects. People seeking treatment for cannabis use–related problems report more negative use outcomes and fewer benefits (Hathaway, Macdonald, and Erickson 2008). Expected differences observed in the degree of problematic cannabis use behaviour between treatment and nontreatment groups are much larger for adverse effects, or symptoms of abuse, and least pronounced for symptoms of dependence. Symptoms such as craving and compulsive use, put otherwise, are less distinctive features of the treatment seeker's profile, as compared to users in the general population, than the greater incidence in treatment populations of self-reporting actual adverse effects of use.

As compared to other drugs more commonly acknowledged as presenting a substantial need for treatment, cannabis users in treatment score consistently lower on all measures of dependence and abuse (Hathaway et al. 2009). The less disruptive nature of cannabis use–related problems means that treatment seekers are often more ambivalent about their need for treatment, which is commonly coerced. Forcing users to submit to coerced treatment, noted Norman Zinberg (1984), perversely ties the therapeutic process to criminal justice and punitive responses in a way that bastardizes and denigrates the mental health system.

This hybridized approach to treating drug use–related problems has profound effects on how drug users view themselves and negatively affects their substance-use behaviour. The mental health of users is affected more adversely by punitive societal conditions and reactions than by the psychological effects of substance use. These observations call for the adoption and expansion of harm-reduction interventions and educational initiatives that acknowledge the benefits of moderate controlled use while addressing self-reported problematic use.

Across samples of experienced users at different levels of consumption, the most frequently reported motivations are relaxation and the enhancement of recreational activities, followed by coping with stress and anxiety. There is a clear association between motives and effects (Hathaway, Kirst, and Erickson 2013). Use for coping, versus relaxation and enjoyment, is related to experiencing more negative effects. There is no clear association between cannabis use problems and the amount or frequency of use (Hathaway 2003). However, fewer use-related problems over time are associated with the adoption of more moderate and stabilized patterns of use (Hathaway 2004).

A recent study of experiences and attitudes toward the use of cannabis among undergraduate students ($N = 1773$) included standard items assessing mental health. Multiple comparisons between groups were conducted to assess the mental health status of nonusers as compared to users, and among those reporting more or less recent cannabis use. Nearly half (47 percent) of students surveyed had used cannabis before, with 80 percent of lifetime users having used in the past year. About two-thirds (65 percent) of past-year users had used in the past month, 40 percent in the past week, and 8 percent daily (Hathaway et al. 2016, 2018).

Nonusers in the study were more often single and reported getting higher grades. Students who used cannabis reported having more close friends, and they were more likely than nonusers to report having very good or excellent social support. The past-year prevalence of use-related problems among users was 20 percent for problems in their family or relationships and 15 percent for work- or school-related problems. Twelve percent reported having health-related problems, and 8 percent had problems due to use in public places. Almost half (47 percent) of past-year users agreed with the statement "I use cannabis to make me feel good."

Tables 7.1 and 7.2 compare the findings on self-reported mental health in different groups of students, beginning with comparison of those who had used cannabis versus those reporting that they had never used.

Comparisons between users and nonusers indicate that users have more positive and fewer negative responses on survey items assessing mental health. Cannabis users overall were just as likely or more likely to respond "not at all" when asked about sleep problems due to worry, having low confidence or self-worth, feeling unhappy or depressed, being under constant strain, and having difficulties they are unable to get over. And conversely, students who never used cannabis were more likely to respond that in the past three months they had been less able to enjoy activities, face problems, or make decisions. Nonusers also more often responded that they had been feeling less useful and less reasonably happy.

To examine differences by level of consumption, Table 7.2 compares responses among users who are grouped according to their frequency of use.

The percent responding "not at all" for indicators of poor mental health are quite consistent between groups. Where larger differences exist, the data show that daily users are less likely to report concerns about their mental health (i.e., losing confidence, feeling worthless, or under constant strain). And daily users surveyed are consistently less likely to report reductions, over the past three months, in each of the five symptoms of robust mental health. Few of the differences between groups are statistically significant. But they are remarkably consistent across items and provide empirical support for the contention that young people who use cannabis, including those who use it often, have just as good or better self-reported mental health.

TABLE 7.1
Cannabis users and nonusers: Self-reported mental health status over the past three months

Symptoms of poor mental health	Responded "not at all" (%) Users	Non-users
Lost much sleep due to worry	18	17
Been losing confidence in yourself	35	30
Been thinking of yourself as a worthless person	61	58
Been feeling unhappy or depressed	25	22
Felt constantly under strain	9	9
Felt you couldn't get over your difficulties	25	21

Symptoms of good mental health	Responded "less" or "much less than usual" (%) Users	Non-users
Been able to enjoy normal day-to-day activities	16	26
Been able to face up to your problems	12	17
Felt capable of making decisions	9	13
Felt that you are playing a useful part in things	17	20
Been reasonably happy, all things considered	20	22
	$N = 830$	$N = 943$

TABLE 7.2
Frequency of cannabis use: Self-reported mental health status over the past three months

	Responding "not at all" by frequency of use (%)			
Symptoms of poor mental health	Over the last year	Over the last month	Over the last week	Over the last day
Lost much sleep due to worry	19	22	23	21
Been losing confidence in yourself	37	36	41	49
Been thinking of yourself as a worthless person	63	64	69	75
Been feeling unhappy or depressed	26	25	24	22
Felt constantly under strain	10	11	12	19
Felt you couldn't get over your difficulties	26	28	29	29

	Responding "less" or "much less than usual" by frequency of use (%)			
Symptoms of good mental health	Over the last year	Over the last month	Over the last week	Over the last day
Been able to enjoy normal day-to-day activities	15	13	13	12
Been able to face up to your problems	12	10	8	6
Felt capable of making decisions	9	8	7	6
Felt that you are playing a useful part in things	16	15	15	12
Been reasonably happy, all things considered	19	17	20	14
	$N = 665$	$N = 434$	$N = 264$	$N = 52$

※

Writing a half century before the introduction of the plan to legalize the use of cannabis in Canada, Alfred Lindesmith observed presciently that

> the histories of alcohol and marihuana suggest that these substances, and others like them, have a psychological value which is beyond the control of legislation and which tends to nullify attempts at prohibition. The destiny of marihuana, like that of alcohol, will probably be determined by the efficiency with which it meets certain common human psychological needs. If,

for example, it is a less dangerous and generally more effective intoxicant than alcohol, no conceivable legislation can alter this fact or prevent it from becoming known. Much of the literature on marihuana is designed primarily to frighten adolescents, but the latter are much less influenced in these matters by what they read or by what adults tell them than they are by what they themselves experience and by what they learn from each other. (Solomon 1966, xxviii)

This chapter adds a sociological perspective to inform policy discussions on the effects of cannabis on users' mental health.

Informal group controls within the subculture of users were also recognized by Howard Becker (1967) and Norman Zinberg (1984) as integral to the harm-reduction practices of users. Subjective drug experience and physiological reactions are primed by social learning among users in a way that minimizes adverse reactions and experiences. Occurrences of negative reactions, labelled as derangement or psychosis up until the 1950s, disappeared entirely from the scientific literature despite the increasing prevalence of use.

Social learning within peer groups provided novice users with alternative explanations of the drug experience. Inexperienced users' interactions with the group counteracted the anxiety of expectations partly formed by the panic-inducing myths of the Reefer Madness era. The suggestion that cannabis causes psychosis has recently enjoyed somewhat of a resurgence (Gage, Hickman, and Zammit 2016; Rabin and George 2017; George, Hill, and Vaccarino 2018). Previous attempts to prove this link have proven futile. As Becker noted long ago, such efforts closely resemble the failure to identify the singular causes of crime.

Nonetheless, as we have seen, the "information out there" for average citizens and scientists is more concerned with documenting the alleged link between cannabis use and mental illness than the link between cannabis use and better mental health. Typing "cannabis use and mental health" into Google or Google Scholar demonstrates the power of the pathologizing lens, through which the haze of Reefer Madness is never far from view. The effect of cannabis use on mental health, according to the Government of Canada, is that it can trigger a psychotic episode and cause anxiety or panic. In the long term, it warns, use of cannabis puts one at greater risk of schizophrenia, anxiety, depression, and psychosis.

The information given by Health Canada is largely echoed in resources hosted on official websites in other countries such as the United States, the

United Kingdom, and Australia. The official source of information tends to be concerned primarily with (re)directing Google searchers' attention to mental health disorders linked with cannabis use – or psychiatric illness as opposed to mental health. Advice to users emphasizes use reduction and diagnosing symptoms of drug use–related problems.

It is noteworthy that the DSM criteria adopted for diagnosing substance-use disorders reflect a dualistic understanding of addiction that is informed by medical and psychosocial factors (see Hathaway 2015). The DSM provides a common language for clinicians and mental health professionals that has played a role in shifting the discourse of drug problems from a moralistic standpoint to a health-oriented view. Although widely praised for standardizing psychiatric diagnoses, the DSM has also been criticized for putting labels on behaviour based on nebulous criteria that are subjective, open to interpretation, and socially defined.

The DSM-5, introduced in 2013, continued the tradition of medicalizing deviant behaviour by lowering the diagnostic threshold that determines whether a drug user has a substance-use disorder. Among the revisions was the introduction of the new criteria of having a "craving," or strong urge to use the drug. The discovery of cannabis withdrawal was another factor that contributed to the creation of the diagnostic label "cannabis use disorder."

The DSM-5 combined previously separate criteria designating substance dependence and abuse and expanded the standard checklist from seven to eleven symptoms. It introduced a new measure of severity by distinguishing between levels of disorder, from mild (two or three symptoms) to moderate (four or five) to severe (six or more). However, by lowering the threshold that triggers diagnosis of a substance-use disorder from three to two symptoms, the modified criteria created a new "need" for treatment.

The changes further blurred the distinction between medical criteria for diagnosing substance use dependence (i.e., increasing tolerance, withdrawal) and psychosocial problems caused by maladaptive use that were previously categorized as symptoms of "abuse." Symptoms of this nature are primarily subjective, determined as they are by societal reactions and the social circumstances in which a drug is used. Definitions of dependence and abuse are shaped by culture. *Substance use disorder* is an even vaguer term that dismisses criticism by removing the distinction between dependence and abuse, and in the process further contributing to widening the diagnostic net.

There is no straightforward relationship between cannabis use levels and use-related problems. Studies show most users have, at one time or another, experienced a strong desire or craving for the drug. Cannabis use–related problems ordinarily have more to do with self-perceptions of immoderate use than the type of adverse outcomes that are associated with other commonly abused drugs. Eschewing a more nuanced understanding of the problem, the DSM has instead been adapted to label a large segment of the population as having a (mild, moderate, or severe) case of cannabis use disorder.

The recent "discovery" of CUD (or MUD in the United States) has already been reified. Self-diagnosis is enabled by online screening tools adopted and adapted for that purpose by Mental Health America. As one of several illustrations of the "information out there," this marks another leap in the DSM's long journey, from a desk resource for clinicians to an incrementally expanding tool for labelling disorders and people who use drugs in ways never meant to fall under its diagnostic gaze.

The alleged link between cannabis use and mental illness has been facilitated by pairing it with discussions of problem use, as diagnosed by DSM criteria. Online information is remarkably consistent in its emphasis on mental health disorders and use-related problems. There is little reference to the benefits of any kind for users seeking information about "cannabis use and mental health."

A Google Scholar search turned up studies that provide a more nuanced, evidence-based understanding of cannabis pathologies than information geared toward non-experts. Despite their emphasis on data and rigid scientific standards of assessing evidence for proof, there is evidently little interest among researchers in providing a better understanding of why so many people use cannabis and what its mental health benefits may be.

The research literature on cannabis use *for* mental health is scarce, as compared to research investigating the harms. To offer a more balanced understanding of the experience of use, de-pathologizing cannabis depends on recognizing something that is often overlooked – people who use cannabis like the way it makes them feel. The limitations of relying on self-reported data are common knowledge among scientists. For social scientists, however, disregarding self-reports that shed light on subjective understandings of reality introduces bias of a very different sort. The association between cannabis and mental illness is socially, historically, and culturally conditioned to such an extent that understandings of these phenomena are informed as much by social science as medical evidence and knowledge.

The next step toward a better understanding of the link between cannabis use and mental health is recognition that "recreational" and "medical" patterns of consumption are not mutually exclusive ways of understanding why people use the drug. The use of cannabis for mental health–related benefits transcends distinctions based on labels that designate use as either for medical conditions or "just for having fun."

Transitioning from rehashed Reefer Madness rhetoric, still very much apparent in the legalization era, suggests a larger role for social scientists whose research illuminates the social history and cultural conditions that have shaped societal reactions to the drug. Engaging in hyperbole about cannabis effects is a harmful tendency that continues a tradition of neglecting decades of sociological research.

As cannabis has shifted from the margins to the mainstream of conventional society, social knowledge and awareness of its uses have evolved. As use becomes more prevalent and society more tolerant, informal group controls will become more nuanced, reflecting the wide array of circumstances in which the drug is used. As society becomes more familiar with a drug, there is less need for ideological commitments to maintaining subcultural connections and support. Informal rituals developed to support drug use become less rigid, notes Zinberg (1984), as social sanctions are internalized and adapted to reflect more individualized use patterns.

Legalizing cannabis supports the harm-reduction practices of users by endorsing the position that not all use is harmful. In an era of renewed concerns about the potency of new strains of cannabis (and concentrates and edibles) – and alarm about their links to mental illness – fostering informal group controls remains the most effective harm-reduction intervention.

Fostering societal conditions that will facilitate the use of cannabis for mental health is equally important. To paraphrase Lindesmith and other early social scientists whose insights are no less relevant today, the frightened discourse of the Reefer Madness era endures, yet it is ultimately less influential than users' understandings based on actual experience and interactions with other users.

Notes

1 The DSM-5 is the current version of the *Diagnostic and Statistical Manual of Mental Disorders* issued by the American Psychiatric Association (2013).
2 Much like Harry Anslinger in the United States, Emily Murphy was a prominent crusader for marijuana prohibition. Using the same themes of unsubstantiated violence and the provocation of interracial fear, this early advocate of voting rights for women campaigned for prohibition by depicting marijuana users as a menace to society (Hathaway 2015; see also Chapter 1, this volume).

Works Cited

American Psychiatric Association. 2013. *The Diagnostic and Statistical Manual of Mental Disorders: DSM 5.* Bookpoint US.

Aspis, Itay, Daniel Feingold, Mark Weiser, Jurgen Rehm, Gal Shoval, and Shaul Lev-Ran. 2015. "Cannabis Use and Mental Health-Related Quality of Life among Individuals with Depressive Disorders." *Psychiatry Research* 230 (2): 341–49.

Baudelaire, Charles. 1971 [c. 1860]. *Artificial Paradise: On Hashish and Wine as a Means of Expanding Individuality.* New York: Herder and Herder.

Becker, Howard S. 1963. *Outsiders: Studies in the Sociology of Deviance.* New York: Free Press.

–. 1967. "History, Culture, and Subjective Experience: An Exploration of the Social Bases of Drug-Induced Experiences." *Journal of Health and Social Behavior* 8 (3): 163–76.

Degenhardt, Louisa, Wayne Hall, and Michael Lynskey. 2001. "The Relationship between Cannabis Use, Depression and Anxiety among Australian Adults: Findings from the National Survey of Mental Health and Well-Being." *Social Psychiatry and Psychiatric Epidemiology* 36 (5): 219–27.

–. 2003. "Exploring the Association between Cannabis Use and Depression." *Addiction* 98 (11): 1493–1504.

Feingold, Daniel, Mark Weiser, Jurgen Rehm, and Shaul Lev-Ran. 2016. "The Association between Cannabis Use and Anxiety Disorders: Results from a Population-Based Representative Sample." *European Neuropsychopharmacology* 26 (3): 493–505.

Gage, Suzanne H., Matthew Hickman, and Stanley Zammit. 2016. "Association between Cannabis and Psychosis: Epidemiologic Evidence." *Biological Psychiatry* 79 (7): 549–56.

Gates, Peter. n.d. "Does Cannabis Cause Mental Illness?" National Drug and Alcohol Research Centre. Originally published in The Conversation, February 24, 2016. https://ndarc.med.unsw.edu.au/blog/does-cannabis-cause-mental-illness\.

George, Tony P., Kevin P. Hill, and Franco J. Vaccarino. 2018. "Cannabis Legalization and Psychiatric Disorders: Caveat 'Hemp-tor.'" *Canadian Journal of Psychiatry* 63 (7): 447–50.

Hall, Wayne, and Nadia Solowij. 1997. "Long-Term Cannabis Use and Mental Health." *British Journal of Psychiatry* 171 (2): 107–8.

Hathaway, Andrew D. 1997. "Marijuana and Lifestyle: Exploring Tolerable Deviance." *Deviant Behavior* 18 (3): 213–32.

–. 2003. "Cannabis Effects and Dependency Concerns in Long-Term Frequent Users: A Missing Piece of the Public Health Puzzle." *Addiction Research and Theory* 11 (6): 441–58.

–. 2004. "Cannabis Careers Reconsidered: Transitions and Trajectories of Committed Long-Term Users." *Contemporary Drug Problems* 31 (3): 401–23.

–. 2015. *Drugs and Society.* Toronto: Oxford University Press.

Hathaway, Andrew D., Russell C. Callaghan, Scott Macdonald, and Patricia G. Erickson. 2009. "Cannabis Dependence as a Primary Drug Use-Related Problem: The

Case for Harm Reduction-Oriented Treatment Options." *Substance Use and Misuse* 44 (7): 990–1008.

Hathaway, Andrew D., Maritt Kirst, and Patricia G. Erickson. 2013. "Marijuana Motives and Associated Outcomes: Relaxation and Enhancement versus Coping Motivations." In *Drug Use and Abuse: Signs/Symptoms, Physical and Psychological Effects and Treatment Approaches*, edited by Marie Claire Van Hout, 119–33. New York: Nova Science.

Hathaway, Andrew D., Scott Macdonald, and Patricia G. Erickson. 2008. "Reprioritizing Dependence and Abuse: A Comparison of Cannabis Clients in Treatment with a Non-treatment Sample of Users." *Addiction Research and Theory* 16 (5): 495–502.

Hathaway, Andrew, Amir Mostaghim, Kat Kolar, Patricia G. Erickson, and Geraint Osborne. 2016. "A Nuanced View of Normalisation: Attitudes of Cannabis Non-users in a Study of Undergraduate Students at Three Canadian Universities." *Drugs: Education, Prevention and Policy* 23 (3): 238–46.

–. 2018. "'It's Really No Big Deal': The Role of Social Supply Networks in Normalizing Use of Cannabis by Students at Canadian Universities." *Deviant Behavior* 39 (12): 1672–80.

Hathaway, Andrew D., and Kate Rossiter. 2007. "Medical Marijuana, Community Building, and Canada's Compassionate Societies." *Contemporary Justice Review* 10 (3): 283–96.

Hathaway, Andrew D., and Justin Sharpley. 2010. "The Cannabis Experience: An Analysis of 'Flow.'" In *Cannabis – Philosophy for Everyone: What Were We Just Talking About?*, edited by Dale Jacquette, 50–61. New York: Wiley-Blackwell.

Health Canada. n.d. "Cannabis and Mental Health." Accessed May 23, 2021. https://www.canada.ca/en/health-canada/services/drugs-medication/cannabis/health-effects/mental-health.html.

Jones, Craig, and Andrew D. Hathaway. 2008. "Marijuana Medicine and Canadian Physicians: Challenges to Meaningful Drug Policy Reform." *Contemporary Justice Review* 11 (2): 165–75.

Lev-Ran, Shaul, Bernard Le Foll, Kwame McKenzie, Tony P. George, and Jurgen Rehm. 2013. "Cannabis Use and Cannabis Use Disorders among Individuals with Mental Illness." *Comprehensive Psychiatry* 54 (6): 589–98.

Lev-Ran, Shaul, Bernard Le Foll, Kwame McKenzie, and Jurgen Rehm. 2012. "Cannabis Use and Mental Health-Related Quality of Life among Individuals with Anxiety Disorders." *Journal of Anxiety Disorders* 26 (8): 799–810.

McGee, Rob, Sheila Williams, Richie Poulton, and Terrie Moffitt. 2000. "A Longitudinal Study of Cannabis Use and Mental Health from Adolescence to Early Adulthood." *Addiction* 95 (4): 491–503.

Mental Health America. n.d. "Risky Business: Marijuana Use." Accessed May 23, 2021. http://www.mentalhealthamerica.net/conditions/risky-business-marijuana-use.

Moore, Teresa H.M., Stanley Zammit, Anne Lingford-Hughes, Thomas R.E. Barnes, Peter B. Jones, Margaret Burke, and Glyn Lewis. 2007. "Cannabis Use and Risk of Psychotic or Affective Mental Health Outcomes: A Systematic Review." *The Lancet* 370 (9584): 319–28.

Moreau, Jacques. 1845. *Du hachisch et de l'aliénation mentale: Études psychologiques.* Paris: Librarie de Fortin Mason. English edition: *On Hashish and Mental Alienation.* New York: Raven Press, 1972.

Müller, Christian P., and Gunter Schumann. 2011. "Drugs as Instruments: A New Framework for Non-addictive Psychoactive Drug Use." *Behavioral and Brain Sciences* 34 (6): 293–347.

Murphy, Emily F. 1922. *The Black Candle.* Toronto: Thomas Allen.

Nahas, Gabriel G. 1992. *Cannabis Physiopathology Epidemiology Detection.* Boca Raton: CRC Press.

National Institute of Health. n.d. "Cannabis Use and Mental Health in Young People: Cohort Study." Accessed May 23, 2021. https://www.ncbi.nlm.nih.gov/pmc/articles/PMC135489/.

Patton, George C., Carolyn Coffey, John B. Carlin, Louisa Degenhardt, Michael Lynskey, and Wayne Hall. 2002. "Cannabis Use and Mental Health in Young People: Cohort Study." *British Medical Journal* 325 (7374): 1195–98.

Rabin, Rachel A., and Tony P. George. 2017. "Understanding the Link between Cannabinoids and Psychosis." *Clinical Pharmacology and Therapeutics* 101 (2): 197–99.

Rey, Joseph M., and Christopher C. Tennant. 2002. "Cannabis and Mental Health: More Evidence Establishes Clear Link between Use of Cannabis and Psychiatric Illness." *British Medical Journal* 325 (7374): 1183–84.

Royal College of Psychiatrists (UK). n.d. "Cannabis and Mental Health: For Young People." Accessed May 23, 2021. https://www.rcpsych.ac.uk/mental-health/parents-and-young-people/young-people/cannabis-and-mental-health-information-for-young-people.

Solomon, David. 1966. *The Marihuana Papers.* New York: New American Library.

Zinberg, Norman E. 1984. *Drug, Set and Setting: The Basis for Controlled Intoxicant Use.* New Haven, CT: Yale University Press.

8

Help Wanted

The Plight of Workers and Consumers under Canada's Legal Cannabis Production Regime

CLAYTON JAMES SMITH McCANN

> I offer my history as evidence.
> – BENNETT JUDKINS, *WE OFFER OURSELVES IN EVIDENCE*

My Story

What is "safe" cannabis? According to Ottawa, it is Health Canada–approved, commercial-grade, mass-produced, seed-to-shelf tracked cannabis. It is fully taxed at two levels of government and sealed in plastic, child-proof packaging approved and excise stamped by the Government of Canada. But what I have described is just the finished product, an inadequate description of the work of cultivating seed to bud to what ends up in the consumer's joint.

My first job in illicit cannabis production was working as a trimmer. The primary duties included receiving, grading, racking and drying, tracking, hand trimming, running auto trimmer and hopper operations, and bagging and tagging. A trimmer can work sixteen to eighteen hours a day, typically in spaces that pose risks to health and safety. This work typically occurs in an underground location or hidden away in buildings that appear nondescript to the untrained observer – and often lack safety features such as fire extinguishers,[1] proper ventilation, and protective gear such as masks and respirators. The only equipment typically provided to workers are protective gloves, Fiskar brand pruning scissors, and isopropyl alcohol (to clean up the residue from all that sticky bud).

Trimmer positions were much sought after at one time, paying upwards of twenty thousand dollars for four to six weeks' labour. The downside includes coughing up particulate matter for months after and repetitive strain injuries from constant crouching and working with scissors. Thankfully, my first trim position was terminated after a few weeks. However, it was not my last.

My next job was as a hiker. In addition to carrying heavy packs on foot, the job of the hiker is to pick and grade. Bizarre work hours are the norm: from 11 p.m. to 3 a.m., I hiked a double stack of XXL totes filled with "wet" cannabis strapped to a frame pack off a mountain in the dark. On arriving at the designated "drop" point, I'd turn around and do it all again. Sometimes this meant hiking a kilometre straight up a mountainside – the only guide being the soles of the worker's boots climbing directly above. The lifespan of this position is five years at most. After that, one's back is shot. I stretched out my five years (and my back) by alternating between being a hiker, fall guy, and maintenance.

The fall guy does not work the harvest in the Rocky Mountains. Rather he (or she) is strapped to an indoor grow operation. The job requires committing to multiple grow cycles that last about nine weeks; eventually, you'll quit for a better cut of the proceeds at another operation. While it looks like a "house" on the outside, the house is really a factory farm that needs an occupant. That was me: the guy outside on weekends cutting the grass, planting flowers, having barbeque cookouts on summer evenings and playing frisbee with friends. Come winter, I was the poor sod shovelling the driveway at the crack of dawn before the neighbours are awake.

Why not be out there shovelling? Sleep did not come easily with all the anxiety. The job is *to be seen* (putting up and taking down Halloween decorations, then Christmas lights, and so on, and so on) and seen often by the neighbours – the same neighbours you will never invite over for a beer. And why not? Because once inside your idyllic suburban home, all they'd smell would be the warm, skunky fart of flowering cannabis.

The job of being the fall guy involves endless paranoia. You can't even go to Costco without constant fear of the house burning down. You must be forever vigilant and careful not to be followed when returning from the grow supply shop. There is never a day off. In addition to evading thugs, and all the rest of it, your job is to hire, train, pick up, pay, and drive home your trimmer crew.[2] You can't be seen with six cars in the driveway once every nine or so weeks. The fall guy also has to cope with the inevitably unnerving experience of dealing with unexpected visitors such as door-to-door salespeople, religious missionaries, and even the odd cop.

And you have to deal with your employer, the house owner, who swears the house can "turn" fifteen pounds a cycle. Never having seen such an impressive yield, you nonetheless must take them at their word. Then, lo and behold, on harvest day you pull eleven pounds. That means you get no bonus (and never will because the house never seems to "turn" more than about a dozen pounds). Not surprisingly, the owner can never seem to keep the same fall guy around for more than four or five months. (One employer actually wept when I told him I was "out"!)

I then moved on to maintaining outdoor grow sites (usually three or four located along a water line, or "trapline," on the south side of a mountain). A good maintenance worker can manage about a dozen sites per grow season (which runs May through October). This is a full-on sprint that involves an array of tasks that must be carried out from start to finish and on schedule, with no firm guarantee of compensation.[3]

Not surprisingly, perhaps, I became concerned about the hazards of fertilizers. On a mountainside overlooking the Castlegar pulp mill, when I was pouring a twenty-five-pound bag of "blue" into an irrigation injector, an employer casually said, "Careful breathing that crap. You could fuck up your kidneys." Fed off the main water line, the irrigation injector permits a set ratio of fertilizer to be mixed into the "dripper" system. I could not help but ask myself: Do all fertilizers contain so much salt? And if so: How could that be healthy for the plants?

My search for answers to these questions led to Matthew Shaffer's (2001) research finding that commercial fertilizers are toxic to human health.[4] Furthermore, according to Julian Karadjov (2011, 3), cannabis is classified as an accumulator plant: "This means it accumulates everything in its environment and these substances remain in the plant, influencing all future development of the sapling, the germ, and even the seed. In fact, cannabis is so effective at accumulating contaminants, that it was even used after the Chernobyl accident to remove radioactive waste from the soil." These discoveries both alarmed me and inspired the present work.

Emptor Caveat

A 2016 *Globe and Mail* article set off alarms that the federal government was failing to act, despite evidence confirming that legal cannabis approved for consumption by licensed medical users contained banned toxins "such as the pesticide Carbamate, which is not permitted for use on cannabis, and

Dodemorph, a fungicide used on roses that is not approved for human consumption" (Robertson 2016b).

It was reported that in March 2014, Kelowna RCMP seized "more than 700 kilograms of B.C. bud stored in 55 hockey bags" destined for Tweed and Mettrum (both now Canopy Growth Corp.) under a legal procurement deal for "plants and seeds" (Quan 2019). RCMP declined to pursue the case against the licensed producers (LPs), citing the "lack of any charges." Yet, presumably, attempting to transport nearly three-quarters of a tonne of illegally grown cannabis across provincial borders, with the intent to traffic, is still a crime in Canada. That is, unless you are a corporation.

When the banned pesticide Myclobutanil was discovered in cannabis produced by Mettrum, Health Canada's response was this: "Exposure to the affected cannabis products would not likely cause any adverse health consequences." This is a curious assessment considering reports that "microbiologists and lawmakers in the United States consider there to be no acceptable level of Myclobutanil in cannabis" (Robertson 2016a).

In 2019, there were over 170 corporations licensed to produce and distribute cannabis and associated products (Health Canada 2019). Considering that LPs essentially police themselves – being permitted, as they are, to self-regulate by choosing product samples to be taken for testing by a licensed third party, whom they pay – it would seem that the honour system regulates worker and consumer safety. As we shall see, however, these concerns are not unique to corporate cannabis production. On the contrary, concerns about toxicity and safety are well documented by researchers and just as commonly ignored by regulators in the North American agricultural food industry.

Neoliberalism and Industrial Cannabis Work

> An individual might choose to make shoes rather than risk life in the cleaning department of a grain mill, but grain would be cleaned, and the working class would clean it.
> – WILLIAM GRAEBNER, "DOING THE WORLD'S UNHEALTHY WORK"

Neoliberalism has been defined as "a large-scale historical project for the transformation of social structures and practices along market lines" (Connell 2010, 33). It has also been described as a "sociocultural logic" of late-stage capitalism "that values individualism ... transferring economic power and control from governments to private markets" (Howse 2017, 97). Among other dire consequences, it has been observed that "these are difficult times for workers. In the wealthy countries of capitalism's center, labor is struggling to maintain existing wages and benefits against a combined assault by corporations and governments, while conditions of workers in the periphery are even more difficult" (Magdoff and Magdoff 2004, 18).

Maximizing profit under late-stage capitalism calls for "flexible" or "variable" labour; it therefore requires a precarious workforce. The sale of labour power is arguably becoming "a political fiction" due to "the inequality of bargaining positions" (Holmstrom 2011, 202), further eroding the rights of workers to refuse unsafe work. *Letting the market decide* is the mantra that justifies more hiring of temporary, part-time, and contract labour. The slogan also rationalizes "the privatization of government functions, and outsourcing portions of industrial and service operations to other locations at home and abroad. All of these contingent or nonstandard work arrangements have the advantage for capital that they further weaken its already weak obligations to workers" (Magdoff and Magdoff 2004, 22).

Occupational social benefits (sickness compensation, occupational accident compensation, and unemployment insurance) declined in all developed countries between 1975 and 1995 (Navarro 2009). Neoliberalism is committed to cost-cutting and the withdrawal of state interventions, including regulations implemented to protect workers (Harvey 2000). This commitment turns the worker "into a mere appendage of capital itself" (Harvey 1982, 97).

Industrial agriculture and greenhouses are among the workplaces that present the greatest risks (Otero and Preibisch 2010), especially to temporary foreign workers (TFWs) and seasonal agricultural workers (SAWs). A worker who refuses unsafe work is likely to end up an unemployed worker. It has also been observed that many workers in agriculture "do not receive adequate workplace health and safety training ... Health and safety in agriculture is undermined by poorly maintained, inadequate farm equipment, deficient hygiene and sanitation at worksites, and lack of personal protective equipment" (Otero and Preibisch 2010).

Work Environments in Cannabis Production
Work environments in industrial cannabis production are determined by the growth cycles of the plant. From seed or clone, the little lady has to "veg" for two weeks then "flower" for seven to nine weeks. Throughout these stages, the plants have to be strictly monitored for pathogens such as "rust" (nutrient deficiencies or "blocks"), "burn" (overfertilization), parasites (e.g.,

thrips, spider mites), and pathogens (powdery mildew, mould), among other maintenance tasks.

Maintenance includes trimming lower fan leaves, "bending" for light, cleaning the canopy, maintaining the pH/electroconductivity of water via chemical applications, "dipping" the entire plant in insecticidal soap, spraying foliar applications (sulphur "smoke," conazoles, soaps, chemicals), staking branches as they become weighted by burdensome flowers, and "punching" nutrients into subsoils. Many of these tasks pose risks to the worker and the plant's health, productivity, and harvest yields, and they must be done on schedule. Consider what a challenge these tasks pose when the plant count runs into the thousands!

Experienced growers have come to rely on chemical applications to make production at scale possible. These applications range from relatively harmless foliar nutrient sprays, to potentially hazardous insecticidal soaps, to more dangerous pesticides and herbicides, to approved but highly toxic applications such as Agrotek Vaporized Sulphur (controls powdery mildew, toxifies the entire workspace for two hours), Rootshield (R) WP (not for use on edible plants or tobacco, contains 98.85 percent "other ingredients"), and Milstop Fungicide (contains 85 percent potassium bicarbonate, can cause severe stomach pain, cramping, nausea, vomiting, and diarrhea).

Work environments in cannabis production are variable and fluctuate from mildly to extremely toxic with no warning to workers. Health Canada permits LPs to employ a range of twenty-odd chemical applications, in accordance with the Pest Control Products Act (PCPA, SC 2002, c 28), in addition to the use of highly toxic fertilizers, to produce commercial cannabis (see Table 8.1 for examples).

And what about "other ingredients"? This is a standard statement on a variety of products like Actinovate SP that are popular with growers. On the label, it states "no harm to plant or human expected." However, while its labelled "active ingredient" is Streptomyces, a whopping 99.9629 percent consists of "other ingredients" (Valent 2017). More generally (and to the point), it is certainly noteworthy that the manufacturer is not required by law to list "other ingredients" on product packaging, nor, apparently, to disclose them when responding to inquiries.

It has already been established that banned chemicals such as Myclobutanil are used widely and routinely by licensed cannabis producers (Bracken 2017; Miller 2017; Robertson 2017; Seibert 2017; Toth 2017).[5] The Dow Chemicals product is so dangerous that workers are warned to wear full hazmat protective clothing and respirators, and controlled access to the

TABLE 8.1
Health Canada–approved pesticide ingredients and known health effects

Product	Health effects
Botanigard 22 WP[a]	Contains petroleum distillate: risk of aspiration and pneumonia
Kopa Insecticidal Soap[b]	Potential reproductive and developmental damage
MilStop Foliar Fungicide	May cause confusion, uneven heartbeat, severe stomach pain, vomiting, diarrhea, and anxiety
Prestop	Potential damage to immune and endocrine systems
Neudosan Commercial[c]	A known carcinogen above 1 percent toxicity; causes coma, hypotension, and respiratory failure; very toxic to aquatic life

Notes:
a Botanigard contains 78 percent "nonactive ingredients." What might these be? Its label states: "Wash thoroughly with soap and water after handling and before eating, drinking, chewing gum, using tobacco or using the toilet. Remove contaminated clothing and wash clothing before reuse" (Biowork Inc. 2019).
b Kopa Insecticidal Soap, a pesticide, lists "other ingredients" at 53 percent and states: "Conditions to avoid: Exposure to excessive heat" (OHP 2017).
c Neudosan Commercial's "active ingredient" is Abamectin (2.2 percent, fatal if inhaled) (Cayman Chemical 2016). Its "other ingredients," accounting for 54.6 percent by volume, are largely composed of potassium salts (Nuedorff 2015), yet its safety data sheet, under "Disposal Considerations," describes the product as "containing dangerous substances."

application site must be strictly enforced. The potential health risk to consumers is no less deadly considering that Myclobutanil turns to hydrogen cyanide and hydrochloric gas when burned (Conrad and Blair 2015).

"Career Opportunities" in Legal Cannabis Production

Like its illicit counterpart and forerunner, the legal cannabis LP industry creates a lot of jobs with the potential to put workers in harm's way. Table 8.2 presents a few help-wanted ads to illustrate the skills required of workers in the industry as well as some common job descriptions indicative of the high level of exposure to toxins in the work environment.

Among other observations, it is evident that some of the language in the industry is changing to reflect a need for more credentials and specialized training in the use of toxic chemicals by production workers. Between 2018 and 2019, for example, the job title for a worker doing pest and weed control and fertilization changed from "community farmhand" to "cultivation technician" at the Green Organic Dutchman. The more recent posting also has a new requirement – the applicant must be qualified to "execute pest manage-

TABLE 8.2
A sample of help-wanted ads for cannabis production workers, 2018–19

LP/posting date	Position and description
The Green Organic Dutchman Jerseyville, Ontario, March 2018	Community farmhand: Preventive management and control of weeds, pests, and pest diseases; fertilization, harvest, and irrigation.
The Green Organic Dutchman Jerseyville, Ontario, May 2019	Cultivation technician – Operations technician III: Execute pest-management protocols.
Up Cannabis Beamsville, Ontario, March 2018	Assistant grower: Pesticide licence considered an asset.
Up Cannabis Beamsville, Ontario, August 2018	Processing manager: Experience in food packaging, pharma, or commercial agriculture a must. Willing to do whatever it takes to get the job done.
Canopy Growth Smiths Falls, ON, 2018	Fertigation (fertilizer/irrigation) specialist: Maintain inventory of all chemicals and fertilizers on-site.
Canopy Growth Smiths Falls, ON, 2018	Irrigation assistant: Maintain inventory of all chemicals and fertilizers on-site.
Canopy Growth Chatham-Kent, ON, 2019	Section grower: Supervise pest-management protocols as directed by integrated pest-management (IPM) specialist.
Canopy Growth Smiths Falls, ON, 2019	Section grower: Execute pest-management protocols as directed by IPM Specialist. Must be bilingual – Spanish and English.
Emblem Cannabis (now Aleafia) Paris, Ontario, February 2018	Regulatory affairs and quality-assurance coordinator: Ensure that only Health Canada–approved pest-control products registered under the Pest Control Products Act (PCPA) are allowed for production uses.

▼ Table 8.2

LP/posting date	Position and description
Organigram Moncton, New Brunswick, May 2019	Production supervisor – Horticulture manager: Responsible for leading the production team through the full plant cycle, including watering (veg/flowering), IPM, propagation, mothers, and so on.
Aurora Cannabis Vancouver, BC, 2019	Plant cultivation tech: Assist in the recognition and response of plant pathogens and pests.
Aurora Cannabis Vancouver, BC, 2019	Coordinator, cultivation: Coordinate timely and effective pest and disease control measures as required.
Aurora Cannabis Vancouver, BC, 2019	Greenhouse manager: Pre-emptively apply approved pesticides, when appropriate, to reduce pathogen pressure.
Aurora Cannabis Vancouver, BC, 2019	Manager, cultivation: Along with the IPM team, coordinate timely and effective pest- and disease-control measures as required.
Zenabis, now Hexo Atholville, NB, January 2019	IPM specialist: Spray applications that require a pesticide applicators licence. Experience using biological applications.
Zenabis, now Hexo Stellarton, NS, May 2019	Integrated pest-management IPM specialist: Utilize traps, allowable chemical and nonchemical methods to manage pests, [including Health Canada–approved] pest-control products for use on Cannabis.

ment protocols as directed by QAP" (Green Organic Dutchman, March 2019).

It is far from reassuring that at least one LP (Up Cannabis) informed potential applicants that the company expected workers "to do whatever it takes to get the job done" (Up Cannabis 2018). It is also noteworthy that at least one other company, Canopy Growth, had a sudden need for section growers who speak Spanish (Canopy 2019). The most prominent pattern is increasing use of the term *integrated pest management* (or, simply, IPM). The Aurora website helpfully defines IPM as "preemptively applying approved pesticides, when appropriate, to reduce pathogen pressure" (Aurora Cannabis 2019).

Is IPM then really just a buzzword used by LPs as they continue to prioritize preventing financial loss over expectations about quality control? As we shall see, the health of workers in the industry does not appear to be a matter of concern for regulators. Nor is it a priority for corporations that neglect or downplay the risks to health and safety of using chemicals at work.

Occupational Health and Safety Provisions
The Ontario Occupational Health and Safety Act (OHSA, RSO 1990, c O.1) is the legislation in the province under which the Workplace Hazardous Materials Information System (WHMIS) falls. The OHSA "does not apply to farming operations" aside from the protections it provides against "workplace violence" and "workplace sexual harassment" (Part 1, 3.2). Precarious workers, including TFWs and SAWs, are routinely exposed to pesticides and other farming chemicals, and they have no legal protections, inadequate drinking water, no access to hand-washing or toilet facilities, and insufficient safety training for use of chemicals at work (Larson 2001; Arcury et al., 2001, 2005).

One Canadian study found that "almost half of all Mexican farm workers who applied pesticides in their jobs did not receive training" (Verduzco and Lozano 2003). Farm workers often fail to wear protective equipment because of a lack of available respirators and safety clothing (Moore 2004; Quandt et al. 2006), and they are not properly trained in the use of hazardous chemicals (Sakala 1987; Arcury et al. 2001; CAISP 2008). Because the OHSA does not apply to farming, farm employees are protected under the Employment Standards Act (ESA, SO 2000, c 41).

It remains to be seen how cannabis production workers will be classified. An inquiry to the Ministry of Labour in Ontario evoked the following response: "It will take a cannabis case going to trial before sufficient precedent exists to categorize it." In the meantime, the ESA applies in the case of wage disputes, like unpaid overtime, unless the worker signed away their legal rights in the farm labour contract. In the case of unsafe work conditions, a farm worker, assuming they have access to a phone and speak fluent English or French, may call 1–800–387–0750, Monday to Friday, from 7:30 a.m. to 5 p.m., to report exposure to a workplace health hazard (WSIB 2019).

Farm labourers employed as TFWs or SAWs remain completely unprotected (Delaney 2008; Canadian Press 2009; Tomlinson 2019), considering the lengthy claim-submission process and strong (quite realistic) suspicion among workers that complainants are deported (Globe Newswire 2018). The stark precarity of migrant labour in Ontario is amply demonstrated by the fact that workplace-safety legislation excludes TFWs and SAWs. A request for information from the WSIB was refused: "My apologies that we cannot provide the data you requested and I will be closing this request" (correspondence with author, June 11, 2019). On previous attempts to access data on TFW and SAW mortality and morbidity (the incidence of injury), it was communicated that "these figures are so low that we cannot share them with you, to protect worker privacy" (correspondence with author, June 6, 2019).

In sum, it seems the system is working as intended: cannabis workers remained uncategorized, claims concerning unsafe working conditions took time, and workers could not file a claim if they had arranged to work as an "independent contractor." As noted by Gerardo Otero and Kerry Preibisch (2010, 34), farm labour contracts put workers at risk, particularly migrant workers, because "the relationship diffuses responsibility regarding health and safety, training, and other workplace rights."

A Few Inquiries

In early 2018, I began writing to the agencies responsible for regulating fertilizers used in cannabis production seeking answers to my questions about "other ingredients," which are not required by law to be listed on products (official correspondence, Pierre Bilodeau, September 6, 2018). On commercial packaging, I queried, there are ratios of nitrogen-phosphorous-potassium (N-P-K) indicating content by volume percentages. A bag of 10–5–7 fertilizer, for example, indicates that the product contains 10 percent nitrogen, 5 percent phosphorous, and 7 percent potassium, adding up to 22 percent of the bag's mass. So the question was this: What makes up the remaining 78 percent?

Inquiries to the ministers of health and agriculture, respectively, the Canadian Food Inspection Agency, and Fertilizer Canada (a lobby group promoting the business interests of manufacturers, wholesalers, and retailers) resulted in the proverbial run-around – replete with buck-passing, lengthy delays, and outright obfuscation. Health Canada's Directorate of Cannabis Compliance eventually responded:

> Paragraph 94 (1) of the *Cannabis Regulations* outlines testing for microbial or chemical contaminants. Cannabis that is a cannabis product or that is contained in a cannabis accessory that is *a cannabis product may contain microbial or chemical contaminants* provided that they are within the generally accepted tolerance limits for herbal medicines for human consumption, as established in any publication referred to in Schedule B to the Food and Drugs Act. (Cannabis Regulations SOR/2018–144, emphasis added)

Similar inquiries to the regulatory agencies "overseeing" use of pesticides in cannabis production (including the Pest Management Regulatory Agency, or PMRA) led to the suggestion that concerned citizens might consult the "Statement from Health Canada on the Testing of Cannabis for Medical Purposes for Unauthorized Pest Control Products" (Health Canada 2017). The statement, from early 2017, proclaimed that Health Canada would strive to "educate" wayward licensed producers. The outdated document refers to working with "38 licensed producers" – there are over 700 LPs in Canada today (Health Canada 2021).

Section 81 of the Cannabis Regulations states: "Cannabis must not be treated with a pest-control product unless the product is registered for use on cannabis under the Pest Control Products Act or is otherwise authorized for use under that Act" (SOR/2018–144, Part 5). Subsection 93(1) states further: "Cannabis that is a cannabis product or that is contained in a cannabis accessory that is a cannabis product must not contain any substance other than the cannabis." But Subsection 93(2) adds: "Despite subsection (1), the cannabis may contain residues of a pest-control product, its components or derivatives, if they do not exceed any maximum residue limit, in relation to cannabis, specified for the pest-control product, its components or derivatives under section 9 or 10 of the Pest Control Products Act."

Sections 9 and 10 of the Pest Control Products Act (SC 2002, c 28) stipulate "maximum residue limits." Section 9 of the Act states: "When making a decision regarding the registration of a pest-control product, the Minister shall, if necessary, specify any maximum residue limits for the product or for its components or derivatives that the Minister considers appropriate in the circumstances." And Section 10(1) states: "The Minister may specify maximum residue limits for an unregistered pest control product or its components or derivatives, or for a registered pest control product or its components or derivatives with respect to a use that is not provided for by its registration, whether or not an application under subsection (2) is made for that purpose."

Particularly alarming was the fact that the product Cyclone was 30.1 percent Paraquat dichloride.[6] Paraquat is so "highly poisonous," according to the Centers for Disease Control and Prevention (2018) that it is sold in the United States dyed an optic blue (so it will not be confused with coffee) and labelled "Danger – One Sip Can Kill." The spraying of Paraquat, manufactured by Chevron, has been linked to Parkinson's disease in farm workers (Tanner et al. 2011), and even low doses can induce symptoms of Parkinson's in rats.

While I was assured by Health Canada's PMRA spokesperson via email in March 2019 that this was a "different" form of Paraquat, I was also reminded on that occasion that "pest control products [PCPs] ... only need to list the active ingredient(s) of their pesticide and [the] concentration" therein. Moreover, the PMRA "knows the identity and formulants of all registered pesticides" but these remain "confidential business information and cannot be made available" to the public.

Here was the critical dilemma presented by the regulator's intransigence: consumers must continue to take the regulator at its word that not a single other ingredient in all twenty-plus PCPs pose any risk to consumer health, regardless of consumption vector (combustion, ingestion, etc.) and regardless of intensification due to processing practices. Furthermore, consumers must also accept that not one other ingredient in all the fertilizers approved for use on cannabis production poses any risk whatsoever, regardless of consumption vector.

This practice protecting the manufacturer over the health of consumers is akin to that of the tobacco era. While Health Canada's PMRA would seem a benevolent public servant in these matters, it should be remembered the regulator approved the soil fumigant chloropicrin in 2021, a trichloronitromethane linked to pulmonary injury and environmental toxicity, for use in outdoor cannabis production contexts (Cesarone 2021). The PMRA, it would seem, considers the petro-chemical producers/venders in Canada to be its constituents, as opposed to the consumers of Canadian agricultural products.

Another cause of concern is the common practice of irradiating cannabis using the radioactive element Cobalt-60 (60Co). The logic of the biopharmaceutical industry is such that complete sterility of production spaces is called-for in the production of all consumer products used by chronically ill consumers with weakened immune systems. The practice, after all, is routinely used in the biomedical industry to sterilize equipment, and it is observed that "pharmaceutical regulations in countries such as The Netherlands and Canada specify that these products must adhere to strict safety standards regarding microbial contamination" (Hazekamp 2016, 1). The threshold established under Canada's regulations is 1,000 CFUs (colony-forming units) of "harmful microbes or fungal spores" per gram of dried cannabis (Hazekamp 2016, 1). In particular, "certain specific pathogens must be completely absent, e.g., Staphylococcus aureus, Pseudomonas aeruginosa, and E. coli" (CEEP 2001–7; USP 2015). Furthermore, the absence of fungal mycotoxins must be confirmed by additional quality-control testing.

Opponents of irradiating cannabis, including the Organic Consumers Association, contend that it results in "breaking molecular chains and creating free radicals, which can then combine to create a variety of toxic substances." It is noted that "irradiation can cause foods to lose up to 85 percent of vitamins as well as their natural digestive enzymes, making them harder to digest by humans" ("Gamma Irradiation" 2017, 1).

Free radicals may very well be generated by gamma irradiation (Crews, Driffield, and Thomas 2012). This is especially concerning considering that cannabis compounds are sought after by informed consumers for their ability to reduce free-radical–induced inflammation and oxidative stress. Martin A. Lee (2012, 212) further notes that "produced when animals use oxygen to burn food for fuel, free radicals are implicated in the formation of protein amyloid plaques, which disrupt neural synapses and prevent normal brain function in Alzheimer's patients." Sources of free-radical stress include herbicides and pesticides, food additives and preservatives, corn syrup and artificial sweeteners, hydrogenated fats, air and water pollutants, synthetic household chemicals, prescription pharmaceuticals, alcohol, radiation, and cigarette smoke (Lee 2012, 213).

This raises the question: Why is nearly *all* of Canada's LP-produced cannabis being irradiated? Research has demonstrated that the practice destroys terpenes in cannabis, which are responsible for many of the plant's characteristics, including its flavour and purported health benefits. Indeed, irradiated cannabis, at least anecdotally, does not "exhibit the same taste, smell, and/or effects as non-irradiated cannabis" ("Gamma Irradiation" 2017). Jessica Rosslee (2018, 1) notes that "terpenes work in symphony with cannabinoids to present what has been dubbed as 'the entourage effect' to mitigate THC's 'tricky psychoactivity.'" Water loss during irradiation may also contribute to reports among users of a loss of pleasurable inhalation effect (Hazekamp 2016, 3).

In summary, although "the jury is still out" on irradiating cannabis, if concern for the health and safety of consumers is insufficient grounds for further scrutiny of regulatory practices, the tastes and preferences of users indicate that measures should be taken to ensure the right of citizens to access nonirradiated products containing a complete cannabis terpene profile.

Toward a Clean Cannabis Manifesto

> Commercial roses that you buy at the store for holidays are not regulated for human consumption. They might look pretty but they're often sprayed with pesticides and/or hazardous chemicals to keep them looking fresh, so only use organic roses or roses from a trusted garden when rolling rose blunts.
> – RAY LEXIS-OLIVIER, "HOW TO ROLL A ROSE BLUNT"

Since cannabis is known to be a bioaccumulator, a plant that absorbs toxins in growing environments, toxic chemicals must not be used in its production (Karadjov 2011).[7] The Government of Canada is not and should not be beholden to chemical corporations for pest-management solutions. The legal cannabis regime requires effective regulation by regulators who know something about cannabis production.[8]

Outdoor growing operations ought to be encouraged. Jorge Cervantes (2006, 344–45) notes that "fungal spores have little time to settle in a breeze, and grow poorly on wind-dried soil, stems, and leaves." So-called IPM solutions should prioritize the use of "natural organic sprays like Pyrethrum and Neem," which do not burn plant foliage, and as one of the masters of cannabis cultivation has urged, "use only contact sprays that are approved for edible plants" (Cervantes 2021, para. 19). Indoor-growing operations require awareness that fungi grow poorly in 40–50 percent relative humidity with good airflow (e.g., horizontal fans) and appropriate HVAC controls. Irrigation measures can be modified to ensure dryer grow conditions, and it is common knowledge that a clean production space is the best defence against powdery and downy mildews. No Myclobutanil required!

Relying on "organics" represents a contradiction for regulators fully familiar with industrial agriculture. Agribusiness models are exploitative of workers and the environment and are committed to the pursuit of profit at all costs. A commitment to less toxic business models would require more rigorous inspections and the power to close facilities, fine LPs, and charge corporate managers and investors with environmental and civil crimes under the Criminal Code. To ensure compliance by well-financed producers, repeated violations would require shutdowns, and continued flaunting of the laws would result in permanent closure.

To facilitate more rigorous inspections, regulators must have access to equipment for testing atmospheric, soil, and aqueous inputs and the surrounding environment. Inspections must include appropriate measures for protecting and monitoring the health of workers – including TFWs and SAWs. Other recommended measures include

- establishing comprehensive, industry-wide health plans for cannabis production workers – with workers having full proprietary ownership of personal health information
- enacting new laws acknowledging the health risks inherent to greenhouse and industrial agriculture applications – with adjudicatory mechanisms that protect the rights of workers
- requiring LPs to pay generously into a funding pool established to compensate workers in a way that is commensurate with severe occupational health hazards.

As we have seen, the properties of cannabis ensure that any toxin used in the production process is likely to end up inside the finished product. Shifting from toxic to organic growing methods, and from artificial to natural light sources, is also necessary for environmental health.[9] Perhaps a greener Canada warrants more incentives, in the form of corporate tax cuts and grants, to shift away from costly LED, high-pressure sodium, and metal halide lighting to solar.

New regulations to enforce industry accountability must include the full disclosure of all ingredients (both listed and "other") in pesticides and fertilizers used by cannabis producers. Finally, in addition to enforcing bans on toxic applications, Health Canada's vague mandate to prohibit all but some "acceptable residue" – which implies that there is some acceptable level of exposure to toxins for workers and consumers – must be revised to make zero tolerance the norm.

This chapter is informed by work experience and ethnographic observation conducted while working in illicit cannabis production for over a decade. The toxic cultivation practices of the illicit industry are being introduced into the legal landscape, putting workers and consumers at risk. Yet an industrial-scale "clean cannabis" model already exists, in the form of "legacy" or craft cannabis producers, and the small-batch production site. Cannabis is an accumulator plant; it soaks up toxins from its production space and passes them on to consumers. Cannabis production in Canada remains a risky undertaking due to toxic work environments, occupational health and safety hazards, and limited protections for workers under the law. Particularly vulnerable are migrant labourers, organized under the rubrics of the TFW Program and the SAW Program. Most vulnerable of all are migrant labouring women, who are exposed to sexual harassment in the workplace and unhygienic working conditions (Otero and Preibisch 2010).

Policy makers' collusion with chemical manufacturing and "big agriculture" places workers in harm's way, without sufficiently enforced legal protections. Despite assurances that "pest-control products" approved by Health Canada are safe for use on cannabis, inquiries into the available ingredients revealed that these products were not intended for use on cannabis. "Other ingredients" in pesticides and fertilizers place workers and consumers at risk. Irradiation of cannabis, the norm in the Canadian cannabis production space, alters the cannabis significantly, destroying "the entourage effect," which aids in mitigating THC's "tricky psychoactivity" (Lee 2012, 171).

A government commitment to the production of clean cannabis would go a long way to ensuring a nontoxic product and prioritizing the promotion of healthy public policy over the interests of licensed producers. For anyone who occasionally indulges, the next time you use legal cannabis, ask yourself this: How did this perfectly trimmed little bud get into its packaging? Someone had to grow it and prepare it for my use. What are the risks involved for those who do that work?!

Notes

1 Drying cannabis involves the application of a heat source in confined spaces to dehydrate the plant materials.
2 The fall guy also shares indoor space with chemicals such as insecticidal soaps, solvents (used to "up" or "down" pH levels), chemical fertilizers, antimicrobial agents,

hydrogen peroxide (to sterilize the water), micronutrients applied locally, pesticides and herbicides sprayed as foliar applications (e.g., Forbid 4F, Avid, Bifenazates, synthetic pyrethroids, sulfur), bleach (to wash down the space after cycling down), miticides (like Avamax), fungicides, and "chems" (used to balance electrical conductivity levels), among other contaminants.

3 Primary maintenance tasks include hacking new sites out of the temperate rainforest, "tempering" new clones in makeshift greenhouses, running water barrels up the mountain, creating reservoirs, cleaning filters, camouflaging operations, laying drip lines, scaring off bears, chatting with conservation officers, repairing water lines (after those same bears have eaten several metres of the black poly hose), cleaning injectors, talking to various weirdos you run into in the bush, hiding the trail head from tourists and "rippers," taking in the harvest, avoiding helicopters, building a dry shack (while trying not to burn it down with a tiger torch), pulling eight hundred pounds of crop from the bush, driving it through the night (while navigating roadblocks), and delivering your final report.

4 In the United States:

> Between 1990 and 1995, 600 companies from 44 different states sent 270 million pounds of toxic waste to farms and fertilizer companies across the country. The steel industry provided 30% of this waste. Used for its high levels of zinc, which is an essential nutrient for plant growth, steel industry wastes can include lead, arsenic, cadmium, chromium, nickel and dioxin, among other toxic substances. (Shaffer 2001, 11)

5 Myclobutanil [a-butyl-a-(chlorophenyl)-1H-1,2,4,triazole-1-propanenitrile] is a fungicide with reported exposure symptoms in rats and dogs that include eye irritation, hypertrophy, hepatocellular necrosis and increased liver weight, bilateral aspermatogenesis, increased incidences of hypospermia and cellular debris in the epididymides, and increased incidences of arteritis/periarteritis in the testes, hepatocellular hypertrophy, and increased alkaline phosphatase (e.g., subchronic exposures) (EPA 2008).

6 The history of cannabis and Paraquat is infamous, the pesticide having been sprayed on Mexican fields in the 1970s at the direction of US president Richard Nixon. The practice was continued under the Carter administration, and in the 1980s, Ronald Reagan adopted the "drug control" strategy domestically, spraying cannabis crops in Georgia and Kentucky. According to Jerome London (2021): "A scandal erupted in the state of Georgia in 1983 when it was uncovered that law enforcement officials had aided in smuggling drugs from south of the border into the USA. They had also facilitated the planting and cultivation of giant weed farms in Georgia's Chattahoochee Forest." This revelation led to Reagan authorizing the spraying of Paraquat on the Chattahoochee and the Daniel Boone National Forest in Kentucky (Russakoff 1983).

7 A wide variety of natural pest-control and fertilization methods are available to reduce the use of chemicals (see Cervantes 2006). Alternative pest-control methods include the use of alcohol (isopropyl), bleach, cinnamon, citrus, garlic, horseradish, hot pepper, hydrated lime, mint oil, vegetable oil, oregano, soap, and tobacco. Diatomaceous earth and *Quassia amara* controls aphids, *Rotenone* (from Derris,

Lonchocarpus, and Tephrosia root) kills flies (maggots), Ryania (of *Ryania speciosa*) kills thrips, and seaweed kills spider mites.

8 Required reading for all growers, and bureaucrats at every level in charge of this portfolio, for example, should include the most authoritative sources on the subject such as *Hemp Diseases and Pests: Management and Biological Control* (McPartland, Clarke, and Watson 2000) and *Marijuana Horticulture* (Cervantes 2006). These sources alone are sufficient to familiarize regulators and all growers with healthy, low-toxicity pest management solutions that are easily transferable to industrial-scale applications.

9 The carbon footprint of cannabis production is such that to produce one plant requires the equivalent of about 265 litres of oil (Hansen 2018). Put otherwise: producing 1 kilogram of finished cannabis product creates approximately "4600 kg of carbon dioxide emissions to the atmosphere, or that of 3 million average US cars when aggregated across all national production" (Mills 2012).

Works Cited

Arcury, Thomas A., Sara A. Quandt, Altha J. Cravey, Rebecca C. Elmore, and Gregory B. Russell. 2001. "Farmworker Reports of Pesticide Safety and Sanitation in the Work Environment." *American Journal of Industrial Medicine* 39 (5): 487–98.

Arcury, Thomas A., Sara A. Quandt, Pamela Rao, Alicia M. Doran, Beverly M. Snively, Dana B. Barr, Jane A. Hoppin, and Stephen W. Davis. 2005. "Organophosphate Pesticide Exposure in Farmworker Family Members in Western North Carolina and Virginia: Case Comparisons." *Human Organization* 64: 40–51.

Aurora Cannabis. 2019. "Wanted: Greenhouse Manager." Accessed May 29, 2019. https://careers.auroramj.com/job/Vancouver-Greenhouse-Manager%2C-Comox-Albe/533725717/.

Bilodeau, Pierre. 2018. Official Correspondence, Canada Food Inspection Agency, Quote: 243846, 244100; Executive Director, Plant Health and Biosecurity Directorate. September 6, 2018.

Biowork Inc. 2019. "Botanigard 22WP." https://www.bioworksinc.com/products/botanigard-22wp/botanigard-22wp-label.pdf.

Bracken, Amber. 2017. "Mysterious Symptoms and Medical Marijuana: Patients Are Looking for Answers." *Globe and Mail*, August 19. https://www.theglobeandmail.com/cannabis/article-mysterious-symptoms-and-medical-marijuana-patients-are-looking-for/.

CAISP (Canadian Agricultural Injury Surveillance Program). 2008. "Foreword and Executive Summary." *Agricultural Fatalities in Canada, 1990–2005*. Kingston: Canadian Agricultural Injury Surveillance Program.

Canadian Press. 2009. "Inquest Jury Says Big Passenger Vans 'High-Risk.'" *CBC News*, December 10. https://www.cbc.ca/news/canada/british-columbia/inquest-jury-says-big-passenger-vans-high-risk-1.811616.

Canopy. 2019. "Section Grower," help-wanted posting. http://jobs.canopygrowth.com.

Cayman Chemical. 2016. "Abamectin," safety data sheet. Accessed June 26, 2019. https://www.caymanchem.com/msdss/19201m.pdf.

Centers for Disease Control and Prevention. 2018. "Facts about Paraquat." https://emergency.cdc.gov/agent/paraquat/basics/facts.asp.

Cervantes, Jorge. 2006. *Marijuana Horticulture*. Vancouver, WA: Van Patten.

—. 2021. "Ch. 14: Pests, Fungi, and Diseases." In *Marijuana Horticulture: The Indoor/Outdoor Medical Grower's Bible*. China: Van Patten.

Cesarone, Travis. 2021. "Health Canada Approves Chloropicrin Fumigant for Cannabis Farms." March 6, https://cannabislifenetwork.com/fumigant-approved-for-cannabis-farms/.

Connell, Raewyn. 2010. "Understanding Neoliberalism." In *Neoliberalism and Everyday Life*, edited by Susan Braedley and Meg Luxton, 22-36. Montreal/Kingston: McGill-Queen's University Press.

Conrad, Frank, and Cindy Blair. 2015. "Eagle 20 and Myclobutanil in the Context of Cannabis Cultivation and Consumption." *Colorado Greenlab* (blog), May 14. http://www.coloradogreenlab.com/blog/eagle-20-and-myclobutanil-in-the-context-of-cannabis-cultivation-and-consumption.

CEEP (Convention on the Elaboration of European Pharmacopoeia). 2001–7. "5.1.4. Microbiological Quality of Non-sterile Pharmaceutical Preparations and Substances for Pharmaceutical Use." *European Pharmacopoeia 7.0*. Strasbourg: Council of Europe.

Crews, Colin, Malcolm Driffield, and Christopher Thomas. 2012. "Analysis of 2-Alkylcyclobutanones for Detection of Food Irradiation: Current Status, Needs and Prospects." *Journal of Food Composition and Analysis* 26 (1–2): 1–11.

Delaney, Joan. 2008. "Poor Safety, Health Standards for B.C. Farmworkers, Study Shows." *Epoch Times*, June 26. Accessed September 29, 2009. http://www.theepochtimes.com/news/8--6--26/72481.html.

"Doktor Doom Formula 420 3-in-1." 2019. Accessed June 25, 2019. http://hawaii.gov/hdoa/labels/8588.3.pdf.

EPA (Environmental Protection Agency). 2006. "Myclobutanil; Pesticide Tolerance." *Federal Register*, December 20. https://www.federalregister.gov/documents/2006/12/20/E6-21489/myclobutanil-pesticide-tolerance.

"Gamma Irradiation on Cannabis: A Controversial Topic." 2017. *Cannabis.info*, July 22. https://manoxblog.com/2019/11/15/gamma-irradiation-on-cannabis-a-controversial-topic/.

Globe Newswire. 2018. "On International Migrants Day, Canada's Food Workers' Union Calls on Government to Reform TFWP." December 18. https://www.globenewswire.com/news-release/2018/12/18/1668855/0/en/On-International-Migrants-Day-Canada-s-food-workers-union-calls-on-government-to-reform-TFWP.html.

Graebner, William. 1984. "Doing the World's Unhealthy Work: The Fiction of Free Choice." *Hastings Center Report* 14 (4): 28–37.

Green Organic Dutchman. 2018. "Community Farmhand," help-wanted posting. Accessed March 5, 2018. https://tgod.bamboohr.com/jobs/view.php?id=12.

Hansen, Luis. 2017. "A Growing Problem: Lightening the Carbon Footprint of Cannabis Farms." *Mercury News,* October 3. https://phys.org/news/2017-10-problem-carbon-footprint-Cannabis-farms.html.

Harvey, David. 1982. "Chapter 8: The Limits to Capital" In *Key Texts in Human Geography.* CA: SAGE Publications.

—. 2000. Chapter 6, "The Body as an Accumulation Strategy." In *Spaces of Hope: California Studies in Critical Human Geography.* Berkeley: University of California Press.

Hazekamp, Arno. 2016. "Evaluating the Effects of Gamma-Irradiation for Decontamination of Medicinal Cannabis." *Frontiers in Pharmacology* 7: 108. https://doi.org/10.3389/fphar.2016.00108.

Health Canada. 2017. "Statement from Health Canada on the Testing of Cannabis for Medical Purposes for Unauthorized Pest Control Products." February 14.

—. 2019. "Licensed Cultivators, Processors and Sellers of Cannabis under the *Cannabis Act*." https://www.canada.ca/en/health-canada/services/drugs-medication/cannabis/industry-licensees-applicants/licensed-cultivators-processors-sellers.html.

—. 2021. "Licensed cultivators, processors and sellers of cannabis under the *Cannabis Act*" In Health Canada webpages, 13 August 2021.

Holmstrom, Nancy. 2011. "Against Capitalism as Theory and as Reality." Chapter 2 in *Capitalism, For and Against: A Feminist Debate,* by Anne E. Cudd and Nancy Holmstrom, 133–260. Cambridge: Cambridge University Press.

Howse, Dana. 2017. "Injured Workers' Moral Engagement in the Compensation System: The Social Production of Problematic Claiming Experience." PhD diss., University of Toronto.

Judkins, Bennett M. 1986. *We Offer Ourselves as Evidence: Towards Workers' Control of Occupational Health.* New York: Greenwood Press.

Karadjov, Julian. 2011. "Eliminating Heavy-Metal Toxicity in Medical Marijuana, to Produce Patients' Medicine Safer Than Drinking Water." A research white paper, Bulgarian Academy of Sciences.

Larson, Alice. 2001. *Environmental/Occupational Safety and Health.* Migrant Health Issues Monograph Series, vol. 2. Buda, TX: National Center for Farmworker Health.

Lee, Martin A. 2012. *Smoke Signals: A Social History of Marijuana – Medical, Recreational, and Scientific.* New York: Scribner.

Lexis-Olivier, Ray. 2019. "How to Roll a Rose Blunt." *L.A. Taco,* May 31. https://www.lataco.com/how-to-roll-a-rose-blunt/.

London, Jerome. 2021. "Paraquat Pot: The True Story Of How The US Government Tried To Kill Weed Smokers With A Toxic Chemical In The 1980s." *Thought Catalog,* February 4. https://thoughtcatalog.com/jeremy-london/2018/08/paraquat-pot/.

Magdoff, Fred, and Harry Magdoff. 2004. "Disposable Workers Today's Reserve Army of Labor." *Monthly Review: An Independent Socialist Magazine* 55 (11): 18–35.

McPartland, J.M., R.C. Clarke, and D.P. Watson. 2000. *Hemp Diseases and Pests: Management and Biological Control.* New York: CAB International.

Miller, Jackie. 2017. "Health Canada Orders Medical Marijuana Growers to Test for Banned Pesticides." *Ottawa Sun*, 2017. https://ottawacitizen.com/news/local-news/health-canada-orders-medical-marijuana-growers-to-test-for-banned-pesticides/.

Mills, Evan. 2012. "The Carbon Footprint of Indoor Cannabis Production." *Energy Policy* 46: 58–67.

Moore, Graeme. 2004. *Hand-Harvesters of Fraser Valley Berry Crops: New Era Protection of Vulnerable Employees*. Vancouver: BC Federation of Labour.

Navarro, Vincente. 2009. "What We Mean by Social Determinants of Health." *Global Health Promotion* 16 (1): 5–16.

Neudorff. 2015. "Neudosan New Blattlausfrei." https://biogrow.co.za/wp-content/uploads/2015/03/MSDS-Neudosan-Neu.pdf.

OHP. 2017. "Kopa Insecticidal Soap." https://www.ohp.com/Labels_MSDS/PDF/kopa_sds.pdf.

Otero, Gerardo, and Kerry Preibisch. 2010. *Farmworker Health and Safety: Challenges for British Columbia*. Vancouver: WorkSafeBC/Simon Fraser University, Department of Sociology.

Quan, Douglas. 2019. "RCMP Went Silent about Massive Pot Bust over Concern for Marijuana Producer's Stock Price, Documents Reveal: There Were Also Concerns the Release of Information Could Embarrass Health Canada and Expose 'Deficiencies' in New Medical Marijuana Regulations." *National Post*, May 31. https://nationalpost.com/news/canada/rcmp-went-silent-about-massive-pot-bust-over-concern-for-marijuana-producers-stock-price-documents-reveal.

Quandt, Sara A., María A. Hernández-Valero, Joseph G. Grzywacz, Joseph D. Hovey, and Melissa Gonzales. 2006. "Workplace, Household, and Personal Predictors of Pesticide Exposure for Farmworkers." *Environmental Health Perspectives* 14: 943–52.

Robertson, Grant. 2016a. "Canadians Not Told about Banned Pesticide Found in Medical Pot Supply." *Globe and Mail*, December 29. https://www.theglobeandmail.com/news/national/canadians-not-told-about-banned-pesticide-found-in-medical-marijuana-supply/article33443887/.

—. 2016b. "Ottawa Failed to Act on Tests Showing Toxins in Retail Pot." *Globe and Mail*, September 21. https://www.theglobeandmail.com/news/national/ottawa-failed-to-act-on-tests-showing-toxins-in-retail-pot/article31980965/.

Robertson, Grant. 2017. "Banned Pesticide Found at Medical Marijuana Company." *Globe and Mail*, May 2. https://www.theglobeandmail.com/news/national/banned-pesticide-found-at-medical-marijuana-company/article34882109/.

Rosslee, Jessica. 2018. "Cannabis Irradiation: Canada's Hot Topic – With the Recent Implementation of Canada's Legalized Cannabis Laws, There Are Stringent Regulations to Ensure the Safe Development of a Healthy Market." *Cannabis Tech*, December. Accessed June 2, 2019. https://www.Cannabistech.com/articles/Cannabis- irradiation-canadas-hot-topic/.

Russakoff, Daniel. 1983. "Use of Paraquat to Kill Marijuana Stirs Protests." *Washington Post*, August 25. https://www.washingtonpost.com/archive/politics/1983/08/25/use-of-paraquat-to-kill-marijuana-stirs-protests/33fc0618-ecb8-4b2c-be2a-9bf71f659553/.

Sakala, Carol. 1987. "Migrant and Seasonal Farmworkers in the United States: A Review of Health Hazards, Status, and Policy." *International Migration Review* 21: 659–87.

Seibert, Amanda. 2017. "Myclobutanil: Why Are Some Licensed Cannabis Producers Using This Banned Pesticide?" *Georgia Straight*, 2017. Accessed April 4, 2018. https://www.straight.com/Cannabis/958891/myclobutanil-why-are-some-licensed-Cannabis-producers-using-banned-pesticide.

Shaffer, Matthew. 2001. *Waste Lands: The Threat of Toxic Fertilizer.* San Francisco, CA: California Public Interest Research Group Charitable Trust.

Tanner, Caroline M., Freya Kamel, G. Webster Ross, Jane A. Hoppin, Samuel M. Goldman, Monica Korell, Connie Marras, et al. 2011. "Rotenone, Paraquat, and Parkinson's Disease." *Environmental Health Perspectives* 119 (6): 866–72.

Tomlinson, Kathy. 2019. "Ottawa Moves to End Employers' Monopoly on Foreign Workers." *Globe and Mail*, June 24. https://www.theglobeandmail.com/politics/article-ottawa-moves-to-end-employers-monopoly-on-foreign-workers/.

Toth, Katie. 2017. "Banned Pesticides Keep Turning Up in Canada's Medical Weed." *Vice News*, April 21. https://motherboard.vice.com/en_us/article/d7bymx/canada-legalized-weed-medicalmarijuana-pesticides-recall-testing-weedweek2017.

Up Cannabis. 2018. "Processing Manager," help-wanted posting, March 15.

USP (US Pharmacopeia). 2015. "1111: Microbiological Attributes of Nonsterile Pharmaceutical Products." *U.S. Pharmacopoeia*. Rockville, MD: USP.

Valent. 2017. "Actinovate SP." Accessed June 25, 2019. https://www.valent.com/Data/Labels/2017-ACSP-0001.pdf.

Verduzco, Gustavo, and María Isabel Lozano. 2003. *Mexican Workers' Participation in CSAWP and Development Consequences in the Workers' Rural Home Communities.* Ottawa: North-South Institute.

WSIB. 2019. "Occupational Disease and Unsafe Workplace Health Hazards." https://www.wsib.ca/en/businesses/claims/occupational-disease-and-workplace-health-hazards.

PART 3
CANNABIS SUBJECTIVITIES
AN ARRAY OF VOICES

9
Women in Corporate Cannabis Work

JEANNETTE VANDERMAREL, KARINA LAHNAKOSKI, and ALISON McMAHON

From a Good:House to Good:Farm
An interview with Jeannette VanderMarel

I first read about Jeannette VanderMarel when the *Hamilton Spectator* ran a piece on women in legal cannabis production in February 2019. As the co-CEO of 48North, she oversaw the acquisition of a 100-acre farm that was Canada's then-largest outdoor cannabis production facility. That farm, and all of 48North, has since been gobbled up by HEXO Corp. in the frantic mergers and acquisitions frenzy of the contemporary moment (New Cannabis Ventures 2021). My interview request by phone was readily accepted, and on April 19, I drove down the 403 to Brantford for our scheduled meeting at Good:House, 48North's new facility just off Wayne Gretzky Parkway.

After being greeted by Jimmy, Jeannette's raucous poodle, she ushered me into her office for a spirited discussion about what makes a successful cannabis licensed producer (LP) CEO tick. Her energy was welcoming, and our conversation about Canada's new burgeoning LP industry was casual and candid. My work experience in the illegal cannabis industry occasionally proved useful as an instrument for gliding past sound bites and talking points of the type commonly prepared to service media inquiries. The year

2018 was fraught with scandal in the industry. In February, charges of insider trading hit Aphria-Nuuvera.[1]

Aurora's hostile bid for CanniMed raised hackles in an industry where such scandalous conduct was common. But nothing rattled investors or angered analysts more than the business practices of Aphria.[2] VanderMarel was both well-informed and frank about such shady dealings in the industry. She disclosed (though she need not have) that all of Good:Farm's cannabis would be irradiated, as per Health Canada's specifications for medicinal cannabis, which specify a maximum of one thousand colony-forming units (CFUs) of mould spores per gram of dried product. This struck me as a startling admission, considering "boutique" cannabis consumers' preference for unadulterated products.

Our lengthy interview that winter was conversational and trusting enough that by the end of it, it seemed entirely fitting to press VanderMarel for a tour of the Good:Farm. Three months later, in late July 2019, she welcomed me onto the property of the production acreage. And there was Jimmy, Jeannette's bellicose poodle, faithfully at her side in the golf cart she used to show visitors around. As we puttered about, we looked on rows and rows of cannabis starts, some in fine shape, others displaying signs of a slow start because of a late spring.

"We're going to pull 40,000 kilograms," Jeannette asserted. "I'd rather underpromise and overdeliver." Although I had my doubts because we were midway through the summer already, I can honestly say that I'd never tried growing 100 acres of *cannabis-ruderalis* cross![3]

On September 10, 2019, VanderMarel stepped down as co-CEO of 48North, citing personal reasons.[4] Perhaps the Canadian LP cannabis sector had, by late 2019, become so toxic as to be uninhabitable? However it continues, VanderMarel's story, a counternarrative of integrity and vision, is worth telling. What follows are selected excerpts from our interview and conversations. — C.J.S.M.

The basic background is a rather long and winding story. I grew up in an agricultural and entrepreneurial family. I ended up going into health care. My daughter, Breanne, was born in 1994 with Dravet Syndrome, which includes uncontrollable epilepsy, unfortunately. Despite her being on twenty different drugs, she never received cannabis. She passed away suddenly in 2003. I don't know if cannabis would have cured her, but I do believe it would have improved her quality of life.

Because of this tragedy, I became interested in the cannabis industry in 2009, when I started seeing families and patients using cannabis for epilepsy and other conditions while I was working at the Pediatric Intensive Care Unit at McMaster Hospital as a registered nurse, charge nurse, team leader.

My husband and I formed a company called the Green Organic Dutchman. It was a long and winding road to get through [Health Canada's legal licensed producer of cannabis] licensing, but we eventually did. I formally left that company in 2017 and contemplated retiring. But I saw there was still a lot of opportunity in the cannabis space, especially for women and diversity and creating a real industry that is not focused on stock promotion but creating great products for patients and consumers. So that inspired me to found Good and Green along with my business partner, Tyne Daniel Goldberg, and we quickly received licensing in October 2018.

Prior to that, I had been working with 48North, and they were an LP with one production space in northern Ontario. They had a northern location in Kirkland Lake, Ontario (a very state-of-the-art production facility) and a head office in Toronto. I vended Good and Green into 48North. We became one company under two licences, my Brantford facility and the Del Shen facility in Kirkland Lake, but at the same time, we were concurrently trying to get an outdoor licence for cultivation for the outdoor farm. I see outdoor cultivation as a real game-changer in the industry.[5]

Fortunately, we received our new outdoor licence a few weeks ago [in April 2019], and we're actively growing on the farm right now. Our products are currently for sale in Quebec, Alberta, and through the Ontario Cannabis Store. We had a landmark agreement; no provincial regulator or distributor has ever purchased outdoor-grown cannabis in Canada. Uniquely, Quebec actually signed the agreement prior to us receiving licensing. They recognized the supply deficit that's currently occurring in the legal market and acted accordingly.

48North is really a health and wellness company focusing on products for a lifestyle that includes cannabis, as well as a healthy lifestyle. That's really the focus of our company at 48North. We will create next-generation products for consumers, such as vape pens, topicals for skincare, sublingual applications, things that are not combustible, as well as continuing with our lines of prerolled "joints" and dried flower.

We've recently announced agreements: we've partnered with three great brands. Avitas is the most popular whole-plant, natural-extract vape pen selling in the Northwest, including California. So we've signed an agreement with them that we will be manufacturing their products in Canada at our Brantford facility, for distribution throughout Canada. They have an amazing team. It allows us to replicate their [US] lab [here] at Brantford. They bring in their science team and advisers.

We've also partnered with Mother and Clone, a brilliant product out of Denver, Colorado. It's a fast-acting sublingual spray, with the efficacy and onset of cannabis without actually smoking. It's a calorie-free, scent-free spray you spray under your tongue. Mother and Clone kicks in in a matter of minutes; it's metered dosing, so you can do as many milligrams as you see fit. It's a great option for consumers compared to edibles, which can take a long time to become bioavailable. A fast-acting spray will hopefully dissuade people from overconsuming. One of the challenges with edibles is the prolonged onset and peak.[6]

There are some emerging markets. We're looking at international expansion, whether it be to license our IP and [cannabis-production] protocols or partnering with other countries to help develop medical programs in their countries and possibly, eventually, going to adult-use therapeutic [legal recreational]. So there's a lot of opportunities in the UK, in the EU, as well as emerging markets such as Central and South America, Australia. So we're certainly looking at those options as well. There also is an opportunity for us to export our products from Canada to countries where medical cannabis is legal, such as Germany.[7]

Also US acquisitions. Currently, obviously, we would never break a US federal law, so we wouldn't be touching the cannabis plant, but with the new US Hemp Act, we can now work with companies in the United States to develop CBD and hemp-use products that we can distribute under our brand and our companies throughout the United States. We have staff in the US every week working on strategy around US legal non-THC production companies.

We're very thankful and pleased that there are other licensed producers in Canada that have received outdoor cultivation licences. But we at 48North remain the only one licensed under the Cannabis Act. We are the largest at this time. There are a couple of things that are beneficial to being covered under the Cannabis Act, the most exciting part is that it has been challenging to the legalized cannabis LP market to obtain and acquire genetic materials for new varietals. Under the Cannabis Act, we were allowed a one-time acquisition of new cultivars [cultivated varieties] and genetics, which we have fully utilized, so the other producers that have been licensed, they have all had their existing licences amended. They weren't granted the same opportunities that we were. So it's allowed us to really increase the genetic cultivars that are available in the licensed industry, and we can then share them among our sites.

So one hundred acres of cannabis. Certainly, there are challenges and great rewards. For me, I grew up in agriculture. Cannabis started outdoors and only moved indoors because it was illegal.

We expect that 80 percent of our crop will be going to the value-added next-generation market. The agriculture industry doesn't grow any other product indoors for an extract market; we don't grow grapes indoors for wine or canola indoors for canola oil. It just doesn't make sense. This is an agricultural commodity, and I think it's really, really important to conceive of cannabis in this way because indoor cannabis cultivation is extremely energy-intensive and a real drain on our ecosystem.

We do have two indoor sites, for dried cannabis, for therapeutic use, for somebody that needs a consistent product [medical-grade cannabis for use by chemotherapy patients, for example, and chronic pain sufferers]. We provide that, if they want to use dried cannabis for a preroll or dried-flower format. For everything else, extracts are the way to go. We've seen in markets that are more developed, like in California and Colorado, that a great preponderance of products being sold are extracts and value-added products. That gives a consistency in products for the consumer.

For us, it's really the ESG – environmental, social, and governance – part of this. We consider ourselves to be a really ESG-focused company, or CSR – corporate social responsibility.

Number one is environment. It is not sustainable or tenable to grow indoors a plant that grows so well organically outdoors. Cannabis is one of the few crops we can grow outdoors without pesticides in our southern Ontario environment. We are so thrilled to be growing 100 percent organically on an organic farm. We're not adding any synthetic pesticides or chemical pesticides or fertilizers to the watershed. We're close to the Grand River, and I think it's really important to protect our natural environment.

About 30 percent of our crop will be autoflower, a *ruderalis* cross, very unique in that they don't require a certain number of hours of light per day in order to flower. We're striving for two crops this year. We've already planted the first crop and harvest in the first week or so of August. A few weeks prior to that, we'll seed the second batch, which we'll harvest in early to mid-October. The remainder is a variety of CBD-dominant strain, and some of high THC and a variety of hybrids. It is very difficult to get a pure *sativa* or pure *indica*, but a lot of the hybrids we're growing are sativa-dominant. I think there's a lot of benefit from the size they can get to, the yield. They are a longer-flowering period; there are challenges with that. But I think we're ready for this challenge.[8]

We've intentionally underestimated our yield. We estimated that we hope to get 40,000 kilograms from our farm. If you study other outdoor growers' expected yields, they are much higher than ours. I would much rather under-promise and overdeliver. I hope we exceed that. I think that was a responsible estimate of our yield for this year.

As to social responsibility, I work on this aspect of our corporate performance every day. Female is very important; women are a priority here at 48North. So many groups have been unreasonably ostracized and unfortunately victimized by the illegality of cannabis: people of colour, minorities, the disproportionate representation of lower socioeconomic status humans in criminal-justice contexts. So it is not just female, though the gendered asymmetry on corporate boards, as CEOs, is a big part of it. This is a unique opportunity to create an industry that is gender-blind, colour-blind, and just brings the best people in.

So we're very pleased that 40 percent of our board currently is female. More than 60 percent of our C-suite is female. I certainly think we're an industry leader in this. But it's also important to see that women need to be empowered, and there's a skill set that comes from investment bankers, junior miners – shell companies, more or less. In the early days of cannabis, all of the companies, like junior miners, were merely speculative. Today, they actually must deliver revenue to be successful. Those executives tend to be all men. And it's really important for us to support and mentor women coming into our company. So I'm certainly hiring some great people but also promoting individuals from within the company who happen to be women.

The challenge is that many women have great skills and transferable skills, but the black-and-grey market has been unduly difficult for women who can't risk freedom for a plant.

When we look at resumés, we look at transferable skills. Any mom that has raised four kids and managed hockey and soccer and breakfast, lunch, and dinner is an amazing executive assistant because, wow! They have amazing time-management skills. It is using a critical lens to look at resumés and applicants and finding those transferable skills. We do undervalue women's work in general, and I think it's very important to really value the skills that somebody has developed by doing domestic work.

If I could do it, anyone can. I had no special skills, just a profound determination and passion to do what I do. And I'm very thankful for my success, but as someone who had no special skills in starting a huge public company, it has been a privilege and an honour to do this, but also I hope to demonstrate that women can and should go forth. People ask, What is my one key message? I always say: "Say yes. Say yes to an opportunity or a challenge. Say yes to taking on a new skill or a new role." Because, so often, as people, often women especially, we tend to be afraid of challenges because we feel we do not have the skill sets, but we do.

Lastly, I feel that outdoor cannabis cultivation can be a real opportunity for Canadian farmers. I think we can revitalize agriculture in Canada. Cannabis can clean soils and remediate land. Let's get to work![19]

Building Consumer Trust in a Nascent Industry
Karina Lahnakoski

I first heard of Karina Lahnakoski in early 2019 while looking through proposals for Canada's forthcoming extracts and edibles regulations. The Cannabis Act mandated that regulations governing edibles and extracts be introduced within one year of the October 2018 legalization date.

Lahnakoski's voice stood out in a cannabis "journalism" sector muddied by dishonesty and "green rush" profiteering. Her twenty-odd years of experience working in regulated industries translated into sound advice concerning the best practices of quality assurance, which are highly relevant to cannabis production. Canada's adoption of the European Union's Good Management Practices (EU GMP), for example, would mean that cannabis products produced in Canada would become viable for sale to a larger global market (the whole European Union and the United States). Meeting and exceeding the GMP is known in regulated industries that pride themselves on quality assurance as being "beyond compliance."

Lahnakoski's contribution to this volume sheds important light on the challenges that face an industry attempting to regulate itself. It remains to be seen whether measures adopted will be sufficient to produce reliably safe products – and spur the level of demand required to sustain the industry beyond the frenetic early days of the so-called green rush. – C.J.S.M.

My perspective comes from being embedded in the cannabis space from 2017 onward after an eighteen-year career in pharmaceuticals. In 2017, cannabis experienced the green rush as Canadian companies ramped up for recreational legalization and the pursuit of the international market.

On Regulations

For pharmaceuticals, Health Canada and international regulators such as the US FDA and European Union spent decades developing regulations for consumer or patient protection, adjusting them when deficiencies (sometimes tragedies) occurred in the industry and progressively making the system stronger. International regulators work together to share information and take action on developments and directions for the industry. The standards we have today for regulatory compliance of drugs are now some of the highest in the world.

The cannabis industry, on the other hand, isn't there yet. The regulations are young in comparison: the Marihuana Medical Access Regulations (MMAR) of 2001 were changed in 2014 to the Marihuana for Medical Purposes Regulations (MMPR), which were changed again in 2016 to the Access to Cannabis for Medical Purposes Regulations (ACMPR), until, finally, the Cannabis Act in 2018 legalized recreational use. And the regulations continue to evolve as additional product classes (such as edible cannabis) are subsequently legalized. Our regulations are still infantile compared to the grandparents of other regulated industries – we don't have decades of experience to draw on, and we don't have international regulators to help us regulate, because, perhaps for the first time in Canada's history, we are breaking new ground.

Canada's regulatory regime is unique. It's not regulated like pharma, and it's not regulated like agriculture. It's somewhere in between – a little bit like medicine but also like a CPG (consumer packaged good) product. We could be grateful for this because the sentiment that a plant shouldn't be regulated exists, and bringing the black market into the regulated space takes a reasonable and achievable level of control. Yet many other countries consider cannabis a medicinal product and are regulating it under existing drug laws. Canada is certainly "going it alone" with a set of regulations that differ from every other jurisdiction in the world.

The frustrating thing to watch is companies making errors that have already been learned in those parallel, regulated industries. We are seeing rampant production issues that could easily have been avoided if the learned history had been extrapolated into this new industry. We see recalls that would have never occurred in other industries with regulatory controls. We also experience the internal struggles of companies that have the experienced quality and regulatory staff they need to avoid these issues, but they are not implementing improvements because they are not required by the Cannabis Act.

We should not have to relearn all these lessons. But because Canada did not take existing regulations from those spaces, we essentially ensured a "square one" approach to the regulation of cannabis production. The cannabis industry will require time to go through the rounds of continuous improvement over many years to get to a sophisticated level of performance. Those companies that have instilled higher levels of compliance and drawn experience from parallel industries such as pharma will have a head start and therefore a clear advantage.

On Corporate Governance

In an emerging industry, started largely by small private companies, establishing corporate governance is not normally a priority for a firm. Operational considerations and maintaining first-mover advantage are priorities for leaders – the green rush during 2016–18 saw companies scrambling to get ahead and stay ahead.

During this time, corporate governance (the system by which companies are directed and controlled, including installation of experienced boards to direct the company) was a lower priority. The boards selected can be wracked with nepotism – choosing friends over experience. With numerous companies building at a rapid clip, in a newly regulated space, with inexperienced boards, big failures are likely to occur. The board is responsible for risk management, which is difficult to do in this environment – certainly, only experienced management teams guided by proper principles can do this well.

Many believe that a reckoning is coming, given the way many companies are conducting themselves within the industry. I don't think it will be a reckoning but rather a slow series of failures and embarrassments – some public but many hidden. Much like relearning best practices in regulatory compliance, corporate governance is also being relearned in cannabis, even though we have learned those lessons before.

Building Trust

Building consumer trust is going to be a slow process. Trust is developed over time with strong branding, a quality product consistently delivered, and a reputable company at the helm. Brands are attempting to build trust in this new industry; however, this is difficult because of the restrictive regulations set for cannabis companies. In this unique case, we also have the challenge of winning over a legacy cannabis market (the black market) that is reluctant to change its purchasing habits. The industry needs help.

There are initiatives. Take, for example, the inaugural C45 Summit, held in Winnipeg in April 2019. The C45 Summit was the first ever meeting of professionals who work at the plant level to maintain quality systems in the very facilities that bring consumers product. This was a critical first step because every other industry – pharma, food, medical devices, and so on – has industry associations in which the people doing the work and making the daily quality decisions can share best practices. There was a sense of relief in the room during the first meetings of the C45, relief that we were finally getting away from stock-pumping business conferences to talking about things that will impact the longevity of the business: quality, regulations, and a strong industry relationship with Health Canada.

Another industry association is the Global Cannabis Partnership (GCP), established in 2018. The GCP was established under the premise that the industry must act responsibly, collaboratively, and transparently and engage in continuous improvement. In other words, we must "behave." Given this goal, the GCP is establishing corporate social responsibility (CSR) standards for the industry, and they are doing this proactively. Most other industries have had to implement CSR reactively to justify their existence to regulators and the public after major disasters. It is still early days, but the success of the GCP and the proactive approach to CSR will be major steps toward building the industry to a reputable place where brands can be trusted.

Where We Go from Here

These initiatives to improve and collaborate are key to serving the needs of the medical and recreational consumer and the public health objectives of Health Canada. Those committed to quality and constant, continuous improvement will become the subset of companies that will build sustainable businesses and become key players in advancing the industry – not only in Canada but globally. In the meantime, Canada is under the magnifying glass. As we roll out legalization, the world is watching this social experiment to determine if they will follow our lead. Let's lead responsibly.

Cannabis Jobs in Canada
Alison McMahon

I first became aware of Alison McMahon's important work in 2018, when I set out to find employment in Canada's then burgeoning but new cannabis industry. Having worked in cannabis production for over a decade and living in Ontario (home to half of all licensed producers), I felt my job prospects were sure to be abundant, if all the hype about jobs in the sector were true (or so I reasoned). In fact, the call-back rate was truly underwhelming. My disappointment led me to look more closely at the job ads. As I documented in Chapter 8 of this volume, there is a high demand for workers with pest-management experience. For the present purposes, however, further context is in order.

The Ontario Liberals were in power at the time and had every intention of completing another term. An early June election date loomed, but it did not deter Premier Kathleen Wynne and her cabinet from designing the province's cannabis distribution regime, a project for which they, and the other provinces and territories, were responsible under the terms of the Cannabis Act. One result was the creation of the Ontario Cannabis Store (OCS), conceived as an arm of the province's massive liquor distribution branch, the LCBO. As the OCS rollout moved into its early stages, I started applying for distribution work.

One position that interested me was as a store manager at the Hamilton OCS. I have a background in retail management and thought this was a good fit. The HR firm retained by the province was McMahon's Cannabis@work. This was my first interaction with the CEO of an HR firm. That an Alberta-based HR firm had been hired by an Ontario government corporation seemed significant. Moreover, the fact that a cannabis-specific HR firm even existed in Canada suggested that a great deal of hiring was indeed underway.

Perhaps I was mistaken in suspecting that the promise of hiring was just another means of shameless self-promotion by the licensed-producer sector, a marketing ploy amounting to all sizzle and no steak. Perhaps the workforce has been increasing after all. Whatever the case may be – and only time will tell – McMahon's contribution to our edited collection sheds important light on the historical formation of the legal cannabis industry in terms of market labour. Here is what an expert on the workforce has to say. – C.J.S.M.

Many things remain uncertain about the exact way cannabis legalization will unfold over the long term in Canada. One thing that is clear is that the cannabis industry has always been a source of jobs, and job creation has been a strong part of the narrative under the legal regime. Let's look at jobs by following the multiyear journey to recreational legalization in Canada.

Pre-Marihuana Medical Access Regulations (MMAR)
Jobs in cannabis have been part of Canada's employment history for decades, both on the right and wrong sides of the law.

Canada has had a black market for cannabis for many decades. Although these are jobs that wouldn't be recognized formally, many Canadians made an income by growing, harvesting, and selling cannabis illegally. Products such as extracts and hash were also produced and sold illegally through drug dealers or online stores.

In addition to jobs in the black market, there were also jobs in quasi-legal dispensaries and compassion clubs in Vancouver and other cities across Canada.

The obvious legal jobs connected to the cannabis industry prior to formal regulations were jobs in head shops, where employees would sell cannabis accessories like pipes, bongs, rolling papers, and other paraphernalia.

The Marihuana Medical Access Regulations (MMAR)

In 2000, the *Parker* case led to the creation of the first medical cannabis regulations in Canada. Parker argued that a total prohibition on cannabis was an infringement of human rights where an individual used the plant for medical purposes. The courts ruled in favour of Parker, and the Marihuana for Medical Purposes Regulations (MMAR) were born.

With the creation of the MMAR also came the first government-sanctioned cannabis cultivation facility, Prairie Plant Systems located in Saskatchewan. This facility received its licence from Health Canada on September 19, 2013. Individuals with a medical authorization for cannabis could purchase their cannabis from Prairie Plant Systems, grow plants in their home, or assign a designated grower to cultivate cannabis on their behalf.

A facility like Prairie Plant Systems creates jobs in cultivation, harvesting and packaging, quality assurance, and corporate services. In 2013, Health Canada issued a total of six licences to other medical cannabis production facilities. These facilities offered employment in similar job categories.

Also, Health Canada created a cannabis office that was another source of jobs connected to the emerging legal cannabis industry.

Interestingly, a loophole in the MMAR also led to the creation of MMAR grows, which were and continue to be a source of employment. Under the MMAR, an individual could receive a medical authorization that allowed them to grow a significant number of plants – in some cases, hundreds. They could grow them on their own or assign the cultivation of the plants to a designated grower or "caregiver." In some cases, designated growers cultivated for multiple patients in one facility. These MMAR grows were usually in a retrofit warehouse or industrial bay. In many cases, the designated grower would hire cultivation staff to manage the plants, harvest them, and distribute them to patients.

A number of concerns have emerged with MMAR grows. First, the cultivation is largely unregulated, and there is no oversight over the chemicals used for plant nutrients or pest management. Additionally, lab testing isn't required, so microbial or pest contaminants are not assessed during the cultivation process. While many MMAR growers are passionate about the plant, concerns about the quality of cannabis exist in any unregulated scenario.

A second issue with MMAR grows is diversion of the product to the black market. While MMAR grows are legal, diversion of product to anyone other than the patient with the medical authorization is not. There has been a history of MMAR growers being charged for cultivation and trafficking.

The Marihuana for Medical Purposes Regulations (MMPR)
In 2014, a new regulatory framework was implemented: the Marijuana for Medical Purposes Regulations (MMPR).

One of the changes under the MMPR was the removal of home growing for patients altogether, a right they enjoyed under the MMAR. The goal was to rectify the issue with MMAR grows – product diversion. The change was immediately challenged, and a case, *Allard v Canada*, was launched to argue for the reinstatement of patients' right to grow at home. The Supreme Court of Canada ruled in favour of Allard in August 2016, reinstating the patients' right to grow at home. However, designated growers were capped at growing for two individuals, rendering many large-scale MMAR grows no longer legal. This reduced employment opportunities in MMAR grows, but the MMPR created more legal opportunities for employment.

The MMPR created the first free market for cannabis cultivation in Canada. Previously, under the MMAR, there was only one government-licensed cultivation facility – Prairie Plant Systems. Under the regulatory oversight of Health Canada, the MMPR allowed for an individual or group of individuals to apply for a cultivation and sale licence for medical cannabis. During the MMPR era, there were sixteen licences awarded, and a market for patient acquisition and the sale of medical cannabis was created. These licence holders came to be known as licensed producers, all of which were a source of jobs.

Jobs emerged in the licensed facilities. The number of staff in each facility was dependent on a number of factors, including the physical size of the operations. Master growers, cultivation staff, quality assurance, processing and packaging, facility maintenance, security, shipping and receiving were all jobs needed to operate a facility. In addition, corporate service roles such as finance, marketing, human resources, IT – to name just a few – were needed to run these businesses.

One characteristic of the MMPR was the requirement that certain staff receive a security clearance from Health Canada. The regulation required there to be a person in charge (PIC) in any room where cannabis and staff with no security clearance were present. This requirement meant that licensed producers needed a critical mass of employees with PIC status for operational efficiency.

I was on a tour of a licensed producer in 2017 when we came across an employee standing in the hallway outside of a grow room. My guide greeted her and asked what she was doing. She did not have PIC status, and her colleague who was security cleared had to use the bathroom, so she had to leave the grow room until he returned.

This raises the question: Why wouldn't a licensed producer just get security clearances for all their employees? I learned it wasn't that easy. Applying for a security clearance is a lengthy process because it involves an investigation into the individual's background to ensure there is no history of illegal activity, namely, cultivation and drug trafficking. These investigations are not fast, and Health Canada has historically taken four to twelve months to issue a ruling.

The other reason that security clearances are an important part of the dialogue about employment is that this requirement has prevented some individuals who have experience from the illegal cannabis sector from crossing over into the legal sector. It should be noted that not all roles require a security clearance, and some people have successfully made the transition from being a MMAR grower, for example, to working for a licensed producer. However, it has remained a barrier for some.

Another consideration for the successful transition from the illegal sector to the legal sector is the fit with the culture. While the legal sector is composed of passionate and entrepreneurial people, cannabis production facilities are highly regulated. The plant is literally tracked from seed or clone to sale. There is a lot of data entry, documentation, and physical security requirements – all required for compliance with the regulations. Not everyone is a fit for this environment. Individuals who grew cannabis in environments not requiring this diligence may find themselves frustrated.

Another sector that emerged was cannabis clinics, where patients could see a physician, acquire an authorization for medical cannabis, and register with a licensed producer to purchase product. These clinics were a source of jobs for physicians, registered nurses, licensed practical nurses, medical office assistants, and cannabis educators.

In addition to licensed producers, more ancillary businesses emerged to support the early market entrants. One example was Ample Organics, which entered the market to provide a technology platform for automated seed-to-sale tracking. Today, Ample Organics has over one hundred employees in software development, account management, education, and corporate services.

During the MMPR era, Justin Trudeau was elected prime minister, and he made a major campaign promise to legalize and regulate cannabis for recreational or adult use. One of his first initiatives was the creation of a task force to research, analyze, and recommend a regulatory framework for the legalization of cannabis. The task force recommendations would form the foundation for the Cannabis Act.

The Access to Cannabis for Medical Purposes Regulations (ACMPR)
The medical cannabis regulations changed once again in August 2016 to the Access to Cannabis for Medical Purposes Regulations (ACMPR). This change didn't have a distinct impact on employment.

However, the ACMPR era did see drastic changes to the employment landscape. These changes were the result of Trudeau's task force and the tabling of the Cannabis Act on April 13, 2017, which signalled to the cannabis industry that the legalization of adult use was not only inevitable but also likely to occur in the near future.

Growth and job creation within the industry noticeably ramped up in early summer 2017 as licensed producers scaled up and Health Canada began to increase the number of licences issued in anticipation of a legal adult-use market.

The Cannabis Act
The Cannabis Act came into effect on October 17, 2018, and the prohibition of cannabis officially ended in Canada. One outcome was continued job growth within the cannabis sector. Leading up to legalization, Canada saw an increase in cannabis jobs in the retail sector, supply chain, marketing, and sales.

Under the Cannabis Act, jobs like cultivation, quality assurance, and other roles within the cultivation facilities continued to be a staple of the industry. However, the Cannabis Act expanded licence categories and the market. For example, standard and micro-processing licences are now available, as well as licences for cannabis nurseries.

The Canadian government released proposed regulations for edibles, extracts, and topicals, which took effect on October 17, 2019. This initiative created additional jobs as processing licence holders hired formulation scientists, food scientists, and extraction specialists in anticipation of the legislation.

Future Outlook
As we look into the future of jobs in cannabis in Canada, I expect to see continued growth as companies reach operational scale and take advantage of market-expansion opportunities, such as in the edibles market.

As cannabis companies continue to invest in automation in their facilities, this will be a trend to watch to see if it has an impact on jobs.

Additionally, the Canadian cannabis market will face pressure from the international cannabis market in the coming years. This may change the employment landscape as other countries catch up to Canada's position in the market and come to offer low-cost cannabis production.

Regardless of what the future holds, cannabis has been a source of employment in Canada and will continue to be a source of job growth for many years to come.

Notes

1 Under then CEO Vic Neufeld and "pump and dump" scammer Andy DeFrancesco, Aphria attempted an acquisition of Nuuvera, but not before obtaining significant shares in the takeover target. The assumption was that Nuuvera's stock value would increase dramatically – and the plan worked, netting the schemers $100-million overnight. The legal problem they encountered was that Aphria insiders did not signal their interest in the takeover until they held the targeted stocks, one day prior to acquisition of these shares.
2 Indications of unethical behaviour in the boardroom include overcharging veterans who use cannabis as medicine. By the end of 2019, the next scheme unravelled when Hindenburg Research, a short seller conducting an analysis of Aphria's operations, publicly accused the company of buying up "useless" holdings in Jamaica and elsewhere, assets conveniently owned by Aphria executives.
3 This is a combinant, auto-flowering strain that flowers and finishes quickly. It's ready for harvest sooner than the typical *indica-sativa* cross, or dominant strains of either varieties favoured in cannabis production. Some time in its ancient progenesis, *ruderalis* likely adapted to the shorter growing seasons associated with the more northern climates of central Asia. Ruderalis is a smaller example of a cannabis plant, with an incredibly brief gestation period: it begins flowering a mere twenty-one to thirty days after seeding.
4 Cision News, "48North Provides Update on Executive Team," news release, September 10, 2019, https://www.newswire.ca/news-releases/48north-provides-update-on-executive-team-857430217.html. Soon after, VanderMarel took up a CEO position at Beleave. This lasted until late December, when she again resigned. When I asked on Twitter: "What had happened? What was [your] next move?," she replied: "Open to any ethical company that is well governed."
5 *Editor's note:* Economies of scale are key to cannabis production. Indoor growing requires humidity and heat controls and very expensive specialized lighting. Maintaining these greenhouse conditions is costly and "carbon heavy." Some estimates indicate that forty-five kilos of oil is required to produce one kilogram of cannabis. Outdoor growing, conversely, means accepting the vagaries of the climate and hedging against calamity with "scale" or large numbers. Hence the size advantage of Good:Farm's 100-acre grow.

6 *Editor's note:* So-called vectors of consumption, or methods of consuming cannabis, are rapidly transforming in the marketplace. New technologies include vaping (the rapid heating of cannabis flower or derived products) in addition to the introduction of a water-soluble, nano-emulsification method, which transforms fat-soluble cannabis into a powder that is more bioavailable to humans with a rapid onset of ten minutes. This technology provides new opportunities for marketing cannabis in the form of drinks, foods, and sublingual sprays that mimic established norms of accepted consumption such as drinking at bars and in restaurants.

7 *Editor's note:* Medical cannabis is considered the "thin edge of the wedge," a necessary precursor to the existing legal market. First came the inevitable constitutional challenge needed to make it accessible medicine. The medical-cannabis sector attracted sufficient investment by lobbying corporate interests to warrant normalizing its nonmedical consumption. Realizing full legalization required incentivizing the deep pockets of global corporations – to start buying up production properties, hiring workers, drafting celebrity executives, all highly publicized in such a way as to convince Canadians that the coming green rush would be good for the economy. Vilifying generations of providers of "black market" cannabis was part of the equation, and it reached new levels of absurdity when it stirred a new panic about carfentanil-laced cannabis and national media accounts of children eating tainted pot. The only antidote for this crisis was to legalize by introducing the Canadian model now on export to the world.

8 The two dominant cannabis subspecies are *sativa* and *indica*. *Sativa* (which means "cultivated" in Latin) has long, thin leaf structures. Named by taxonomist Karl Linnaeus, this subspecies was likely developed in premodern times, being known for its "head high" or dreamy quality. *Indica* originated in India. It is more common than *sativa*, has relatively stubby leaves, and is known to be sedating. Hybrid strains combining *indica* and *sativa* are preferred by most producers, who select among varieties of the subspecies for genetic traits with possibly endless combinations.

9 *Editor's note:* VanderMarel's call for the expansion of outdoor cannabis production, radical as it may seem for many industry proponents, may very well be unavoidable as the costs of indoor growing continue to soar. Unsustainable practices, and impossible per-gram price points in retail, may ultimately usher in an exciting new age of craft cannabis. The boutique model would look more like microbreweries or small-batch wineries. The benefits of locally produced cannabis include local job creation (as opposed to centralized, large-scale factory production) and local economic growth. The potential contribution to communities in Canada is in stark contrast to the ethically ambiguous global profiteering of the corporate LP sector.

Work Cited

New Cannabis Ventures. 2021. "Hexo Completes Acquisition of 48 North." September 1. https://www.newcannabisventures.com/hexo-completes-acquisition-of-48north/.

10

Last Stop before Hopeless

KELLY INSLEY

This chapter offers searing insight into the public health care practitioner's lifeworld at work: the sort of people she encounters, the evidence for a system failing our most vulnerable citizens, and the reported benefits of cannabis use by clients. Kelly Insley works on the front line of health care for target populations that consist of substance users: ex-convicts and mental health patients primarily. She provides a haunting view of a world incomprehensible to many of us, a world in which cannabis gives people hope:

> "When would be a good time to call?" I asked.
> "How about right now!"

Our first call ran on for two hours or more, during which we spoke of the injustices and lies being perpetrated in the name of legal cannabis. Insley, as it turns out, is particularly critical of the purported "public health approach" to legalization that seems a half-hearted effort at best.

I heard her words so deeply that by the time the call was over, I was certain she could tell us something we had overlooked. The way I heard her words was reminiscent of the way the narrator listens to the piano work in James Baldwin's "Sonny's Blues." In it, he hears the heartbreak and injustice of growing up Black in one of

America's poorest cities and the prejudice that African Americans are confronted with every day. Beneath it all, he also hears the deep tonality of the human being, alive and demanding decency, kindness, dignity, and respect. Gabor Maté's *In the Realm of Hungry Ghosts: Close Encounters with Addiction* (2008) includes a similarly haunting account from the medical front lines that situates addiction in an epidemic of hopelessness that results from social dislocation in a variety of forms.

We need to know more about the human costs of social engineering and the fractured lives it leaves behind, despite the best efforts of people forced to compromise as they participate in health care systems every day.

Two hours after our first phone call, I received a twelve-page screed from Insley that exceeded expectations. I slipped off to sleep in a state of half-delirium. And by morning I had devised a plan. Why not get Insley to walk us through a day at her clinic?

This approach provided structure for her roaming narrative, and vivid renderings soon followed that documented her experience as a health care worker in a system that appears to care little for the people who are most in need of care.

Throughout a process of meticulous reviews, revisions, and rewrites (that often appeared in my inbox in the middle of the night!), we became fast friends and collaborated to present her contribution as a *sotto voce* achievement. What follows provides a glimpse of Insley's world in an authentic, immersive voice. – C.J.S.M.

> Drug reformers get seduced by politicians who co-opt our language but who make no meaningful change. And when we don't hold politicians accountable, we contribute to harm.
> – DR. CARL HART, COLUMBIA UNIVERSITY

In the morning before work, my resilience feels tenuous. I grab a cup of coffee, dress in the closest thing I have to pyjamas, and start the ten-kilometre slog to work, transitioning from a bucolic landscape to a concrete, dilapidated section of the city. While driving, I imagine the end of my shift, where I'm sitting on my deck with a cold glass of beer, a time-travelling coping mechanism to assure myself I will make it through the day.

Rounding the last stretch, I take a deep breath and roll into the clinic parking lot. The clinic's location stands as a stark contrast to the home community I occupy: a gentrified Pleasantville where folks build fortresses, bicker over hedge heights, and abhor the influx of newcomers, despite newly arriving themselves. I sit a few minutes in my M&M's–sized car and take in the Hieronymus Bosch–depiction of hell unfolding outside. A procession of human suitcases, many casualties of system failure, drift across the parking lot to corral their life's belongings on the concrete steps.

Many arrive in altered states. A woman, tanned and wild-eyed, moves like a cat on fire. She leans against our clinic window, lights a crack pipe then searches her bags, blocking the main entrance. On the steps, a young man fixes his bike while others share grief over recent overdose deaths. Across the street, sex workers, arms akimbo, discuss the day's business with clients. Beside my car, an elderly woman smokes a cigarette. Through my car window, she warns me of the metal screws strewn across the parking lot and, with yellow fingers, plucks one from behind my tire.

※

I first glimpsed the cannabis landscape while taking extensive patient histories for people with chronic diseases such as obesity, diabetes, heart disease, and hypertension. I knew nothing. They knew more. Curious and humbled, I cannonballed to the university library to cram for my patients' "Inquisition for Cannabis Ignoramuses."

The more I learned, the more I suffered cognitive dissonance. Cannabis, a seductress, knocked off her knickers to reveal a one-hundred-year sin: an ongoing racket of harmful drug policies rooted in racism, greed, colonialism, and free-market-generated mass dislocation as well as the nether regions of our semantics and our narrow, Western, xenophobic lens. I was smitten.

Like a parturient bride hot-footing it to a drive-thru chapel in Vegas, I abandoned my job and spent the next two years chasing the romance of a weed. Navigating a *cannabyss* vortex to subjects not taken, I cold-called researchers, devoured papers, enrolled in courses, and toured medical conferences like a groupie. Through her bodacious botany, I knew I'd found my MILP, the mother I'd like to plant. I hungered for more.

The public's thirst for knowledge renewed my vigour and strengthened my resolve to understand client perspectives, but I needed practical experience. To translate my learning, I started a job at a collaborative, trauma-informed, medical clinic specializing in cannabinoid therapies: a treatment team exclusive of law enforcement or politicians as educators and experts. And yet we make this bizarre exception in drug-policy development and school education, letting politicized opinion act as corrosive on what our civilization desperately needs: to help humans in pain. Our patient demographic spans from the prepubescent to the senior. I see patients with rare diseases, cancer, chronic disease syndromes, mental health challenges, and men newly released from incarceration. We often serve as the last stop before hopelessness.

I reach for my briefcase and walk through the crowd. I try to make eye contact and say good morning. I enter through the business next door to avoid agitating the person blocking the entrance. Inside our clinic, patients shuffle in their seats, elbow to elbow, filling out lengthy questionnaires; a modern Norman Rockwell motif minus sentimentality but with all the diversity in facial expressions, comportment, and attire.

My first patient, a senior dressed in her Sunday best, finishes her cup of tea and walks cross-kneed to the bathroom to take a urine drug screen, part of our intake process. Any woman of child-bearing age must take a pregnancy test. For women who are celibate, sterile, queer, or who've been sexually abused, asking for this test can cause trauma. In the wake of the developing, dystopian "handmaid's tale" to the South, our civilization suffers from a miraculous misconception: a woman with a uterus serves only as a potential fetal-containment unit.

Relieved, my patient enters my office. I ask her to get on the scale and note her body language and visible anxiety. I ask her to face away from the numbered beam, and I explain my background in eating disorders, opening up an opportunity to gauge her reaction. She tells me she had anorexia as a teen and thanks me for my sensitivity.

I proceed to review her intake forms, ask questions to flesh out details, ruling out any possible contraindicated, or untreated, health conditions. Our clinic collects data for research and to understand how patients employ cannabis to help with symptoms as well as any reported positive or adverse effects.

As I take notes, her face contorts, and she struggles to find words. She tells me the questionnaires as well as interactions with healthcare professionals induce shame through institutional discourse and medical surveillance.

Among the many questionnaires that screen for mental health and medical contraindications, the CUDIT-R (Cannabis Use Disorder Identification

Test) uses semantics with little room to define, explore, or understand the patient's unique and subjective experiences or intent. Our colonial, North American semantics fence patients into binary streams, *medical* or *recreational:* the latter originally meant "to refresh, restore, make anew, revive and invigorate" but is now synonymous with negative connotations and drug taking. Many patients abandon the questionnaire because it makes them feel pigeon-holed, degraded, humiliated, ashamed, and like a teen under parental interrogation. Instead, they follow up with me in dialogue to clarify responses.

I summarize some of the typical patient reactions to the CUDIT-R questionnaire and assessment questions as follows:

1 How often do you use cannabis?

- It depends on how much pain or how anxious I'm feeling.
- Anywhere from daily to 3 times a month, depending on triggers.
- I don't like the word "use," it makes me feel weird like I shoot up drugs. Like I'm guilty of doing something before I even see the doctor.

2 How many hours were you "stoned" on a typical day when you had been using cannabis?

I don't feel stoned, I feel

- relaxed.
- happy, more social, more in the moment. It's the first time I felt normal. No paranoia, no nightmares. And my rash, it's completely gone!
- peace. The busy thoughts stop, and I can fall asleep.
- focused. I can watch TV and not feel distracted by pain and nausea.
- detached. The pain doesn't bother me anymore. It's still there, but I can carry on and do my work
- a little happy just before I go to bed. Is that bad?[(From a senior]
- in the moment. My husband and I have some in the evening, and we focus on each other, laugh, and talk. It has helped us in our marriage and in bed.
- nothing. I put it on my skin.

3 How often during the past six months did you find that you were not able to stop using cannabis once you had started?

- What do they mean by this?

- Why would I stop taking it if it helps me with my symptoms?
- I had to stop when travelling to the States. I had no issue other than my pain worsened, and I had to return to taking my old meds.
- If I stop, the migraine symptoms return. I'm taking CBD. I'm off all the meds (meds for pain, anxiety, sleep, and nausea). My work has zero tolerance for cannabis, so now, if I want to work, I have to resume taking all my meds.

4 How often during the past six months did you fail to do what was normally expected from you because of using cannabis?

- I didn't do my errands. I took cannabis for pain and was told not to drive after taking it. [Yet they often drive after taking Gravol, an opioid, an antihistamine, or while wearing a Fentanyl patch, and so on.]
- I took cannabis for pain. It helped. I altered my plans accordingly.
- Who's doing the expecting? What am I, twelve?

5 How often in the past six months have you devoted a great deal of your time to getting, using, or recovering from cannabis?

- Of course, I spend a great deal of time trying to get it. I had to track down a similar product because the licensed producer ran out.
- Recovering? I don't get a "hangover" from cannabis.
- I take my medication three times a day. How do I even answer this?

6 How often in the past six months have you had a problem with your memory or concentration after using cannabis?

- That can be a side effect right?
- I'm asleep after I take it. How would I know?
- I have fibromyalgia. I'm menopausal, stressed, grieving, and overwhelmed. Of course, I'm forgetful!

7 How often do you use cannabis in situations that could be physically hazardous, such as driving, operating machinery, or caring for children?

- I'm a mother. I have pain. I also have children. And your point is ... ?
- People drink wine at the dinner table with their kids. How is this different? I don't feel stoned, whatever that means.

8   Have you ever thought about cutting down, or stopping, your use of cannabis?

- Yes, after the symptoms improve, I'd like to cut the dosing down if possible.
- No, I haven't. I can't drink alcohol, so I substitute cannabis for social occasions and take it for pain and sleep.

On average, patients never endure such a bureaucratic gauntlet to access hypnotics, opiates, stimulants, and other medications. In gathering client histories with the intent to understand, I developed a sensitivity to the semantics we commonly use as healthcare professionals. I switched to nonjudgmental, person-first language and adopted a curious, exploratory mindset. I ask one question when taking a social history: What do you do to enjoy life or cope with life's challenges? This question places all coping mechanisms, "healthy" or otherwise, under one umbrella, levelling the field between substances and behaviours. I let the patient define their experiences inclusive of joy, euphoria, spirituality, creativity, connection, and communion.

In response, my patients not only open up about taking cannabis but also about other issues such as mental health, marital problems, financial stresses, and maladaptive coping behaviours, including those laden with stigma and shame. The approach puts the focus on the person and upstream causes so one can collaborate on finding solutions, if and when they are ready.

※

On the whole, patients taking cannabis formulations defy the pothead stereotype. I ask an elderly, Mexican female with diabetic neuropathic pain if she ever "takes" cannabis to treat her symptoms. She smiles and recounts childhood memories of her mother and aunts making cannabis formulations for their family pharmacy. To her, cannabis, a harm reduction from other pharmaceuticals, reflects her unique family culture and customs.

Another patient, an erudite healthcare professional, lectures in her home country, India, to challenge colonialist attitudes toward a plant her culture once deemed holy. Her great-grandmother harvested the young flower buds to cook in family meals and avoided taking cannabis during her menstruation because of conscientious observation. In India, the patient's treasured, multigenerational, family records painstakingly document this personal ethnobotanical history. She confides that when she came to Canada, she "shook inside" when faced with our attitudes. With both women, I talk about how our colonial, binary, moralistic lens precludes them from speaking openly to their doctors or friends.

Many patient histories include trauma. While listening, I attempt neutrality, donning armour to deflect darkness without sound, weight, or edges. One person, molested throughout childhood, says they experienced multiple murders of family members and later managed trauma and despair with street-sourced medication. Tragically, later in life, under the influence, during a fight that spiralled out of control, a blow caused death, and the person spent decades incarcerated.

Another person recounts rapes that occurred from toddlerhood to adulthood, sometimes by more than two individuals in a day. She later lost her unborn babies to an assault with intent to cause miscarriage. She looks at me and mimes holding her infants in her arms, describing how she said goodbye. Days later, she lost her last living child in an accident. The trauma continued in various forms for years, leaving her so physically scarred she can't bear weight. She takes cannabis to help with the triggers and nightmares. As she speaks, I sit in silence and cry, apologizing for losing my composure. Where is her badge for resilience and courage for rising from misogyny, corruption, and systemic health inequities?

Another patient – the victim of childhood neglect and physical, emotional, and sexual trauma and later a gang rape – tells me that they succumbed to managing with street-sourced medication. Both their parents managed despair through alcohol. From my assessment, they failed to receive support and treatment for fetal alcohol syndrome, severe mental health challenges, childhood abuse, and poverty.

At times, when facing these patients, bereft of words, I repeat over and over, "I'm so sorry this happened. I'm so sorry you had to go through this without support."

Our "euphoriaphobic" one-size-fits-all approach to cannabis for therapeutic intent denies these patients respite from PTSD and a little joy. To call any of these patients an addict, substance user, or even misuser completely nullifies, negates, and ignores the events and issues that lead to maladaptive coping mechanisms.

If we employ the term *use* to denote "*problematic* drug" consumption, we must also apply the same language to other coping mechanisms. Are we "users" of gambling, pornography, food, technology, or other compulsions to numb out or fill the void of despair or boredom? We are not "users of substances," much the same way as we are not "users" of aspirin or anxiety medications. We "take" them. It's the porous and fluid intentions, reasons, situations, and settings at the time of consumption that differ.

When was the last time you were asked to define your intent when buying wine? Come to my virtual cash register, and I'll call you a wine user. Are you using wine for medical purposes such as decompressing or quelling anxiety? Are you drinking recreationally? I hope so. It would be a drag to drink for miserable purposes. Did you combine the intents? Are you using wine for a sacrament or rum for Christmas pudding edibles? If you happen to be pregnant or you're taking other substances, please take the urine and drug tests before purchasing liquor. If you test positive and deem your situation problematic, you're on your own, as we lack adequate, affordable resources to support you. But we'll stigmatize you with our language even as we ignore your history and mental health and focus on the outcome, especially if you medicate your physical and emotional pain (both of which show up in many of the same areas of the brain) with substances.

Why don't you tell me about last night? Did granny get high on sherry at the wedding? I bet she did. I'll assume one outcome: she drank to get pissed. Did she feel euphoric? Trousered? Was it an adverse side effect, or were there nuances and personal experiences she can describe? Later, at a family dinner, while drinking ethanol in the presence of children, you'll laugh about Granny and how cute it was when she was "tipsy" and bumfuzzled. I'll bet you'll post some Facebook videos and cherish the movies for years to come.

We don't *use* alcohol unless we're referring to the "alcoholic," "drug addict," "druggie," or "substance user." We *drink* it, or we *have a drink*, a phrase not synonymous with simply having a glass of any beverage. We never *take* alcohol either.

A Framework for the Legalization and Regulation of Cannabis in Canada – developed by a task "force" consisting of three medical doctors, two politicians (with arts, law, and engineering backgrounds), two career law enforcers (with law/administration backgrounds), three researchers/professors (with law and drug-policy backgrounds) – addresses the social and structural determinants to health under "further recommendations" with few details outlining specific actions or goals. They state the objective: "To protect vulnerable citizens, particularly youth; to implement evidence-based policy; and to put public health, safety and welfare at the heart of a balanced approach to treaty implementation" (Canada 2016). According to the Public Health Agency of Canada (2016), Key Element 4, "Increase Upstream

Investments," is important because "it has the potential to achieve the greatest influence on population health and it can result in great savings, as prevention tends to be less expensive than treatment."

The Canadian Council on Social Determinants of Health (2015, 2) states that the "frameworks most effective at informing policy and decision-making will also illustrate who, when, where, and how action can be taken to improve the health trajectory of an individual or community." The Task Force on Cannabis Legalization and Regulation addresses the roof tiles rather than the foundational heart on which the walls and roof must be built.

Many of my patients don't suffer from addictions, substance use, or misuse disorders – they suffer from system failure maladaptive coping mechanisms, an umbrella term that includes all behaviours, from problematic gambling, shopping, eating behaviours, and pornography consumption to taking street-sourced medication to manage living in a fractured system. *System failure maladaptive coping mechanisms,* as a label, levels the field, decreases stigma, is person-first, and puts the focus squarely on the fundamental upstream causes. We need to comprehensively increase the sphere of public-knowledge in understanding the upstream interconnection to the downstream pathways of human suffering and maladaptive coping. Only then can voting civilians and health care professionals confidently support a comprehensive person-centred approach and widen the possibilities for transformation, healing, and social justice.

In closing, I quote the wisdom of Bruce Alexander (2010, 68):

> The medical-criminal dichotomy is false because addiction is neither a medical nor a criminal problem. Addicted people are neither suffering from a disease that can be cured nor engaging in criminal behaviour that should be punished. Rather, they are *adapting,* as well as they are able, to the rising tide of dislocation that threatens to engulf them. Adaptation is neither a disease nor a criminal act, but this does not mean that it is not a problem. In free-market society, addiction is best understood as a *political* problem, rather than a medical or criminal one. If the political process does not find new wellsprings of social meaning and membership to replace those that have been paved over by globalising free-market society, ever more people will become addicted, ever more severely with terrible consequences for society.

Works Cited

Alexander, Bruce K. 2010. *The Globalization of Addiction: A Study in the Poverty of the Spirit.* New York: Oxford University Press.

Canada. 2016. *A Framework for the Legalization and Regulation of Cannabis: The Final Report of the Task Force on Cannabis Legalization and Regulation.* https://www.canada.ca/content/dam/hc-sc/healthy-canadians/migration/task-force-marijuana-groupe-etude/framework-cadre/alt/framework-cadre-eng.pdf.

Canadian Council on Social Determinants of Health. 2015. *A Review of Frameworks on the Determinants of Health.* May 20. https://nccdh.ca/images/uploads/comments/CCSDH_A-review-of-frameworks-on-the-determinants-of-health_EN.pdf.

Public Health Agency of Canada. 2016. "Key Element 4: Increase Upstream Investments." *Population Health Approach: The Organization Framework,* Canadian Best Practices Portal. https://cbpp-pcpe.phac-aspc.gc.ca/population-health-approach-organizing-framework/key-element-4-increase-upstream-investments/.

11

Dusting Off the Path – Tsi Nionkwarihotens

KANENHARIYO SETH LEFORT with
CLAYTON JAMES SMITH McCANN

"Dusting Off the Path" in Context
Clayton James Smith McCann

This chapter offers an Indigenous response to the Cannabis Act. It offers a competing vision of what cannabis distribution in Ontario might look like. Canada's most populous province was home to a failed distribution rollout in October 2018. Its game plan was to have twenty-four "brick-and-mortar" cannabis retail storefronts to service 14.5 million people.

Seth LeFort is a cannabis-policy author and owner of the Recreational Cannabis Farmers Market in Tyendinaga Mohawk Territory, Shannonville, Ontario. The cannabis distribution regime implemented by Tyendinaga Mohawk Territory, located in eastern Ontario between Belleville and Kingston, is perhaps the most successful in Canada. Others may point out that the territory isn't in Canada at all; rather, it is land that belongs to the Mohawks of the Bay of Quinte First Nation. Over sixty dispensaries occupy a small reserve of just over seventy-six square kilometres, creating over four hundred jobs (Edwards 2018; Hunter 2019).

To provide some perspective, the former per-capita national leader, Hamilton, Ontario, had over eighty dispensaries at the height of demand in the months leading up to legalization. Hamilton is situated on a much larger land plot – 1,117 square kilometres, or one dispensary for every twelve square kilometres. The ratio in Tyendinaga is one to one.

Hamilton sought to shutter dispensaries both prior to and especially following October 17, 2018. At the time, I just so happened to be working for the city in the role of volunteer cannabis-policy consultant in its Licensing and By-law Services Division, Planning and Economic Development. The director of licensing, a former deputy police chief, made it clear to me what he thought of dispensaries: "If you are working in an illegal business, you are also part of the problem" (correspondence with author, October 29, 2018).

Our correspondence concerned an October 25 police raid of the Georgia Peach dispensary. One of my concerns was that young wage workers, not management or owners, were the ones being punished. The raid resulted in six arrests on charges of "possession of cannabis for the purpose of selling." A conviction can carry a fourteen-year maximum sentence.

Having been rebuffed by the director, I took my concerns to City Council. At the council's December 18, 2018, meeting, I issued an appeal to reconsider the unofficial city policy of arresting dispensary workers in raids. These kids aren't criminals, I argued. They're merely seeking a working wage. Turning them into criminals will only serve to further marginalize young people and restrict their opportunities. Alas, for all the effect my words had, I may as well have been speaking to the cormorants of Hamilton Harbour, who congregate on the islets and in marshier places around the Burlington Skyway, heedless of the screaming transports hurtling past at all hours of the day and night.

The council decided – behind closed doors, it seems, with pressure from municipal and provincial law enforcement – to squeeze what many feared to be the last "war on drugs" funds to keep up the fight at street level. The human cost is staggering. But my protest (like so many others) to high-ranking members of the Doug Ford government continued to go unanswered.

Ontario's cannabis distribution regime got off to a rocky start. The online ordering system, as the only avenue through which to obtain cannabis, stumbled along until April 1, 2019, at which time the focus shifted to brick-and-mortar retail opportunities. The Ford government's mismanagement myopia was total: evidence suggests upwards of 88 percent of cannabis sales happen in interpersonal contexts (OCS 2019). Online sales remained the only form of consumer access from legalization day in October 2018 until April 1, 2019. At the end of October 2018, the Ontario Cannabis Store announced a data breach involving the personal information of over 4,500 customers. Soon after, the Allocation Lottery Selection scheme was announced for awarding retail store allocation licences (RSAs). The initial lottery saw over 17,000 submissions for twenty-five RSAs. (The winners of the lottery were all wooed by corporate interests to sell off their licences for millions of dollars. Despite Premier Ford's announcement that the aim was to enable "the little guy" to participate in the new cannabis economy, this was not the outcome of the first, second, or third lottery.)

Getting more directly to the point of this preamble, the second lottery was designated as the "Cannabis Retail Store Allocation Process for Stores on First Nations Reserves." Eight licences were issued to serve a population estimated at 220,000 to 375,000, or one store per 27,000 to 47,000 Indigenous customers. Unlike Ontario's abysmal cannabis distribution rollout, in general, in Tyendinaga, the practised politics of self-determination resulted in a wholly different policy formation. Informed by principles established in a February 2018 announcement by the federal government (Canada 2018), cannabis distribution policy in Tyendinaga fell under local control:

> For too long, Indigenous Peoples in Canada have had to prove their rights exist and fight to have them recognized and fully implemented ... The Prime Minister, Justin Trudeau, today announced ... a Recognition and Implementation of Rights Framework ... The Framework can also include new measures to support the rebuilding of Indigenous nations and governments, and advance Indigenous self-determination, including the inherent right of self-government.

Just a few weeks earlier, in December 2017, at the Assembly of First Nations Chiefs in Ottawa, the Ontario Regional Chief, Isadore Day, stated: "Our people are going to say, 'Listen, we have aboriginal treaty rights, we have economic rights as First Nations people. Who is Canada to say our community can't have a dispensary?'" Moreover, self-determination means administrative support from local band managers, whose community members may 'want in on the economic benefit to create jobs and earn revenue,' said Donald Maracle, Chief of the Mohawks of the Bay of Quinte" (Galloway 2017).

Could it be that the "Cannabis Retail Store Allocation Process for Stores on First Nations Reserves" was an attempt to destabilize efforts to establish local authority on reserves in Ontario? As raids targeting Indigenous dispensaries continued,[1] my attention turned to Kanenhariyo Seth LeFort. Police raided his storefront with automatic assault weapons drawn and pointed at him. He observed that "they came in like they were robbing a bank." The CCTV video evidence provided to the CBC unequivocally corroborates his point of view (Barrera 2018a).

I wrote Seth a letter, hoping to persuade him to share something of his story in this book. On February 20, 2018, he wrote:

> Kwe kwe Clay McCann. I am writing to tell you I received your letter. It was nice getting a hand written letter. I can't remember how long it's been since I received one. I have been thinking a lot about your request. And I have decided I would like to speak with you further. But I am certainly interested in co-authoring a chapter.

What followed was a series of texts, phone calls, and conversations ranging from what the contribution would look like, to Seth's return to Tyendinaga to open the Recreational Cannabis Farmers Market, among other initiatives. By early spring 2019, he had forwarded a series of audio interviews. The topics ranged from a Bear Clan Band Mother urging him to generate a policy statement for cannabis distribution on reserve to considerations of community security. Administrative and security concerns included the real possibility that cannabis retail would succeed wildly in Tyendinaga and that organized crime – in the form of Hell's Angels, Rock Machine, or tong Mafia from nearby cities such as Montreal and Toronto – could descend on the community with the intention of extortion, violence, or gleaning tributary arrangements with local Indigenous retailers.

The solution, for Seth, was community-based security. Everyone involved in local cannabis distribution would donate some time each week to operating a *de facto*, unarmed security force. Seth pushed for appropriate training and vehicles and for implementing strict administrative procedures. Cannabis distribution at Tyendinaga under his watch is now, first and foremost, a community effort.[2]

As for the charges laid against him in connection with the November 2017 raid, Seth remained committed to the endgame:

> LeFort said he would have faced a fine in the thousands of dollars on a guilty plea, but he chose to launch the constitutional challenge as a matter of principle. "The issue I am raising is we have an inherent right as Onkwehón:we [the Indigenous peoples of North America] to make medicine and to have an economy," said LeFort. "We have a right to add new technology and knowledge to our medicine chest." (CBC News 2018b)

But by March 2019, the Crown had dropped the charges. To avoid a scandal in the press perhaps? Moreover, a Supreme Court ruling might have sent

C-45 back to the proverbial drawing board with a new mandate to include provisions for First Nations to collect taxes on cannabis purchases to be shared with the province. Instead, much like Seth himself, the victory was a quiet one that is nonetheless significant in Canadian legal history.

How will governments respond to the green rush in Tyendinaga? Cease-and-desist orders seem likely – one hopes next time without the neocolonial spectacle of automatic weapons being aimed at peaceful citizens.[3]

Today, Tyendinaga, with its sixty-plus dispensaries, is still undergoing "a cannabis-infused economic boom in [a] Mohawk community of 2,100" (Barrera 2019). "The community is dotted with renovation and construction projects, including several new gas stations and at least one new franchise restaurant," all indicators of just how successful this experiment has become (Barrera 2019). Local cannabis production and distribution can be highly profitable when run according to the Tyendinaga model, which has sustained a ten-fold markup between production and retail.

For further context and perspective, it is worth noting that Ontario, like every other province or territory, assumes responsibility for distribution of cannabis under the terms of the Cannabis Act. Its failure is partly due to a structural disconnect caused by a change of government. In June 2018, five months prior to legalization, the Ontario Liberals lost the provincial election. Doug Ford's Progressive Conservatives formed a government that was virtually untested after the Liberals' fifteen-year run in office. Ford, Attorney General Caroline Mulroney, and Minister of Finance Vic Fedeli were handed the challenging cannabis file, along with the rest of their provincial duties, with little governance experience. His corporation-friendly "Open for Business" slogan, which adorns licence plates across the province, is as unconvincing as it is a brash and bold claim, considering that neither Ford nor anyone on his team was equipped to oversee the cannabis portfolio.

Premier Ford's alleged entrepreneurial activities (selling hash from a van in the 1980s) didn't lend him the business acumen required to be successful in the mass distribution of cannabis as a retail commodity. Not surprisingly, perhaps, his first concern was to distance his government from the Liberal cannabis distribution model.[4]

Opting for online sales only – putting offline distribution on hold until April 2019, a full six months after legalization went into effect – the Ontario Cannabis Store's (OCS) debut was marred by the ordering system malfunctioning (Draaisma 2018). The OCS went on to post a $42-million loss for the fiscal year ending March 31, 2019, with a staggering $106 million in expenses (Aversa, Hernandez, and Jacobson 2021).

Meanwhile, Indigenous entrepreneurs across the province began opening cannabis dispensaries on band territories in 2017. Seth LeFort's Mohawk Medicine was one such dispensary. His constitutional challenge in response to the November 2017 raid on his shop asserted his people's right to self-governance and Indigenous prosperity through sovereignty and full participation in the green rush. His efforts in Tyendinga in the legalization era are at the very centre of the profound transformation taking place in postcolonial relations in Canada today.[5]

To more fully illustrate the Tyendinaga model, Seth's contribution to this collection, titled "Dusting Off the Path," was generated by his community to articulate their worldview and the need for local administration of cannabis distribution:

> The purpose of this document is to remove the dust, which has apparently settled on Kanyen'kehà:ka customs with respect to our culture, economy, and medicine. The intent of this document is to articulate in written form the customs and laws regulating our economic activities and medicines in our territories that are pre-existing and that cannot be extinguished. The document has been designed to be improved upon, modified, and reprinted; and the ideas expressed within it belong to all Onkwehon:we who claim them.

These views and vision of the future are integral and vital to creating a broader vision of community health and welfare that works for the betterment of all Onkwehon:we (The People).

Figure 11.1 Chapter illustration for Dusting Off the Path
Source: Courtesy Kanenhariyo Seth LeFort

Dusting Off the Path – Tsi Nionkwarihotens
(Or, Customary Law and Practice regarding Economy and Medicine for the Kanyen'kehà:ka)

Preamble

a Recently, many Band Council lawyers advised that where Band Council bylaws and regulations have not been enacted on reserves according to the Indian Act, provincial laws of the Canadian government apply – including motor vehicle regulation, public health and safety, tobacco and cannabis regulation, gaming, and child protection services.

b In fall 2018, numerous Indian Act Band Councils introduced draft "laws" to prohibit, tax, and extensively regulate cannabis production and sale in Kanyen'kehà:ka communities, including Kahnawake, Akwesasne, Tyendinaga, and Six Nations.

c Some Band Councils have stated they would pass bylaws to ward off the imposition of provincial law on reserve and to protect the rights of the people. However, these Band Council cannabis laws usurp the people's jurisdiction and authority and seek to prohibit, tax, and extensively regulate cannabis production and sale, all while ignoring the existing customs and conventions of the Onkwehon:we.

d The regulatory systems they have proposed are fundamentally incompatible with Onkwehon:we customs and conventions. In the Kanyen'kehà:ka world, we do not pay a fee or a tax to a higher authority in order to gain a right to do something. We have responsibilities to take action, and we have rights that protect our existence, peace, and well-being (*Sken:nen*). Our responsibilities have been passed down to us by our ancestors and are defined through our customs and culture. Our rights are the shelter we enjoy under the branches of the *Tsyonneratasekowa* – the unique system of political governance that belongs to us.

e If we accept a system of tax collection and state-sanctioned regulation or licensing, then we are allowing a foreign power (Canada's Indian Act, the Band Council system) to take away our power as free people and corrode our rights, responsibilities, and identity as Kanyen'kehà:ka.

f Band Councils operating within the Canadian Indian Act system have been claiming to be the ultimate authority and sovereign power with the rights to make rules and laws governing Kanyen'kehà:ka people and our territory. In doing so, Band Council authorities are acting contrary to the United Nations Declaration on the Rights of Indigenous Peoples [UNDRIP], the

Universal Declaration of Human Rights, and breaking Kanyen'kehà:ka laws, customs, and traditions.

g The purpose of this document is to remove the dust which has apparently settled on Kanyen'kehà:ka customs with respect to our culture, economy, and medicine. The intent of this document is to articulate in written form the customs and laws regulating our economic activities and medicines in our territories that are pre-existing and that cannot be extinguished. The path our ancestors laid down for us is still visible in our culture and customs as Kanyen'kehà:ka people.

h In our oral tradition, it is our custom to focus on the words of the speaker rather than the speaker's appearance or identity. We do this so as not to be prejudiced against the speaker and to be able to consider the words on their own merits. To protect the integrity and merit of the words in this document, no authorship of this document has been claimed.

i Use this document if it is helpful in articulating your rights and responsibilities. If there is something missing from this text, pass it through your minds and add what has been missed to your articulation of our ways as a people. This document may be improved upon, modified, and freely reprinted.

The United Nations Declaration on the Rights of Indigenous People

In addition to our culturally specific Kanyen'kehà:ka ways, the international community of nations has come to a global consensus concerning the rights of Indigenous peoples through UNDRIP, which was adopted by the United Nations General Assembly on Thursday, September 13, 2007. Of particular relevance to this document are the following articles, which are consistent with our understanding of our rights and responsibilities concerning the self-regulation of our economy and medicines:

18 Indigenous peoples have the right to participate in decision-making in matters which would affect their rights, through representatives chosen by themselves in accordance with their own procedures, as well as to maintain and develop their own indigenous decision-making institutions.

19 States shall consult and cooperate in good faith with the indigenous peoples concerned through their own representative institutions in order to obtain their free, prior and informed consent before adopting and implementing legislative or administrative measures that may affect them.

20 1. Indigenous peoples have the right to maintain and develop their political, economic and social systems or institutions, to be secure in the enjoyment of their own means of subsistence and development, and to engage freely in all their traditional and other economic activities. 2. Indigenous peoples deprived of their means of subsistence and development are entitled to just and fair redress.

21 1. Indigenous peoples have the right, without discrimination, to the improvement of their economic and social conditions, including, inter alia, in the areas of education, employment, vocational training and retraining, housing, sanitation, health and social security. 2. States shall take effective measures and, where appropriate, special measures to ensure continuing improvement of their economic and social conditions. Particular attention shall be paid to the rights and special needs of indigenous elders, women, youth, children and persons with disabilities.

23 Indigenous peoples have the right to determine and develop priorities and strategies for exercising their right to development. In particular, Indigenous peoples have the right to be actively involved in developing and determining health, housing and other economic and social programmes affecting them and, as far as possible, to administer such programmes through their own institutions.

24 1. Indigenous peoples have the right to their traditional medicines and to maintain their health practices, including the conservation of their vital medicinal plants, animals and minerals. Indigenous individuals also have the right to access, without any discrimination, all social and health services.

In the Canadian context, the state structures of the colonizers were forcibly introduced through the Band Council systems of the Indian Act. Such systems of governance are those of a foreign occupying power and have no legitimacy for Kanyen'kehà:ka. The elected Indian Act system of governance is an extension of the Canadian state and is not integrated within our customs and laws and therefore does not have sovereign authority over us. The election of leadership within the Indian Act structures does not make them a legitimate authority over our lands or our people, as they are not participating within our customary legal framework. Those individuals belonging to our Nation who are working within these structures should be encouraged to take steps to steer governance back to traditional customary systems and to abandon the Indian Act system.

The regulatory bylaws and rules created by the Band Council system are not only in violation of Kanyen'kehà:ka governance systems and customs, they are also in violation of international law as it concerns the relationship of state-based societies and Indigenous peoples.

Conventions
a   Everything in the world is interconnected. We have a responsibility to care for and safeguard all of creation and a specific responsibility to Kanonhsonnion:we (Our Territory). We have been given the duty to live in balance and harmony with one another and all living beings.
b   The Kanyen'kehà:ka are a free people. Each individual is "sovereign" – a free and equal decider on all matters concerning their life and path in this world. The only limits to our freedom exist where we harm or interfere in the lives of others or where we are in conflict with the customs of our people.
c   Kanyen'kehà:ka are born of our Mother, the Earth, here on Turtle Island. We are not capable of surrendering our collective or individual liberty. Because we are free individuals, our people may leave our society behind and join another. However, those who leave our circle leave naked, leaving behind everything that makes them Kanyen'kehà:ka, including their name, their clan, their birthright, and their rights and responsibilities in the Kanyen'kehà:ka world.
d   Within Kanyen'kehà:ka society, there is no hierarchy. Everybody – women and men, young and old – is "of the same height." All have the right to have their voice taken into consideration in the deliberations of the people when making decisions that affect them.
e   Kanyen'kehà:ka governance is guided by *Sken:nen* (peace), *Kanikonriio* (a righteous mind), and *Kanoronhkwathsera* (Lovingfullness).
f   Kanyen'kehà:ka systems of governance enable the people to come to one mind and make decisions. They also assist in maintaining continuity with the political and social direction of the people. The Kayenereko:wa is the path of powerful positive energy (*Kasastenhtsera*) that our ancestors left for us to follow for the benefit of our people and creation as a whole.
g   An inclusive, consensus-based decision-making process of the people is the ultimate authority within our territories. The people's council fire is ever-burning and ever-ready to make decisions.
h   The upkeep of the rules in our society is the collective responsibility of the people. When someone has broken the rules, the people have the

responsibility to come together and address the issue in accordance with the Kayenereko:wa and the specific customs of that community.

i   Therefore, when Kanyen'kehà:ka exercising the freedoms of their birthright are interfered with by enemies – foreign or domestic – we have a collective and individual responsibility to drive out the enemy and support the freedom and liberty of our people. Failure to come to one another's defence will endanger our collective liberty and freedoms in our territory.

j   Our customs and traditions do not require Chiefs and Clan Mothers to be in place for the people to make decisions and maintain our laws. In some circumstances, decision-making happens at the Chiefs' Council or amongst Clan Mothers, but in other cases it may fall on head men and women, clans, and the people in general to make decisions and uphold them.

k   How we as Kanyen'kehà:ka people exercise control and maintain our customary practices in relationship to the outside world rests upon the Tyohate (the Two-Row Wampum). The Tyohate is a means to create mutual benefit and balance between different entities (including individuals, groups, nations, and even species). The Tyohate is the relationship of Sken:nen (peace), Kanikonriio (a righteous mind), and Kasastenhtsera (power) between two parties. It acts as a mechanism to assist noninterference and harmony between them as they drift down the river of life together.

l   The whole of creation – plants, animals, air, water, earth, etc. – is accessible freely and without prohibition to all *Onkweshon'a* (human beings in all of their various forms).

m   All Kanyen'kehà:ka have the right to be free and to govern our own lives.

n   All Kanyen'kehà:ka have the right to equality of opportunity within the human-made institutions and structures of the Kanyen'kehà:ka world.

o   All Kanyen'kehà:ka have the right to adapt and use new technologies and elements of creation as long as they are beneficial to our people and creation.

p   Kanyen'kehà:ka have differing responsibilities related to our gender, maturity, family, clan, nation, society, and politically appointed duties and responsibilities.

q   Kanyen'kehà:ka have common responsibilities with respect to creation. We have the responsibility to assist creation in flourishing. None of the various elements of creation need us, but we cannot survive without them. The elements of creation help us because we assist them in harmonizing with creation and thereby improve the fecundity of our entire territory.

r   In the Kanyen'kehà:ka way of life (*Tsi niyokwa-rihotens*), our responsibilities change and evolve over the course of our lives, affecting the nature of our economic, social, and political activities. These life changes can occur for many reasons, including

- i *The passing on of knowledge and skills.* Often, knowledge keepers – whoever they may be – choose people with certain traits and abilities that lend themselves to the mastery of the particular knowledge and skills to be passed on. Once the learner is accepted as learned, they have the responsibility to practise, extend, and pass on their skills and knowledge to others.
- ii *Physical changes relating to ability.* When those chosen to fulfill particular roles are no longer able to meet certain physical criteria, then there is an obligation for their people to lift the burden of responsibility and honourably release them from their duties.
- iii *Gender roles.* Men and women have a gendered division of responsibility on matters such as child rearing; the provision of shelter, food, and medicine; diplomacy; politics; harvesting; trade and economics; security; and ceremony.
- iv *Political appointments.* People may be appointed to make medicine or to assist in knowledge transmission through our political decision-making systems.
- v *Spiritual obligation.* The responsibility for the use and application of medicine and healing can be realized through spiritual means such as dreams, illness, or the process of a fast during a rite of passage. Those healed by medicine societies gain the responsibility of healing those with the same illness using the same medicine. Those guided through their fast in the transition to adulthood who become medicine people gain the spiritual responsibility to heal others through that same process.

s   All Kanyen'kehà:ka have equal responsibilities to uphold the ceremonies, treaties, and the political and economic structures that sustain our people and that provide for all seven generations and the faces yet to come.

t   All Kanyen'kehà:ka have the responsibility to follow our laws and customs and do not need to seek permission from any outside authority or institution to uphold them.

General Economic Principles of the Kanyen'kehà:ka

a   No individual has the right to monopolize nature or natural resources in general, but specific families may have rights to a particular harvesting area. When harvesting resources, one must always take with a spirit of thankfulness and humility and leave enough to regenerate the resource.

b   Kanyen'kehà:ka trading relationships are based on principles of mutually beneficial trade and exchange between friends. We don't trade with our enemies.

c   In Kanyen'kehà:ka economics, we differentiate between the exchanges made with those outside of our system and exchanges happening internally among Kanyen'kehà:ka. In external exchanges, when we negotiate a sale or a purchase, we set our price. The exchange is not required to be mutually beneficial, but it must be advantageous to ourselves and coming generations. Generally, in these types of exchanges, we trade something that we have in great abundance for something that is rare to us.

d   Internal trade among the Kanyen'kehà:ka occurs as a reciprocal relationship with a spiritual component. In cases where the commodity has come from the earth, or where the technology has come from our ancestors, or where the source is part of our national treasure (collective knowledge, land and collective resources, etc.), then the purchaser sets the price of what they are prepared to pay with something that is precious to them. The purchaser's offer comes in the context of information sharing between the parties and the effort, hardship, and specialized knowledge the provider has invested in the product should be weighed.

e   In respect to medicine, the seller may decline the offer made by the purchaser and instead add additional value in the negotiation, or they can gift it to the purchaser, and the purchaser will be expected to fulfill a future need of the seller.

f   The purchaser is also expected to offer something sacred such as a gift of tobacco, seeds, or a precious item to complete the deal. The value of this spiritual item will be reflected in the spiritual value and hoped-for effect of the trade. We offer to buy something valuable with things that are dear to us. The parties must also agree not to allow the product to spoil or waste. The seller must be transparent about the product and will have bad luck should they withhold knowledge of the product. The value and effect produced by the exchange are maximized through the exchange being honest, spiritually correct, and carried out in good faith.

g   Kanyen'kehà:ka people pay for the exchange of products or services as a mutually beneficial exchange. This exchange may take a variety of forms and may include the trade of labour, a service, a product, currency, or technology. The one who accepts the payment isn't supposed to set the price. The one who pays makes the offer based on their honour and how much the exchange is of value to them. A generous price is an acknowledgment and appreciation of the graciousness of the seller in providing the product and ensures that the provider will continue to provide that product or service in the future.

h   Since time immemorial, Kanyen'kehà:ka have traded, exchanged, and sold various commodities, services, and technologies with one another and with outsiders. We have used universal trade currencies (such as tobacco, seeds, wampum beads, foreign currencies, and rare items such as precious metals, stones, and even fossils) to hold and exchange value, but these market relations are always embedded in our culture and customs.

i   In our language, we can only claim ownership over things that we can actually possess or create through our own labour. We can sell our own labour and skills, as well as commodities that we have produced or purchased. We are not allowed to sell items that have not been gathered or produced by human hands, and we can't commoditize another's right to the land. We cannot sell a licence to capture the fish in the river or to harvest a deer or a tree in the forest, because we can't sell a right to access another being. However, we can catch a fish and sell the fish as long as we fulfill our responsibilities to ensuring the fecundity of creation.

j   In gardening and agriculture, if we choose to grow plants, we have to ensure that we improve the soil and make it more fertile. If we're taking up space for a garden, then we also need to leave some of the produce for the beings we have excluded from the garden.

k   When harvesting, we are to use as much of the plant or animal as we can and share the remainder with creation. For example, when we hunt a deer in the woods, we are supposed to take what we're going to use and leave behind what we don't use (such as the entrails) so that other parts of creation can benefit. When we harvest a medicine plant, we take only the portion of the plant we are to use (leaves, flowers, or some bark or roots) and leave the rest so that it may return to the earth or be used by another being.

l   We have the obligation to contribute common labour in our defence of one another and the enforcement of our rules and laws, and in the creation and development of national infrastructure and collective gender- or clan-related economic endeavours.

m   The renewable flow of resources in nature that Kanyen'kehà:ka economies are dependent on (fish, trees, plants, animals, etc.) have their own responsibilities and are accessed collectively by the people in a nonexclusionary way. All Kanyen'kehà:ka have equal opportunity to access those resources based on their free interactions with Mother Nature. The "Thanksgiving Address" is an explicit means of expressing our common relationship to creation.

n   Kanyen'kehà:ka economies are not based on the extraction of nonrenewable stocks of resources. The energy and raw materials buried in the earth should remain there, as utilizing them will cause sickness and suffering.

o   The Kanyen'kehà:ka have customs for economic sharing, collection, trade, and redistribution. It is our custom to offer food to visitors. We also help one another to harvest resources. We are always to maintain an awareness that we live in an interconnected web of shared responsibilities and reciprocal expectations with one another and all other life forms.

p   People have the right to do little work or to live frugally, as long as they are fulfilling their specific responsibilities and not causing harm or interfering with other Kanyen'kehà:ka people.

Rules for Kanyen'kehà:ka Medicines

a   Kanyen'kehà:ka people have our own unique medicinal practice and system of knowledge that we carry in our collective cultural consciousness.

b   The particular rules concerning the harvesting, making, and distributing of medicines do not involve any kind of licensing system and do not involve paying a tax or levy to another human or human-created institution.

c   Bear Clan people have special responsibilities concerning medicines. The Bear Clan was gifted with medicinal knowledge to understand sickness and to remedy it through plant medicine. With that knowledge came the responsibility to preserve our medical knowledge, add to it, and make it available to those who are in need of it.

d   All people are allowed to grow, harvest, and trade medicines in keeping with the Onkwehon:we relationship to Mother Earth. People of clans other than the Bear Clan are not obligated to provide or exchange medicines with others or to be actively involved in preserving and passing down medicinal knowledge.

e   In approaching a plant as medicine, we are to intentionally connect with the plant's spirit and ask it to assist us in healing an individual or a particular illness. We ask the "leader" of that particular grouping of medicines. We speak to that leader and inform them of who we are and what our intentions are. We say who we're planning to pick it for, what sickness or ailment the plant will be used to treat, and in what way it will be prepared. We say that to the group of medicines and speak to the biggest one by name. We introduce the people doing the harvesting, and we ask the plants if they'll offer some of their people as medicine the way our Onkwasotk'owakenha (our great-grandparents who've passed) instructed us to do.

f When we grow medicines for specific purposes, we spiritually explain to them what we're growing them for. We also speak to the soil and the water and all the other elements of creation. We put those words into the tobacco we burn and thereby communicate our intentions to the rest of creation.

g Our relationship to our medicines is reciprocal. We make an offering of tobacco when we harvest medicines, and we also help those medicines to have a place where they can thrive. We ask the "leader" to ask its relatives to volunteer themselves and to make themselves visible to us for harvesting. We don't over pick medicines, and we do what we can to make their world more hospitable to ensure their continued reproduction and growth. We also transplant medicine plants to more beneficial environments and different locations to ensure their continued existence. Medicine plants such as sweet flag, yellow lily, and burdock benefit from fire, so we burn marshes to encourage the medicines to grow back healthily.

h Medicine people do not go out looking for sick people to heal. They wait for people to ask them for medicine. Medicine people are not to refuse treatment to anyone – even their worst enemy. If they come seeking medicine, they are obligated to help them. Not helping others may result in the medicines refusing to work for medicine people.

i Medicine people have an obligation to not provide medicines that will harm the recipient.

j Medicine is not offered for free but is received in a mutually beneficial exchange. This exchange usually involves a gift of tobacco and an exchange of labour or trade goods. It may also include a financial offering. Sometimes, the person seeking medicine is unable to make an exchange at that time and thus incurs an obligatory spiritual debt to the medicine person, which will be paid when they're well again or by their family at their ten-day feast.

On the Issue of Ka'nikonhratenyen or "Mind changers"

a Despite the arguments of the adherents of the religious sect known as Handsome Lake, Kanyen'kehà:ka people are free to consume Ka'nikonhratenyen, or mind changers, as long as we do not harm others in doing so and as long as we are able to carry out our personal and collective responsibilities. Everything that we consume in our bodies has mind-changing effects because, as it is metabolized, it interacts with and affects our digestive and nervous systems and general sense of well-being. This effect is evident not only in the consumption of cannabis, tobacco, alcohol, and other drugs but also in the consumption of sugar, coffee, tea, and, especially, highly processed and refined foods.

b Kanyen'kehà:ka customs do not prohibit individuals from consuming psychoactive substances, but they do require all Kanyen'kehà:ka to be clear-minded and free from such influences when gathered to make political or business decisions or to conduct ceremonies or carry out public responsibilities.

c There is a common misconception that Europeans introduced fermentation processes to Turtle Island, when in fact, prior to the arrival of Europeans, North Americans throughout the hemisphere produced fermented beverages. The fermented drink *chicha* continues to be popular in Indigenous communities from the US Southwest to Southern Chile. Chicha is made from a wide variety of sources, including corn, quinoa, kañiwa, peanut, manioc root, palm fruit, potato, and other fruits and vegetables. Iroquoian people have produced fermented beverages such as corn and cranberry beer, root beer, ginger ale, and "wines" from crab apples and berries since time immemorial. A fermented crabapple beverage is associated with our Moccasin Dance.

d Through colonial prohibition and cultural genocide, Kanyen'kehà:ka continue to live under the Indian Act's prohibition of fermentation processes and the consumption and sale of alcohol on our territories. This is part of the colonial apparatus that attempts to dominate and control our society.

e Another common racial stereotype is that Indigenous people on Turtle Island do not have the genetic capacity to effectively metabolize alcohol and that this is the reason for alcoholism in our communities. However, as in other cultures across the globe, such substance abuse is closely correlated to the effects of trauma and colonial genocide on our populations, and the colonizers have regularly funnelled highly addictive substances into communities to encourage dependence and self-destruction among the populations they seek to control.

f Onkwehon:we fermented drinks are fundamentally different from the refined spirits such as whisky and rum that European colonists traded with the Onkwehon:we. Distilled spirits are considerably stronger in their effects and can generate a 180-degree turn of mind, disrupting our culture and customs and unravelling the social fabric of the people when overconsumed.

g The term *mind changers* refers to the transformation of one's mind to a fundamentally different way of functioning. The context of Handsome Lake's prohibition of "mind changers" such as alcohol was one in which unscrupulous white traders and government agents imported distilled spirits and hard liquor for the purpose of getting inebriated Onkwehon:we to sign over rights to their territory or to cheat them in trade.

h When the Europeans came with whisky, the men would go and trade, returning drunk with whisky. The women and old people would hear them singing the Atahkwakayon and go and hide as the men were wild and deranged from the whisky. It was passed in Mohawk Council that the men were no longer allowed to sing the Atahkwakayon. The song was banned for so long in our villages that we forgot it completely. During the time of the wars with the Americans, the Oneida taught the song back to the Mohawks on the condition that we would never drink alcohol and sing this song.

i The really dangerous mind changers that Onkwehon:we people should abstain from are ideological in form and come from outside societies seeking to disrupt and weaken our way of life. Such mind changers include foreign religions, political ideologies, and economic programs that hack away at the basis of our Sken:nen and way of life. The irony is that the Handsome Lake ideology is a kind of mind changer, in that it has introduced much of the framework of the Christian system – the concepts of heaven, hell, angels, God, the devil, repentance, and pacifism – to our culture and communities. This mind changer has caused strife and led to a cold war throughout Kanonshonni'onhwe Wisk Niyowentsyake.

Rules for Kanyen'kehà:ka Economy and Industry

a In Kanyen'kehà:ka economies, internal trade is a distribution of wealth among a web of interconnected and mutually reinforcing obligations. Wealth is gained from external trading relations, while the internal economy is redistributive and aimed at raising one another up. Internally, wealth is "banked" by increasing the fertility and fecundity of Our Mother, the Earth, and she is available to all, free of charge.

b Every Kanyen'kehà:ka has the right to involve themselves in industry and business through their own industriousness and initiative so long as they follow the customs and laws of our nation and community. This includes participation in a nearly endless array of economic opportunities, including activities such as the harvesting and processing of fish and deer; the cultivating, processing, and selling of agricultural cash crops such as tobacco, corn, and cannabis; the harvesting and production of ash baskets; and the production and resale of clothing, arts, and crafts; the production of various media; and the construction of buildings and infrastructure.

c   We, as the living generation, have the responsibility to continue, cultivate, process, consume, and share *Tyonhekwen* (the domesticated plants that humans rely on and that need human intervention to reproduce themselves) for the benefit of ourselves and the faces yet to come. Out of respect for the relationship our ancestors made with these plants, it is our responsibility to ensure their propagation and success as they support our existence.

d   The safeguarding of the integrity of the genetics of Tyonhekwen is the responsibility of the descendants of those who cared for them. Onkwehon:we have the collective ownership and responsibility to cultivate, propagate, and develop the genetic identity of the plants passed on to us by our ancestors so as to continue their vitality and health and to develop new cultivars to suit our changing needs. Likewise, we can hold, change, and pass on new genetics to the collectivity of future generations. The plant's responsibilities are to the collective, and the collective's responsibility is to the plants.

e   Should the activities of any Kanyen'kehà:ka industry (including tobacco, gaming, gas stations, cannabis, etc.) cause harm to the people, the Kanyen'kehà:ka people in that community have the ability to meet and address the problems in ways that those affected can all accept and live with. The discussion and resolution of problems in Kanyen'kehà:ka culture are well known and follow an inclusive consensus-based, decision-making process centred on peace, a good mind, and lovingness.

f   Each community has the right to set up its own specific rules and customs about how it chooses to deal with the political economy of its territory. It is our custom that every person is free, and every village can govern itself as it chooses. When people do not agree with the decisions being made in their territory, they are free to leave and found a new village instead of breaking the peace.

g   With the decline of our ecosystem's ability to sustain us, we have increasingly become more reliant on trade with the outsiders passing through our territories. In essence, the wealth of the outsiders has become a resource for us to sustain ourselves. The rules for harvesting this new resource are not fundamentally different from the rules that apply to harvesting other flows of resources, such as the fish who come to spawn in our rivers or the game in our forests.

Sewatohkwat: The Dish with One Spoon or Beaver Bowl Treaties

a   In addition to our economic customs as outlined above, there are some specific peace and friendship treaties made between ourselves and other original peoples that specify rules and protocols to be followed when harvesting resources (including medicines) within each other's territories. One of the most commonly referred to of these agreements is the Sewatohkwat (Dish with One Spoon/Beaver Bowl Treaties), which applies in the Great Lakes watershed. The Beaver Bowl is represented in a white wampum belt seven beads wide and consists of a black diamond symbol in the middle with a white bead in the centre.

b Many of the protocols within Sewatohkwat have an ancient history stretching back to the foundation of the Kayenere:kowa, the constitution developed by the Rotinonhsonnitonh (They Who Have Built the House). As part of this political and economic agreement between Iroquoian people, the Kayenere:kowa stipulates that when a new Chief has been stood up by his Clan Mother through his clan, all the other Chiefs are to welcome his instalment with a feast of beaver tail soup or roasted beaver tail. The Beaver Tail Feast is to be eaten from a single bowl without the use of sharp utensils – to ensure that no blood is accidentally spilled.

The participants must be careful to not use sharp tongues and to ensure that no hard feelings are caused among one another. This ceremonial meal is an expression of the economic rules of sharing resources and maintaining peace in a common territory Kanonhsonni Wisk Niyohwentsyake (The House of the Five Lands).

c Sewatohkwat treaties describe the harvesting territories and the protocols for non-Iroquoian peoples to access hunting territory within Kanonhsonni Wisk Niyohwentsyake and for Iroquoian people to access harvesting within non-Iroquoian territories. Such Sewatohkwat agreements have been made by the Iroquois with many other Indigenous nations, including the Anishinaabe, Cree, Petun, Potawatomi, Miami, Mississaugas, Nippissing, Odawa, and Lakota. The agreements ensure that all parties may access, share, and use the land, provided that they take only what they need and leave enough to regenerate the resources they take. The injunction not to use "sharp utensils" in the Beaver Bowl Feast means that the weapons (and mentality) of warfare should not be brought into the harvesting areas, so as to preserve the peace.

d The Sewatohkwat protocol to be followed when approaching the group of Indigenous people who have jurisdiction over the area from which you wish to harvest is as follows. When a group seeks to harvest from a particular area outside of its people's jurisdiction, they shall meet with the ones responsible for the area and provide a feast of either roasted beaver tail or beaver soup with the headmen and leaders of that people. At this gathering, the two groups are to sit together and eat from and share the beaver tail dish without using sharp utensils. Those coming to harvest must explain what the specific resource is that they are looking for (moose, deer, fish, wild rice, birch bark, etc.) and state how long they are planning to stay in the area and how much they need to harvest to meet their needs. The people with the jurisdiction over the area tell the ones coming in where to harvest, how much can be taken in an ecologically sustainable fashion, and what harvesting techniques are suitable and acceptable in the region. They will also provide guidance as to appropriate or acceptable behaviour so as not to end up in conflict with others. The guests should also bring gifts to compensate the hosts for their time in meeting with them and sharing their knowledge of the land.

e   For example, the area of land to the north of Lake Ontario is jointly shared by the Iroquois and the Algonquin and Anishinaabe. The watershed on the north side of the Ottawa River belongs to the Algonquin and Anishinaabe, while the watershed north of Lake Ontario is under the jurisdiction of the Iroquois, but both peoples can harvest in each other's territories according to the Beaver Bowl Treaty. So, if a party of Mohawks from Six Nations wanted to hunt moose in Algonquin Territory north of Ottawa, they would then host a Beaver Bowl Feast for the local Algonquin people in, say, Barriere Lake, whose territory they wish to hunt in. The proceedings would unfold as described above, and with any luck the Mohawks would return with a moose.

f   Sewatohkwat covers a huge territory that involves a stretch of land reaching from Albany in the East to Fort Detroit in the West and Iroquois Falls in the north, where the watershed changes direction and flows into the Arctic. Others describe the territory as stretching from Montreal to Detroit, and some consider it as occupying the whole watershed of the Great Lakes.

g   Because of Sewatohkwat, there is no need to have border ports of entry and rules about where people can travel in the territories. The rules of jurisdiction about where Indigenous peoples can harvest, establish villages, and carry out trade were already made between Indigenous peoples before Europeans negotiated land treaties in the region.

h   In today's context, the same protocols apply in terms of land use and access. Application of Sewatohkwat also applies to modern business developments where the guest meets with the host jurisdiction to discuss land-use parameters and requests for economic activities in their territory. This could include planting, transporting goods, importing and exporting, and brick-and-mortar trade and commerce. Meetings should be happening

Dusting Off the Path – Tsi Nionkwarihotens 263

with people feasting in each other's territory if they want to do business there or use the land in some way in accordance with the protocols established within the Sewatohkwat.

i   The protocols of the Sewatohkwat are so ancient that it is unclear as to their origin. It is possible that some of these protocols were brought to Onkwehon:we people by other nations as a solution for peace or vice versa. It is likely that other nations used these sorts of protocols for peaceful resolutions of harvesting conflicts independent of Onkwehon:we people. In today's context, other Indigenous Nations, if they so choose, could adopt such protocols within their own agreements.

Resource Allocation and Public Works Contracts

a   When more than one party (a clan, two competing communities, or a group of individuals) wish to have a seasonally limited but exclusive access to a collective resource or means of production that is too limited to be used by everyone, a contest may take place to determine which party will gain access to the opportunity or singular activity.

b   These contests are a means of settling tenders for public works such as hosting ceremonies, producing maple syrup, the planting of communal cash crops, the harvesting and processing of communal crops, the building of a road, the construction of a well or public building, and so on. In all of these cases, the winning party gains a payment and a responsibility to complete the task for the public good.

c   In cases where a surplus is created through the public work (such as the growing of crops or the production of maple syrup, etc.), the winning party keeps the surplus that was produced after sharing what is required by custom.

d   For example, in the case of cooking for a communal meal, the people assigned the task of preparing the food eat last. They must provide enough food for all the people. After everyone has had their share, the cooks eat. In the event that there's not enough food, the cooks don't eat. In the event that there's a surplus, the cooks get as big a bowl as they can eat.

e   Contests are often used to resolve differences between competing interests to access resources and provide civic public works. We play dice or the seed game when there are multiple parties competing. *Kayentowanen* (the Peach Stone Game) is played when the job requires a lot of participants and there are only two parties involved (for example, to decide who will win the payment for hosting the ceremonies for the year or what gender will do the planting for the community gardens). *Ohwenta* (Mudcat or Short

Snow Snake) and Snow Snake are also contests played to determine the winning party in bids that require fewer numbers of people to complete the bid and when it is to happen in the spring. *Tewa'arathonh* (lacrosse) and *Tahontsikwa'eks* or *Ahki* (hockey) might be played to resolve disputes between two villages or Nations over which will have access to limited resources such as a sugar bush or fishing grounds or a certain hunting area. These sorts of dispute-resolution mechanisms are often employed on an annual or recurring basis to reopen the opportunity for access.

f   The result of these various decision-making contests occurs on a spiritual level and are understood to be ultimately determined by Creation itself.

In Closing

This is a working document based on living knowledge from the path walked by our ancestors. Like all living knowledge, this collection is incomplete as we as a people are still contributing to this body of knowledge, and laying down our path into the future. We encourage you to add new rafters of knowledge to our ways as you walk your path as an ancestor of the generations yet to come.

Ehtho Nikawennake, Tahnon Onen Ehtho

Notes

1. Jorge Barrera, "First Nations Entrepreneurs Are Asserting Sovereignty and Seizing the New Cannabis Economy," *CBC News*, January 10, 2018. https://www.cbc.ca/news/indigenous/first-nations-entrepreneurs-are-asserting-sovereignty-and-seizing-the-new-cannabis-economy-1.4481747.
2. The success of local cannabis distribution in Tyendinaga is contingent on the way that the community has rallied behind efforts such as spaghetti dinners hosted at the local hall to raise funds much-needed for local initiatives. In 2018, there were more than forty cannabis dispensaries in Tyendinaga. That number is stable in 2021. Unlike the schemes cooked up by bureaucrats, they must be doing something right.
3. Although the days of the Oka Crisis and the Gustafsen Lake Standoff appear to be behind us, we are haunted by fresh images such as the 2017 fiasco of RCMP dismantling a Wet'suwet'en Nation protest camp at gunpoint. Or the 2019 RCMP raid against the Gidimt'en Access Point. Or the 2020 Coastal Gas Link stand-off that garnered international attention. The echoes of colonialism reverberate strongly when law enforcement inflicts violence in support of corporate interests.
4. On taking power, Ford immediately cancelled construction of forty brick-and-mortar Ontario Cannabis Store (OCS) distribution sites. In hindsight, this was probably his biggest mistake. The move was overseen by the finance minister, Vic Fedeli, who was later removed from the position. Permitting these retail locations to be built and "open for business" would have put Ontario on par with many other provincial

distribution plans but far from emulating Alberta's more aggressive retail distribution model.

5 Tim Barnhart, owner of Legacy 420, a Tyendinaga cannabis dispensary, put the vision for local control of cannabis distribution another way: "We built [this system of self-governance] to prevent [the federal government] from building it for us ... Our whole lives they've been coming in and building everything for us, and telling us what our nations need. We're telling them that's not working anymore. We want to assert our rights and show Canada we can strive and move forward" (Barber 2018).

Works Cited

Aversa, Joseph, Tony Hernandez, and Jenna Jacobson. 2021. "Canada Provides Lessons to the World on Selling Weed." the oz.newsletter, September 23. https://okanaganz.com/oz/features/canada-provides-lessons-to-the-world-on-selling-weed/.

Barber, John. 2018. "Indigenous Pot Superstore Drives Profound Transformation on Tyendinaga Mohawk Territory." *Toronto Star*, October 14.

Barrera, Jorge. 2018a. "First Nations Entrepreneurs Are Asserting Sovereignty and Seizing the New Cannabis Economy." *CBC News*, January 10.

—. 2018b. "It's Business as Usual for This Mohawk First Nation's Marijuana Stores While Court Challenges Planned." *CBC News*, October 17.

—. 2019. "THC Slushies, Pirate Radio and the Cannabis-Driven Boom in a Mohawk Community." *CBC News*, July 21.

Canada. 2018. "Government of Canada to Create Recognition and Implementation of Rights Framework." News release, February 14. https://pm.gc.ca/en/news/news-releases/2018/02/14/government-canada-create-recognition-and-implementation-rights.

Draaisma, Muriel. 2018. "4,500 Ontario Cannabis Customers Have Personal Data Stolen." *CBC News*, November 8. www.cbc.ca/news/canada/toronto/ontario-cannabis-store-data-breach-canada-post-customer-orders-1.4895619.

Edwards, Kyle. 2018. "No Recreational Pot Shops in Ontario? This Place Didn't Get the Memo: Dozens of Dispensaries on Tyendinaga Mohawk Territory Are Selling Marijuana According to Their Own Rules – and So Far There Don't Seem to Be Many." *Maclean's*, October 17.

Galloway, Gloria. 2017. "First Nations Demand Control over Cannabis Sales." *Globe and Mail*, December 6. https://www.theglobeandmail.com/news/politics/first-nations-want-to-set-own-rules-for-cannabis-sales/article37231232/.

Hunter, Brad. 2019. "Weed Wonderland: What Mohawks Can Teach Us about Cannabis." *Toronto Sun*, June 29, 2019.

12

Slow Cannabis

KELLY COULTER

Relatively new to Twitter in 2018, I began to notice several consistencies with the feed I had created for myself. Among my observations was that Kelly Coulter tweets the most stimulating online content about cannabis in Canada. When I contacted her for comment, she responded enthusiastically, seeming to know everyone connected to the industry in Canada. In later conversation, she spoke insightfully about the importance of women in the cannabis industry making the transition to the legal economy.

What follows provides an answer to the question: Where do we go from here if we are to reclaim cannabis culture and remake it in Canada with a human face? Echoing concerns raised by others in this volume, she presents a compelling case for pursuing more organic cannabis production on family-owned farms. Smaller-scale, community-minded operators – who adhere to water-use and quality agreements and who use sustainable methods of production (such as 100 percent renewable-energy sources) and organic certification regimes – are the suggested antidote to the fast-cash ethos of Big Cannabis. Much like the world-class wines of the Okanagan Valley, regions that produce cannabis have their own terroir that reflects the unique characteristics of the environment. Appellations are geographical regions whose agricultural products are synonymous with place. Champagne is one example. In addition to protecting branding rights and local economies, Stoa (2018, 16) observes that appellations also "provide a mechanism for local farmers to get together and work on local issues." Consumers gain transparency, better options, and higher quality due to local producers' adherence to cultivation and sustainability standards.

As an advocate for Slow Cannabis, Coulter stubbornly refuses to diminish the integrity of cannabis enthusiasts by passively accepting industrial agriculture fuelled by the engine of Big Cannabis. – C.J.S.M.

At the entrance to a farm in the Cowichan Valley on Vancouver Island, there is a sign that reads "SLOW DOWN." It shows a picture of horses and children playing, but it is the words that really grab you. The drive is long, surrounded by pastures and majestic trees with the sparkle of a lake in the distance. By the time you reach the sign telling you to slow down, your mind has already done it. Your shoulders have relaxed, and you're smiling as you breathe in the fresh country air. The horses greet you with flicks of their tails, and life seems suddenly simple. As you lean against the fence, taking in the beauty of your surroundings and your first blissful toke, you wonder if this is what it is really all about.

Cannabis wants you to slow down. She wants to make you think and question and ultimately answer those questions. But she also wants you to relax and laugh and share her with others in the enjoyments of life – food, music, nature, love, friendship, and healing.

As we enter into the new paradigm of legal cannabis in Canada and around the world (hallelujah), now is the time to re-examine what this "perfect plant" is really trying to teach us. In *The Botany of Desire* (2002), Michael Pollan writes about the genius of plant life and how humans have much to learn from them, including cannabis. I believe cannabis will eventually lead us back to a more natural way of living in harmony with the seasons, not only as farmers but also as consumers.

The Farmers

In 1978, Masanobu Fukuoka wrote *The One-Straw Revolution*, a treatise on how food could and should be grown. It's a manifesto about farming, eating, and how the limits of human knowledge will require a radical change to preserve our planet and the systems we rely on for our food. Masanobu was a rice farmer who chose a less labour-intensive farming style because he wanted his life to be a happy, healthy, and fulfilling one. He believed and proved that farmers could grow to sustain themselves without breaking their backs, their minds, and their spirits. Cannabis farmers of the future who share these values are gathering now in the United States and Canada to embrace these same principles of permaculture, which not only serve the natural environment but also produce what some might argue is the "highest-end" cannabis – seasonal, regenerative, organic, and fair.

Brittny Anderson of the Cannabis Conservancy is currently working with others to help develop more sustainable criteria for cannabis growers. Her commitment to the regenerative movement was solidified during her time as an intern at Bija Vidyapeeth, Vandana Shiva's farm in India:

> Regenerative agriculture is the path we must take if we want to renew our communities and reverse climate change. I believe this is a critical moment in time and we must build the world we envision. Regenerative cannabis cultivation is going to be a big part of creating a sustainable future and inspiring other agricultural sectors to do the same. Together we will change the world. The Cannabis Conservancy's certification allows farmers to differentiate themselves in the marketplace so consumers can choose products aligned with their values. (Personal conversation, 2018)

Cannabis was not always grown indoors, which is, surprisingly, a radical notion to many. It was grown covertly, because it was illegal, on forest floors, in swamps, and among rows of other crops. It was hidden and untended for the most part, which is probably, if not definitely, why outdoor cannabis has gotten a bit of a bad rap. The good farmers of northern California, who have been growing legal medical cannabis for the rest of the state for decades, were able to hone their techniques, strains, and philosophies around cannabis cultivation and have proven that sun-grown is not only friendlier to the planet and less costly to grow but also deliciously effective.

Casey O'Neil of HappyDay Farms is one of those "good farmers" who believes his farm is meant for a higher purpose: "As a diversified cannabis and vegetable farmer, it is important to me to see thriving small farms that build soil and community. I look forward to learning and sharing with other farmers as we move towards a more regenerative form of agriculture" (Personal conversation, 2017).

Amanda Reiman is the communications director for Flow Kana, a distribution company in California known for its support of small farms:

> We work with sun-grown farmers in Mendocino and Humboldt counties who go beyond organic by using regenerative farming practices, literally improving the quality of the soil with every harvest. Flow Kana was the first company to connect the public with this small community of farmers, who, because of prohibition, have existed in the shadows until now. Flow Kana is proud to give them a platform to tell their stories, and an opportunity to brand themselves, their region and their cannabis for a whole new group of consumers. With offices in southern CA, the Bay Area and Mendocino County, Flow Kana brings the farm to the dispensary along with opportunities to meet the farmers who produce the world's best cannabis. Flow Kana is also in the process of renovating an eighty-acre property in Mendocino, formerly home to a winery, for centralized processing, manufacturing, testing and distribution for the local farmers. The Flow Cannabis Institute will also provide an opportunity for the public to visit, tour the facility and interact with farmers on their farms. The institute will be a source of education, not only about cannabis, but about prohibition and its associated harms. Additionally, Flow Kana advocates on the local, state and national level, for policies that support small, traditional, sun-grown farmers and lessen barriers for their success in the new marketplace. (Flow Kana 2018)

The work of these visionaries and others will be critical for small, sustainable cannabis farmers throughout North America and beyond. The good news is that the world is getting woke to the harms of the industrialization of agriculture, and the slow food movement has been gaining momentous speed. This is partly due to the incredible work of Carlo Petrini, who wrote the Slow Food manifesto, but also to the support of the worlds' greatest chefs, including Jamie Oliver and Dan Barber, who are major proponents of more sustainable food consumption. Not long ago, Netflix might have had one documentary devoted to food culture. Now, there are dozens – and the list grows longer every day. The idea that people are more in tune with where their food comes from and how it is grown will naturally converge with the consumer values of the future cannabis consumer. They will have choice, transparency, and, above all else, more education. Farming documentaries – which reveal some of the harms of monocultures, pesticide use, and the importance of supporting local food producers – could soon be focusing on cannabis farms in the not too distant future.

You

But it is not simply lofty ideals about the industrialization of agriculture and the importance of preserving our soils that will help restore the old ways of growing cannabis ... it will be you. Going to farmers' markets is fun. Meeting and getting to know the farmers who produce your food is rewarding in many ways. You are supporting other humans and not big, multinational corporations. You are eating fresh and healthier food. You are helping communities. You are being kind to the environment by purchasing food with less to zero packaging. You are learning about farming and educating yourself about where your food comes from. You are supporting a slower pace in life that is reflective of life. You are sticking it to the machine.

Cannabis is at the very root of this ethos because it has endured a legacy of demonization. In its future incarnation as a legal plant (feels odd even writing this), the values of radical self-sufficiency and true futurism could and should be embraced and supported. Ideally, we should all be consuming our cannabis as we should be consuming our food, by growing our own. The next best thing is to vote with your wallet. If the trends we are seeing in other sectors, including food, wine, beer, and alcohol, are any indication, the future looks promising for small cannabis farms committed to quality, craftsmanship, and community.

There are regions throughout Europe with small, sought-after, and profitable vineyards. The farms are typically hundreds of years old and have been passed down through generations. These farms have not only survived but have thrived, and the lessons are infinitely valuable. First of all – they remained small, less than five acres in most cases, a practice that lends itself to a more manageable infrastructure. Second, they had a loyal following, winemakers who knew that the grapes grown were of the finest quality, intimately tended to, and expertly harvested. Those same winemakers in turn have loyal followings, and so every vintage is spoken for pre-harvest. Finally, we have the craftsmanship of the farmer.

This applies not only to stewardship of the land but also to the methodology of the harvest and translates to the principles of slow cannabis farming. Is the soil healthy? Is the cannabis hang-dried and properly cured? Will it be hand-trimmed? Are the workers paid a fair living wage? Does the farm aim to benefit the environment and the community?

Cannabis can teach us so many things about how we interact with our natural world, and I truly believe that is where we are heading. Friedrich Nietzsche alludes to a similar idea in *The Birth of Tragedy* (1967), and Michael Pollan expands on it in *The Botany of Desire*.

Michael Pollan (2002) notes that in *The Birth of Tragedy*, Nietzsche (1967) describes intoxication as "nature over power and mind, nature having her way with us" (2002, 178). The Greeks understood that this was not something to be undertaken lightly or too often. Intoxication for them was a carefully circumscribed ritual, never a way to live, because they understood that Dionysus can make angels or animals of us. It all depends. Even so, letting nature have her way with us now and again still seems like a useful thing to do, if only as a check on our hubris, if only to bring our abstracted upward gaze back down to Earth for a time. What a re-enchantment of the world that would be, to look around us and see that the plant and the trees of knowledge grow in the garden still.

Good farmers know this. Slow cannabis, like slow food, is about working with the natural rhythms of life. In the spring, we plant; in the summer, we tend; in the fall, we harvest and share; and in the winter, we rest. We live sustainably and regeneratively so that generations who come after us will also be able to do the same. We are going slow.

Works Cited

Fukuoka, Masanobu. 1978. *The One-Straw Revolution: An Introduction to Natural Farming*. Emmaus, PA: Rodale.

Nietzsche, Friedrich. 1967. *The Birth of Tragedy*. New York: Random House.

Pollan, Michael. 2002. *The Botany of Desire: A Plant's-Eye View of the World*. New York: Random House.

13
Illicit Cannabis Market Folklore

CLAYTON JAMES SMITH McCANN and "SAL"

Having worked for several years in the cannabis folk market – toiling as a trimmer, driver, and maintenance guy on outdoor grow sites – the time had finally come to "return to the field." As I started checking in with some of my connections in the Central Kootenay and Central Okanagan regions, I was reminded of the astonishing variation in cannabis-growing operations one encounters when meeting new collaborators, especially as I wandered into converted outbuildings, outdoor operation sites, and residences throughout the regions. I was fortunate enough, in a word, to "help a friend" one early morning, far up in a subalpine "patch" just a few hundred feet off a logging main.

It had been years since I set foot in one of these outlaw farms, and this one was classic: it had a trickle-feed reservoir watering system, on timers, irrigating through drippers. Thousands of plants, with two distinct strains, accompanied by that overwhelming punch of sensory overload: the smell of it all. Tightly packed together, it seemed impossible that the plants could get enough sunlight. This occurred to me as I, too, stood in a temperate rainforest, the conifers densely packed around me.

To be honest, my back ached just looking at all that produce, and my heart was saddened that the end of an era had passed without comment: none of the hundred-odd pounds that would be harvested from this site would make it to drying racks and into the hands of trimmers. Those days were gone, for now, maybe forever. It would all be turned into "crude oil," my friend informed me. It would be dried deep in the bush in a dry shack and pulverized into a powdery substrate. Later, in another processing site, it would be made into a slurry. Finally, various extraction techniques would be applied to the watery goo and the valuable oils distilled off, to be refined off-site.

Such an ignominious end to the gloriously romantic age of "outdoor" gave me pause. My time in this industry sector had defined me; it was more a part of me than my long-vanished youth. Had I not been there to bid it farewell, I likely would never have believed in its passing. I stood and stared at the compact field, so cleverly hidden away: a mere decade prior, it would have yielded upwards of $250,000 in profits and paid for the winter's survival of an army of trimmers, hikers, and transporters. I stared dolefully at it, and very much like in the now-famous song "Rivers of Babylon," I sat upon the nearest stump and wept for what we had lost.

There we sat down.
Yeah, yeah, we wept
when we remembered Zion.

Shifting from something sacred into a commodity of folk capitalism, marijuana became an industrial agriculture initiative, then an aggressive financial capitalist cannabis overtaken by powerful elites, toward what seems for now to be a dismal flailing by those same elites, hampered by greed.

These folk capitalism sentiments are captured, in my own words, in the poem "Guilty Republic." To conclude this chapter, "For the Discriminating Traveller" recounts another harrowing encounter, as told by "Sal" the smuggler, from the storied history of Canada's cannabis folk market. – C.J.S.M.

Guilty Republic
Clayton James Smith McCann

> The government can never be more than the government of words.
> — WILLIAM CARLOS WILLIAMS, LETTER TO ROBERT CREELEY, c. 1960s

For Canada's 2021 census, I worked the backroads, hills, and switchbacks of the lower Slocan Valley, British Columbia. This census was different, due to COVID-19. One new protocol was the use of "door droppers," security-sealed access codes specific to addresses that had no postal box registered at the local post office.

And around the lower Slocan, there were a lot of folks who weren't interested in the government knowing where they lived. The area was, at one time in the mid-1990s, home to Canada's illicit cannabis industry. Cannabis was grown elsewhere in Canada, but never in such abundance, nor so enthusiastically, as there. Two of every three homes in the region had been retrofitted to be indoor cannabis production spaces in some capacity or other. But "indoor" was not what distinguished the Slocan.

Named after a Sinixt or Ktunaxa word for "spear piercing the head of the fish," the southeastern British Columbia Kootenay region, home to the Slocan, was once spawning grounds for coastal salmon, but generations of hydroelectric dam projects along the Columbia and Kootenay Rivers have rent such resources from the land and people.

The Sinixt and Ktunaxa have lived in continuous occupation of the region in excess of ten thousand years (Barley 2007, 6). Seasonal migratory patterns resulted in some Sinixt and Ktunaxa residing permanently in what is now Idaho, Montana, and Washington States. Some continue to live in the Slocan, having recently won a pitched battle to be declared a surviving Indigenous group. Sinixt are now recognized by the Government of Canada (Metcalf 2021).

One of the first contact points between European settler-invaders and these Slocan peoples was the Lewis and Clark Expedition (1803–06), when the bearded explorers appeared on the shores of the Kootenay River, rather the worse for wear and in need of sustenance. Offered salmon by the Sinixt, the newcomers didn't like the looks of the bright orange fish flesh and refused. Instead, the haggard Eurocentric wanderers killed a nearby dog and ate it. History remains silent as to which party the dog belonged.

Not all contact has been this amicable. The smallpox epidemic of 1858 wiped out thousands of Indigenous people across what is now British Columbia, and it was only one of several successive waves of biological ethnic cleansing. Ethnographer James Teit's voice reaches out to us from the late 1800s, noting that the *Variola major* plague found its way into the Slocan Valley: "All interior tribes have decreased in number ... and are only about one-third as numerous as in former times: Kutenai, between 500 and 600 [are dead]" (Wickwire 2019, 179).

Further, the colonial project of clearing Indigenous groups from their ancestral lands, combined with continuous eras of rigorous and destructive resource extraction, has had an apocalyptic effect on Indigenous groups in BC, a phenomenon that continues today, with the BC NDP endeavouring to destroy 128 kilometres of West Moberly First Nations land in the Peace River Valley, as part of the disastrous Site C hydroelectric project, the most expensive, and violent, dam project in Canadian history (Cox 2021).

I worked the 2021 census out of financial necessity. Yet it gave me the opportunity to do what I always wanted: venture onto the properties and laneways of "grower palaces" throughout the lower Slocan. I wanted to see for myself the bizarre and wonderful creations – the residences – of cannabis growers who, for upwards of five decades, prospered by cultivating cannabis in high mountain sites, clustered around reliable water sources in a series of traplines, on approximately south-facing slopes.

With each year's "winnings," a new room would be added to the "palace," and after a number of successful seasons, what was once a one-room shack, hunkered out in the bush, was suddenly a sprawling, arcane monstrosity, a byzantine maze of studios, hallways, and yet another bedroom.

I filled my boots, as the saying goes, and was saddened to see example after example of the faded glory of a bygone era. Many of the "palaces" were overgrown, abandoned even, to wood rot and infestations of termites and carpenter ants. The odd bear seemed to be the only resident nowadays. Where had the growers gone? They were difficult to spot in Winlaw, Crescent Valley, Shore Acres, Bonnington, and Nelson. Where, indeed, were they among all the private home-holders, small-business owners, restaurateurs, retail store proprietors, notary publics, city councillors, and mayors?

I wrote the poem that follows, "Guilty Republic," to contend with a figure that history has certainly passed over – the illicit cannabis worker. Such a character as she – a "trimmer," an indoor cultivation labourer, a "hiker" from back when "outdoor" cannabis was still profitable enough to warrant the risks – where has she vanished to? Surely, we may find her yet, toiling in the pubs and kitchens of the cities of the empire, or perhaps she, too, has entered the shrinking middle class and now resides "on the coast," in some quaint little village that stands to be exploited by hipsters fleeing the impossible rents and mortgages of Vancouver.

I wrote "Guilty Republic" for those who contributed the lion's share of the labour required to get enough perfectly shaved, robust little buds to fill a half-pound Ziploc yet received the mouse's portion of the profits. Even under the "pure capitalism" of the illicit sector, exploitation was rife, and workers were ill-treated. Not all, of course, but I was witness to more than my fair share of examples of how the game was rigged: the house always wins.

Cowering in the bush as RCMP helicopters thunder overhead. Hiking out into the dark hills with only a water bottle, a fruit and nut bar, and a headlamp to see you through "fertigation" during hunting season out on the open altiplano, gunshots ringing in your ears. "Night dropped" near a patch only to find a curious grizzly staring you down (in a place where mosquitoes and no-see-ums are the *real* monsters). These are the offices of the outdoor cannabis worker. These and endless hours of hauling seventy-pound "bales" up a slope, or double totes down. A fistful of twenties for your troubles.

We don't yet know where cannabis legalization will lead us, but we may have seen the last of the illicit worker in this sector. I, for one, will miss them. The Slocan was also home to a vibrancy of spirit once. It was a creative play space for those who dared to run the blockades in a redux of "Thunder/Copperhead Road" – running down the mountainsides with a truck full of rapidly decaying plant matter, risking liberty and limb for a few hundred dollars and the bragging rights of one who knows, who can make the boldest of claims. "I, too, once was there. I saw it all."

> *Dear (deleted): the*
> *Valley looks cold*
> *to me. How will*
> *you make a life there*
>
> *For your lady, yourself, the*
> *baby? Should this poem be*
> *more positive? I can't get my*
> *head around the prob*
>
> *Lem, this dream of hope and*
> *happiness. I write to*

*fight, because poems are
bullets are nurses are*

*Soldiers in the war, this
war against (what shall we
name it?) against the sin of wages
against monstrous*

*Greed, against our own
sorrow. Dear (your lover's name):
winter's coming I can
feel it in my bones. People can't eat*

*The dread of want, no matter
how much wood they cut. Days
are shorter now – already cold
way up where*

*We built the zombie-proof
box. My dear (Prime Minister) we
sense your headless machine tonight, that
which our joyous forces*

*Must wrestle blind on the razor
rim of history. This thing you've
made: screams stillborn, rich white
rage at our resolve. We smell your robot*

*Fear, this brute, scaled torso of
isolation – and we're holding this
thing by the ears. But, sooth, my child's
up in the loft, sick and*

Hungry. I can hardly see to write the

*Words: "Dear Me: the Valley
seems dark tonight, go ask the
obviously-extant, extinct Sinixt –"
lay lines shifting... You say there's*

*The harvest, twenty days in the
hills (I'm not allowed to name them), but*

*will it get you through? Will the grower make
advances? And will you really risk*

*Prison? Won't the rippers get
it first? Aren't there deer on the
road? By the singular beam of your
headlamp! And Conversation Officers*

*Everywhere?! Oh, the Arnica, Emergen-C, knee-
brace, tree-planter tape, the tensor, mole-
skin, propolis – sing a song of aging
labour. Are you not, in point of*

*Fact, selling your body piece-
meal? Plantar fasciitis, your lower
back spins a tail of disaster – 'cause
when it goes, it be gone: no*

*Worker's comp, nor re-
training: "Name?"
" (Yours)."
"Occupation?"*

*"Pot grower."
"Age?"
"38."
"Oh ... you look much*

*Older." And what justice would you
find, in a province where everyone's complicit in the good
times; but the cops hunt YOU*

*Down. And you're just a
worker, a hiker, a trimmer, the
driver who'll never get rich – I ask it
again: WILL IT GET YOU*

THROUGH? These words seem to be typing

*Me. Dearest Mother; I'm back in
school and what a con. The walls are grey*

and featureless, so too the lectures, but
just below the surface, the ancient

Insects stir, inchoate, jealous
over bits of rusted chain. The academy
is sick and dying. By (your god here), the
Valley looks good just now. As a

Joke, I want to start burning Business
books, Economics texts, journals of
Commerce, 'cause they're not
worth the trees they cut down to

Print such obscenities upon. As a lark I want
to offer a course called "Anthropology of the
Murderous Rich 100" or may
be "Oral Traditions of Technocrat Doublespeak" (TBA).

And there's "Art for Bigots, Art for Pervs" (seminar
only). I think I'll die in this paper
mine and no one will ever
know. Dear (Milton Friedman): your economy

In tatters is like war coming down, dog-men
are gathering (I see guns in their eyes), America
is broken forever and Canada's not far
behind: a few breaths from collapse and I guess

We're to eat the dead? I can't walk to Pass
more with a sucking chest-
wound, And I wish I'd listened
harder to my grand-folks who survived

The Great Depression. But I do re-
call my Granny and her final,
asthmatic skies: The Valley looks warm to
me, the Valley looks warm and

Bright. Dear (everyone): Maybe you'll
Make it. This poem wants you to
be happy. We've seen others survive and they
don't work at Kaleshnikov's they don't go

Off to the tar sands. You only ask
For a winter cabin, to make art, a muffler
for your shit-box, a big bag of rice – perhaps
there's green enough? The

Mountain looks smart to me, like a
victorious insurgency: a Chiapas of
the mind, a Confederacy
of the forest, Resistance piney-scented,

Florets of illicit statehood. And the
Valley looks righteous tonight.

For the Discriminating Traveller
"Sal"

Meeting "Sal" seemed opportune for both of us. I had in my possession a packet of Zig-Zags and some tobacco, and she had a story to tell. Sal was a professional cannabis smuggler of the pre-legalization era who had no reservations about telling her "work stories" to a stranger at a party. Her story gives a glimpse into the precarity endured by the cross-border smuggler, a person beyond the rule of law and state protections granted citizens, a person abandoned in search of big payoffs and thrills.

"I suppose we were rum-runners once," Sal confided, referring to the Prohibition era in the United States (1919–33), which created high-stakes opportunities for Canadians to get into the smuggling business. "We smuggled whiskey way back when," she added. While this era of high-speed automobiles (precursors to NASCAR!) and powerboats outrunning Canadian and US Customs agents makes for great folklore, one hears very little about cannabis smugglers.

Cannabis smugglers such as Clay "Boss Weed" Roueche or Sam Brown are often characterized as criminals or thrill-seekers. But Sal was far from two-dimensional. Her home was paid off, and she led a respectable lifestyle as a local small-business owner. But she went on to describe a time "back when" when she was hustling BC bud in San Francisco for four thousand dollars a pound. Hockey bags (of course!) loaded with dried cannabis were flown and dropped across the border by a single-engine plane. A hiking team dispatched the day before waited at the drop point to pick up the contraband (if all went well).

Of course, this worked only if the pilot and the hikers were at the same drop point. "Sometimes you just lose $100,000 worth of weed. And it's gone forever. And sometimes the bag encounters some obstacles on the way down, and you have to climb two hundred feet into the forest canopy, the clock ticking. US Border Patrol takes a keen interest in low-flying aircraft criss-crossing the northern border."

Prior to all this, "Sal" had been an elementary school teacher for a number of years. She left the profession when it became too corporatized. "We had a remarkable education system in Canada at one time," she confided, "but the priorities have changed. We no longer aspire to be a nation of freethinkers. Instead, we have created a school system that produces consumers. It's a top-down administrative model that promotes stupidity at the top and deep mistrust at the bottom. When I saw the chance to have a different sort of life, I took it." Blunt, forthright, strong, and kind – some might look on Sal as a reckless adventurer.

But cannabis smugglers are a very cautious lot who are known to leave nothing to chance – apart from the daunting multitude of factors that of course are entirely beyond their control – as they step (or drive, fly, snowmobile, ski, float, or even submarine) across the border.

Imagine the rewards, especially when decent BC bud was in great demand in California. For the intrepid few who could make a living in this hair-raising career, the profits – and pitfalls – were considerable. Just look to Canada's Marc Emery, who served five years in a US federal prison for mailing cannabis seeds across the border.

With the passing and implementation of California's Proposition 64 in 2016, this career path was effectively closed for good. Another era of profiteering from smuggled goods was over. Perhaps now is the time to start celebrating the men and women who smuggled Canada's finest green into America. Sal's tale is but one story, included here to give a more palpable sense of the harrowing realities of the high rewards and risks of the smuggler's way of life. – C.J.S.M.

> In all versions of "Tom Thumb," a child tricks a giant.
> – WILLIAM MARLING, *THE AMERICAN ROMAN NOIR: HAMMETT, CAIN, AND CHANDLER*

Crossing over the Lions Gate Bridge and leaving North Van. It's pouring rain, getting dark, and we're on our way to the border mountains. It's the middle of summer. The back of the truck is fully loaded with three massive packs. One hundred and fifty pounds of high-end weed that take up the whole rear seat. We hit a roadblock on the other side of the bridge. No way to turn around, nowhere to go.

When we pull up to the police officers, one of them leans into the window to look us over. There's two of us, and our American friend in the vehicle. The whole package. They could have had a beautiful night with us.

We have a meditation moment, where we just focus on being the Jedi. There's nothing to see here. Pull on up.

"'Been drinking tonight?"

"No."

"Have a great evening."

The Jedi flows.

From there, we go down the highway, head toward the mountain at the edge of the border.

Just having lost two of my nine lives at the bridge, we get to the mountain, and there's a bunch of rednecks having a huge party right on the trail we have to drive up. Alright. Round two. Back to the Jedi. Just drive on up. Ask the guys if they knew of any great fishing holes. They tell us of a couple they knew. We go right through. Unbelievable. I've changed diapers about ten times at this point.

Now we have to make it up this mountain. Totally summertime, but the rain turns to slush as we drive, then snow. It's snow at the top. We hadn't anticipated that. The storm had gone through and dumped up there because it's higher up. So we have to hike through snow now. To get stateside.

I'm, like, okay, I guess we should try. We park the truck, dig into our bags. We have all kinds of gear and are prepared for whatever, just in case. Strap-on snowshoes. All sorts of gear. But for some stupid reason, we don't have proper jackets or anything like that, gloves, or proper headgear.

We have about a six-hour hike ahead of us, so we throw on every piece of clothing that we can possibly manage. We pull crap out from under the seats, looking for socks, gloves, anything. I find a windbreaker, pull it over everything I'm already wearing, which isn't much, and that is about it. Headlamps. We have headlamps. And the moon, a nearly full moon. Clear night. It's like daylight. We start hiking, with my friend's dog in the lead.

Through the snow, through the snow. This dog is doing totally fine. We kind of follow it 'cause it's done the trail so many times? We move up this ravine and into shadow, the moon is obscured by the ridge wall. Pretty steep, lots of weight, like seventy pounds each. Falling up the mountain. We get so into the rhythm, we can't really hear anything else.

Four hours in, we're all of us totally exhausted, totally, like, sweat-drenched. It's freezing out. But we're warm, for a while. We come out at the top of the ravine, more like a couloir. We enter a rounded section, trees scattered. Hiking keeps us going, 'cause our body temperatures are up. And we are kind of following the dog, tired and not really paying attention.

We catch up to the dog in this one area. For some reason, it stopped. Then it goes off in this direction, and we're, like, okay. So we just follow it, thinking that it knows where it's going. An hour later, we come across tracks. We're pretty freaked out at first. My Canadian friend says: "Those are our tracks. Those are the dog's prints in there." We figure out that they're our own tracks. We have done a loop. Panic starts to set in. We really weren't prepared for a night up here, and we sure as fuck can't be here in the morning.

Five hours, we trace back, we're totally exhausted. Another Jedi moment of just honing in. So we retrace right to the couloir. Then we start again, and we figure at one point, you know, this was where the dog went off path. So we take a different path, what looks like a trail. And we make our way through there. It's okay. It's rough at points. I fall, lose my compass in the snow. My hands are pretty cold after that.

We get through to the other side. We make it to where we know we have to hike out to get to the American guy's vehicle. Going down the trail toward where our base is, we hear a vehicle. There should be no vehicles around here. Freaking out. Another Jedi moment. Is this ever going to end? Now we are in the US, so we're, like, double up the creek if anything happens. We go down, sit and wait a little while, because the vehicle proceeded in the opposite direction. We wait for a good half hour. I'm getting cold. I have one of those emergency blankets, the worst thing in the bush when you're trying to be nondescript, like tinfoil, but I wrap it around me. I pass out a couple of times from cold and exhaustion while we're waiting for this vehicle thing to leave. I probably pass out twice then snap back to wakefulness: "Where am I?"

The vehicle ends up being nothing. Somebody driving up a road. Just happened to be when we're coming down. We wait long enough, there's nothing. We start moving again, which is good, warming us. We hike down to where we think we're supposed to be, and my Canadian friend sees a light. Definitely not supposed to be a light. Like a porch light or something. We move closer. It's a pump-house or something. Nobody around.

My American friend says, "I really have no idea where we are." Do we go back up? Do we keep going down?

We decide we can't go back. We're running out of time, out of darkness? So we go down this trail and we come to a road. A logging road. And there's a pickup parked on the side. Like, what the hell do we do?

My American friend leaves his bags with us and moves up to the truck. There is nobody. He runs back: "The keys are in it!" So we load our bags and drive away. I was just waiting for the gunshots? Some hunter, or whatever, sees us stealing his truck.

We're squished in the cab. Small truck, and my Canadian friend says there's something sticking in his lower back. He reaches around and finds a handgun. He rolls down the window and throws it into the bush. It's gun country. We're in gun country now.

We drive around, sweating the fact that the sky is getting light, like just enough light to make you nervous, not full-on morning. And my American friend realizes that he knows where we are. So we backtrack and come around a bend, and there is his vehicle.

This calms me. The Jedi mind returns. We load up and travel down a main logging road, down to the highway to get out. We started driving down, and there are these two cars on the other side of this backroad bridge. And we're, like: "Fuck, like, is that *them* waiting for us? Is it Border Patrol?" Do we cross the bridge? Do we drive in a different direction and just wait it out? What do we do? I just want to get out of the vehicle and run.

We decide to cross the bridge. The vehicles are empty, nobody around. Must have been some other hikers. We drive and drive and, after another hour, we make it to this guy's house.

We pass out from exhaustion, sleep for two hours, and then get up, organize. We're gone by six a.m., to drive the bags to California. That's the time of day when you're in the flow of rush hour. You're blending in. You're a part of the larger process. You don't stand out.

For it to work, you have to keep with the flow of road traffic. Know when to pull over. It might not be convenient, but you do it. You wait it out.

But we go through some really crazy areas of the highway, where it seems certain sections are designated as cop alleys. You drive through and there's, like, eyeballs. It's really interesting. I know of a few areas on the coast that have these pockets. It might be a town you're driving through, or a section of the highway. Creepy.

So we go through Washington, Oregon, and into northern California. When we get to California, we have to go through the agricultural border. They pull you over and can search your vehicle if they feel like it. They want to know if you're bringing in any fruits or vegetables. I'm thinking, I don't think this qualifies as fruit, right? Ha-ha! And I'm hoping that we don't get some tweaky little border guard who can ruin our lives just because he's having a bad day.

So we're in a rental vehicle. We tried to pick one without a BC plate. We have one that has a Washington plate, which probably isn't the best idea. We tried to get one with California plates, but none were available. Fifteen hours out in the open like that, along the highway, all the way down. In that part of the state, you're driving through little *puzzly* California towns where, you know, the police are like ten times as crazy. You drive into these towns, and the local cop pulls out, and he follows you, right behind you. Jedi moment after Jedi moment. 'Cause you know, if he flicks those lights, your life's over. For a long time.

We go down to the Bay Area, get a hotel, wait for the sale.

I made that trip about thirty times.

Works Cited

Barkley, Lori. 2007. "Archeology and Pre-History of Brilliant, B.C." In *Being on the Land: Histories at the Confluence,* Symposium on the People of the Kootenay and Columbia Rivers, Centre for Peace at Selkirk College, June 19, 1–4. http://selkirk.ca/sites/default/files/Mir/Selkirk-College-Mir-Centre-for-Peace-People-of-the-Kootenay-Columbia-Rivers.pdf.

Cox, Sarah. 2021. "BC Hydro, Province Ordered to Release Secret Site C Dam Docs to West Moberly First Nations." *The Narwhal,* May 6. https://thenarwhal.ca/bc-supreme-court-site-c-documents/.

Metcalfe, Bill. 2021. "Sinixt, First Nation Bordering Canada-U.S., Can Claim Indigenous Rights, Top Court Rules: The Decision Essentially Reverses a 1956 Declaration the Sinixt Were Extinct." *Victoria News,* April 23.

Wickwire, Wendy. 2019. *At the Bridge: James Teit and an Anthropology of Belonging.* Vancouver: UBC Press.

14

Cannabis Activism in Canada
Reflections on a Movement in Transition
JODIE EMERY

> As the most well-known of us, it seems only fitting that Jodie Emery be presented with the proverbial last word. Her contribution provides another needed voice – that of the tireless activist, evidently still committed to fighting the good fight. She writes with foresight and conviction and as one who has made history, with a sweeping vision of the road we took to get here. What follows is arguably the most comprehensive and coherent answer to the question that has driven our inquiry from the outset of this book: What the hell just happened? Can someone explain this legalizing of cannabis to me? Whatever happened here has happened, though we just got here ourselves, because of (and perhaps in spite of) proud *cannabians* such as Jodie and so many others we have heard from and met along the way. So now we have a better understanding. Now we know. – C.J.S.M

We are living in a world where cannabis is finally legal for many people who have a relationship with the plant. Global drug-policy shifts are underway, with cannabis at the forefront. Canada's federal law change was significant and inspired other countries to begin reforming their own cannabis laws and regulations.

While cannabis legalization is sometimes seen as a political inevitability, history demonstrates that that is not true. In fact, opposition to cannabis law reform came from those with political power and influence, and they spent significant time and resources preventing cannabis legalization efforts worldwide.

Governments and industrial powerhouses were only quick to support law reform when they determined that with the right restrictive regulations, there would be enormous financial opportunities, tax revenues, and market dominance available for a select few participants. They were focused on the money and control. But the push for cannabis legalization came from a longtime outcry against governments using harmful laws to hurt harmless people. Cannabis was already everywhere, but so, too, was cannabis law enforcement, and policing organizations repeatedly condemned efforts to legalize.

The societal mainstreaming of what was long considered a deviant subculture also helped force changes to cannabis laws. Medical marijuana activists created various forms of access through civil disobedience and court victories. An increasing number of people came out of the cannabis closet, and stigma began to fade as law reform came to light. But behind the upbeat progress taking place, there remains a significant, and often ignored, story of trauma, oppression, and persecution. We must understand the history of cannabis activism and law reform and be aware of the risks involved when governments and wealthy profit-driven corporations create policy together.

Waging War on Peaceful People and Plants

Cannabis prohibition is an enormous global government war of propaganda and punishment enforced against peaceful people for their relationship with a plant. This plant has evolved with humankind for tens of thousands of years and has long been used to liberate people's health, minds, and spirits; some advocates might say that those are the real reasons for its criminalization and demonization worldwide. Despite decades of real war and significant penalties, including execution, there are still hundreds of millions of people consuming and growing cannabis everywhere on Earth.

Countless citizens have suffered, and many have even died, while campaigning and working for cannabis freedom. Thousands of heroic individuals have devoted their lives to the long, hard battle for the liberty of our fellow citizens, using peaceful civil disobedience and numerous other tactics to encourage cannabis law reform. This powerful human passion for the cannabis plant, combined with relentless activism efforts and campaigning, is the real reason that legalization has finally started to become a reality. We would not be seeing cannabis law reform without the constant bravery and struggle of the marijuana movement – a global activist collective that continues to grow stronger despite brutal, deeply entrenched government opposition.

As Canada, the United States, and other nations begin to significantly reform cannabis laws, we must remember and rectify the traumatic, costly, and destructive history of cannabis criminalization. Legalization is meant to liberate people from being punished for using cannabis. If unjustifiable prohibitions and recriminalization punishments are still enforced, and if people are deprived of their civil liberties and human rights, the work of this global movement isn't complete.

Cannabis legalization must make right the wrongs of the past. Law reform must ensure that the victims of prohibition and pioneers of the industry are not excluded from taking part in the legal landscape. The first legalization regimes so far have not honoured or achieved those goals. They even hinder them. Amnesty and opportunities must be granted to the millions of citizens who have suffered as victims of prohibition. Activists around the world cannot stop our calls for freedom until true justice is delivered and no one is ever again punished for any activities related to the cannabis plant.

The Roots of the Movement

Canada is credited with being the first G20 country to legalize cannabis. The news headlines went around the world, and the symbolic nature of this shift encouraged other governments to reconsider their cannabis laws. It is easy to assume that cannabis law reform was inevitable. For decades, the plant was already being used on a wide scale and was regularly represented in movies, music, and other forms of media. Despite harsh criminal laws, cannabis flourished in an underground economy and subculture and became increasingly available for anyone seeking medical relief or recreational pleasure.

Cannabis law reform did not happen without tremendous resistance from various opponents, especially governments. Elected officials, public servants, law enforcement, and other authorities consistently supported and maintained criminalization and denied the validity of medical cannabis. This bureaucratic refusal to reduce restrictions and penalization, in combination with the criminalization of citizens, meant law change would have to be achieved in courts.

Medical cannabis prohibition laws were declared unconstitutional by various levels of courts across Canada, repeatedly, including the Supreme Court of Canada on a number of occasions. Official medical cannabis access regulations were born of court orders directing the government to cease violating the Charter rights of medical cannabis patients across Canada. This only happened because patients and their access providers refused to follow the law, which prohibited cannabis in every way, and chose to break the law.

Most of these cannabis lawbreakers did so privately, because of legitimate fears of being arrested, charged, and imprisoned. Some provided access openly, choosing to break the law publicly in order to provide essential services to people in need. Medical cannabis dispensaries, also known as compassion clubs, were created in the 1990s to deliver medicine to patients suffering from a variety of ailments. They were run by advocates who risked their liberty to provide health care support to people in need.

Lawbreaking has always been necessary to change cannabis laws. High-profile activists broke laws publicly, none more so than Marc Emery, known worldwide for his leadership in the early days of cannabis culture and advocacy. His earliest social and political activism challenged censorship of music and print media, Sunday shopping bans, and other prohibitions on free choice and free speech.

As a bookseller and radio host in the 1990s, Marc discovered that Canada banned marijuana books and magazines under section 462.2 of the Criminal Code, with harsher punishments for cannabis information than for cannabis itself. To raise awareness of this absurd law, and to challenge it, he openly sold illegal *High Times* magazines, Jack Herer's famous tome, *The Emperor Wears No Clothes*, and the only growing books available at the time and asked to be arrested and charged. Public peaceful civil disobedience was a tactic that proved successful in many of his campaigns, including his court case for illegally selling 2 Live Crew rap music cassette tapes – changes that forced law reform in the courts and through government legislation.

Marc broke many cannabis laws publicly to force a debate and political action. He began with marijuana books and magazines and then moved on to selling illegal bongs, pipes, and vapourizers during a time when it was almost impossible to find a head shop that openly embraced cannabis with no "for tobacco use only" signs on display. He sold marijuana seeds and growing equipment and told people to "Plant the Seeds of Freedom to Overgrow the Government." He was constantly raided, arrested, and charged. He helped open Canada's first head shops and used his businesses to finance other activists, court cases, challenges by medical marijuana patients, rallies and marches, and so much more.

Everything was illegal, but unjustly so, and that's why peaceful civil disobedience was useful. It demonstrated that the laws were absurd, unfair, discriminatory, costly, and harmful. Activists who got arrested made the news, and that made people talk, and that made change happen. Cannabis lawbreakers were essential, and they were also courageous, because criminal-justice-system punishments and repercussions are significant.

The prohibition of cannabis has always relied on government control, brute force, and coercion. Medical cannabis growers, access providers, and activists have been victims of prohibition law enforcement for many decades. Raids were carried out with police in tactical uniforms and weapons drawn, resulting in handcuffs being snapped shut on the wrists of harmless people, unconstitutional strip searches in custody, and other indignities and abuses.

For frail and weak patients and their compassionate caregivers, these arrests came with charges and detention inside jail cells. Every activist, access provider, and grower had to retain expensive lawyers, because extraordinarily harsh punishments were heavily enforced for cannabis crimes. This was additionally punitive for people already struggling on disability and with other health care expenses.

Compassion clubs and dispensaries limited their services to people who were in dire circumstances, because court decisions had ruled in favour of medical access. Being forced to choose between your liberty and your health meant medical patients who used cannabis were being forced to break the law and jeopardize their security. This violation of constitutional rights resulted in court decisions ordering the government to allow patients or designated caregivers to grow cannabis for medical purposes.

Many of those court cases were financed in part or in full by Marc Emery, using his Emery Direct Seeds marijuana-seed business profits. He always said that cannabis businesses were essential to pay the costs of legal challenges, and no one made more donations and financial contributions to Canada's cannabis court cases than Marc and his Emery Seeds and *Cannabis Culture* magazine, store, and related companies. He donated hundreds of thousands of seeds to medical patients too.

For many patients, however, growing their own cannabis wasn't possible. Disabilities, living-space restrictions, and other obstacles meant most patients would seek knowledgeable gardeners to become their legal designated growers. To get a personal or designated production licence, patients needed approval from their doctors, which usually meant referrals from specialists. Finding a cannabis-friendly doctor was nearly impossible, leaving many patients in the realm of illegality.

Many doctors were unknowledgeable about, or unwilling to provide, the authorizations needed for patients to get legal access, due to decades of prohibition propaganda and misinformation about cannabis. This resulted in a select few health care practitioners being the gatekeepers for patients and a lot of risk for those who did approve of medical cannabis use.

The limited availability of cannabis-friendly doctors and designated growers helped lead to the growth and acceptance of compassion clubs and dispensaries, which provided plentiful quality cannabis and related products. Patients were still being forced to break the law to obtain the medicine that worked for them, and their access providers in compassion clubs were also breaking the law, and so too were most of the growers, but a mutual and consensual relationship existed between patients and providers. Court cases in favour of medical access made the participants more comfortable, knowing that they had a legal defence if they were arrested and charged. After all, cannabis criminalization was still prohibitively violating the Charter rights of sick and dying Canadians, and judges were on the side of patients.

Aside from medical cannabis activism in the courts, a very small but devoted group of activists had to fight an uphill battle against widespread demonization and stigma against cannabis. Media news stories about grow-ops were as much attention as cannabis would get for many years, and it was always sensationalized and portrayed in a negative way. Rebuttals to propaganda became the key to clearing misconceptions about cannabis. Before the widespread growth and popularity of social media, cannabis education took place in newspapers and on radio and television. Writing letter-to-the-editor submissions was a huge part of activism, and it was how I began my own advocacy.

The internet was useful for finding newspaper articles and sending responses to misinformation and propaganda about cannabis. One of my greatest pleasures was seeing my letters in print – and there were nearly two hundred published over time. Whether we were writing about grow-op hysteria, or lies about health impacts, or "Reefer Madness" editorials condemning cannabis in so many ways, activists like myself had endless opportunities to set the record straight.

Cannabis advocates had to tirelessly promote medical marijuana, hemp, and legalization in an environment where activists were written off as fringe stoners. Despite facing challenges and risks of enormous variety and harm, we spent decades writing letters to the editors of newspapers; calling into radio shows; holding press conferences; forming political parties; running for office; marching in the streets for many protests, including the international Global Marijuana March; organizing large rallies such as the decades-old 4/20 Vancouver and Cannabis Day events; hosting information sessions, conferences, and expos; meeting elected officials; and publishing magazines and other forms of media, among many more methods of engagement and advocacy. I personally engaged in every one of those tactics and earned numerous interviews to discuss laws and the marijuana movement.

Cannabis law reform only happened because of passionate, compassionate lawbreakers using peaceful civil disobedience to challenge and change unjust laws and educating the public and establishment through outreach and political interactions. These leaders and pioneers endured tremendous harm and paid enormous costs for their dedication to cannabis liberation, including long prison sentences and many other violations of rights.

An Expensive and Brutal War

Cannabis law enforcement causes widespread harm at an enormous cost. For decades, hundreds of millions of dollars in law-enforcement budgets went toward cannabis crackdowns in every province and territory across Canada. Taxpayer dollars were being spent on numerous anticannabis initiatives, including helicopter raids, medical cannabis garden tear-downs, and militarized police seizures wherever cannabis was grown.

The increased risk meant there was more reward for those who were willing to grow or sell cannabis. Laws do not change human desire, and cannabis prohibition did not reduce the demand for supply. Prohibitive and exceedingly harsh laws resulted in unsavoury individuals becoming more likely to take advantage of supplying the constant public desire and demand for cannabis. Peaceful participants in the cannabis industry are less likely to engage when laws get tougher – meaning, tough laws and cannabis criminalization only serve to incentivize criminal organizations and gangs.

Thankfully, the cannabis community believes in peace and nonviolence, and because cannabis isn't addictive like harder, more expensive drugs, consumers aren't engaging in theft or violence or other crimes to obtain it. The Justice Department of Canada analyzed court cases for growing and providing access to cannabis and determined that 95 percent of all accused were otherwise law-abiding and not connected to gangs or organized crime. This information was presented to the Liberal government during the consultations about legalization but was ignored – because it didn't fit the narrative that the government was depending on.

The government's misleading messaging about cannabis being controlled by gangs continued to be repeated in official advertisements and information campaigns. Even though it wasn't true, government officials had to perpetuate the "gangs and cannabis" myth to justify tough laws and ever-increasing enforcement budgets. British Columbia's cannabis industry has long been an undeniable pillar holding up the province's economy, and it employs hundreds of thousands of people directly and indirectly. Reports estimate that it was one of the top revenue generators for years, and the vast majority of growers, sellers, and buyers were regular citizens engaging in peaceful consensual transactions.

The massive cannabis economy was essential for the survival of the rest of the economy and boosted all kinds of businesses: real estate, restaurants, tourism, cars, clothing, coffee, wine, music, arts, and everything else that people spend money on. Taxpaying citizens were choosing to buy cannabis but were also being forced to finance cannabis prohibition through taxpayer-funded law-enforcement crackdowns and criminal-justice-system costs. With so much public acceptance of medical cannabis use, and non-medical cannabis use, the idea of legalization – ending cannabis criminalization – continued to gain support.

The cannabis legalization rallying cry for years was "Legalize It!" Cannabis legalization was supposed to legalize the massive pre-existing industry that had been operating for decades. Tens of thousands of skilled, knowledgeable growers and access providers spent many years seeking liberation from criminalization.

This widespread underground market and collective, combined with the critical mass of societal acceptance and promotion of cannabis, pushed government officials into accepting law reform. But as the next few years would prove, prohibition profiteers would fight hard to prevent true legalization from happening.

Flawed Cannabis Reform

For decades, legalization was an issue that most political parties shied away from. It was dismissed as a fringe concern, and any elected official who championed cannabis law reform became an easy target for attacks by prohibitionists in positions of influence. The 2003 Liberal government under Prime Minister Jean Chrétien flirted with decriminalization, announcing a one hundred dollar fine for simple possession, but it was quashed after threats from the United States made the Canadian government nervous. The New Democratic Party under Jack Layton was initially supportive of cannabis, and Layton was publicly in favour of law reform, even going on Marc Emery's Pot TV network to announce his vision of the future. Sadly, that pronouncement didn't evolve into meaningful change. When it comes to cannabis, political cowardice often becomes an obstacle.

The United States started the biggest rumblings about legalization in 2010, when California put forward Proposition 19. That was the same year that Marc Emery was extradited to the United States to face a five-year prison sentence for his many years of selling cannabis seeds and donating millions of dollars to cannabis activism and court cases in the United States. His tactics had been hugely successful from 1994 to 2005, when he was arrested in Canada by US Drug Enforcement Administration agents and Canadian police.

Even though Marc hadn't gone to the United States, the governments of both countries worked together to ensure he faced a very severe punishment for having helped finance and lead the marijuana movement. Marc had indeed planted the seeds of freedom to overgrow the government, but he would have to be sent into the heart of the Drug War's birth nation to oversee its downfall, from within the Drug War–dependent US prison system. Those were long, difficult years for me and everyone who knew us. But we persevered.

When Marc began his prison sentence in 2010, I stepped up my activism. In 2009, I had run for office with the BC Green Party (after two BC Marijuana Party election campaigns) because the BC Greens were the first provincial party to openly support ending cannabis prohibition. In 2010, I entertained the idea of a federal election run with the Green Party of Canada, as it had also expressed support for ending cannabis prohibition.

However, I was unable to run that time around because I was so burdened with the heavy load of running *Cannabis Culture* magazine, Cannabis Culture Headquarters head shop, Pot TV, and our many events and activism organizations. I couldn't run for office again on top of taking care of Marc in prison – a nightmarish experience that saw him sent to six different facilities across the nation, including institutions run by private for-profit companies GEO Group and Corrections Corporation of America, and medium-security federal Bureau of Prisons compounds. I visited him eighty-one times and spent more than five months inside prison walls, witnessing first-hand the horrors of the Drug War and mass incarceration.

Being a prohibition victim made me even more relentless in my activism. For California's Proposition 19 effort in 2010, I went to the election headquarters at Oaksterdam University and made phone calls, and I took part in a press conference with the campaign team. We broadcast the election night live on *Cannabis Culture* and Pot TV. Sadly, Proposition 19 failed to pass, but it was followed up by Colorado and Washington introducing legalization proposals in 2012.

When Washington approved Initiative 502 and Colorado passed Amendment 64 in 2012, the momentum helped buoy the cannabis law reform movement in Canada. Marc and I were official endorsers for Washington State's I-502, and I spent a lot of time working online and in person to ensure these initiatives and amendments passed, despite the flaws and concerns from cannabis advocates in those states. To me, the importance of the "Legalization" headline and message was more important for the world than the devil in the details. In retrospect, with Canada's own Cannabis Act introducing such brutally flawed legalization, I better understand the worries of those cannabis activists who didn't support I-502. However, I knew then – and still know now – that the symbolism would have far-reaching beneficial impacts that we couldn't afford to lose.

In 2011, Justin Trudeau, as leader of the Liberal Party of Canada and prime minister hopeful, said he opposed legalization and even voted in favour of the Conservative government's mandatory minimum prison sentences for cannabis. He then adjusted his stance and said he supported decriminalization, which was a positive step, but he took more time to come around to full legalization. The Liberal Party membership voted in favour of a cannabis legalization resolution at their annual convention in January 2012, so that helped ensure it became part of the campaign platform for the 2015 election. Justin Trudeau's initial comments were focused on using decriminalization and legalization to end the harm caused by cannabis criminalization. That messaging got my attention, and many other Canadians' attention too. He said Canada should cease the wasteful law-enforcement spending and criminal records given to peaceful Canadians. These were the main reasons to legalize cannabis, which was generally supported by the majority of Canadian citizens and Liberal Party members.

I believed what Justin Trudeau was saying, and he even admitted to using cannabis himself as a Member of Parliament, so it seemed like the legalization dream was finally arriving. Perhaps he would finish the job that previous Liberal prime ministers had failed to accomplish, so, with hope in my heart, I hesitantly accepted an invitation to seek a federal Liberal nomination in the riding of Vancouver East for the 2015 election. Trudeau had said anyone could apply to run, so with the urging of many members of the public and political establishment, I began my nomination campaign.

My second BC Green Party provincial run in 2013 had helped raise my profile as a cannabis-activist politician, and the media coverage of my federal Liberal nomination campaign was intense. The best part of it was that the excitement of my run ensured that cannabis law reform was front and centre in the national news cycle, especially given the uncertainty about whether my nomination would get approved by the Liberal Party brass. The strange strategic dance between myself and the Liberal headquarters resulted in endless media discussions about legalization and cannabis information, and I was thrilled with the chance to talk about civil liberties and the Charter of Rights and Freedoms in Canada.

It seemed like my job as an activist was disappearing, as it seemed everyone was in favour of legalization. There wasn't much debate about it, but the Liberals were still behaving nervously, and Trudeau was all but running away from being seen anywhere with me. Understandably, it was because the Conservative government and members of Parliament were attacking the Liberals for being associated with a marijuana activist, but the Liberals were also being cowardly – and perhaps it was a silent alarm signal that "legalization" was just a populist ploy to get votes, not to defend and promote cannabis access. The political battles about cannabis waged on between the parties, even though cannabis consumers, growers, patients, access providers, and novice potential users were all ready for liberation and normalization.

In 2014, when Marc was finishing his US prison sentence and preparing to return home to Canada, the Conservative government replaced the federal medical marijuana program – the Marihuana Medical Access Regulations, or MMAR – with a new regime, the Marihuana for Medical Purposes Regulations, or MMPR. In 2016, the newly elected Liberal government of Canada replaced the MMPR with the Access to Cannabis for Medical Purposes Regulations, the ACMPR. These medical marijuana regulations established the creation of the licensed-producer system, or LP system. These federally regulated LP companies were given exclusive licences to grow medical cannabis for patients authorized by their doctors and the ability to mail the product to medical consumers. The regulations did not allow for dispensaries or any in-person access.

While public support for cannabis legalization kept growing, and as dispensaries and cannabis-related businesses began to open up across Canada in preparation for legalization, corporate LP lobbying efforts and other insider activities were taking place behind the scenes. The program for medical cannabis access was in constant flux because of court challenges and political shifts, but many politicians, law-enforcement officials, and venture capitalists saw opportunities to make money for themselves and cement their position in the upcoming "legal cannabis" landscape. The first news stories that covered this insider preparation showed up in 2013, and there were no political party alliances involved. Everyone in a position of power wanted to get in on the developing "legalization" landscape that was appearing on the horizon.

Dozens of public officials and police began joining and creating medical cannabis companies from 2014 onward. More than fifty former prime ministers, premiers, mayors, drug-enforcement officers, RCMP heads, and other public officials began getting paid for being part of the LP industry, as documented by media reports and cannabis advocates. My own Twitter compilation of names has been referenced many times; the "Unfairness List" kept growing during the hyped-up slow crawl toward legalization.

The first LP companies listed themselves on the Canadian stock market beginning in 2014 and raised capital from investors, which was encouraged by government officials. The following year saw the Liberal Party elected to govern Canada, and LPs began lobbying the newly elected government – especially the new "legalization czar," Bill Blair, the former Toronto police chief in charge of G20 violations in 2010. Blair became a member of Parliament as a Liberal in 2015 and took positions as the parliamentary secretary to the justice minister and the parliamentary secretary to the health minister.

The LP lobbying efforts directed at Blair and the federal government asked governments to raid, arrest, and charge cannabis dispensaries and access providers to force consumers to buy from LPs instead. This lobbying was soon followed by the biggest LP companies receiving public and media endorsements from the very same government officials responsible for creating cannabis legislation. Those officials promised that heavy-handed measures would be used to ensure that the original cannabis industry would be criminalized and eliminated, to be replaced by government-approved corporations.

The Liberal government's legalization task force head, Anne McLellan, was the former Liberal government health minister and justice minister. She had passionately opposed medical cannabis access, even calling marijuana a "scourge" when she was a public servant elected to office. She then went on to work for Bennett Jones Law, a legal firm that represented many LPs. No surprise to anyone, the Liberal government task force report concluded that LPs should be the only legal growers of recreational cannabis. I had tried many times to be on the task force, as an official member or just to provide testimony, and my request was originally tentatively approved by the health minister, Jane Philpott – only to be vetoed by Bill Blair the next day, as covered by the media during the Liberal ministerial retreat they were attending at the time.

After Justin Trudeau became prime minister in October 2015, the Liberal messaging about legalization began to shift away from it being an issue of social justice and civil liberties and toward promoting a continued criminalization regime with tougher penalties and more law-enforcement funding. Liberal officials, including Blair and Trudeau, used the same anticannabis talking points as those used by the former Steven Harper Conservative government. It may have been a political effort to deflect the inevitable Conservative attacks, by repeating their opponents' concerns, but it also served to promote continued prohibitive legislation.

Cannabis activists began to note and critique the changing messages regarding "legalization." Many of them publicly predicted that it seemed the Liberal government was leaning toward a restrictive, prohibitive, and punitive regime that would continue to perpetuate the harms of cannabis criminalization. The appointment of anticannabis prohibitionist Bill Blair as the chief of the legalization file, and the following years of disastrous legislation and implementation, confirms that these concerns were valid. The Liberal government began to focus on a "restrict and limit cannabis access" approach in Bill C-45, the Cannabis Act, perpetuating falsehoods about organized crime dominating the cannabis industry. Even though the government claimed to be open to consultation and "evidence-based policy," it was increasingly clear that ideology was the dominant deciding factor.

Marc and I were both invited to provide expert testimony to the House of Commons Standing Committee on Health in September 2017, alongside a number of other cannabis experts like Dana Larsen. The best possible knowledge about cannabis was present in that committee hearing. My testimony included my personal experience with cannabis as medicine, and I even pulled out a joint during my presentation to demonstrate that all the fear about cannabis was absurd and that it was outrageous to severely punish people for flowers. I provided endless studies and numerous citations to disprove every falsehood and propaganda point in the Cannabis Act. Despite all of the studies and evidence I presented, Bill Blair and other Liberal members of Parliament present at the committee hearing chose to gloss over it all and stick with their original prohibition plans.

Insider Advantages, Opportunism, and Hypocrisy

Beginning in 2013, former law-enforcement officials and politicians from every level of government began to run, and get paid by, medical marijuana LPs, knowing that in a few years' time those companies would very likely become the sole producers of recreational cannabis. Insider opportunities were being created and taken advantage of by serving and retired law enforcement and public officials.

Media reports in 2016 revealed that the LPs of cannabis were lobbying government officials, including Bill Blair, to demand that medical cannabis dispensaries be raided and closed. The reasoning was that Canadian medical cannabis patients were choosing dispensaries and traditional access instead of ordering through the mail from LPs. They were concerned about losing revenues and made it clear that they needed the government to step in and eliminate the competition.

Canadians were quickly investing their money into LP cannabis stocks, encouraged by government officials such as Blair, who stated that these stock market companies would be the only legally authorized producers of recreational cannabis. Stock market values went up with every law-enforcement crackdown, especially the massive Toronto Police "Project Claudia" raids in 2016, and Project Gator raids on Cannabis Culture in 2017.

After Trudeau was elected in October 2015, the cannabis movement was excited about the chance to finally be legalized and liberated. Trudeau had noted in Winnipeg that illegal dispensaries would soon be legal. Compassion clubs and dispensaries had been opening up across Canada rapidly, because it was clear that everyone wanted access, everyone was already buying and using cannabis, and thousands of entrepreneurs were ready and willing to supply the high demand.

In March 2016, Forum Poll found that 57 percent of Toronto citizens thought marijuana dispensaries – which were then illegal, awaiting legalization – should be allowed to operate, and that included not just medical marijuana, but all adult use. Dispensaries were flourishing in Toronto; approximately two hundred had opened and were serving happy customers. Everyone felt that legalization would mean that these businesses could simply apply for a permit like a restaurant, café, or bar would and that would support economic growth and opportunities for small businesses and entrepreneurs.

During this period, I was running Cannabis Culture media and our head shop and lounge, but we were struggling to stay afloat. Marc's five-year US imprisonment had been extremely expensive, and I worked nonstop to ensure he was as safe as possible behind bars. Being a full-time activist speaking at events and conferences across Canada and abroad meant that my businesses were just getting by – but I relished the opportunity to excel at work and activism. There wasn't time for anything else, and our companies demanded full attention, but we needed to make a change to survive.

The spring season of 2016 saw the launch of a new approach for Cannabis Culture: cannabis dispensaries for all, not just medical access. Up until then, almost every dispensary required clients to see a doctor in person or via internet video, which would give them a membership to that specific dispensary. Other dispensaries would allow for self-declaration, which was useful for conditions that medical cannabis wasn't yet legally applicable for. These dispensary doctor referrals and memberships were not federal ACMPR authorizations but simply cannabis recommendations. Getting proper ACMPR coverage was difficult, even impossible for many, and some LPs began opening up clinics to force patients to pay high costs to get ACMPR licences. They then demanded that the patient purchase from the LP that owned the clinic. The LP medicine would only be sent in the mail, as required by law, and cannabis medicine was not legal in any storefronts or in-person access points.

These barriers meant many consumers chose to get their cannabis at illegal dispensaries. And because they knew the laws were in flux, dispensary consumers wanted some kind of security, so declaring that they were using cannabis for medical purposes meant there were precedents in court for Charter rights protections. Many cannabis consumers who were not sick or in need medically felt guilty about going through the process. As I watched the growing dispensary landscape, I realized that Cannabis Culture could set an example for everyone else and open up dispensaries that did not require customers to have – or lie about having – medical issues. Non-discriminatory access for all, with the company profits going toward cannabis activism efforts, as always.

Cannabis legalization was supposed to mean job creation, and I was hopeful that small-business participants would have a chance to get established after so many years of obstacles and outright prohibitions and punishments. Our brand, Cannabis Culture, was recognized worldwide, but we had no money after all those hard years, so I created a franchise model that would allow entrepreneurs in cities across Canada to open up a cannabis retail business with extremely reasonable costs, to serve all Canadians age nineteen and over. We would provide the vision and the guidance, and they would create jobs and opportunities for their local communities. It was a perfect plan, and with Trudeau promising to legalize dispensaries, it seemed like a good way to demonstrate what the future could hold.

In April 2016, we opened our first Cannabis Culture dispensary in Vancouver, a city where cannabis retail regulations were being tinkered with by municipal officials despite objections from LPs like Tweed, part of Canopy Growth. Cannabis Culture launched the first Toronto shop in May 2016 – coincidentally the day after the massive "Project Claudia" dispensary raids in Toronto, a multimillion-dollar police exercise that stunned the entire country. Hundreds of arrests and charges, enormous seizures, massive protests, and endless media coverage sparked a big debate about cannabis and the then-under-development legislation being worked on by the Liberal government.

I protested the raids alongside local activists and patients, and we got plenty of news coverage and interviews about how cannabis legalization was supposed to mean an end to such destructive and wasteful enforcement. The Toronto Police Headquarters press conference was an infamous scene; after being grilled by reporters, the police chief stuttered and turned to Health Canada officials, trying to explain the massive crackdown on dispensaries, given there had been massive and obvious public support for them. I was present and began to ask questions, which turned into accidentally taking over the press conference. The entire interaction was broadcast live across Canada on every news network, and that was the day the police began their investigation into me and my brand-new Cannabis Culture venture.

The day of the press conference, May 27, was also the day of our first Toronto store opening on Queen Street West. Our unique and bold approach to serving all adults, not just medical patients, made national and even international news headlines. "This is what legalization should look like," I said at every dispensary opening, and we promised to use peaceful civil disobedience to publicly show everyone how legal cannabis should be handled. "This is what is supposed to be legalized" was the main message. Lineups went out the door and down the block, and this was repeated numerous times during 2016. There were ultimately over thirty Cannabis Culture dispensary locations, and hundreds of franchisee requests poured in. Unfortunately, the majority of new Cannabis Culture locations were closed by raids and other enforcement because, despite legalization being promised, the many levels of government prohibitions and anticannabis propaganda were getting even worse.

After the "Project Claudia" raids in May 2016, it was my turn to face the firing squad. I was arrested and charged in March 2017 alongside Marc. Dozens of Cannabis Culture employees were arrested, and many faced severe penalties. Of course, I accepted a plea deal that ensured I would avoid prison time, and it let eighteen employees go home free with all charges repealed. My coaccused included fellow activists and Cannabis Culture franchisees Marc Emery, Chris and Erin Goodwin, and Britney Guerra, and we all received fines and probation after our lawyer, Jack Lloyd, managed to arrange the plea deal.

My fine was nearly two hundred thousand dollars, and Marc paid the same. The penalty was substantial, and the government and police knew it was a serious hit because they were aware – after having investigated and followed me for ten months – that I didn't have any assets. They found my activism notes and a journal with notes about how I wanted to liberate people and protect civil liberties. My business model was meant to finance activism, as Cannabis Culture had always operated that way, but this enforcement and punishment ensured I was locked out of the legal system and would be locked up if I dared try to participate again.

It became clear that government-connected LP companies would be designated as the only legal cannabis access providers for both medical and recreational cannabis, and government officials and law-enforcement crackdowns would ensure that pre-existing providers would be criminalized and displaced. The very prohibitionists who had been paid by taxpayers to enforce cannabis laws and ruin lives were now getting paid to ensure that they and their cronies would be legally allowed to grow and sell cannabis and that everyone else would be subject to criminal persecution. The Government of Ontario introduced its own tough regulations, which I testified against at the Ontario Legislature's Justice Committee in 2017, making it clear that the new prohibition was trickling down from the top level of government to every level below.

The thing that was most concerning about the crackdowns and raids on the grassroots industry was that many of the big corporate LP companies were being founded and run by former police officers, drug law-enforcement officials, public servants, and politicians – including former prime ministers, premiers, and mayors. These companies went public on the stock market, and Liberal government officials assured Canadians they would financially benefit from a massive transfer of wealth, taken from the pioneering cannabis industry that was supposed to be legalized, and handed over to a newly created corporate regime that did nothing to advance legalization efforts in the past.

Some of the most egregious cannabis company operators were former police and politicians who didn't just abstain from cannabis law reform advocacy but outright opposed and condemned any efforts to modernize legislation. Many prohibitionists inserted themselves into the new cannabis businesses that were being promised government protectionism in the form of taxpayer subsidies and criminal crackdowns on the competition.

Conservative health minister Leona Aglukkaq sought to ban medical cannabis-growing licences and went on to form a medical marijuana corporation, which would seek funding and support from government contracts. Former disgraced police chief Julian Fantino and fellow drug narc officer Raf Souccar – also a friend of Bill Blair and a member of the Liberal legalization task force – started a medical marijuana company, too, even though Fantino, as a minister in the Harper Conservative government, had said he would "never" do so and that legalizing cannabis was akin to legalizing murder. These were just some of the dozens of hypocrites cashing in on cannabis under the new regime being installed.

Media outlets and Canadian citizens began to take note of the collusion between law enforcement, government, and LPs. Not only were these entities working on legislation together to ensure the continuation of criminalization, but they were promoting LP pot stocks to investors and pledging many millions of dollars in taxpayer handouts to the richest LP corporations.

Restrict and Limit Access

When LPs were just starting up, they sought millions of dollars in funding from investors on the stock market because the cannabis production regulations were so prohibitive and costly that there was no other way to afford to participate. Many of these LPs helped create excessive regulations with their lobbying efforts, however, and benefitted from the restricted and limited access model in place. Creating a cannabis regulation regime that includes punitive, prohibitive, and costly barriers is not an improvement on cannabis prohibition. But corporate profits depend on an artificially limited supply, to ensure that the value of the limited supply remains high. Stock market profits require ever-increasing profit margins and shareholder returns, meaning the product of LPs changed from being medical and recreational cannabis into being stock market profits based on mergers and acquisitions – not actual services or products.

Shortages of legal cannabis plagued the LPs when it came to their obligation to serve medical patients, and the same happened for recreational consumers. This had been predicted by many advocates and cannabis experts who truly understand the cannabis market and community and who had experienced legal medical cannabis shortages firsthand. There is no feasible way for a newly created mass-production factory farm regime to displace a diverse, decentralized, deeply entrenched, decades-old industry that thrived despite harsh criminal laws. Using tough criminal penalties to try to attack and eliminate cannabis didn't work under prohibition, and it won't work under faux legalization. Any kind of recriminalization of the cannabis industry only serves to perpetuate the same issues and harms of the previous criminalization laws.

The movement to "legalize it" included marches, protests, election campaigns, media outreach, and much more activism. The *it* portion of the phrase *legalize it* refers to the massive culture and industry that existed long before LPs or the Cannabis Act – a culture and industry that suffered punishments and exclusion. Legalization is supposed to liberate the victims of prohibition, not maintain their oppression and reward their oppressors.

The concerns about legal cannabis supply shortages are especially frustrating for consumers and cannabis advocates. For many years, legalization campaigns explained that one of the top reasons to legalize was to acknowledge that despite prohibition, there was so much cannabis supply available that it didn't make sense to prohibit it. Dispensaries that suffered raids and seizures lost many pounds of high-quality cannabis, only to replace it within hours – because there's so much cannabis in Canada, and it's readily available everywhere.

Liberating the grassroots cannabis market, and letting it be part of the mainstream economy without stigma or prohibitions, would be a disaster for the new government LP cannabis regime and would reduce the stock market values of the limited number of LPs approved by Health Canada. This is why the "restrict and limit" model was created. And as a result, the traditional cannabis industry remains illegal, allowing the police to continue getting paid to enforce cannabis criminalization laws against harmless Canadians.

Great Historical Injustices

With cannabis law reform underway in the form of Bill C-45, the Liberal government wanted to appeal to voters who saw criminalization as a failed policy. Canadians had increasingly expressed support for ending the arrests and criminal records of peaceful people involved with cannabis and had criticized the wasteful spending of tax dollars on cannabis enforcement. Harsh criminal laws and billions of tax dollars spent on criminalization failed to slow or stop the growth of the cannabis industry – and they failed to prevent growing support for law reform. Activists pointed out that spending money to punish harmless people meant resources were being diverted from investigating real crimes, like theft, assault, and violent offences. It didn't make sense to devote police time and money to cannabis enforcement and investigations when victims of real crimes were waiting for resolutions and justice. I gave a deposition to the Toronto Police Board in 2017, explaining how the public and police would be better served by less prohibitive laws and regulations, but silence was the only response provided.

The Liberal Party knew that legalization was going to be a vote winner in the 2015 election, so they promoted it and invited support from cannabis consumers. The messages were initially in line with what Canadians and cannabis advocates wanted: no more criminal records for peaceful people and no more spending limited resources on cannabis law enforcement. Justin Trudeau admitted to possessing, consuming, and trafficking cannabis. Simply passing a joint, which was his confessed activity, constituted "trafficking" as defined by the law at the time. He noted publicly that his father, the former prime minister, Pierre Trudeau, helped make a possession charge "go away" when Justin's late brother, Michel, was busted with cannabis. He admitted this during a VICE News broadcast in April 2017, during which Bill Blair, Prime Minister Trudeau, me, and three other selected citizens discussed legalization. Trudeau and Blair were dismissive of me, and Trudeau told a young Black man that it was a shame he got busted for working at a dispensary, but things wouldn't change. The message was that the class system and racially biased policing related to cannabis were too deeply entrenched.

Blair had already acknowledged that cannabis law enforcement's disproportionate targeting of marginalized, Indigenous, and radicalized Canadians was a "great historical injustice." He said so at Parliament's Liberal Senate forum on legalization in February 2016, where I met Blair for the first time, as I provided testimony to the senators about cannabis, law reform, civil liberties, and what legalization should look like. Senator Jim Munson echoed my requests for a moratorium on marijuana arrests and amnesty for Canadians with cannabis criminal records, but that was brushed off by Senator Larry Campbell – who also worked for a medical marijuana LP company at the time. Blair was interviewed at the forum and insisted that cannabis arrests would continue, even for possession, until the day legalization became official years later. The Liberal government knew that Canadians wanted cannabis legalization because it was widely understood that criminalization was not only unfair, and expensive, but also racially biased – proven by statistics and information requests made by media reporters. When the Cannabis Act was introduced and being promoted as a way to "restrict and limit access to cannabis," which is the same goal of prohibition, the Liberal government struggled to reconcile its fearmongering messaging about cannabis being a "threat to public health and public safety" with the supposed goal of ending unjust criminalization.

Calls for cannabis amnesty for criminal record holders and prohibition victims began to grow even louder, with endorsements from lawyers, civil liberties experts, and elected officials from the New Democratic Party. In early 2018, I helped found the nonprofit advocacy group Cannabis Amnesty, with the goal of expunging all criminal records for the 2 million peaceful Canadians who had received cannabis convictions in the past sixty years of prohibition. With endorsements from the federal New Democratic Party, even more pressure was placed on the federal government to take action. It was indisputable that cannabis law enforcement was racially discriminatory and unfairly harmful toward the most vulnerable in society.

The Liberal public safety minister, Ralph Goodale, found himself in a contradictory position. While the Liberal government had just issued legislation to provide criminal record expungements for men convicted in antihomosexual legislation, and made clear that it was because those laws represented a "great historical injustice," Goodale stated that cannabis prohibition enforcement was not a "great historical injustice." This was not aligned with what Bill Blair had already said. It was the opposite.

These contradictions became transparent as it became clear that the criminalization of cannabis was not over. The Cannabis Act – with forty-five new federal criminal offences for cannabis, and the driving force behind extremely prohibitive, punitive regulations introduced by provincial, territorial, and municipal governments – was not legalizing anything that had been illegal before. It simply legalized the ability of LPs of medical cannabis to become the exclusive providers of recreational cannabis. Everything else was now deemed "illicit" and became the target of an expanded, and increasingly funded, criminal law-enforcement regime.

The great historical injustice of cannabis criminalization couldn't be addressed in Canada because the new criminalization of cannabis meant the same harms, costs, and injustices were going to continue. The government couldn't admit that cannabis shouldn't have been criminalized, because they were, in fact, continuing criminalization. It was a Catch 22, and the Trudeau Liberal government was stuck in a hypocritical position. Cannabis legalization was supposedly coming soon, but I and others were asking: Legalization of what, and for whom?

Cashing In on Cannabis and Criminalization

To make matters even worse, more and more former police and anti-cannabis drug officials were taking over the "legal cannabis" landscape while their uniformed comrades were using tough new laws and budgets to raid and close down access to providers and activists who had built the cannabis industry. These prohibition victims were peaceful people who suffered great persecution and trauma because of their courageous and necessary work. This conflict of interest meant that a lot of beneficiaries of prohibition were ensuring they would profit from continued criminalization and exclusive legislation. Government law-enforcement efforts displaced the original pioneers to replace them with profiteers, and this was not lost on Canadians or people worldwide. Questions about the Cannabis Act touched on the curiosity that cannabis law-enforcement budgets were being increased, not decreased, across Canada. It seemed peculiar that it would cost more money to enforce the law against cannabis under legalization than it did under prohibition.

For years, police forces across Canada were asking for cannabis legislation delays in order to "figure out" how to proceed. It is not difficult to stop arresting people. But it is more difficult to set up a regime that maintains criminalization under the guise of legalization.

Policing across Canada depends on cannabis prohibition and drug prohibition. Statistics Canada charts show that of all crime in Canada, the majority of arrests are for drugs – and the bulk of that is cannabis, and most of that is possession. In 2013, news reports documented that 70 percent of federal court time and resources went toward cannabis. As the number of crimes with real victims decreased in Canada, cannabis-related criminal law enforcement was increasing.

But when law enforcement caught LPs committing crimes as far back as 2014, they covered it up to protect the stock value of those companies. In 2019, after five years of making Freedom of Information Requests and official complaints to the federal information commissioner, journalist Douglas Quan revealed that Canopy and Mettrum (which would later be bought by Canopy) were engaging in illegal cannabis trafficking, including a significant bust and seizure at the Kelowna airport and an ensuing cover-up by the RCMP. What wasn't mentioned in the news coverage was that the former head of the RCMP, Norman Inkster, was involved in running Mettrum.

Douglas Quan's investigation found that the RCMP bust and decision to not pursue charges were related to protecting the stock market value of the companies, as they were just about to go public – the first of many LPs to do so. Officials worried that the information would make Canadians question the validity of the government's marijuana regulations, for both medical and recreational cannabis. Government officials, police, and Bill Blair had repeatedly claimed that the new "legal" regime would not be like the pre-existing "criminal" market that had to be punished with harsh new laws and penalties. They needed to maintain that narrative to prop up the new criminalization regime, the Cannabis Act. And they needed to ensure that the system they spent years establishing – a system that enriched the already rich as well as the prohibitionists of the past – wouldn't fail to reap the stock market financial rewards they were promised.

Activists, Exclusion, and the Future of Legalization

While former prohibitionists cashed in, and current officials passed restrictive and punitive new laws and regulations, the advocates and activists responsible for forcing cannabis law reform found themselves being persecuted and sidelined. Compassion clubs and dispensaries were newly targeted by reinvigorated law-enforcement crackdown units with new powers and budgets. Government propaganda spread misinformation and fear about dispensaries and the traditional cannabis industry. The public was being lied to with discriminatory policies and messages, and the government made no apology for the harm it did previously and continues to do.

I publicly promoted many attempts to have the prime minister issue a moratorium on marijuana arrests, given that legalization was supposedly going to end those arrests in months or the coming years. Members of Parliament received letters, emails, and in-person visits. I attended appointments armed with information about cannabis and delivered letters to government officials in Toronto and beyond, all of which were covered in the news. My hope was that my continued high-profile activism would encourage others to take a stand, and if we couldn't stop the harm from taking place, at least we would have spoken the truth and warned everyone in advance.

Legalization was supposed to liberate millions of peaceful people from unjust and cruel cannabis criminalization laws. Legalization was supposed to legalize the existing market and culture that had been long oppressed and subjected to gross violations and indignities. Legalization was supposed to acknowledge and undo the harms of prohibition and allow traditionally marginalized people an opportunity to take part in a blossoming industry. But legalization that simply recriminalizes cannabis and perpetuates the harms of prohibition is not legitimate.

Cannabis amnesty and liberation are essential for true legalization. People should not be getting arrested, going to jail, losing their housing, losing their jobs, losing their children, losing their travel rights, and being forced to endure discriminatory drug testing and other stigma and demonization. New rules and regulations are causing widespread harm to harmless people across Canada, impacting families and communities in numerous negative ways.

The entire point of legalization was to end all of these horrific injustices. However, when police and prohibition profiteers are put in charge of creating "legalization" laws, the only things being legalized are corporate and government control and profit from a fake industry based on hype, stock-market greed, and cartel-style elimination of a culture and community. Fairness in cannabis laws and regulations would see activists, pioneers, and prohibition victims being granted the first legal licences for cannabis. But they aren't at the front of the line and are even prohibited from participation. They must sit on the sidelines, being locked out and locked up, while their oppressors cash in on a new "legal cannabis" regime designed by the rich, for the rich, to enrich the rich. The excessive costs and requirements to become a "legal" cannabis business make it impossible for most people, especially those who have had everything taken away from them due to prohibition enforcement and punishments. Legalization is supposed to mean freedom, justice, equality, dignity, and peace for the cannabis community and culture. If law reform fails to provide these essential elements, and fails to liberate the prohibition victims and advocates who created the cannabis industry and suffered great persecution from governments for it, then that form of legalization is a fraud.

The cannabis movement worldwide is watching as Canada fails in its legalization regime. The licensed-producer supply is poor-quality and grown only for profit, without any of the care or love that traditional – and still criminalized – craft cannabis growers use in their gardens. Factory farm grow-ops run by LPs are producing a fraction of the supply in Canada, with the traditional market supplying the rest, as always. Taxpayers and middle-class investors are losing hundreds of millions of dollars as the Cannabis Act house of cards comes tumbling down. Despite failing in Canada, the LPs are exporting the horrific Canadian model of fraudulent legalization to countries abroad, lobbying governments to create prohibitive and restrictive legalization to allow only a few select rich corporations the right to grow and sell cannabis, while continuing to criminalize the global cannabis grassroots industry and community. This greed-driven motive is destroying the cannabis culture and creating a monopolized industry focused on profits and devoted to destroying the lives and livelihoods of the majority of cannabis enthusiasts and patients.

Human rights violations have often been carried out based on cannabis criminalization, leading to countless gross individual abuses and civil liberties infringements. Renewed cannabis prohibition under the guise of legalization, resulting in even greater harms and injustice, is a crime against humanity. Legalization activists need to ensure that no matter what regulations are introduced, that the main point of law reform is to protect people from the harms caused by governments. The civil liberties and human rights violations perpetrated by cannabis criminalization are widespread and affect every person, even those who don't use cannabis or have any relationship to it. Law enforcement continues to squander billions of dollars fighting a war against a plant that brings peace and health to millions of consumers and patients. Politicians who support the continued criminalization of cannabis are supporting the continued destruction and devastation of harmless people.

Cannabis has evolved with humanity for thousands of years. This has been well documented by historians and anthropologists, and fascinating new information is discovered regularly. Cannabis saves lives; it has certainly saved mine and the lives of many people I know. Cannabis helps people, of all ages. The incredibly versatile cannabis plant is food, fuel, fibre, medicine, and so much more. There is no legitimate justification for making it the target of the brutal global Drug War. Cannabis legalization should be the first step in ending the criminalization of all plants and herbs and stopping the terror of the murderous and militarized war on drugs worldwide.

Legalization and law reform don't come easily, and they require constant vigilance to maintain. As we continue moving forward in a world where cannabis is growing more popular and helping more people than ever before, we must push even harder to ensure that legalization means liberation and freedom for cannabis and the people who love it. Even though it's taken decades to get to this point, it will take decades more to continue making things better for individuals and humanity. Nothing ever stays the same when it comes to laws and societal trends, and even positive progress can be pulled back. True legalization will mean full liberation, amnesty, and reparations for prohibition victims too. It might take time, but it can happen.

The cannabis culture, community, and industry must persevere in our pursuit of legitimate law reform and never give up fighting for what's right. Step by step, we are moving forward, even if we're forced to take a few steps back on occasion. Relentless positivity, passion, and hope are what make change possible. As I always say to my fellow advocates who seek to make a difference: take what you can get, and always ask for more. We are indeed changing the world.

Postscript

"Craft" Cannabis and a New Kind of Canadian Farm

ANDREW D. HATHAWAY and CLAYTON JAMES SMITH McCANN

In 2001, Brazilian *garimpeiros* (independent prospectors) unearthed a 752-pound cluster of emeralds with an estimated value of up to US$925 million. Thus began the Bahia Emerald's rather convoluted journey[1] from the Carnaiba Mine in northern Brazil to a police evidence locker (Weil 2017). As the story goes, along the way, the gem's transporters were attacked by jaguars, which killed several cartage mules. This would be the first in a long line of disasters, some of which included the conning of investors, theft, being coveted by Bernie Madoff, theft again, and kidnapping.

In 2015, Brazil claimed ownership, but at the time of writing, the ultra-precious gem had been briefly awarded to FM Holdings only to be restrained under the Los Angeles County Sheriff's Department at the order of a US federal judge (Cesar 2015). Could this be a cautionary tale denouncing greed and the disruption of relationships to rival Tolkien's grotesque Gollum? If it has anything to do with the story we have told about cannabis legalization in Canada, one might view the present moment as the "attacked by jaguars" stage. Or to put the argument more plainly:

> The world is watching Canada blow this once-in-a-lifetime opportunity to legalize cannabis. What bothers me is all the goodwill, all the free advertising, and all the established demand for high-end Canadian bud: *that* goes down the drain with our reputation as garbage weed made by these LPs floods the global market.[2]

As portended in the Introduction to this volume, the lessons of cannabis legalization are not altogether different, in so many ways, than other observations made about the marketing of drugs. That is to say: "One did not succeed entrepreneurially by making *better* crack." The stories of malfeasance in the industry that have emerged to excoriate legal cannabis in Canada are troubling. But, naturally, there is much more to say.

The laboratory of the social sciences, where description and analysis of social phenomena must be conducted, is, of course, the living world. And in the living world, things tend to remain in motion, despite our best attempts to arrest that momentum and hold the phenomenon up to the light, or even slow its gyrations and examine it in flight. Canada's legalization of cannabis for nonmedical use has been a bit like the Big Bang; it started from a putative single point and exploded outward at the speed of light in all directions at once.

Such a metastasizing nature renders the careful, slow determinations of academic inquiry inadequate. Like astronomers, we who study the events preceding legalization, legalization itself, and the ensuing months and years are required to deduce one atomic structure at a time from the infinite layers of emerging celestial bodies, even as they hurtle away, frustratingly diminishing into their own quadrant of the night sky. Having laid hold of one such particle, pausing in its mad tumble through the cosmos, we derive meaning from its progress, assess its historical formation *in media res* (in the midst of things) to determine – if we're lucky – where it might be headed.

The legal cannabis phenomenon in Canada has spawned a multitudinous and intricate array of related phenomena for analysts to ponder. Among other subjects covered here, considerable attention is devoted to detailing the rise of the for-profit legal production sector with its attendant successes and scandals. We juxtapose this intricate and wide-ranging inquiry of the legal industry with analysis of the current reigning champion of production and distribution, the traditional folk market or black market (the term you favour will depend on your point of view).

Among other topics for discussion moving forward, it is worth noting that at the time of writing, global demand for CBD outstripped demand for THC. This would suggest that consumers of legal cannabis would rather get a good night's sleep than "summit blazed as fuck" (current product ratios of THC to CBD tend to average about 27.5 to 1) (Laba 2020). Thus, it is conceivable that many more nonusers of cannabis in Canada might yet be beguiled by potential new uses that will translate into new meanings.[3]

The persistent failings of neoliberal governance mean we must continue, at the same time, to contend with the human costs of waging war on (certain) drugs. Four years after the Cannabis Act came into force, the government has yet to expunge the criminal records of Canadians who had suffered untold hardships because of the war on cannabis. The offer of federal pardons and waiving application fees does not go far enough. For persons convicted of cannabis possession, who have already more than paid their "debt" to society, a pardon does not ensure housing or employment security, the right to travel internationally, or even freedom from discrimination, prejudice, and exploitation.

The new mandate to "restrict and regulate" the use of cannabis in Canada is a modern manifestation of the control of pleasure. In the name of what? we ask, along with Frederic Jameson. Pleasure, suggests Jameson, means reconciling the human body with something akin to nature. As he contends: "Maybe indeed the deeper subject is here not 'pleasure' ... but the libidinal body itself *and its* peculiar politics" (Jameson 1983, 9).

The Canadian government, in presumptively assuming that it has the moral authority to "restrict and regulate," has also sought to seize the moral high ground through repetition of the mantra that its primary objectives are to keep "cannabis out of the hands of children" and "cannabis proceeds out of the hands of criminals." The first objective is pure fiction. Youth who care enough to seek it will continue to obtain it through an array of sources – as they always have – and new sources will continue to become available as expanded access to legal cannabis evolves.

Quashing the "black market," we might add, has always been a neoliberal fantasy rooted in the need for taxes. Succeeding in that quest requires us to regulate our way out of a moral quagmire created by those same forces and authority structures that first cast cannabis as a villain in 1923. What hope, after all, does authority have to succeed in regulating pleasure? Pleasure is what Jameson describes as a "radical weapon" that was long ago harnessed to consumption as a reward under industrial production: what one "works for" when one labours, the pleasure of consuming.

Part of the history of cannabis documented here is the history of consumers demanding access to its pleasures. Another aspect of the story we tell is its history of force and coercion, of the kind described by Gramsci, on behalf of power and its monopoly on violence. The Canadian criminal justice system became addicted to ballooning war on drugs budgets. When this could no longer be ignored by even the most conservative of observers, the pundits, policy makers, and police switched sides and joined the boards of newly minted legal cannabis production corporations.

So much for exercising the intellectual and moral leadership that critical theorists such as Gramsci call for from the state and corporations. That would require building alliances based on trust and making compromises with a variety of stakeholders and interest groups that go beyond financial vested interests. Instead, we get increasingly alarming tales about malfeasance in the industry (and production binges of a magnitude capable of stockpiling four hundred tonnes of low-quality cannabis) (Meyer 2019).

Licensed producers (LPs) have not been satisfied to operate within the regulations restricting cannabis product promotion. And LPs were not satisfied with rules requiring they attract the needed capital investment to pay for producing legal cannabis "at scale." Instead, the green rush resulted in a bubble that caused valuations to soar (Williams 2019).[4] This scenario is eerily familiar, of course, to the not-long-ago housing and dot.com bubbles that also left investors holding worthless scrip.

Have we gathered enough evidence to confidently argue that the whole green rush is actually a greed crash? To further illustrate, in early February 2020, Aurora's CEO Terry Booth stepped down and announced the elimination of five hundred jobs (George-Cosh 2020a; Aurora).[5] Then, on February 11, the other shoe dropped. *BNN Bloomberg* reported that several of Canada's top-tier cannabis LPs – once worth billions, with hundreds of millions of dollars in liquidity – were now mere months away from being stone-cold broke (Owram 2020).[6] What has become of many of these firms since may yet prove anecdotal, as federal legalization efforts loom in the United States. With the advent of the SAFE Banking Act and, perhaps even more significantly, the MORE Act, it appeared Americans were at last prepping to light the six-foot bong with their toes. But 2021 came and went with only minor nods in such directions. The prison industrial complex and carceral capitalism (Jackie Wang 2019) notwithstanding, the tragedy continues much as Joseph McNamara suggested: "In a holy war, you don't have to win. You just keep on fighting."

Writedowns are common in capitalism. As are layoffs. Yet many cash-poor LPs are now cap in hand, begging investors to return to the sector (Maccke 2020). So, what happened? Flashback to the ebullient days of early 2018, in the lead-up to legalization that October. Optimism ran so high throughout investor circles that cash flowed to LPs that often lacked the proven capacity to produce cannabis at scale (Roman 2019). These firms were pushing hype, only interested in optics or keeping up appearances to spur demand for LP stocks.

A key factor that investors assess when deciding where to place their bets is market capitalization, or the market value of a publicly traded company's outstanding shares, arrived on by multiplying share price by the number of outstanding shares. But what determines market value when investors are less interested in the current value of a company than what that value might become? Enthusiasm remained high because it was a brand-new industry.

The malfeasant practices determining the valuation of LP inventories first came to the attention of industry analysts in late 2017, one year prior to legalization, before the blush was off the rose for investors looking to cash in on the green rush.[7] Joe Castaldo's article in *MacLean's* in January 2018 should have been a critical wake-up call to regulators, and investors, that something was very amiss in the accounting practices of new Canadian cannabis production firms.

But they all slept in. The story came at a moment when the entire corporate media apparatus was working in concert, hyping the new LP sector with legal weed on the horizon. The resulting "noise" was tremendous, and the story went away. Or did it? Malfeasance by licensed producers had to be egregious indeed to warrant coverage. But that did not stop the tide of damning media reports.[8] Volatility in the subsector started to come into focus when just a few days after cannabis legalization came into force in October 2018, LP stocks lost $10 billion in value (Milstead 2018).

By 2019, the legal cannabis production sector was finally beginning to face the reality that cannabis demand did not live up to investment hype. Many of the nearly three hundred brand-new Canadian legal cannabis corporations turned out to be "pump-and-dump" investment scams, with no intention of producing cannabis at scale. The bottomless cash supply for the green rush was drying up. And larger investors were beginning to wonder just how safe their money was.

In September 2019, Constellation Brands – the US firm that invested over $1 billion in Canopy Growth – discovered it had lost hundreds of millions on its investment. Canopy CEO Bruce Linton was sent packing, albeit with a $200 million golden parachute. By December, more grim reports began emerging in Canadian media coverage of the LP subsector.[9]

Addicted to cash, Canada's "capital-hungry" legal cannabis subsector began 2020 on a starvation diet.[10] And the latest shake-up was already underway. As cannabis companies began filing for credit protection, others were getting sued for unpaid bills and cutting jobs; reckless, irresponsible use of investor funds was increasingly apparent in the struggling industry (George-Cosh 2020b; Shreve 2020; Saminather 2020; West 2020; Aspiri 2020). Just three weeks into the new year, it was reported that "at least nine U.S. law firms are pursuing [class action] cases against Canopy Growth, Aurora Cannabis and HEXO Corp. in American courts"; each stands accused of "misleading investors or failing to disclose certain problems with their businesses" to the tune of $500 million in claimed damages (Southwick 2020; see also Subramaniam 2020a).

Two facts emerge from this dizzying narrative of an industry seemingly circling the drain. First, many LPs licensed by Health Canada had no intention of producing cannabis "at scale" or to industrial-scale volumes. The objective, rather, was to lure investment in a "pump and dump" scheme to attract cash. Second, the use of IFRS accounting methods enabled LPs to publish market capitalization "data" as fact, giving them the credibility investors were looking for. The system rewards guessing at inventory valuation and gives firms too much latitude to be creative with their estimates. When firms with no intention of producing cannabis at scale use IFRS to value their companies, "gross margins in the sector are distorted as a result, making firms look more profitable than they really are" (Castaldo 2018).[11]

It seems entirely reasonable to speculate that the LP subsector's financial activities remain unregulated for a reason: to make a pile of cash for those first through the door (ex-MPs, ex-cops, and other privileged insiders) (*Potfacts* 2017). Canada had every opportunity to structure this regulatory system with adequate protections to deter the culture of malfeasance in the industry.[12] But other vested interests continue to predominate, to the detriment of all. Somewhat more optimistically, a well-informed US observer has made the case that "there is very little standing in the way of a public effort to create an agricultural model for the marijuana industry that represents the public interest. Of course, there isn't yet a [clear] consensus on what constitutes the public interest" (Stoa 2018, 190). One might imagine that the exact opposite of the current tobacco model might be a good place to start.

Looking forward to the future, it is worth asking if anything further can be gleaned from the experiences of the United States. Ryan Stoa (2018), for example, notes that the lion's share of the legal cannabis markets of Colorado, Oregon, and Washington comprise sales of high-quality, boutique raw bud. All the more so if pre-rolls are included. Thus, the low-cost cannabis produced by Big Marijuana might be destined for "next-gen" products such as vape cartridges, edibles, oils, topicals, and tinctures. Rising demand for organic, wholesome products includes demand for healthy cannabis as much as healthy food. Thus, the future customers of Big Marijuana will likely be the most price-conscious with no desire for boutique cannabis (or those content to eat "shwag" weed concealed within a candied gummy). But the intensification of toxicities, which is the result of extraction and distillation methods, might make such a gamble untenable.

Elizabeth Bennett's (2017, 2019) work in the US supports the view that the demand for "wholesome" products is a trend that carries over into cannabis consumption. She observes: "Ethical purchasing initiatives that emerged after legalization largely mimicked initiatives already in place for other agri-food products" (Bennett 2019, 753). Sustainable agriculture is starting to crop up in diverse Canadian contexts, such as Ontario (Tignanelli 2021), where "agro-tourism [is seen as] a way to engage with the community while encouraging people to take an interest in sustainable farming and food practices." But since surveillance of the supply chain in the legal market has not sought to ensure organic or no-spray growing methods, claims by unethical producers of healthy practices are dubious. As it stands, the practice of "greenwashing," (mis)labelling or misrepresenting products to appeal to health-conscious consumers, is pervasive in the industry.

The observed momentum (Regennabis 2021) toward demand for more "environmentally friendly or socially responsible cannabis" has largely mimicked trends seen with other agri-food products: "Ethical consumerism in cannabis was similar to other sectors in terms of demographics of supply and demand, prioritization of ethical issues, and [recognition of] pervasive false claims" (Bennett 2017, 17). The latest data tracking global trends toward organic farming methods show "a twenty percent growth [in 2017] – the largest ever recorded – over 2016 numbers" to keep up with demand for healthy, wholesome products (Willer and Lernould 2019).

Stoa's work, as noted previously, identifies a number of distinct advantages to small-scale cannabis farming. A system of appellations (much like the famous wine-growing region of Champagne) would help sustain rural economies and local jobs – and even promote agri-tourism – in addition to reducing energy consumption; protecting ecosystems, soil, and the integrity of agricultural products; and preventing price collapses in agricultural commodities.

For readers interested in countering the well-documented trend of malfeasance in the legal cannabis industry in Canada, with Stoa, one might start by asking: "What do we want the marijuana farm of the future to look like?" Are we standing at the precipice of "a once-in-a-lifetime opportunity to spark the rebirth of the [North] American family farm" (Stoa 2018, 189)?

If one thing is for sure, it is that "legacy" producers[13] are still moving product and playing by their own rules, despite the best-laid plans of governments and LPs (Ross 2019). Why not incentivize producers to start making the shift from the so-called legacy market to the regulated market? For skilled growers who have managed to be profitable for decades, what sort of inducement would it take for them to transition to working in a regime where autonomy vanishes, where the supply chain is strictly surveilled, and where there is no semblance of collective benefits?

In early 2020, Health Canada held "consultations" in the Kootenay region (and Vancouver and Vancouver Island, among others) to encourage "legacy" producers of high-quality craft cannabis, as well as medical cannabis production licence holders (of which there are about 250,000 nationwide) – both of which can engage in the supply of the illicit market – to transition to legal production. On February 13, 2020, the regulator's representatives met a select group of producers in a closed meeting in Nelson, BC, seeking input on what the group perceived to be structural barriers to the licensing process (McCann 2022).

But Health Canada did not attend in good faith, as attested by minor changes made to the Cannabis Tracking and Licensing System (CTLS) webpages some eight months later. In truth, it held a fake consultation in the vein of those perpetrated by contemporary neoliberal governments such as the Canadian government, which had failed to adequately consult with Indigenous groups in BC prior to construction of Site C dam, the Coastal Gas Link project, or even the Trans Mountain pipeline twinning project (Cox 2021). This pseudo-consultation evinced that Canada's federal government is currently not interested in facilitating access to licences and markets for the country's brightest and best cannabis producers. Indeed, it is a government intent on instituting a corporatized cannabis production model (Harvey 2021).

Such claims may be substantiated by the regulator's decision to make the licensing process even more difficult for would-be transitioning producers when, in May 2019, Health Canada included the "build-out" provision in the micro-producer (i.e., the cultivator or processor) application process. This provision meant producers would have to build their facilities in accordance with the regulator's Good Production Practices (GPP) specs before they could be considered for a licence. Applicants would then typically have to come up with about $1 million, hire Quality Assurance Professionals (QAPs) to help them build to spec, submit an application, then wait upwards of a year, all before they would be permitted to grow a single bud (Rendell 2019).

In the meantime, moving forward with due caution and a dose of healthy optimism, the following words of wisdom warrant sharing as corporate cannabis and governments contemplate the steps ahead: "A few LPs believe they can bulldoze their way to the top. But, many know this isn't so, and live to cultivate beautiful flowers, tend to and harvest with care, cure their rewards, and will always outwit, outplay and outlast the greedy."[14] In sum, this book tells part of the story of what happens when a sacred object of inestimable value is misappropriated and given a new form.

Once governments become involved as profiteers and shills, promoting corporate interests via regulatory processes, promises and forecasts of billions of dollars of economic activity inevitably follow. The need to raise investment capital is met by further promises to overlook certain indiscretions, allowing for reporting loopholes, the free "mobility" of profits, and what amounts to immunity from prosecution for licensed producers. To put it bluntly, the corporate cannabis sector is astonishingly corrupt and produces a commodity that few consumers seem to want.

The organizing logic of late capitalism, after all, does not centre on production but rather on the goal of financialization (making money from money). Thus, we have arrived at what has also been described as the cancer stage of capitalism, indiscriminately devouring entire cultures and humanity itself (McMurtry 2013). But what is the corrective for this quandary? To begin with, there is an urgent need to understand the bigger picture. And to that end, we could do worse than echo the words of Christian Wiman (2013, 120) advising humanity to "more fully inhabit our lives and the world in which we live them, and that if we more fully inhabit these things, we might be less apt to destroy both."

Notes
1 Our thanks to Ian Carpendale for suggesting the analogy.
2 Statement by David Robinson, owner of Pacific North West garden supply, during a consultation between Health Canada and illicit cannabis producers, February 13, 2020, Nelson, British Columbia.
3 As noted previously, new technologies include nanoemulsification, which produces a fast-acting, water-soluble powder that can be used in any number of ways and tooled to produce any number of effects: a CBC powder for neuronal stimulation and potential neuroplasticity, possibly a treatment for Alzheimer's and dementia

patients; a THCA powder, possibly efficacious for reducing and slowing the progress of tumour production in the body; or a CBD/melatonin transdermal patch for the slow-release of sleep-inducing elements, permitting a long and restful sleep for an anxious civilization. Or, for those who eschew such "silver bullet," single-molecule solutions, which are so favoured by the pharmaceutical industry, there will always be the "entourage effect" of the whole cannabis plant: for its anxiolytic (anxiety-reducing) or analgesic (pain-reducing) effects.

4 When Canopy Growth stock exceeded the sixty-five dollars per share threshold in 2018, and the company was valued at $10 billion, one observer's quip highlighted the incredulity evoked: "Canopy is now worth more than Air Canada [but] at least the airline has some planes" (Jagielski 2018).

5 Days prior, Tilray, another LP, announced it was cutting about 150 jobs. David George-Cosh (2020a) reported that same week: "Hexo Corp., CannTrust Holdings Inc. and Sundial Growers Inc. have all announced similar staff reductions in the past several months." Around the same time, Toronto-based "asset management" firm Evolve was shutting down its two cannabis ETFs, which had lost more than 50 percent of their value in less than two years (Ferreira 2020). And the LP Wayland Group (formerly Maricann) declared "fire-sale" levels of asset liquidation, teetering on the brink of bankruptcy (Lutz 2020).

6 Although among the heaviest hitters in the LP subsector, it was reported that Aurora possessed just 2.3 months of cash before insolvency; Tilray, 3.7 months; the Green Organic Dutchman, 3.9 months; Hexo, 6.5 months; and Canopy, 7.7 months (Owram 2020).

7 LPs were employing a European accounting method called IFRS (International Financial Reporting Standards), which created problems: "Companies have to put a value on their marijuana plants for accounting purposes, even though pricing and future demand are not yet known. As a result ... financial statements rely heavily on managers' estimates, and are wildly inconsistent" (Castaldo 2018).

8 First, the New Brunswick–based LP Organigram was discovered to have been applying a banned pesticide, Myclobutanil, to cannabis plants, causing medical users to become seriously ill (Robertson 2017). Then Ontario-based Aphria was caught inflating medical cannabis prices for Canadian veterans and became embroiled in a scandal for insider trading (Hindenburgh Investment Research 2018). That same year, 2018, Aphria was the subject of a US-based financial analyst's "short" report, which revealed Aphria executives were selling their own international acquisitions (e.g., worthless real estate holdings) to the company at grossly inflated prices. Embroiled in the Aphria scandal was Andy DeFrancesco, a "pump-and-dump" con artist who fled to Florida ("a 'homestead' state, [where] it is hard to attach a person's main residence in case of judgments of liens") with his "winnings," accrued from selling relatively worthless Latin American "assets" to Aphria for US$150,616,833, activities described in media accounts as "massive fraud committed by senior management" (Tilson 2019; Pomerantz LLP 2019).

9 Stephen McBride (2019) relayed the situation rather bluntly: "It's a bloodbath." He reported that Canopy's stock value had dropped 65 percent since April, that Cronos Group's had dropped 71 percent over the same period, and that Aurora's had dropped by an astounding 74 percent.

10 "'I don't think we've seen any indication yet that the broader capital raising environment for cannabis is going to improve in the short term,' said Jamie Nagy, Canaccord Genuity's cohead of mergers and acquisitions and a point person for the firm's cannabis deals" (Subramaniam 2020b).

11 As further explained by Castaldo (2018):

> IFRS allows agricultural firms to use the estimated increase in the value of their biological assets, such as plants, to offset costs when calculating gross margins. It's a little bit like counting chickens before they've hatched. For mature agricultural industries, that can make sense. The market for tomatoes is well-established, prices are not in dispute, and a producer can enter into future sales contracts. That's not the case with recreational marijuana sales, an industry that doesn't even exist yet.

12 For example, through a system that requires performance bonds to ensure that only those firms capable of producing "scale" receive production licences, and a system far more stringent in its security-clearance-vetting procedures to keep international crime out of the LP subsector. One of the great ironies of the LP era is that organized crime continues to profit from cannabis sales under legalization, despite all of Bill Blair's tough-on-crime rhetoric.

13 This is a relatively recent elision being employed in place of the traditional pejorative black market.

14 A statement by Wayne King, a Chatham-Kent, Ontario-based cannabis pundit.

Works Cited

Aspiri, Jon. 2020. "Cannabis Producer Canopy Growth Shuts Down 2 B.C. Facilities, Leaving Hundreds Out of Work." *Global News,* March 4. https://globalnews.ca/news/6630628/cannabis-producer-canopy-growth-shutter-facilities/.

Aurora. 2020. "Aurora Cannabis Announces CEO Retirement and Succession, Board of Directors Expansion, and Business Transformation Plan." *Cision,* February 6. https://www.newswire.ca/news-releases/aurora-cannabis-announces-ceo-retirement-and-succession-board-of-directors-expansion-and-business-transformation-plan-869307955.html.

Bennett, Elizabeth A. 2017. "Extending Ethical Consumerism Theory to Semi-legal Sectors: Insights from Recreational Cannabis." *Agriculture and Human Values* 35 (2): 295–317.

—. 2019. "Prohibition, Legalization, and Political Consumerism: Insights from the U.S. and Canadian Cannabis Markets." In *The Oxford Handbook of Political Consumerism,* edited by Magnus Boström, Michele Micheletti, and Peter Oosterveer, 741–72. New York: Oxford University Press.

Castaldo, Joe. 2018. "Canadian Weed Stocks Have a Serious Accounting Problem: Investors Risk Being Misled by Financial Statements That Are "a Bloody Mess," Says Forensic Accountant." *Maclean's,* January 23. https://www.macleans.ca/economy/canadian-weed-stocks-have-a-serious-accounting-problem/.

Cesar, Stephen. 2015. "Federal Judge Halts Release of Massive Brazilian Emerald." *Los Angeles Times,* June 25. https://www.latimes.com/local/lanow/la-me-ln--brazilian-bahia-emerald-20150625-story.html.

Cox, Sarah. 2021. "UN Committee Rebukes Canada for Failing to Get Indigenous Peoples' Consent for Industrial Projects." *The Narwhal*, January 15. https://thenarwhal.ca/un-rebukes-canada-industrial-projects/.

Ferreira, Victor. 2020. "Evolve Terminating Its Two Cannabis ETFs after Less Than Two Years As Funds Drop More Than 50%: Doubts Whether Pot Stocks Will Ever Return to the Trading Highs They Hit in March 2019." *Financial Post*, January 27. https://financialpost.com/investing/evolve-etfs-terminating-its-two-cannabis-etfs-less-than-two-years-after-they-launchedhttps://financialpost.com/investing/evolve-etfs-terminating-its-two-cannabis-etfs-less-than-two-years-after-they-launched.

George-Cosh, David. 2020a. "Aurora Plans to Lay Off 10% of Staff amid Profitability Push: Source." *BNN Bloomberg*, February 5. https://www.bnnbloomberg.ca/aurora-plans-to-lay-off-10-of-staff-amid-profitability-push-source-1.1385552.

–. 2020b. "Medipharm Sues Hexo Claiming Breach for $9.8M in Unpaid Bills." *BNN Bloomberg*, January 27. https://www.bnnbloomberg.ca/medipharm-sues-hexo-after-claiming-breach-of-contract-for-9-8m-in-unpaid-bills-1.1380458.

Harvey, Tracey. 2021. "Weed, Greed, and the Need for Reconciliation: Cannabis Legalization and the Case of the Rural Kootenay, BC Region." PhD diss., Department of Rural Studies, University of Guelph, Guelph, ON.

Hindenburgh Investment Research. 2018. "Aphria Insiders Disclose Stake in Nuuvera's Initial Financing Round Just 1 Day before Expected Deal Closing." *Seeking Alpha*, March 22. https://seekingalpha.com/article/4158361-aphria-insiders-disclose-stake-in-nuuveras-initial-financing-round-just-1-day-expected-deal.

Jagielski, David. 2018. "Is Canopy Growth Corp. a $10 Billion Company?" *Motley Fool*, January 11. https://www.fool.ca/2018/01/11/is-canopy-growth-corp-a-10-billion-company/.

Jameson, Frederic. 1983. "Pleasure: A Political Issue." In *Formations of Pleasure*, edited by the Editorial Collective, 1–14. London: Routledge/Kegan Paul.

Laba, Nick. 2020. "First Clinically Verified Cannabis Insomnia Treatment Set to Release This Year: A University-Run Clinical Trial Showed a Significant Reduction of Insomnia with Minimal Side Effects." *Mugglehead*, February 19. https://mugglehead.com/first-clinically-verified-cannabis-insomnia-treatment-set-to-release-this-year/.

Lutz, Jay. "Wayland Group Sells Colombian, Swiss Assets at Major Loss." *Deep Dive*, February 15. https://thedeepdive.ca/wayland-group-sells-colombian-swiss-assets-at-major-loss/.

Maccke, Bruce. 2020. "Aurora Cannabis: What Happened?" *Deep Dive*, February 9. https://thedeepdive.ca/aurora-cannabis-what-happened/.

McBride, Stephen. 2019. "Canopy Growth Has Hit a Dead End." *Forbes*, December 9. https://www.forbes.com/sites/stephenmcbride1/2019/12/09/canopy-growth-has-hit-a-dead-end/?sh=3c1de3c1628b.

McCann, Clayton. 2022. "Canadian Cannabis – One Hot Mess: Orthodoxies of Access and Exclusion." PhD. diss., Department of Anthropology, McMaster University, Hamilton, ON.

McMurtry, John. 2013. *The Cancer Stage of Capitalism: From Crisis to Cure*. London: Pluto Press.

Meyer, Gregory. 2019. "Canada Racks Up 400-Tonne Cannabis Mountain after Production Binge." *Financial Times*, November 22. https://www.ft.com/content/546b9226-0c7b-11ea-bb52-34c8d9dc6d84.

Milstead, David. 2018. "The $10-Billion Wipe Out: What's Bothering Investors As Pot Stocks Suffer Worst Day of 2018." *Globe and Mail*, October 22. https://www.theglobeandmail.com/investing/markets/inside-the-market/article-pot-stocks-swept-up-in-across-the-board-selloff/.

Mulgrew, Ian. 2006. *Bud Inc: Inside Canada's Marijuana Industry*. Toronto: Vintage Canada.

Owram, Kristine. 2020. "Some Pot Companies Are Months Away from Running Out of Cash." *BNN Bloomberg*, February 11. https://www.bloomberg.com/news/articles/2020-02-11/some-pot-companies-are-months-away-from-running-out-of-cash.

Pomerantz LLP. 2019. "Shareholder Alert: Pomerantz Law Firm Reminds Shareholders with Losses on Their Investment in Aphria Inc. of Class Action Lawsuit and Upcoming Deadline – Apha." *MarketWatch*, January 19. https://www.globenewswire.com/news-release/2019/01/11/1690688/1087/en/SHAREHOLDER-ALERT-Pomerantz-Law-Firm-Reminds-Shareholders-with-Losses-on-their-Investment-in-Aphria-Inc-of-Class-Action-Lawsuit-and-Upcoming-Deadline-APHA.html.

Potfacts. 2017. "The Liberal Party Elite Is Heavily Invested in the Medical Marijuana Licensed Producers Mail-Order Business." May 12. http://pot-facts.ca/the-liberal-party-elite-is-heavily-invested-in-the-medical-marijuana-licensed-producers-mail-order-business/.

Regennabis. 2021. "Regenerative Growth for All in the Cannabis Industry." https://theinvestorscoliseum.com/regennabis-blog-2/.

Rendell, Mark. 2019. "Micro Madness: How BC's Craft Cannabis Industry Is Losing Out on Legalization." *Globe and Mail*, May 13. https://www.theglobeandmail.com/robcannabispro/article-micro-madness-how-bcs-craft-cannabis-industry-is-losing-out-on/.

Robertson, Grant. 2017. "Marijuana Producer Details Source of Banned Pesticide Problem." *Globe and Mail*, June 5. https://www.theglobeandmail.com/news/national/marijuana-producer-details-source-of-banned-pesticide-problem/article35211067/.

Ross, Selena. 2019. "Canada Legalized Pot in October. But Its Black Market Is Still Going Strong." *Washington Post*, January 4. https://www.washingtonpost.com/world/the_americas/canada-legalized-pot-in-october-but-its-black-market-is-still-going-strong/2019/01/04/ca09a3b0-fe53-11e8-a17e-162b712e8fc2_story.html.

Saminather, Nichola. 2020. "More Pain in Store for Canadian Marijuana Companies after Aurora Cannabis, Tilray Cut Jobs." *Reuters*, February 7. https://www.reuters.com/article/us-canada-marijuana-cuts-idUSKBN2012JQ.

Shreve, Ellwood. 2020. "Former Agmedica Employees in Same Boat as Company's Creditors." *Chatham Daily News*, January 6. https://www.chathamdailynews.ca/news/local-news/former-agmedica-employees-in-same-boat-as-companys-creditors.

Southwick, Reid. 2020. "Major Canadian Pot Companies Facing Proposed Class-Action Lawsuits in the United States: Each Producer Is Accused of Misleading Investors or Failing to Disclose Certain Problems with Their Businesses." *CBC News*, January 19. https://www.cbc.ca/news/canada/calgary/major-canadian-pot-companies-facing-proposed-class-action-lawsuits-in-the-u-s-1.5431520.

Stoa, Ryan. 2018. *Craft Weed: Family Farming and the Future of the Marijuana Industry.* Cambridge, MA: MIT Press.

Subramaniam, Vanmala. 2020a. "Cannabis Companies Face a Slew of Lawsuits amid Investor Ire: Lawyer Dimitri Lascaris Speaks about a Proposed Class-Action by Investors against Canntrust." *Financial Post*, February 18. https://financialpost.com/cannabis/cannabis-business/cannabis-investing/cannabis-companies-face-a-slew-of-lawsuits-amid-investor-ire.

—. 2020b. "FP Dealmakers: 'There Are Going to Be Bankruptcies,' Cannabis Deals Plunge by Third after Dizzying Rally." *Financial Post*, January 30. https://financialpost.com/news/fp-street/fp-dealmakers-these-are-early-innings-dealers-shift-gear-as-cannabis-bankruptcies-emerge-on-the-horizon.

Tignanelli, Vanessa. 2021. "The Sustainable Family Farm: How a Mother-Daughter Team Built a New Life in Rural Ontario." *Globe and Mail*, September 19. https://www.theglobeandmail.com/canada/article-the-sustainable-family-farm-how-a-mother-daughter-team-built-a-new/.

Tilson, Whitney. 2019. "Defrancesco Sued for Securities Fraud for Role in Aphria." *Empire Financial Daily*, June 6. https://empirefinancialresearch.com/articles/michaels-has-collapsed-defrancesco-sued-for-securities-fraud-for-role-in-aphria-hindenburg-research-exposes-yangtze-river-fraud-chinese-crypto-pioneer-pays-4-57-million-for-lunch-with-warren-buffe.

Weil, Elizabeth. 2017. "The Curse of the Bahia Emerald, a Giant Green Rock That Ruins Lives." *Wired*, March 2. https://www.wired.com/2017/03/curse-bahia-emerald-giant-green-rock-wreaks-havoc-ruins-lives/.

West, James. 2020. "Green Relief Inc: Unprecedented Corporate Malfeasance Brought to Light." *MidasLetter LIVE*, January 27. https://midasletter.com/2020/01/green-relief-inc-unprecedented-corporate-malfeasance-brought-to-light/.

Willer, Helga, and Julia Lernoud, eds. *The World of Organic Agriculture: Statistics and Emerging Trends 2019*. Frick/Bonn: Research Institute of Organic Agriculture FiBL and IFOAM Organics International. https://orgprints.org/id/eprint/34570/10/WILLER-LERNOUD-2018-final-PDF-low.pdf.

Williams, Sean. 2019. "Marijuana Companies Lied to You, Major Pot CEO Alleges." *Motley Fool*, May 19. https://www.fool.com/investing/2019/05/19/marijuana-companies-lied-to-you-major-pot-ceo-alle.aspx.

Wiman, Christian. 2013. *Ambition and Survival: Becoming a Poet.* Port Townsend, WA: Copper Canyon Press.

Contributors

Catherine Carstairs is a professor in the Department of History at the University of Guelph.

Jason Childs is an associate professor in the Department of Economics at the University of Regina.

Kelly Coulter is a writer, environmentalist, advocate, and founder of Slo Farms, a future regenerative cannabis and forest food garden. In 2010, she joined NORML Canada as the national campaign director and was the first female board member. She later cofounded the NORML Women's Alliance of Canada, which is credited with convincing Justin Trudeau's government to legalize cannabis.

Sarah Daniels completed a BA with Honours in the Department of Psychology at the University of British Columbia, Okanagan Campus.

Michael DeVillaer is an assistant professor in the Department of Psychiatry and Behavioural Neurosciences at McMaster University, and a faculty associate with the Peter Boris Centre for Addictions Research and the Centre for Medicinal Cannabis Research at McMaster and St Joseph's Healthcare in Hamilton, Ontario.

Jodie Emery is a Canadian cannabis rights activist and politician. She has run a cannabis legalization platform for the Green Party of British Columbia and the British Columbia Marijuana Party and, in 2014, she unsuccessfully filed a nomination for the federal Liberal Party in the riding of Vancouver East.

George Hartner is a lecturer in the Department of Economics at the University of Regina.

Andrew D. Hathaway is a professor in the Department of Sociology and Anthropology at the University of Guelph.

Kelly Insley is a Canadian registered nurse who is interested in the emerging research on cannabinoid medicine. She lives and works in Victoria, British Columbia.

Karina Lahnakoski is the former vice president of quality and regulatory at Cannabis Compliance Incorporated in Mississauga, Ontario. She is currently a partner with the management consulting firm Deloitte Canada.

Kanenhariyo Seth LeFort is a Kanyen'kéha (Mohawk) man from the Tehana'karineh family of the Bear Clan. He is from Tyendinaga Mohawk Territory.

Clayton James Smith McCann is a PhD student in the Department of Anthropology at McMaster University. He is a former cannabis production worker, in illicit cannabis "outdoor" and "indoor" production contexts. He currently resides in the lower Slocan Valley, British Columbia, where he conducts social sciences inquiry into the effects of legalization on former illicit production communities.

Alison McMahon is the founder and CEO of Cannabis At Work, a recruitment firm founded in 2015 that helps cannabis companies hire employees.

"*Sal*" is a former cross-border cannabis smuggler, much like her grandfather who smuggled "solvents" from British Columbia to the United States between 1920 and 1933, making a career for himself and a fishing boat for his family.

Michelle St. Pierre is a PhD student in the Department of Psychology at the University of British Columbia, Okanagan Campus.

Ryan Stoa is the author of *Craft Weed: Family Farming and the Future of the Marijuana Industry* (MIT Press, 2018).

Jenna Valleriani completed her PhD at the University of Toronto, and a postdoctoral fellowship at UBC Medicine and the BC Centre on Substance Use. She is currently Director, Social Impact and Advocacy, at Canopy Growth Corporation.

Jeannette VanderMarel is the former CEO of 48North cannabis production facilities (Toronto, Kirkland Lake, and Brantford, Ontario) and former CEO of Beleave Kannabis Corp. (Oakville and Hamilton, Ontario).

Zach Walsh is a professor in the Department of Psychology at the University of British Columbia, Okanagan Campus.

Jared J. Wesley is an associate professor and associate chair of graduate studies in the Department of Political Science at the University of Alberta.

Index

Notes: "(t)" after a page number indicates a table; "(f)" after a page number indicates a figure

A Framework for the Legalization and Regulation of Cannabis in Canada, 239
Access to Cannabis for Medical Purposes Regulations (ACMPR), 76, 97, 98, 102, 220, 228, 296
acquired immunodeficiency syndrome (AIDS), 40, 41, 99–100, 148
Actinovate SP fungicide, 193
activism, 287–311
Addiction Research Foundation of Ontario, 37, 39
addictions: attitudes toward, 152, 156, 232, 240; cannabis rate, 165; criteria, 166, 182–83, 184n1; opiates, 18, 156, 157; survey, 39, 40; terminology, 23n3
African Americans, 232
agriculture: accounting methods, 322n11; agro-tourism, 318; greenwashing, 318; industrial operations, 192, 197–98; organic and community-minded, 267–69; regenerative, 268–69; slow food movement, 269–71; sustainable and small, 267–71, 318; workplace safety, 192, 197–98
Agrima Botanicals Corporation, 133
Agrotek Vaporized Sulphur fungicide, 193
Alberta: market-share data, 88; online sales, 64; private retail outlets, 80; retail outlets restrictions (number of), 78, 80(t); variety data, 94
alcohol and tobacco: advertising impacts, 127; attitudes toward, 33, 152, 239; cannabis vs alcohol use, 32–33, 154–56, 159, 170–73, 176; colonialism, 258–59; consumption by women, 15; harms and economic costs, 60, 73, 114–15, 146, 148, 155–56, 159; minimum age requirements, 79; regulatory framework, 52, 57, 59–62(t), 64, 65, 67; tobacco industry lawsuits, 135

Aleafia Health medical cannabis company, 125
Alexander, Bruce, 240
Allard v Canada, 102, 226
Alzheimer's disease, 201, 320n3
Ambrose, Rona, 98
Ample Organics, 227
Anderson, Brittny, 268
antidrug campaigns, 37–39
Aphria Inc., 120–21, 214, 229nn1–2, 321n8. *See also* Nuuvera Inc.
Aglukkaq, Leona, 303
Arthur, Brian, 57
Assembly of First Nations, 244
Aurora Cannabis (CanniMed/Prairie Plant Systems): finances, 321n6, 321n9; government lobbying and influence, 124; integrated pest management (IPM), 196(t), 197; lawsuits against, 317; layoffs, 315; stock valuations, 321n9; takeover, 76, 214
Australia, 168–69, 170–71, 182
autoethnography, 9
Avitas vape pens, 216

Bakhtin, Mikhail, 10
Baldwin, James, 231–32
Barnhart, Tim, 265n5
Barthes, Roland, 8–9
Baudelaire, Charles, 174
BC Green Party, 294, 296
BC Marijuana Party, 39
Becker, Howard, 4–5, 173, 175, 181
Bennett, Elizabeth, 318
Bennett Jones law firm, 124, 298
Bertrand, Marie-Claude, 35
Black, Hilary, 41, 101
Black Canadians, 29, 44–45, 305
black market. *See* illicit cannabis market
Blair, Bill, 6, 297–99, 305, 308
Bloc Pot political party (Quebec), 39
Blyth, Sarah, 149, 154, 157–58, 161
Bonify cannabis producer, 132
Booth, Terry, 315
Bourgois, Philippe, 13

Brazilian emeralds analogy, 312
British Columbia: cannabis economy, 293; cannabis legalization advocates, 39; Downtown Eastside dispensaries (Vancouver), 148–49; hydroelectric dam project, 275; illicit cannabis production, 272–80; illicit vs legal market share and variety, 88, 91, 93–94; medical cannabis dispensaries (compassion clubs), 41, 98, 101, 103–4, 147, 148–49, 151, 224; overdose prevention sites (Vancouver), 149; political parties, 39, 294, 296; private/public retail outlets, 80; retail outlets restrictions (number of), 78
British Columbia Centre on Substance Use (BCCSU), 147
British Columbia Compassionate Club Society (BCCCS), 101
Brown, Sam, 280
Burawoy, Michael, 13

C45 Summit, 222
Cairney, Paul, 66
Campbell, Ian L., 35
Campbell, Larry, 306
Canaccord Genuity, 322n10
Canada: cannabis activism, 287–311; cannabis attitudes, 34, 41, 45–46; cannabis exports, 40, 216, 220, 230n7, 312; cannabis possession statistics, 42, 307; cannabis prohibition origins, 30–32; cannabis reputation, 40; cannabis smuggling (to USA), 280–85; cannabis use statistics, 42–43(t); cannabis use surveys, 40; cannabis use by youth, 43–44; flags, 40; opinion polls, 34, 41; poets, 11; racial profiling, 29, 44–45, 305; securities practices, 121; social assistance and health care system, 56; social issues, 11. *See also* federal government
Canadian Addiction Survey, 40
Canadian Association of Chiefs of Police, 38, 41–42

Canadian Association of Medical Cannabis Dispensaries ([CAMCD] Association of Canadian Cannabis Retailers [ACCRES]), 102
Canadian Council on Social Determinants of Health, 240
Canadian Drug Strategy, 38
Canadian Food Inspection Agency, 198
Canadian Medical Association Journal, 42
Canadian Offensive for Drug Education (CODE) antidrug campaign, 38
Canadian Securities Administrators (CSA), 132
Canadian Substance Use Costs and Harms Scientific Working Group (CSUCH), 114, 115
Canadian Tobacco, Alcohol and Drugs Survey, 43
cannabis: autoflower strain (*ruderalis cross*), 218, 229n3; colony-forming units (CFUs), 214; as commodity, 6, 14–15; as contamination accumulator plant, 190, 202, 204; culture, 266, 289, 310, 311; dried, 217; edibles, 105, 117, 129–30, 216, 219, 228, 230n6; extracts, 217; free radicals formation, 201; growth stages, 192; hybrid varieties, 218; pathogens, 192–93, 201, 202, 214; product quality, 317–18; *ruderalis* strain, 214, 218, 229n3; strains/varieties of, 214, 218, 229n3, 230n8; terminology (names for), 4, 5, 23n2, 58. *See also* medical cannabis; recreational cannabis use
Cannabis Act (Bill C-45): about, 22, 44, 76, 97–98, 134, 220, 228; cannabis promotion, 128–29; edibles and extracts, 219, 228; employment growth, 228; genetic cultivars, 217; Indigenous provisions, 246; intergovernmental regulatory framework, 74, 78, 223, 246; law enforcement, 298, 306–8, 314; licensed producers, 217, 221, 306; objectives, 298–99; task force, 5–6, 59–61, 113, 124–31, 228, 297–98. *See also* recreational cannabis legalization
cannabis activism: advocacy group, 44, 306; arrests and fines, 281, 289, 294, 300, 302; civil disobedience, 288–92; criminalization amnesty, 44, 288, 306, 308–9, 314; human rights, 310–11; legalization attitudes, 286–87, 310–11; media engagement, 291–92, 295, 301; politics of, 294–99. *See also* recreational cannabis legalization
Cannabis Amnesty advocacy group, 44, 306
Cannabis As Living Medicine (CALM), 101
Cannabis Buyer's Club (CBC), 99
Cannabis Compassion Club, 101
Cannabis Conservancy, 268
Cannabis Culture (Cannabis Canada) magazine, 39, 290, 294, 295
Cannabis Culture (dispensaries), 103, 294, 299, 300–2
Cannabis Day (4/20), 40, 292
cannabis legalization. *See* recreational cannabis legalization
cannabis regulation. *See* provincial and territorial governments (cannabis regulation); recreational cannabis legalization; *individual names of legislation or regulations*
Cannabis Retail Store Allocation Process for Stores on First Nations Reserves, 244
Cannabis Tracking and Licensing System (CTLS), 319
Cannabis Trade Alliance of Canada, 127
cannabis use. *See* medical cannabis use; recreational cannabis use
cannabis use disorder (CUD), 5, 23n5
CanniMed (Prairie Plant Systems/ Aurora Cannabis), 76, 214. *See also* Aurora Cannabis (CanniMed/Prairie Plant Systems)

CannTrust Inc., 132–33, 321n5
Canopy Growth Corporation: about, 125, 301; cash funds, 321n6; government lobbying and influence, 124; illegal cannabis trafficking, 308; inventory and sales calculation method, 94n4; lawsuits against, 317; losses, 316, 321n9; production workers, 195(t), 197; valuations, 321n4, 321n9
Canopy Health Innovations (Canopy Growth Corporation), 125
capitalism, 14–15, 192, 276, 315, 320
Capler, Rielle, 147, 151, 161
Carstairs, Catherine, 16
Castaldo, Joe, 316, 322n11
Centre for Addiction and Mental Health (CAMH), 42
chemicals. *See* fertilizers; pesticides
children. *See* youth
Childs, Jason, 17, 84
Chrétien, Jean, 293
Clifford, James, 10, 12, 13
Cobalt-60, 201
commercial drug industries, 114–16
commodity fetishism, 21
compassion clubs. *See* medical cannabis dispensaries (compassion clubs)
Constellation Brands, 316
Controlled Drugs and Substances Act (CDSA), 41, 97–98
Coulter, Kelly, 20, 266–67
craft cannabis production: appellation cultivation, 21–22, 266–67; cultivation standards, 21–22; licensing transitions, 136, 230n9, 319; organic and community-minded, 266–71, 318; regenerative agriculture, 268–69; sustainable and small, 21–22, 266–71. *See also* licensed cannabis producers (LPs)
Criminal Code, 34, 53, 58, 97, 203, 289
criminal justice system: cannabis possession amnesty, 42, 44, 288, 306, 308–9, 314; cannabis possession statistics, 42, 44, 45, 307; cannabis prohibition origins, 30–32; drug act, 34, 35–36, 147; racial profiling, 44–45; record suspensions/pardons, 7, 23n8; sentence disparities, 34
Cronos Group, 321n9
Crosby, Kim, 150, 151–52, 156, 161
CUDIT-R (Cannabis Use Disorder Identification Test), 234–37
Cyclone chemical, 200

Daniels, Sarah, 18–19
DARE antidrug campaign, 38
Day, Chief Isadore, 244
DeFrancesco, Andy, 229n1, 321n8
Degenhardt, Louisa, 170
Denzin, Norman, 10
DeVillaer, Michael, 18
Di Fiore, James, 122–23
Diagnostic and Statistical Manual of Mental Disorders (DSM-5) criteria, 166, 182–83, 184n1
Dow Chemicals, 193–94
drug use: attitudes, 5, 164, 177; crime, 5, 23n4, 42; experiences and motivations, 33, 148, 174–75; mental health, 177, 182; othering, 5; survey, 39; terminology, 23n3

Egypt, 31
Emery, Jodie, 20, 287–311
Emery, Marc, 39, 281, 289–90, 294, 298, 300
Emery Direct Seeds, 290
Employment Standards Act (ESA Ontario), 197
ethnography, 8–13
European Union Good Management Practices (EU GMP), 220
Evolve licensed cannabis producer, 321n5

Fantino, Julian, 303
farming. *See* agriculture
Federal Court of Appeal, 76, 102
federal government: antidrug campaigns, 38; cannabis attitudes, 6, 298; cannabis criminalization as failure,

305–7; cannabis industry lobbying and influence, 123–24, 297–98, 299; cannabis legalization task force (McLellan Report [Anne McLellan]), 5–6, 59–61, 113, 124–31, 297–98; drug policy, 35–37, 134–36; House of Commons committees, 42, 298–99; Indigenous self-government, 244; justice department arrests report, 6–7; legislative bills, 35–36, 42, 122; medical cannabis program, 41; Parliamentary Budget Officer (PBO), 87(t)–88; Schedule of Restricted Drugs, 30–31; Senate Committee on Illicit Drugs, 42, 44; tax revenue, 84, 104, 123. *See also* Health Canada; Liberal Party of Canada; licensed cannabis producers (LPs); recreational cannabis legalization

federal intergovernmental policy (cannabis regulation), 52–69; about, 52–53; analysis, 66–69; decentralization approach, 52–69; directional policy, 55–56; impediments, 57–63; policy alignment vs path dependence, 56–57; policy objectives, 59; policy statement, 58–59; policy-making levels, 53–54(f), 55–56; regulation evolution, 75–77(t); regulation objectives, 77; task force discussion paper, 59–60; task force timeline, 58–61. *See also* provincial and territorial (PT) governments; recreational cannabis legalization

Feingold, Daniel, 170–71
Fertilizer Canada, 198–99
fertilizers, 24n13, 190, 193, 198–200, 203–4, 204n2, 205n4
Floodgate, William, 24n13
Flow Kana company, 269
folk capitalism, 273
folk market. *See* illicit cannabis market
Food and Drugs Act, 35–36, 98, 199
Ford, Doug, 244, 246, 264n4
4/20 (April 20), 40, 292

48North Cannabis Corp., 213–19
France, 21, 136
Fukuoka, Masanobu, 267–68

Gates, Peter, 168–69
Geneva Convention, 31
Georgia Peach dispensary, 243
Global Cannabis Partnership (GCP), 222–23
Global Marijuana March, 292
Globe and Mail newspaper, 36, 119, 190
Goffman, Alice, 13
Goldberg, Tyne Daniel, 215
Gonzalez, Adolfo, 148–49, 153, 161
Good and Green company, 215
Goodale, Ralph, 6, 306
Goodwin, Chris and Erin, 302
Google Scholar, 169–71, 183
Gramsci, Antonio, 12, 314–15
Green Organic Dutchman, 194, 195(t), 215, 321n6
Green Party, 122, 294, 296
Guerra, Britney, 302

Hague Convention, 31
Hall, Wayne, 169, 170
HappyDay Farms, 268
Harichy, Lynn and Mike, 41, 101
Harm Reduction Club, 40
Harper, Stephen, 42, 298
Hartner, George, 17
Hathaway, Andrew, 19
Hayward, Benji, 38
Headmasters' Council of Ontario, 37
Health Canada: cannabis effects, 164–65; cannabis office, 225; cannabis use survey, 43; drug identification number (DIN), 118; licence suspensions and revocations, 132–33; licensed producers, 76–77(t), 94n2, 226–27; licensing program process, 64, 319–20; organized crime cultivation licences, 121; other ingredients regulations, 203, 204; person in charge (PIC) regulations, 226–27; pest-control statement, 199–200;

pesticides ingredients and safety, 193–94(t); product promotion regulations, 135–36; product recalls, 83–84, 119, 131, 135; quality control, 130–31, 135; regulatory evolution, 220–21; on "safe" cannabis, 188; staff security clearances, 226–27. *See also* federal government; public health
HEXO Corp., 213, 317, 321nn5–6
High Hopes Foundation, 149
High Times magazine, 36, 289
historical institutionalism (HI), 57
Hossick, K.C., 31

illicit cannabis market: accessories, 33, 224, 289; background, ix, 224, 288–92; criminal types, 7; dispensary numbers, 242, 264n2; folk capitalism shift, 273; as folk market, 7, 23n9, 313; law enforcement costs, 292, 295; as legacy producer, 319, 322n13; vs legal market, 75, 82–83(t), 84, 87(t), 90(t), 317–18; legal production transition, 319; licensing process consultations, 319; market estimates data, 75, 87(t); organized crime, 6–7, 44, 292–93, 295, 298; portrayals, 6–7; price ratio to legal, 83(t), 84; quality, 82–83(t), 84, 312; record suspensions and pardons, 7, 23n8; supply, 304; workers, 224. *See also* legal cannabis market
illicit cannabis production: about, 188–90, 204nn1–2, 205n3; drying, 204n1, 273; fall guy, 189–90, 204n2; fertilizers, 190, 204n2; indoor grow operations (house as factory farm), 189–90, 274, 275; oil extraction, 273; outdoor grow operations, 188–90, 205n3, 273, 275–80; poem about ("Guilty Republic"), 273, 275–80; recollections of, 272–85; smuggler recollections, 280–85; trimmers and hikers, 188–90, 275; worker health and safety harms (chemicals),
188–90, 204n2. *See also* licensed cannabis producers (LPs)
India, 237, 268
Indian Act, 248, 250–51, 258
Indigenous people: authority, 248, 250–53; cannabis distribution dispensaries, 242–47, 265n5; cannabis distribution document ("Dusting Off the Path"), 247(f)–264; cannabis possession convictions, 29, 44, 45; colonialism effects, 20, 246, 264n3, 274–75; community-based security, 245; constitutional challenge, 245–46, 247; ethnic cleansing, 275; government-led consultations, 319; police raids, 243, 244, 245; retail store allocation licences (RSAs), 244; self-government rights, 244–53, 265n5; smallpox epidemic, 275; treaties, 260–63. *See also* Kanyen'kehà:ka customary law and practices ("Dusting Off the Path" document – Tsi Nionkwarihotens)
indoor cannabis production: house as grow-op, 189–90, 274, 275; vs outdoor cannabis production, 215, 217, 229n5, 230n9. *See also* illicit cannabis production; licensed cannabis producers (LPs); outdoor cannabis production
Inkster, Norman, 308
Insley, Kelly, 20, 231–40
interdisciplinarity, 8–9
International Financial Reporting Standards (IFRS), 317, 321n7, 322n11

Jameson, Frederic, 314
"Just Say No" antidrug campaign, 37–38

Kanyen'kehà:ka customary law and practices ("Dusting Off the Path" document – Tsi Nionkwarihotens), 247(f)–264; about, 247; Atahkwakayon song ban, 259; band council bylaws and regulations, 248,

250–51; cannabis regulatory rights, 248–49; colonialism and alcohol attitudes, 258–59; colonialism and religion, 259; conventions, 251–53; environmental responsibilities, 255–56, 260; fermented drink (chicha), 258; general economic principles, 253–56; medicine plant customs and practices, 256–57; "mind changers" consumption (Ka'nikonhratenyen), 257–59; political governance, 248, 251–53; preamble, 248–49; vs religious sect (Handsome Lake), 257–59; resource allocation and public works contracts (dispute-resolution contests), 263–64; resource harvesting, 260–63; self-government and authority, 248, 249–53; trade economy and industry rules, 259–60, 262–63; treaties (Sewatohkwat: The Dish with One Spoon/Beaver Bowl Treaties), 260–63. *See also* Indigenous people

Karadjov, Julian, 190

Ktunaxa peoples, 274

Lahnakoski, Karina, 20, 219–23

Lalonde, Marc, 36

Langton, Jerry, 44

Larsen, Dana, 298

law enforcement. *See* police

Layton, Jack, 294

Le Dain Commission of Inquiry into the Non-Medical Use of Drugs report, 33, 35–36

Leary, Timothy, 33

Lee, Martin A., 201

LeFort, Kanenhariyo Seth, 20, 242, 244–46, 247

Legacy 420 dispensary, 265n5

legal cannabis market: accessibility data, 84–85(t), 90–91(t), 93; cannabis demand forecast data, 87(t)–88; challenges, ix–x; clean cannabis manifesto, 19, 202–4; consumer choice considerations, 82–83(t), 84–86(t); data analysis, 86–94, 94n3; dispensary numbers, 242, 264n2; dry flower sales, 86, 94n4; employment, 223–29, 293; vs illicit market, 75, 82–83(t), 84, 87(t), 90(t), 317–18; market share data, 17, 87(t)–90(t); oils sales, 86, 94n4; pricing data, 83(t), 84, 89–90(t), 93; product quality, 82–83(t), 84, 89–90(t), 317–18; product recalls, 83(t)–84, 93; regulatory practices, 219–23; retail outlets data, 84–85(t), 93; retail ownership models, 89(t); retail store allocation licences (RSAs), 243–44; social constructionist perspective, 7–8; variety data, 85–86(t), 91–92(t), 93–94. *See also* illicit cannabis market; licensed cannabis producers (LPs)

Lewis and Clark Expedition, 274

Liberal Party of Canada: cannabis legalization resolution, 295; cannabis legalization slogan, 134; cannabis legalization strategy objectives, 121–22; chief financial officer, 122, 123, 124; decriminalization legislation, 122; election platform, 58–59, 122–23, 227–28, 305; fundraising events (cannabis industry lobbying), 124. *See also* federal government

licensed cannabis producers (LPs): accounting methods, 316–17, 321n7, 322n11; alternative (natural) pest control, 202, 205n7; "at scale" vs "pump-and-dump" production, 316–17, 322n12; carbon footprint, 203, 206n9; celebrity partnerships, 120; consulting agreements, 125; corporate directors (women), 213–30, 229n4; corporate governance, 221–22; corporate social responsibility (CSR), 217–19, 222–23; documentation compliance, 227; employment, 225–29, 315, 321n5; environmental, social, and governance (ESG), 217–19; ethics vs corruption, 120–21, 318, 320; exports, 216, 220, 230n7, 312; fertilizers, 198–99; future outlook, 228–29; genetic cultivars availability, 217; health and wellness products, 215–16; help-wanted ads, 194–95(t), 196(t)–197; illegal cannabis trafficking, 132–33, 308; ingredients disclosure, 203; insider trading, 214, 229n1, 321n8; integrated pest management (IPM) positions, 195(t)–197; irradiation practices, 201–2, 204, 214; lawsuits against, 132, 317; layoffs, 315, 321n5; legal firms, 124, 134, 298; licence holders data, 76–77(t), 94n2; licence suspensions and revocations, 132–33; lobbying, 123–24, 297–98, 299; losses, 315–16, 321n9, 321nn5–6; market capitalization, 316; medical cannabis exports, 216, 230n7; medical cannabis licences regulation, 296; occupational health and safety, 19, 193–94(t), 203; organic methods, 202–3, 205n7, 217–18; organized crime, 121, 132–33, 322n12; "other ingredients" (chemicals), 190–91, 193–94(t), 198–99, 203, 321n8; outdoor vs indoor production, 215, 217, 229n5, 230n9; pathogens regulation, 192–93, 201, 202, 214; person in charge (PIC) regulations, 226–27; pest management practices, 202, 206n8; product promotion practices, 120–21, 127–29, 133; product quality, 130–31, 312; production inspections, 131; production practices, 131, 193, 201, 202, 214; public officials and police as owners/investors, 123, 297–303, 306, 307–8, 309; regulatory framework, 225–28, 296, 317, 322n12; regulatory practices literature, 206n8; regulatory practices recommendations, 202–4, 206n8; "restrict and limit" supply model, 303–4; securities practices, 121, 132; staff security clearances, 226–27; stock valuations, 299, 303, 308, 315–17, 321n4, 321n9, 322n10; sublingual sprays, 216; summit conferences, 222; supply shortages, 304, 310; technology platforms, 227; vape pens, 216; women (corporate directors), 213–30, 229n4; yields, 214, 218. *See also* craft cannabis production; illicit cannabis production; legal cannabis market

Lindesmith, Alfred, 180–81
Linnaeus, Karl, 230n8
Linton, Bruce, 316
London, Jerome, 205n6
Lucas, Philippe, 148, 152, 155–56, 158, 161–62
Luscombe, Alex, 45
Lynskey, Michael, 170

MacEachen, Allan, 35
Mad Max movie, 3
Malmo-Levine, David, 40
Manitoba: illicit vs legal market pricing, 84; online sales, 81; price data, 89; private retail outlets, 80; product recalls, 83, 93; retail outlets restrictions (number of), 80(t); variety data, 94
Maracle, Chief Donald, 244
Marcuse, Herbert, 14
Marihuana Medical Access Regulations (MMAR), 75–76, 94n1, 100, 102, 118, 220, 225, 296
Marihuana for Medical Purposes Regulations (MMPR), 76, 102, 118, 120, 220, 226–28, 296
marijuana. *See* cannabis
Marijuana Party of Canada, 39
marijuana use disorder (MUD), 166–67, 183
Marley, Bob, 4
Marling, William, 15

Index

Martel, Marcel, 35
Marx, Karl, 21
Maté, Gabor, 232
McBride, Stephen, 321n9
McCann, Clayton James Smith: cannabis-policy consultant, 243; cultural folklore and myths, 20; environmental health, 19; grow-operations recollections, 188–90, 272–80; "Guilty Republic" poem, 273, 275–80; police raids and arrests policy, 243; research program, 13
McLellan Report ([Anne McLellan] Task Force on Cannabis/Marijuana Legalization and Regulation), 5–6, 59–61, 113, 124–31, 297–98
McMahon, Alison, 20, 223–29
McNamara, Joseph, 5, 23n4, 315
medical cannabis: advocates, 40–41, 291; affordability, 104–5; drug identification number (DIN), 104, 118; exports, 216, 230n7; home cultivation, 54, 61–62(t), 76, 225, 226; licences, 102, 118, 225–28, 296–97; opinion polls, 41; organized crime, 121, 132–33; physician knowledge, 106, 152, 155, 156, 291; product diversity, 105; product quality and safety, 105–6, 117, 119; product recalls, 119; supply, 105, 304; tax revenue, 104, 123; taxation, 104. *See also* cannabis; medical cannabis use
medical cannabis dispensaries (compassion clubs), 97–106; about, 99, 289; accessibility, 17–18, 99–101, 102, 105, 290–91, 300; association, 102; business-licensing agreements, 98; challenges, 106; criticisms of, 103; first, 41, 101, 147; franchise model, 300–2; licence exclusion, 102; members, 100–1; numbers of, 102–3, 299; online sales, 97, 105, 106; opinion polls, 299; origins and overview, 99; police raids and closures, 103–4, 290, 299; product affordability, 104–5; regulation of, 97–98; support for, 98, 99; tax evasion, 117
medical cannabis substitution (opioids therapy), 146–61; accessibility barriers, 151, 152, 154; affordability barriers, 151, 152, 153, 156, 159–60; vs alcohol use, 154–56, 159; attitudes toward (as barrier), 151, 152; awareness and education (as barrier), 151, 152, 156; behavioural economics, 150; benefits of, 157–59; clinical trials, 158, 159; data collection, 149–50, 155, 156; Downtown Eastside Vancouver, 148–49, 153, 154; interviews about (observational research), 146–61; legalization impact, 153–56; marginalized (as barrier), 154, 160–61; medical education, 152, 155; methadone clinics, 149; scholarship on, 146; social structural barriers, 152–53
medical cannabis use: accessibility, 99–101, 102, 105, 290–91, 300; advocates, 40–41; AIDS/HIV, 40, 41, 99–100, 148; vs alcohol use, 154–56, 159, 171–72; attitudes, 41; CBD, 156, 157, 313, 320n3; client registrations, 102, 227; clinical trials, 106, 118–19, 136; court challenges, 40, 41, 75, 99–101, 102, 118, 147, 225, 226, 289; edibles, 105, 117; epilepsy, 41, 100, 106, 147, 215; federal program, 41; glaucoma, 40; hepatitis C, 148; home cultivation, 54, 61–62(t), 76, 225, 226; legalization, 118–21; multiple sclerosis (MS), 41; physician knowledge, 106, 148, 155, 156, 291; physician prescriptions, 148, 152, 155; therapeutic effectiveness, 118–19; veterans, 120. *See also* medical cannabis; mental health and cannabis use; recreational cannabis use
medical marijuana. *See* medical cannabis
Medical Marijuana Buyer's Clubs of Ontario, 101

Medical Marijuana Resource Centre (MMRC), 101
medicinal psychedelic drugs, 136
MedReleaf, 120
Mental Health America (MHA), 165–67, 183
mental health and cannabis use, 164–84; vs alcohol use, 171–72; anecdotal evidence, 176–80(t); anxiety disorders, 170–71; cannabis use benefits, 171–76; cannabis use effects, 164–69, 176–84; cannabis use study (non-users vs users), 178–80(t); consumption frequency, 179–80(t); cultural attitudes toward, 172–76, 184n2; depression, 170; marijuana use disorder (MUD), 166–67; recreational vs medical use, 183–84; relationship between, 169–76, 183; research literature, 169–71, 183; societal behaviour, 172–76; sociological perspective analysis, 180–84; substance disorder diagnosis criteria, 166, 182–83, 184n1; symptoms observations, 174–75; website information, 164–69, 181–82; women, 170, 171, 237. See also medical cannabis use; recreational cannabis use
Mettrum Ltd., 119, 125, 191, 308
Mikuriya, Dr. Tod, 148
Milloy, M.-J., 149–50, 152–53, 154–55, 158–59, 162
Milstop Fungicide, 193, 194(t)
Mintz, Sidney, 15
Model, Karen, 148
Mohawk Medicine, 247
Moreau, Jacques, 174
Morrison, Alexander B., 31
Mother and Clone sublingual spray, 216
Mulroney, Brian, 66
municipal government: cannabis policy-making authority, 54(t)–55, 63, 97–99, 101, 102–3; law enforcement, 33, 103–4, 243, 301
Munro, John C., 35
Munson, Jim, 305–6

Murphy, Emily, 30, 31, 173, 184n2
Myclobutanil pesticide, 191, 193, 194, 205n5, 321n8

Nagy, Jamie, 322n10
Narcotic Control Act, 35–36
National Advisory Committee on Prescription Drug Misuse, 115
National Cannabis Survey (Statistics Canada): consumer choice factors, 82–83(t), 84–86(t); data performance analysis, 17, 75, 86–94, 94n3; price score, 84; quality score, 82–83(t), 84; retail accessibility score, 84–85(t); variety score, 85–86(t)
National Drug and Alcohol Research Centre (Australia), 168–69
National Drug Strategy, 42
National Organization for the Reform of Marijuana Laws (NORML), 36
neoinstitutionalism, 56–57
neoliberalism, 12, 191–92, 314, 319
Neufeld, Vic, 229n1
New Brunswick, 80
Newfoundland and Labrador, 80, 82, 89, 93
Nietzsche, Friedrich, 270–71
Nova Scotia, 78, 80, 94
Nuuvera Inc., 214, 229n1. See also Aphria Inc.

O'Cannabiz event, 133
occupational health and safety: cannabis production, 193–94(t), 203; capitalism and neoliberalism, 192; employee provisions, 197–98, 203, 204; industrial agriculture, 192, 197–98; seasonal and temporary workers, 192, 197–98, 203, 204; women, 204
O'Neil, Casey, 268
Ontario: agro-tourism, 318; Allocation Lottery Selection, 243–44; cannabis accessibility, 90, 93; cannabis employment, 223–24; Indigenous cannabis distribution, 242–47; medical cannabis dispensaries (compassion

clubs), 101–3; medical cannabis dispensaries, police raids and closures, 103–4; online sales, 243, 246, 264n4; private retail outlets, 80, 90; prohibition regulations, 302; retail outlets restrictions (number of), 80(t); retail store allocation licences (RSAs), 243–44; systemic racism and justice report, 44
Ontario Cannabis Store (OCS), 223–24, 243, 246–47, 264n4
Ontario Court of Appeal, 75, 100, 147
Ontario Medical Association, 37
Ontario Occupational Health and Safety Act (OHSA), 197–98
opioid crisis: about, 115; class action lawsuits, 134–35; medical cannabis as substitute therapy, 146–61. *See also* medical cannabis substitution (opioids therapy)
Opium and Narcotics Drug Act, 147
Organic Consumers Association, 201
Organigram licensed cannabis producer, 196(t), 321n8
organized crime: illicit cannabis market, 6–7, 44, 292–93, 295, 298; licensed producers, 121, 132–33, 322n12
Otero, Gerardo, 12, 198
outdoor cannabis production: attitudes toward, 268; grower recollections, 272–80; illicit market, 272–85; vs indoor production, 215, 217, 229n5, 230n9; licensed producers, 213–19; smuggler recollections, 280–85. *See also* illicit cannabis production; indoor cannabis production; licensed cannabis producers (LPs)
Owusu-Bempah, Akwasi, 45

Paraquat dichloride, 200, 205n6
Parents Against Drugs, 37
Parents Resource Institute for Drug Education (PRIDE) Canada, 37, 38
Pareto's Law, 24n13
Parker, Terrance (Terry), 41, 100, 147, 225

Parkinson's disease, 200
Parliamentary Budget Officer (PBO), 87(t)–88
Peron, Dennis, 99
Pest Control Products Act (PCPA), 193, 199–200
Pest Management Regulatory Agency (PMRA), 199–200
pesticides: bans, 191, 193, 194, 205n5, 321n8; cannabis contamination, 24n13, 117, 120, 190–91; environment, 205n7, 217–18; exposure to, 200, 204n2, 205n6; integrated pest management (IPM), 195(t)–197; "other ingredients" approvals, 193–94(t), 198–201
Peters, Arnold, 34
Petitpas-Taylor, Ginette, 115
pharmaceutical industry, 115, 134–35, 201
Philpott, Jane, 298
poets and poems, 11, 273–80
police: antidrug campaigns, 38; cannabis dispensaries raids, 103–4, 243, 244, 245, 290, 299, 301–2, 307; decriminalization recommendations, 41–42; licensed cannabis company owners/investors, 123, 297–303, 306, 307–8, 309; racial profiling, 44–45
politicians: cannabis attitudes, 6, 36, 298; cannabis use, 36–37, 295, 305; licensed cannabis company owners/investors, 123, 297–303, 306, 307–8, 309
Pollan, Michael, 267, 270–71
Pot TV network, 39, 294, 295
Prairie Plant Systems (CanniMed/Aurora Cannabis), 76, 100, 225
Preibisch, Kerry, 12, 198
Prince Edward Island, 78, 80, 89
"Project Claudia" dispensary police raids, 299, 301, 302
provincial and territorial governments (cannabis regulation): alignment vs path dependence, 56–57; approaches,

75; authority, 55; consultation process, 60–61; consumption restrictions, 62(t)–63; distribution framework, 63, 74, 77–80(t), 81(t)–82, 90; vs federal government objectives, 55, 65–66, 77; home production, 61–62(t); hybrid outlets (private/public), 79–81(t); jurisdictional responsibilities, 53–54(f), 55–56; market share data, 87(t)–89(t); minimum age, 62(t)–63; monopsony market, 81; online purchases, 80–81(t); operational policy, 56, 57, 58, 60, 61–62(t), 63; policy-making analysis, 66–69; private vs public outlets, 78–81(t); producers and direct sales, 82; product accessibility data, 84–85(t), 90–91(t); product quality and price data, 82–83(t), 84, 89–90(t); product variety data, 91–92(t); replication vs alignment, 52–53, 56–57, 63–66; retail outlets restrictions (number of), 78, 80(t)–81(t); retail ownership model, 80(t)–81(t), 89(t); set-up costs, 64; strategic policy, 56, 60. *See also* federal intergovernmental policy (cannabis regulation); recreational cannabis legalization; *individual names of provinces*

Provincial-Territorial Working Group on Cannabis Legalization, 61, 63

psychedelic drugs, 136

public health: cannabis advertising limits, 127–29; cannabis legalization safeguards, 113–14, 122; cannabis market expansion vs public health protection, 126–31; drug policy reform objectives, 122, 134–36. *See also* Health Canada

Public Health Agency of Canada (PHAC), 115, 239–40

public health medical clinic (cannabis therapy), 231–40; CUDIT-R (Cannabis Use Disorder Identification Test), 234–37; intake process, 234–38; intake process test (patient responses), 234–37; patient demographics, 232, 234, 237–38; patient histories, 237–38; patient trauma, 238; patients and *system failure maladaptive coping mechanisms*, 240; practitioner experience, 231–40; *problematic consumption terminology*, 238–39

Purdue Pharma, 134–35

Quan, Douglas, 308

Quebec: cannabis legalization advocates, 39–40; cannabis tax revenue, 135; illicit vs legal market pricing, 84; illicit vs legal market share and variety, 88, 91; minimum age (possession), 135; online sales, 90; political parties, 39–40; pricing data, 84, 89, 93; public retail outlets, 80; retail outlets restrictions (number of), 78, 93

R v Parker case, 41, 100, 147, 225
RAND Corporation, 116
Randall, Robert, 40
Rankin, Murray, 130
Reagan, Nancy, 37–38
"Really Me" antidrug campaign, 38–39
Rebagliati, Ross, 39
Recreational Cannabis Farmers Market, 242, 245

recreational cannabis legalization:
– background: about, 29–46; antidrug campaigns, 37–39; criminalization amnesty, 44, 288, 306, 308–9, 314; criminalization as historical injustice, 305–7; cultivation prohibition, 32; decriminalization efforts, 34–36, 41–42, 122, 130, 293–94; law enforcement costs, 33, 292, 295, 305, 310; medical use legalization, 118–21; possession demographics, 33–34; possession fines, 34–35, 293; possession sentences, 33–35; prohibition origins, 30–32;
– legislation: analysis, 3–4, 21–22, 132–37, 312–20; attitudes toward,

Index   341

39–41, 46, 286–87, 293, 298; conflicts of interest, 124–26; corporate interests, 18, 21–22; effectiveness, 74–75; emeralds analogy, 312; expert testimony on, 298–99; market expansion vs public health protection, 126–31; objectives, 55–56, 59, 77, 121–22, 298–99; politics of, 293–99; public health risks, 126; rationale for, 73–74; safeguards, 113; slogan, 134; Task Force on Cannabis/Marijuana Legalization and Regulation, 5–6, 59–61, 113, 124–31, 297–98;
– regulation: analysis, 66–69; authority, 55; background, 75–82; consumer considerations (choice factors), 75, 82–83(t), 84–86(t); consumption, 62(t)–63; distribution, 62(t)–63; edibles and oils, 129–30; federal objectives, 77; home production, 61–62(t); intergovernmental policy integration, 16–17, 52–53, 66–69; jurisdictional responsibilities, 53–54(f), 55–56; maximum possession amount, 55; minimum age, 55, 62(t)–63, 126–27, 135; not-for-profit vs private market, 136; operational policy, 56, 57, 58, 60, 61–62(t), 63; pesticides, 199–200; policy alignment vs path dependence, 56–57; policy-making consultation process, 60–61; product promotion, 127–29, 135; product quality, 130–31, 199–200; production practices, 131; provincial-territorial working group, 61; replication vs alignment costs, 63–66; set-up costs, 64; strategic policy, 56, 60; tax revenue, 84, 123; tobacco and alcohol as model policy, 59, 64–65, 73. *See also* Cannabis Act (Bill C-45); cannabis activism; federal government; provincial and territorial governments (cannabis regulation)
recreational cannabis use: accessories, 33, 289; vs addictive drugs, 292; vs alcohol use, 32–33, 154–56, 159, 170–73, 176, 237, 238–39; attitudes, 6, 34, 45–46, 237, 238–39; background, 4–6; books and magazines bans, 289; CBD, 85, 132, 156–58, 216, 218, 313, 320n3; consumption statistics, 24n13, 36, 40, 42–43(t); countercultural resurgence, 4, 32–33, 39–41; daily users, 92; decline, 39; edibles, 129–30, 216, 219, 228, 230n6; flag, 40; good vs bad drugs, 6; head shops, 33, 101, 103, 224, 289–90, 294, 300–2; vs medical use, 183–84; mental health study, 19, 170, 171, 178–80(t), 183–84, 237; movies about, 33, 36, 39; music about, 33; musicians, 4, 39; new users, 92; Olympic athletes, 39; politicians, 36–37, 295, 305; portrayal as gateway drug, 36; possession statistics, 42, 44, 45, 307; *problematic* consumption terminology, 238–39; social harms, 22, 24n13; social history, 4–5, 16, 287; television about, 39; terminology, 4, 23n2; THC, 24n13, 85, 91, 105, 132, 202, 204, 216, 218, 313; youth, 37–39, 43–44, 314. *See also* cannabis; medical cannabis use; mental health and cannabis use
Reefer Madness era, 5, 6, 122, 181, 184, 291
reflexive ethnography, 9–10
Reiman, Amanda, 269
Report of the Commission on Systemic Racism in the Ontario Criminal Justice System, 44
research methodology, 8–13; autoethnography, 9; ethnographic autobiography, 9; interdisciplinarity, 8–9; reflexive ethnography, 9–10; role, 11–13; truth-telling, 11–13
Rifici, Chuck, 122, 123, 124
Robertson, Gregor, 98
Rootshield (R) WP fungicide, 193
Rose, Dan, 10–11, 13
Rosslee, Jessica, 202

Roueche, Clay "Boss Weed," 280
Royal Canadian Mounted Police (RCMP): anti-drug campaign, 38; on cannabis and crime, 6, 36, 134; cannabis plant destruction, 32; cannabis and tobacco contamination, 83; drug squad, 33; former officers (as licensed producers), 125, 297, 308; Indigenous relations, 264n3; letters to (medical cannabis dispensaries [MCDs]), 98; raids and seizures, 103–4, 191, 308
Royal College of Psychiatrists (RCP), 167–68

"Sal" (cannabis smuggler), 280–85
Saskatchewan: online sales, 81, 90; price data, 89; private retail outlets, 80, 81; producers and direct sales, 82; product recalls, 83, 93; retail outlets restrictions (number of), 78, 80(t)
Schedule of Restricted Drugs, 30–31
Scott, Joan, 12
seasonal agricultural workers (SAWs), 192, 197–98, 203, 204
Seddon, Toby, 24n13
Shafer Commission on Marijuana and Drug Abuse, 35
Shaffer, Matthew, 190
Shiva, Vandana, 268
Shoppers Drug Mart, 105
Single Convention on Narcotic Drugs, 35
Sinixt peoples, 274
Slocan peoples, 274–75
Snoop Dogg, 39, 86, 120
social research, 8–13
Solowij, Nadia, 169
Souccar, Raf, 125, 303
St. Maurice, Marc-Boris, 39–40
St. Pierre, Michelle, 18–19
Statistics Canada: cannabis possession, 307; cannabis survey, 17, 75, 82–83(t), 84–86(t), 87–94, 94n3
Stevens, J., 84

Stoa, Ryan, 21–22, 267, 317, 318–19
Sundial Growers Inc., 321n5
Supreme Court of Canada (SCC), 40, 67, 101, 118, 226, 245, 289

Task Force on Cannabis/Marijuana Legalization and Regulation (McLellan Report [Anne McLellan]), 5–6, 59–61, 113, 124–31, 297–98
temporary foreign workers (TFWs), 192, 197–98, 203, 204
Tilray licensed cannabis producer, 321nn5–6
tobacco. *See* alcohol and tobacco
Toronto Compassion Club (TCC), 101
Toronto Hemp Company, 101
Toronto Star newspaper, 45, 124
Trudeau, Justin: cannabis use, 295, 305; illegal dispensaries legalization, 299; Indigenous self-government, 244; legalization message, 122, 298; legalization opposition, 295; legalization task force, 123, 227–28
Trudeau, Margaret, 36
Trudeau, Michel, 305
Trudeau, Pierre, 36, 305
Tweed Inc., 120, 122, 123, 124,125, 191, 301
Tyendinaga Mohawk Territory: cannabis dispensaries, 242–47, 265n5; cannabis dispensaries numbers, 242, 264n2; cannabis distribution control, 244, 265n5; community-based security, 245, 264n2; economic boom, 246; retail store allocation licences (RSAs), 244

UNICEF report, 43–44
United Kingdom, 167–68, 182
United Nations Declaration on the Rights of Indigenous Peoples [UNDRIP], 248, 249–51
United States: cannabis legalization, 77, 116–17, 216, 294–95, 315; cannabis prohibition, 31, 35, 37, 42, 294–95;

cannabis smuggling into, 280–85; cannabis use, 32; child-proof packaging, 117; class action lawsuits, 134–35; corporate practices, 117; initiatives, 117, 295; medical cannabis dispensaries, 99, 117; medical cannabis use advocates, 40–41; mental health and cannabis use, 165–67, 173, 181; National Institute of Health, 165; pesticides, 117, 200, 205n6; product quality and safety, 116–17; propositions, 99, 281, 294, 295; tax evasion, 117; toxic waste, 205n4
Up Cannabis, 195(t), 197

Valleriani, Jenna, 17–18
Vancouver. *See* British Columbia
VanderMarel, Jeannette, 20, 213–19, 229n4, 230n9
Vice magazine, 45
Vision Vancouver, 98

Wakeford, James (Jim), 41, 99
Walsh, Zach, 18–19
Walters, John, 42
Ware, Mark, 125
Watson, Lilla, 11, 24n11
Wayland Group (Maricann), 321n5
Weissman, Eric, 9, 12

Wesley, Jared, 16–17
West Moberly First Nations, 275
Wilson-Raybould, Jody, 130
Wiman, Christian, 320
women: alcohol and tobacco consumption, 15; cannabis use and mental health, 170, 171, 237–38; corporate directors, 213–30, 229n4; corporate social responsibility, 218–19; occupational health and safety, 204; therapy intake process (urine drug screen), 234
Woolliams, Eldon, 34
Workplace Hazardous Materials Information System (WHMIS), 197

Young, Alan, 101
youth: anti-drug campaigns toward, 38–39; cannabis accessibility, 73–74, 77–78, 79, 127–28, 314; cannabis advertising limits, 127–30; cannabis legalization as protection of, 58, 120, 128, 130, 134, 239, 314; cannabis use, 130, 170, 314; criminal convictions, 5, 7, 34, 44–45; edibles ingestion, 117, 130; mental health and cannabis use, 170

Zinberg, Norman, 177, 181, 184